CLASH

CLASH

Presidents and the Press in Times of Crisis

Jon Marshall

Potomac Books AN IMPRINT OF THE UNIVERSITY OF NEBRASKA PRESS

♾

Library of Congress Cataloging-in-Publication Data
Names: Marshall, Jon, 1963– author.
Title: Clash: presidents and the press
in times of crisis / Jon Marshall.
Description: Lincoln: Potomac Books, an imprint
of the University of Nebraska Press, 2022. |
Includes bibliographical references and index.
Identifiers: LCCN 2021036669
ISBN 9781640123854 (hardback)
ISBN 9781640125261 (epub)
ISBN 9781640125278 (pdf)
Subjects: LCSH: Presidents—Press coverage—United
States—History. | Press and politics—United
States—History. | Mass media—Political aspects—
United States. | BISAC: POLITICAL SCIENCE /
American Government / General |
SOCIAL SCIENCE / Media Studies
Classification: LCC JK554 .M37
2022 | DDC 973.09/9—dc23
LC record available at https://lccn
.loc.gov/2021036669

Set in Adobe Garamond by Laura Buis.
Designed by N. Putens.

To Laurie, Justin, Andrew, and Zachary,
who bring joy to every day

And to all of the journalists
who have been threatened,
assaulted, imprisoned, or killed
for doing their jobs of informing us

If the press does not tell us, who will?

—Ronald Reagan, 40th president of the United States, *An American Life*, 1990

Journalists are accused of being lapdogs when they don't ask the hard questions, but then accused of being rude when they do. Good thing we have tough hides.

—Gwen Ifill, former *PBS NewsHour* anchorwoman, *Rediscovering Black History*, 2016

The true enemies of the people—and democracy—are those who try to suffocate truth by vilifying and demonizing the messenger. The response to that cannot be silence.

—*Des Moines Register*, 2018

CONTENTS

CLASH

Introduction

The President and the Peculiar Press Conference

The White House press corps had tough questions for President Donald Trump and his Coronavirus Task Force at their briefing on March 19, 2020. The virus was spreading rapidly through the United States with 4,777 confirmed cases.[1] Hospitals were running out of ICU beds, and some governors were requiring schools and businesses to close to stop the disease's spread. "Why was the United States not prepared with more testing and supplies?" NBC News's Kristen Welker asked the president.

Trump responded as he often did when faced with an uncomfortable question. He blamed the press. "We were very prepared," the president said. "The only thing we weren't prepared for was the media. The media has not treated it fairly."

Trump then pointed at Chanel Rion of the upstart One America News Network—known as both OAN and OANN—to ask the next question. OAN was owned by Robert Herring, a San Diego multimillionaire who wore socks with Trump's image on them. Loyalty to Trump was Rion's strong suit; accuracy wasn't. She had previously promoted false conspiracy theories that the coronavirus was created in a North Carolina laboratory, Democratic presidential candidate Joe Biden was senile, and former president Bill Clinton and First Lady Hillary Rodham Clinton were responsible for the death of a Democratic National Committee employee.[2]

"OAN," Trump said after pointing to Rion. "They treat me very nicely."

Rion proved they did as she began one of the most bizarre exchanges in the history of presidents and the press. "Do you consider the term 'Chinese food' racist?" she asked.

"I don't think it's racist at all," Trump replied.

"On that note," Rion continued, "major left-wing news media, even in this room, have teamed up with Chinese Communist Party narratives and they're claiming you are racist for making these claims about the Chinese virus. Is it alarming that major media players, just to oppose you, are consistently siding with foreign state propaganda, Islamic radicals, and Latin gangs and cartels, and they work right here, at the White House, with direct access to you and your team?"

Trump loved the question. It allowed him to rant about one of his favorite themes, his anger toward the press. He attacked the *Wall Street Journal*, a staunchly conservative newspaper owned by the same company that ran Fox News, one of his most aggressive promoters. Other reporters in the room looked startled, and members of the Coronavirus Task Force squirmed behind him. He also blasted the *New York Times* and *Washington Post*, two of the newspapers that had investigated him the most. "Because, you see, I know the truth," Trump declared. "And people out there in the world, they really don't know the truth."

As he often did, Trump accused the press of dishonesty. Rion eagerly agreed. "But more than dishonest, they're siding with state propaganda overseas," she said.

"Well, I think they do," Trump replied. "I mean, they are siding with—they are siding with China. They are doing things that they shouldn't be doing."[3]

Without any evidence, the president had just accused the press of lying and engaging in a treasonous conspiracy. Like a cult leader, Trump claimed he was the only person who knew the truth while evading responsibility for his administration's failure to counter the coronavirus pandemic. In any previous presidency, his exchange with Rion would have stood out for its strangeness, inaccuracy, and dangerousness. But by the fourth year of his presidency, it barely caused a ripple. It was just another day in the tumultuous presidency of Donald Trump. The unbelievable was normalized, and conspiracy theories had become the coin of the president's realm.

Throughout his presidency Trump encouraged hostility toward journalists. He called them "dishonest," "disgusting," and an "enemy of the people." He referred to negative but accurate stories about him as "fake news." He demeaned journalists who asked tough questions, threatened to sue news companies, barred some correspondents from covering government events, and taunted reporters kept in pens at his campaign rallies as if they were prisoners. His press secretaries went more than a year without holding a regular news briefing. At the same time, he used the media to spread disinformation and outright lies to boost his own political fortunes.[4]

Trump's ugly relationship with the press weakened U.S. democracy and contributed to a deep and angry polarization in American society. On an almost daily basis during his one term, the relationship reached a new low. Reporters without Borders, a group that usually focuses on abuses against journalists in authoritarian countries such as Iran, China, and Azerbaijan, concluded that the Trump administration "demonstrated the United States is no longer a champion of press freedom at home or abroad."[5]

Despite the attacks against it, the press continued to serve as democracy's watchdog, doing crucial investigative reporting and keeping a close eye on Trump and other powerful people and institutions. Meanwhile, journalism itself was in crisis. Many newspapers, magazines, and broadcast stations had been hobbled by economic downturns and the migration of their audiences to social media. Mostly white and mostly male newsrooms offered a skewed view of reality because of their lack of diversity. Commentators on cable news channels, talk radio, and the web sensationalized the news, spread conspiracy theories, and vilified their opponents. Facebook, Twitter, Reddit, and other social media platforms distributed disinformation created by foreign agents and other bad actors determined to sow confusion.[6] Americans often chose to live in media bubbles that reinforced their preexisting beliefs. It was no coincidence that the public's trust in the presidency and the media plummeted, leaving the foundations of democracy highly vulnerable.

What caused this tumultuous and perilous relationship between the president and the press? Trump was a uniquely toxic leader; blaming it all on him would be easy enough. His lack of respect for democratic norms, his fondness for disinformation, his constant need for attention, his obsession with grievances, and his instinct to go for the jugular all contributed to the dysfunction. But much deeper forces, which this book describes, led us to this point. Trump's unhealthy relationship with the press didn't happen by chance and wasn't completely unprecedented. In fact, there were plenty of precedents. They stretch back to the days of George Washington and John Adams when the United States was first deciding what role the press should play in its democratic experiment. What made Trump's presidency unusual was that these historic forces came into play all at once with a president who was determined to sabotage the fact-based process—embodied by the press—for determining vital information needed for democracy to function.

This book explores the political, economic, social, and technological pressures that have shaped the relationship between U.S. presidents and the press during times of crisis. In addition to Trump, it examines the presidencies of John Adams, Abraham Lincoln, Woodrow Wilson, Franklin Roosevelt, Richard Nixon, Ronald Reagan, Bill Clinton, George W. Bush, and Barack Obama. These presidencies were pivotal in molding the current relationship. Some of them faced military or international crises. For others, the traumas were economic. Sometimes the survival of our system of government was at stake. And during some of their presidencies, multiple crises threatened the nation. By examining what happened between presidents and the press during these critical times, this book helps us understand how we arrived at our current state of affairs. It concludes with recommendations for strengthening journalism's role in keeping presidents accountable.

Obviously, other people and institutions besides the press—Congress, the courts, political parties, lobbyists, the military, and many others—have influenced the presidency. This book focuses on the press because of its ability to communicate presidents' agendas, serve as a check on their power, and frame their policies and images in the public's mind. Throughout *Clash*, I use the word "press" to mean journalism as a whole. Originally, the term just referred to materials produced by printing presses, including newspapers, pamphlets, and magazines. But it has come to mean the wide spectrum of news media encompassing not only printed words and images but also journalism distributed by film, radio, television, the web, and now social media. By concentrating on presidents and the press, this book mostly describes the actions of white men. All of the presidents with the exception of Barack Obama have been white, and none have been female. During most of American history, White House reporters were also almost exclusively white men. This racism and sexism in journalism must finally end if we want to truly strengthen the press.

While researching this book, I was blessed by a wealth of primary sources. Thanks to the wonders of digitization, I was able to study the content of more than ninety newspapers, magazines, news websites, broadcast outlets, and social media feeds. I also examined documents in the collections of presidential libraries, the Library of Congress, the National Archives and Records Administration, the White House, the U.S. Senate and House of Representatives, the University of Virginia's Miller Center on the presidency, and the University of California at Santa Barbara's American Presidency Project. The C-SPAN and Vanderbilt Television Archives offered views of original broadcasts, and the Internet Archive provided old web pages as they originally appeared. In addition, public opinion polls, speeches, congressional reports and testimony, letters, and memoirs proved valuable. And I learned a great deal from the books and articles of the many brilliant scholars and journalists who've studied presidents and the press.

From this research, eight themes emerged that *Clash* explores in detail:

- Since the nation's early years, presidents have frequently tried to attack, restrict, manipulate, and demonize the press in order to strengthen their own power.

- Technological advances have fragmented the media and enhanced presidents' ability to avoid the White House press corps and communicate directly to the public.

- Presidents who nurture respectful relationships with reporters have more long-term success than those who don't.

- Although sometimes sloppy, partisan, and sensationalistic, journalists have often courageously served the public when covering presidents despite formidable forces trying to stop them.

- Journalists who champion political and social movements have influenced presidents to dramatically change their policies.

- Changes in laws during the Reagan presidency released a powerful wave of partisan, divisive journalism that intensified the nation's polarization.

- A growing disregard for the truth by some recent presidents and their media allies has eroded trust in important institutions.

- The declining economic health of the news business has sapped its ability to hold presidents accountable.

All of these dynamics came into play during Trump's presidency. By the end of his term, Trump's penchant for disinformation led to bloodshed at the U.S. Capitol and a direct attack on democracy. All the while, he vilified journalists and even advocated sending some of them to prison.[7] The first chapter discusses a president whose administration did exactly that.

1

John Adams and the Imprisoned Press

Leaders of the new Republican Party gathered for a banquet in August 1800 at Lovett's Hotel in Philadelphia, the U.S. capital at the time. They were there to praise William Duane, editor of the *Aurora*, one of America's most influential newspapers. Duane never backed down from a fight, whether it be on the rowdy streets of Philadelphia or in the pages of the *Aurora*. Once he was arrested after a brawl over politics in a churchyard. Earlier that summer he accused the Federalist administration of President John Adams of engaging in a long series of "abuses and waste of the public money." His *Aurora* also mocked Adams's new secretary of war for being "as well qualified for the office of feeder of the Chinese Emperor's Crocodiles" as he was for his cabinet position. Soon Duane and other Republican editors would help bring an end to the Adams presidency.[1]

Duane and other editors had increasingly challenged the president's power, and the Federalists had done their best to muzzle them. A Federalist militia beat and whipped Duane after he accused them of abusive behavior. Secretary of State Timothy Pickering told Adams the *Aurora* was "an uninterrupted stream of slander on the American Government." Pickering recommended that the administration sue the *Aurora* for libel and banish Duane from the United States. Adams agreed, complaining of the editor's "matchless effrontery."[2] But the case was quietly dropped when Duane threatened to use letters from Adams and Pickering to prove what he had published about them was true.[3]

No wonder the Republicans at the banquet were eager to cheer Duane. To complete their evening of eating, drinking, and singing patriotic songs, they gave a round of toasts. After wishing Adams "a speedy and honorable retirement," they lifted their glasses to honor "William Duane—the firm and enlightened Editor of the Aurora—virtuous and undaunted in the worst of times—the friend of his country, and the scourge of her enemies."[4]

As the banquet made clear, political rivalries were already rampant during the nation's early years, and the increasingly powerful press encouraged them. The roots of today's media partisanship stretch back through the Adams presidency, a period tense with foreign policy crises and bitter domestic disputes. Newspapers and pamphlets carried the passionate arguments of party leaders who believed the fragile nation's survival was at stake, justifying any means necessary to save it. Insults flew back and forth in the press, each more colorful than the last. Adams was called "a repulsive pedant, a gross hypocrite, and an unprecedented oppressor." Republicans were described as "frog-eating, man-eating blood drinking cannibals." Historian Ron Chernow called it "a time of political savagery with few parallels in American history, a season of paranoia in which the two parties surrendered all trust in each other."[5] The viciousness in the press resembled in many ways some of our own era's partisan media.

Newspapers and pamphlets had such a strong impact on government and politics that Adams and other Federalist leaders dangerously tried to suppress them. Adams was the first in a long line of presidents who in times of crisis tried to intimidate, manipulate, and silence journalists. He and his Federalist supporters jailed dozens of writers, printers, and editors, but they ultimately failed to control the press. Their botched effort led to their political demise and set the precedent that it was legal—and indeed important—for the press to challenge those with power. At the same time, journalists—sometimes bravely and sometimes irresponsibly—proved they could help determine a president's fate, a lesson that many of Adams's successors would also learn.

John Adams was a ripe target for the slings and arrows of the press. Although he was bright, hardworking, and devoted to family and friends, he wasn't a natural politician. He lacked the heroic reputation and commanding stature of George Washington, who preceded Adams as president. Adams was stubborn, vain, and irritable, and his strong opinions often led him to continue arguing no matter how much he annoyed his listeners. Years earlier Benjamin Franklin described Adams as someone who "means well for his country, is always an honest man, often a wise one, but sometimes and in some things, absolutely out of his senses."[6] He would display this lack of sense in his dealings with the press.

Adams did possess sterling patriotic credentials. As a leader of the First Continental Congress, he gave the crucial speech that swayed delegates to pass the Declaration of Independence. He twice made the harrowing trip across the Atlantic during the Revolutionary War to serve as a diplomat in Europe, winning critical military and financial support from the French and Dutch. In 1782 he was one of the signers of the treaty to end the war, gaining nearly everything the Americans wanted in the negotiations. He then served as the first U.S. minister to its former enemy, Great Britain, before coming home in 1788 to a hero's welcome. Deeply religious in the Puritan tradition, Adams refused to own enslaved people, unlike some of his Massachusetts neighbors and so many of the nation's other founders.[7]

Eight months after he returned to America, Adams finished second to Washington in the voting for president, making him the first U.S. vice president. He assumed he would be in the thick of decision making, but Washington relied more on Alexander Hamilton, his brilliant treasury secretary.[8] Adams didn't help his cause when he recommended that Congress refer to the president as "His Highness" or "His Majesty" to show proper respect. Adams's idea was ridiculed by a public that a few short years earlier had freed itself from the pompous British monarchy. Congress rejected his suggestion. Adams was accused of being a monarchist, and critics suggested the vice president, known for his plumpness, be called "His Rotundity."[9]

Like many politicians who followed him, Adams's blunders were widely covered in the press, sometimes accurately and often unfairly. Newspapers were becoming increasingly aggressive as their numbers soared during the 1790s from 91 to 234 by one estimate. In those days newspapers were small operations, typically consisting of a printer, maybe some family members, and perhaps an assistant or two. Printing presses were operated by hand, making mass production impossible. Newspapers were usually four pages consisting primarily of letters, advertisements, essays, local news briefs, and dispatches from Europe and around the country. It was rare for any publication to have more than a thousand subscribers, but many more people read each issue as copies were passed from person to person and discussed in coffee houses and taverns. Newspapers were mailed around the country, and editors copied news and opinions from each other. In this way ideas printed in a small newspaper in one town could reverberate through society.[10]

The fledgling newspapers struggled to survive, and many of them turned to political leaders for financial support and content. The ruling Federalists' newspaper of choice was the *Gazette of the United States*, launched just before Washington's inauguration. The Federalists subsidized the newspaper by making its editor, John Fenno, the Senate's and Treasury Department's official printer. Hamilton also gave Fenno a personal loan without asking for repayment. In return, the *Gazette of the United States* flattered Washington with a complete lack of subtlety. When the president visited New York City, it reported that many in the crowd declared "they should now die contented—nothing being wanted to complete their happiness, previous to this auspicious period, but the sight of the Savior of his Country."[11]

Not everyone thought Washington was their savior. Thomas Jefferson and James Madison vehemently opposed his policies and decided they needed a newspaper to spread their views. They helped Philip Freneau, a college friend of Madison's, start the *National Gazette* in 1791. To finance the newspaper, Jefferson used his position as secretary of state to give Freneau printing contracts and hired him as a government translator. Madison, who was then a congressman, became a frequent *National Gazette* contributor, writing a series of anonymous essays accusing Washington's administration of acting "contrary to the will and subversive of the authority of the people."[12]

For the first time, the press was attempting to restrain a president's power. Washington's opponents could communicate their grievances and policies to the public, setting the stage for political parties to form. In the early 1790s, supporters of Jefferson and Madison started creating clubs known as Democratic-Republican societies. By the end of the century, these societies had evolved into the Republican Party, which in the 1820s became known as the Democratic Party. To avoid confusion, this chapter refers to them as Republicans.[13]

In the minds of Adams and other Federalists, challenges to government policies by Republicans and their newspaper allies weren't the acts of a loyal opposition in a healthy democracy. Instead, the Federalists believed the challenges were potentially treasonous and threatened the nation. Adams told his most trusted adviser, his wife, Abigail, that the press should carry more content "in favor of the government than there has been, or the sour, angry, peevish, fretful, lying paragraphs which assail it on every side will make an impression on many weak and ignorant people." Adams's disdain for the press would be shared by many other presidents. His distress over the political rancor, however, was exceeded by his compulsion to argue, and he eagerly joined the jousting in the press. While vice president, he wrote thirty-one essays for Fenno's *Gazette of the United States* warning against the unruliness of pure democracy.[14]

Adams and Washington easily won second terms in 1792. Soon afterward, the two great European powers—France and Britain—began a war that would last twenty-two years. Whether America should back one side or the other became the nation's biggest foreign policy question. Tensions with Britain mounted after it seized hundreds of neutral U.S. ships and forced their sailors to serve in its navy. As more Americans clamored for war, Washington sent Chief Justice of the Supreme Court John Jay to negotiate a treaty with Britain.[15]

The Republicans, who distrusted Britain and Washington's administration, turned to the *Philadelphia Aurora* to try to scuttle the treaty. In what may have been the first leak of a U.S. government document to the press, the *Aurora*—published at that time by Franklin's grandson Benjamin Franklin Bache—printed a copy of the treaty. Its disclosure caused an uproar against Washington's government. The Republican press claimed that America was abandoning its friend France by making peace with Britain. "We are taken from the embraces of a loving wife," the *Boston Independent Chronicle* declared, "and find ourselves in the arms of a detestable and abandoned whore, covered with crimes, rottenness and corruption." It wouldn't be the last time that a partisan publication tried to stoke fear and division during a time of crisis.[16]

Some newspapers tried to remain even-handed, but few were able to stay impartial for long. Believing the fate of the young republic depended on who won the war of words, writers hurled vivid insults back and forth: "skunk," "jackal," "debaucher," "assassin," "addled cat's paw," and "toad-eater," for example. Washington was practically immune from personal attacks during his first years in office, but the increasingly vigorous Republican press spread its vitriol against him during his second term, calling him "a dictator," "spoiled child," and "tyrannical monster." The criticism took its toll on Washington. He said he wouldn't seek a third term because he was tired of being assailed in the press "by a set of infamous scribblers." It was a lament that future presidents could understand.[17]

The election of 1796 was the first in which the press influenced who won. With Washington not running, the top contenders were Adams and his frenemy Jefferson. Fenno's *Gazette of the United States* published a series of essays by Hamilton skewering Jefferson and praising Adams's "intrepid, faithful, persevering, and comprehensively useful services" to the nation. Meanwhile, Bache's *Aurora* predicted that if Adams were elected, he would turn America into a hereditary monarchy with his son John Quincy Adams in line to succeed him. After Adams narrowly won with seventy-one electoral votes compared with sixty-eight for Jefferson, Bache derisively referred to Adams as "President by three votes."[18]

By the time Adams became president at age sixty-one, his teeth were rotting and his eyes were often red from too much reading. For his inauguration he wore a plain gray suit, but a ceremonial sword dangled by his side, perhaps an attempt to match Washington's legendary military bearing. In contrast, Jefferson and Washington looked resplendent in the latest fashions as they towered over Adams. Washington appeared serene as many in the room wept at the thought that their hero would no longer be president. Under the rules of the day, Jefferson became vice president as the second-place finisher even though he had opposed Adams. Silver-tongued and graceful, Jefferson continued to profess his deep friendship for Adams while he quietly prepared to betray him.[19]

Adams entered the presidency facing steep challenges. The possibility of war with France loomed over the fragile new nation. With no national currency, trading was difficult, and stark economic and social inequalities stirred discontent. Wages were low, roads were terrible, and epidemics were common. For all their talk of freedom and liberty, white colonizers continued to invade indigenous people's land, while much of the economy relied on the forced labor of about seven hundred thousand enslaved people.[20] Adams was ill-equipped to handle these problems. His sterling record of patriotic service couldn't overcome a lack of executive experience beyond managing the five workers on his family farm. He didn't have hundreds of aides as presidents do today, not even a chief of staff or someone to deal with the press.[21] The idea that journalists could influence the ideas of the public and communicate their interests and needs was a novel concept that Adams didn't grasp, leaving him unprepared to handle an aggressive, deeply partisan press.

Bache's *Aurora* was one of the most partisan of those newspapers. Bache castigated Adams when he proposed spending more on the military and arming merchant ships in case of war with France. Bache falsely claimed Adams was leading the country with a "war whoop" and leaning toward the British because of the time he'd spent in England. "From the time of his appointment to the present moment," the *Aurora* said, "he has completely deceived the people, who were led by his inauguration speech and other circumstances to believe, that he was of *no party*, and that he was under no *extraneous influence*."[22]

Jefferson was the first U.S. opposition leader to understand that a hostile press could weaken the president. While serving as vice president, Jefferson deviously encouraged the *Aurora*'s attacks on Adams, as did fellow Republican leaders Madison and James Monroe. They urged their friends to subscribe, met with Bache, and loaned him money. The *Aurora* delivered for them, inaccurately mocking Adams as being Hamilton's puppet and describing his policies as "the extravagant and barbarous schemes of a weak old man." Less than three months after Adams's inauguration, the *Aurora* concluded that it was time for the president to resign. The *Aurora* demonstrated an emerging radical belief among Republicans that people (or at least the white men who could vote in those days) had a right to challenge their elected leaders.[23]

Bache was far from the nastiest or most partisan of the Republican writers. That honor belonged to James Callender. Constantly broke and often drunk, Callender was once banished from congressional proceedings for being filthy and covered with lice. But he was a lively writer. As Jefferson paid him, Callender produced a series of pamphlets in the summer of 1797 revealing that Hamilton was having an extramarital affair and accusing him of rampant corruption. Hamilton denied the corruption but admitted the adultery, damaging his future political prospects. At Jefferson's request Callender then wrote a pamphlet alleging that Adams was scheming to become president for life, trying to trick Americans into war with France, and burdening the people with taxes, debt, and despotism. Callender called Adams "one of the most egregious fools upon the continent."[24]

The partisan battles in the press had reached new depths of savagery. Federalist newspapers responded to Callender's and Bache's denunciations of Adams with their own stream of accusations and insults against the Republicans. The most aggressive of the Federalist editors was William Cobbett, a burly English immigrant who called himself Peter Porcupine. His *Porcupine's Gazette* said Callender was a "nasty beast," a "mangy Scottsman," and "a little reptile." Cobbett saved his sharpest attacks for Bache, labeling him "a liar and infamous scoundrel" whose readers were "ignorant deluded partisans." Cobbett's barbed style was an immediate success, and *Porcupine's Gazette*'s circulation nearly tripled within eight months to an impressive three thousand copies a day.[25]

Adams tried not to react publicly to the rancor and insults in the press. He once even joined volunteers passing buckets of water to put out a fire roaring through the Philadelphia home of a newspaper publisher who had attacked the president in print. But the criticism in the press hurt Adams, and in private he seethed. "Bache's paper which is nearly as bad as Freneau's begins to join in concert with it to maul the President," he complained in his diary. The presidency exhausted Adams, and he flew into fits of rage when stressed. Jefferson described the president becoming so angry one time that he trampled his wig on the floor.[26]

Adams frustrated the extreme members of both parties and their allies in the press by refusing to go to war. France had begun seizing American boats carrying cargo to the British, leading to ongoing confrontations at sea known as the Quasi-War. Federalist newspapers wanted the United Sates to declare war on France. The Republican press urged Adams to continue America's friendship with its Revolutionary War ally and accused him of having a secret alliance with the English.[27] But after agents of France's foreign minister demanded bribes from U.S. diplomats, American popular opinion turned against France in a fit of xenophobia. The French foreign minister was burned in effigy, and rumors swirled that French agents were sneaking through the South to stir up revolts of enslaved workers.[28]

The ruling Federalists began to see all opposition as dangerous and civil war as a real possibility. Federalist newspapers fueled the fear with rumors and paranoia as some in the media still do today. The "demons of anarchy and confusion are attempting to organize treason and death," warned the *Courier of New Hampshire*, a Federalist newspaper. "He that is not for us, is against us." Before he returned to England, Peter Porcupine described the French as "Infamous monsters" preparing to attack the United States. "Take care," he wrote, "or, when your blood runs down the gutters, don't say you were not forewarned of the danger."[29]

Adams was winning the war for public support in the press. Because Federalists controlled every branch of government, the documents filling many newspaper pages—presidential speeches, congressional proceedings, government announcements—reflected their worldview. The majority of newspapers leaned toward the Federalists, and Republican newspapers struggled to survive. The *Aurora*, for instance, lost subscriptions and advertising as anger against the French rose. A pro-Federalist mob attempted to burn down Bache's home. Historian Jeffrey Pasley notes that the Republican press at the time was "unstable, widely scattered, vastly outnumbered, and in many cases, unsure of its mission."[30]

Then the Federalists overplayed their hand.[31] As the crisis with France mounted, Congress passed four bills in July 1798 known as the Alien and Sedition Acts. Adams hadn't asked for the new laws, but he still signed them. He and most Federalists in Congress feared that immigrants from France and Ireland were conspiring to spread instability and endanger the nation's security in case of war with France. Adams and other Federalists worried that attacks by the press against the government threatened to rip apart the young republic. And so the Federalists targeted immigrants and the press.[32]

Under the three Alien Acts, Adams had the power to deport, jail, or disenfranchise any immigrant he deemed dangerous or suspicious. No hearings would be held. The laws also created a federal registry of aliens, banned states from naturalizing immigrants, and lengthened the residency requirement for citizenship from five to fourteen years. It wasn't a coincidence that the laws primarily targeted Republicans, including journalists, who had recently arrived in the United States.[33]

For the press, the Sedition Act was even more dangerous. It allowed the government to prosecute anyone who wrote, printed, or uttered "any false, scandalous and malicious writing or writings against the Government of the United States . . . with intent to defame the said government . . . or the said President, or to bring them . . . into contempt or disrepute; or to excite against them . . . the hatred of the good people of the United States." The act also made it illegal "to conspire" to "oppose any measure or measures of the government." In other words, it was now illegal to insult, criticize, or protest the president and government. People convicted under the Sedition Act faced up to two years in prison and heavy fines. Charles Holt, editor of the *New London Bee*, observed that the law "wholly annihilated" the "liberty of speech, printing and writing."[34]

The Sedition Act gave the federal government sweeping new powers over cases that had previously been handled in state courts. Adams and his congressional allies knew that all of the Supreme Court justices and other federal judges were Federalists and could be counted on to use the law against Republican dissidents. The law protected the president but not the vice president, so Federalist critics of Jefferson didn't have to worry. It also was set to conveniently expire at the end of Adams's first term to make sure its power wasn't used against Federalists if a Republican became president.[35]

The Sedition Act, however, had the unintended consequence of strengthening the Republican newspapers' opposition to Adams. James Madison called the law "a monster that must forever disgrace its parents." The stakes were indeed high. The ensuing battle over the Sedition Act would answer fundamental questions about the new nation and the relationship of presidents and the press.[36] Could there be such a thing as a loyal opposition to the government? Should the press be allowed to dissent against an elected government? Could its criticisms go too far? Should a president have the power to imprison editors he considered dangerous?

Adams's answer to the last question was yes. The thin-skinned president approved the arrest of journalists, sometimes sending suggestions to prosecutors of which ones should be indicted. "A meaner, a more artful, or a more malicious libel has not appeared," the president commented about an essay criticizing him. "As far it alludes to me, I despise it; but I have no doubt it is a libel against the whole government, and as such ought to be prosecuted."[37]

The first journalist to be prosecuted was Matthew Lyon of Vermont. Tough, crude, and an outspoken Republican, Lyon had launched a newspaper, the *Farmers' Library*, to criticize local Federalist leaders and boost his own political ambitions. He won a congressional seat in 1796, making him the first newspaper publisher ever elected to the House of Representatives. Because Lyon was an Irish immigrant and former indentured servant, the aristocratic Federalists scorned him. Peter Porcupine called him an "infamous and beastly wretch." On the floor of the House of Representatives in early 1798, Lyon boasted that he could help defeat Connecticut's Federalist congressmen if he started a newspaper in their state. Overhearing those remarks, Representative Roger Griswold of Connecticut insulted Lyon's Revolutionary War record. Lyon reacted by spitting in Griswold's face. Afterward, Griswold snuck up on Lyon, called him a scoundrel, and began whacking him on the head with a hickory cane. Lyon defended himself with a pair of fire tongs, and the two of them brawled on the floor of Congress until they were separated.[38]

Lyon switched from punching Federalists on the floor of Congress to attacking them in his new magazine, the *Scourge of Aristocracy*. He accurately predicted that, under the Sedition Act, opinions critical of the government and its leaders would be open to prosecution. People "had better hold their tongues and make toothpicks of their pens," Lyon warned.[39] He didn't heed his own advice, however, and wrote scathing denunciations of Adams and the Federalists while campaigning for reelection in 1798. In a letter to the editor of a Vermont newspaper, Lyon accused Adams of harming the public welfare "in a continual grasp for power, in an unbounded thirst for ridiculous pomp, foolish adulation, or selfish avarice." Adams, he suggested in another letter, should be sent to a "madhouse" because of his policies toward France.

The Federalists turned to the Sedition Act to silence Lyon, and he was arrested a month before the election. The indictment described Lyon as "a malicious and seditious person, and of a depraved mind and a wicked and diabolical disposition."[40] He stood little chance of being found innocent at his trial, which opened only four days after his arrest. He didn't have time to find a lawyer he liked, the jury was full of Federalists, and one of the two judges had run against him for Congress. Ignoring the fact that one of the letters in question was written before the Sedition Act became law, the jury deliberated for an hour before convicting Lyon of sedition against the president. He was sentenced to four months in prison and fined $1,000.[41]

But Lyon's conviction didn't silence him. From a freezing jail cell, he continued to write denunciations of the Sedition Act that were reprinted in newspapers around the country. His fellow Republicans helped pay his fine and made Lyon a martyr for the cause of free expression. Lyon's jailing created sympathy for him as he campaigned for reelection, and he handily defeated his opponent by a two-to-one margin. After his victory, several thousand Vermont residents petitioned Adams to pardon Lyon, but the president refused. When the editor finally finished his jail time, his supporters paraded behind him in a procession that stretched twelve miles, singing odes in praise of his courage and the Bill of Rights.[42]

Lyon was hardly the only editor or writer prosecuted under the Sedition Act. New York's leading Republican newspaper, *The Argus*, had to be sold after its owner and one of its workers were indicted for making accusations against Hamilton and printing that "the federal government was corrupt and inimical to the preservation of liberty." The *New York*

Time-Piece shut down after its editor was arrested and its main financial backer quit in fear of further government persecution. Thomas Cooper, editor of the *Northumberland (PA) Gazette*, was convicted and thrown in prison for writing a handbill attacking Adams and his policies.[43]

The suppression of the press became so severe that Charles Holt of the *New London Bee*, the leading Republican newspaper in Connecticut, was arrested for printing a letter criticizing the president. The letter suggested that a provisional army created by Adams would become a standing army aimed at suppressing internal rebellions. It referred to Hamilton, whom Adams had named as second-in-command of the army, as "the adulterous Commander." It wondered whether his troops would also be "found in the bed of adultery." Holt was indicted for discouraging recruitment and being a "wicked, malicious, seditious and ill-disposed person" who was fueling discontent against the government. At the trial the district attorney conceded that what the *Bee* published about Hamilton's "amours" was accurate. He argued, however, that referring to the troops as a standing army rather than a provisional one was false. Holt was convicted in April of 1800, sentenced to three months in prison, and fined $550.[44]

In the end more than one hundred people—all of them Republicans—were prosecuted under the Sedition Act or similar common law in less than two years.[45] During the critical election campaign of 1800, several opposition newspapers such as Holt's were forced to close as their editors were locked in disease-ridden jails. The hypocrisy of the Federalists was exposed when Hamilton wrote a scathing letter about Adams that was widely circulated; Hamilton, the powerful Federalist, wasn't prosecuted.[46]

Freedom of speech was squelched as well as freedom of the press. The prosecutions reached their most absurd depths in the case of Luther Baldwin. A Revolutionary War veteran who made his living piloting a garbage boat, Baldwin was drinking in a Newark, New Jersey, tavern one day when Adams passed through town. While Adams was greeted with a sixteen-canon salute, a drunken Baldwin said he didn't care if the canons fired through the president's "arse." The tavern owner, a Federalist, overheard the comment and accused Baldwin, a Republican, of sedition. Baldwin was indicted, pled guilty, and remained in jail until he could pay his $150 fine.[47]

The Alien and Sedition Acts eventually backfired on the Federalists as they became perhaps the most despised laws in the country's history up to that point. The harsh Alien Acts didn't target only French immigrants. They also threatened recent arrivals from Germany and Ireland who responded by giving their enthusiastic allegiance to the Republicans. The obvious partisanship and excesses of the Sedition Act created sympathy for persecuted editors such as Holt and Lyon, making them heroes in their communities. Meanwhile, Adams's popularity declined.[48]

The attempt to suppress the press hadn't worked, at least this time. Thirty Republican newspapers were launched in the election year of 1800, more than the number that stopped printing. A few of these new newspapers were simply trying to make money by appealing to the rapidly growing Republican readership at the end of Adams's term. But for many editors, the hated Alien and Sedition Acts spurred them to become more partisan, and Adams would soon pay the price at the ballot box.[49]

The two political parties, now fully formed, took campaigning to a new level of intensity during the election of 1800, which once again pitted Adams against Jefferson. The press covered the race with a savagery and recklessness never before seen in an election. Federalist newspapers called Jefferson an infidel, atheist, coward, and swindler who was more French than American. If Jefferson won, a New York newspaper predicted, Irish and French immigrants would flood the country, and the nation would descend into civil war. The *Connecticut Courant* warned that if Republicans were victorious, "murder, robbery, rape, adultery, and incest, will be openly taught and practiced." The language was remarkably similar to what Donald Trump used about Mexican immigrants during his 2016 presidential campaign.[50]

Republican newspapers campaigned against Adams with equal vehemence. The president was criticized for creating the provisional army, imposing new taxes, and signing the Alien and Sedition Acts. James Callender, now spreading his venom with Jefferson's financial support for the *Richmond Examiner* in Virginia, assailed Adams as a "wretch" and a "hideous hermaphroditical character." For those words and others, Callender was charged under the Sedition Act, found guilty, and sentenced to nine months in prison.[51]

The election was close. Adams won 65 electoral votes, while Jefferson and his running mate Aaron Burr each received 73. The outcome was finally decided in Jefferson's favor by the House of Representatives. If Adams had won just 250 more votes in New York City, he would have earned a second term. He also would have won if the electoral votes of southern states weren't inflated because enslaved adults were counted as three-fifths of a person even though they were banned from casting ballots.[52] Adams's defeat marked the beginning of the end of the Federalist Party, which never again held national power. He recognized that the press played a major role in his loss and remained bitter about it. Still embracing the xenophobia that marked his presidency, Adams complained that Republican editors were "the most influential men in the country, all foreigners and all degraded characters."[53]

Adams had one last great achievement before leaving office, however. Two years before his term ended, he had sent another diplomatic delegation to France, much to the surprise of his Republican opponents and the fury of many Federalists who were ready for war. The press on both sides of the partisan divide derided the attempt. But after more than a year of frustration, the diplomats successfully negotiated a treaty that ended the naval skirmishes between the United States and France. Adams had ended the crisis and allowed the United States to remain neutral in its foreign policy. Because news of the success had to voyage slowly by boat across the Atlantic, it didn't reach the shores of America until November 1800, too late to help Adams with the election. If the news had traveled faster, he might well have won a second term.

Adams's reelection campaign was doomed by his unwillingness to engage in party politics and his decision to prosecute journalists rather than develop a productive relationship with them. As he prepared to leave the new capital of Washington DC, the *Aurora*—now edited by William Duane after Bache died of yellow fever in 1798—took one more shot at him. God, the newspaper said, had cast Adams away like "polluted water out at the back door." It wished him a safe trip home where "Mrs. Adams may wash his befuddled brains clear."[54]

But that was nothing compared with what Callender had in store for the new president. Once Jefferson took office, Callender expected to be rewarded for promoting his campaign and for serving time in jail under the Sedition Act in service of the Republican cause. He asked the new administration to make him postmaster of Richmond, but he didn't get the job. In revenge Callender switched sides and became editor of a Federalist newspaper. He then revealed that Jefferson had fathered several children with Sally Hemings, one of the women he kept enslaved. The story quickly spread to Federalist newspapers around the country.[55]

Callender wasn't the only editor cut loose by Jefferson once he became president. Duane, who'd been cheered heartily at the Republican banquet in the summer of 1800, moved to Washington with the expectation that the *Aurora* would become an official Republican newspaper. He also hoped to receive lucrative government printing contracts as a reward for his partisan service. But Jefferson thought Duane was too untrustworthy for official responsibilities. The disappointed editor returned to Philadelphia, where he turned his pen against the city's Republican leaders.[56]

With Adams out of office, Duane, Callender, and other journalists no longer needed to worry that the federal government would prosecute them. Long before he became president, Jefferson vowed that if it were "left to me to decide whether we should have a government without newspapers, or newspapers without government, I should not hesitate a moment to prefer the latter." In his inaugural address he proclaimed that freedom of the press was essential to American government. Once he took office, Jefferson and his allies allowed the Sedition Act to expire even though some Federalists tried to renew it. He soon released from jail everyone who had been convicted of violating the act.[57]

Jefferson's relationship with the press wasn't all sweetness, however. His opinion of newspapers soured as some continued their attacks on him. Within a couple of years of becoming president, he began to encourage political allies to use state libel laws to prosecute several Federalist editors. "Nothing can now be believed which is seen in a newspaper," he wrote toward the end of his presidency. "Truth itself becomes suspicious by being put into that polluted vehicle."[58] The champion of the press was no longer certain he wanted it to be completely free.

Despite Jefferson's change of heart, American journalism had survived the crisis of the Adams presidency when First Amendment rights were severely threatened. The Sedition Act's demise established the principle that criticizing presidents isn't disloyal. It meant the press—no matter how partisan or irresponsible it might be—could keep serving as a watchdog over presidents and other powerful officials. The viciousness of the press and the repression of the government also demonstrated that presidents and the press could find ways to justify extreme words and actions during tense times.

Adams discovered the hard way that presidents tangled with journalists at their own risk. It was a lesson that some of his successors would also learn as debate continued over what exactly First Amendment freedoms meant. Those freedoms, however, were not granted to everyone. For all their talk of liberty, Jefferson, Madison, and their allies belonged to the party of slavery. It would be left to a new generation of activist journalists to boldly pressure a president, during a crisis that nearly destroyed the nation, to end America's greatest sin.

2

Abraham Lincoln and the Power
of an Advocating Press

On New Year's Day of 1863, more than two thousand people gathered under the ornate ceiling and columns of the Tremont Temple in downtown Boston. Some of America's leading abolitionist journalists, Black and white, crowded the temple awaiting news from President Abraham Lincoln that would change the nation. Frederick Douglass, who had escaped slavery to become one of America's most famous editors and orators, was there. Wendell Phillips, the Harvard Law School graduate who'd sacrificed his legal career to become a fiery abolitionist writer and speaker, also attended. So did twenty-year-old Anna Dickinson, a Quaker who had published her first antislavery article at age thirteen.[1]

The crowd was expecting to receive word that Lincoln had finally issued the Emancipation Proclamation declaring an end to slavery in the Confederate states of the South. The abolitionists had seen an earlier draft of the proclamation, and they didn't think it went far enough. For instance, it continued to allow slavery in the border states that had stayed loyal to the Union. Even so, they knew the proclamation would mark the first time an American president had moved toward eliminating slavery's horrors.[2]

Douglass, Phillips, Dickinson, and the others waited anxiously. As the afternoon turned into evening, they began to worry. Lincoln had been reluctant to take bold steps before, stubbornly refusing to translate his antislavery feelings into meaningful change. Perhaps he'd changed his mind and disappointed them once again. They had no way of knowing the proclamation had been delayed by a printing error.[3]

And then, after ten p.m., a messenger ran in with news from the telegraph office—the Emancipation Proclamation had been issued! Freedom—at least in theory—had arrived for more than three million people who lived in the Confederacy (although not for enslaved people in the Union states of Delaware, Missouri, Kentucky, and Maryland). The crowd at the Tremont Temple jumped to their feet and threw their hats in the air, cheering for Lincoln and the proclamation. With tears in many of their eyes, they prayed and sang before walking a few blocks through the midnight snow to the Twelfth Baptist Church, Boston's leading Black congregation. They continued feasting and praying until dawn because surely God had blessed the words these activists for freedom had published and spoken for more than four decades.[4]

The abolitionists believed in the power of the press to generate change, and they were right. They played a pivotal role in persuading Lincoln to issue the Emancipation Proclamation. Unlike most newspapers of its era, the abolitionist press was part of an advocacy tradition in journalism that unabashedly champions social movements and marginalized groups and has the ability to influence presidential policies.

In the early 1800s, most publications were aligned with political parties and either ignored slavery, accepted it as inevitable, or praised it as biblically commanded—and profitable. Small antislavery groups existed but were scattered around the country with little money and many disagreements over policies and tactics. The abolitionist press was essential for developing and communicating their ideas. Abolitionist newspapers and pamphlets printed descriptions of slavery's brutality, published accounts of those who had escaped, and publicized petition drives to sway the government. Gradually, antislavery writers and editors persuaded others to join their movement and pushed their ideas into the mainstream. They did so at great personal risk as they were attacked by mobs, threatened with jail, and even murdered. Once Lincoln was

elected, there was finally a president who read the words of the abolitionists and paid attention to their ideas, reluctantly at first, but then
with growing respect. Eventually his moral compass aligned with his
military strategy to save the nation from its greatest crisis.[5]

When the abolitionist press began expanding in the 1820s, most white
Americans spurned it, not just in the slaveholding South but also in many
parts of the North. The abolitionists were labeled as radical, fanatical,
and dangerous. Prior to the Civil War, they certainly didn't get much
support from the White House. After all, for more than two-thirds
of the years between Washington's first inauguration and Lincoln's, a
slaveholder was president. Even among the few government leaders
who condemned slavery on moral grounds, it was considered political
suicide to advocate for immediate freedom for America's nearly four
million enslaved people.[6]

One of the early publications to advocate for slavery's abolishment
was *Freedom's Journal*, the first newspaper written, edited, and published
completely by Black Americans. The Rev. Samuel Cornish, a Presbyterian minister, and John B. Russwurm, the nation's second Black college
graduate, launched the weekly publication in New York City in 1827.
"We wish to plead our own cause," Cornish and Russwurm announced
in the first issue. "Too long have others spoken for us."

Freedom's Journal didn't look much different than the text-filled
newspapers of Peter Porcupine and William Duane in the 1790s, but
the content was revolutionary. Along with literature, profiles of Black
leaders, and news about politics, religion, crime, and culture, nearly
every issue featured at least one article or letter about slavery. There were
accounts of enslaved workers fighting back against their tormentors,
the abolitionist movement in Britain, the capturing of escapees from
forced plantation labor, and the strangling, stabbing, and lynching of
enslaved men.[7]

Plagued with financial troubles and disagreements between Cornish
and Russwurm, *Freedom's Journal* lasted little more than two years. But

it made an impact, adding African American voices to the public debate over slavery, allowing far-flung Black communities to communicate, and laying the groundwork for future abolitionist efforts. By the end of the Civil War, about three dozen Black newspapers were published in the United States. Their names reflected their commitment to abolitionism: *Mirror of Liberty, Genius of Freedom*, and *Northern Star and Freeman's Advocate*, for instance. Like *Freedom's Journal*, the other Black newspapers struggled to survive, rarely selling more than three thousand copies a week and often fewer. But the newspapers were passed from person to person and read aloud to those who couldn't read, each copy sometimes reaching a few dozen people.[8]

Even more radical than *Freedom's Journal* was *Walker's Appeal, in Four Articles: An Address to the Slaves of the United States of America*. It was published in 1829 by David Walker, a Black clothing store owner in Boston who wrote with the vehemence of a biblical prophet. "You may do your best to keep us in wretchedness and misery, to enrich you and your children but God will deliver us from under you," he warned slaveholders. "And wo, wo, will be to you if we have to obtain our freedom from fighting."[9] Walker died a year after publishing his *Appeal*, but his words of resistance continued to spread, shocking many white people, including some abolitionists unsettled by the idea of an actual slave revolt. In the South, rumors spread that Walker's supporters were sneaking into slave quarters and sharing copies of his pamphlet. Terrified enslavers demanded that anyone caught carrying Walker's *Appeal* should be arrested. Virginia's legislature outlawed literacy among its enslaved population. When ships arrived at Georgia's harbors, sailors were quarantined in case they had a copy of the pamphlet on them.[10]

Slaveholders also feared William Lloyd Garrison, a mild-looking white man with a receding hairline, whose blue eyes flashed with passion when he discussed his hatred for slavery. Two years after Walker published his *Appeal*, Garrison began his newspaper, *The Liberator*, in Boston using a fiery style that one admirer said resembled "a newly discovered chapter of Ezekiel."[11] Just as he wouldn't expect a man with a burning house to give "a moderate alarm," Garrison promised not to be subdued about slavery. "I will not equivocate," he declared. "I will not excuse—I will not retreat a single inch—and I WILL BE HEARD."[12]

Garrison and other abolitionist leaders used their newspapers, pamphlets, and books to help organize the growing abolitionist movement. They formed the American Anti-Slavery Society in 1833, and within five years it had a quarter-million members and more than a thousand affiliates. Thanks partly to the efforts of abolitionist editors, the emancipation of all enslaved people, once considered an impossibility by American leaders, was increasingly a matter of public debate.[13]

One of Garrison's avid readers was Frederick Douglass, who had escaped slavery in 1838 and settled in Massachusetts. While doing odd jobs to survive, Douglass began reading *The Liberator* and attending abolitionist meetings. Three years after his flight to freedom, Douglass spoke at the Massachusetts Anti-Slavery Society convention where, one witness said, "flinty hearts were pierced, and cold ones melted by his eloquence." From then on, Douglass's stirring words, powerful baritone voice, and graceful speaking style made him a star on the abolitionist lecture circuit.

Douglass used funds from British admirers to launch a new weekly publication, the *North Star*, in 1847. Based in Rochester, New York, the *North Star* featured correspondents from around the United States as well as Europe and the West Indies. Its best writer was Douglass himself, who didn't mince words when it came to defending freedom.[14] "Every colored man in the country should sleep with his *revolver under his head*, loaded and ready for use," he urged his readers.[15] In addition to abolitionism, Douglass advocated for women's suffrage and played an active role in the 1848 Seneca Falls Convention for female rights. Douglass published the financially struggling *North Star* despite constant threats. Mobs of slavery supporters threw rocks and eggs at him, shouted racist taunts during his lectures, and knocked him off stage as he tried to speak.[16]

The nation's proslavery power structure was terrified of the growing strength of the abolitionist press. Postmaster General Amos Kendall decided that local postmasters could choose to stop distributing "inflammatory" antislavery materials. Towns in Alabama, Mississippi, Virginia, Maine, Pennsylvania, New Hampshire, New Jersey, and Massachusetts approved resolutions encouraging their postmasters to destroy antislavery literature. Every southern state except Kentucky passed laws preventing the distribution of abolitionist newspapers. John Calhoun, the powerful South Carolina senator, tried to ban newspapers with images of slavery from the mail after *The Liberator* put an image of a slave auction at the top of each edition's front page. The Georgia legislature offered a $5,000 reward for Garrison's capture. But Garrison and other editors weren't intimidated. When a supporter suggested that Garrison tone down his heated rhetoric, he responded, "I have need to be on fire, for I have mountains of ice to melt."[17]

On a November night in 1837, Presbyterian minister Elijah Lovejoy stood with a rifle in his hands inside a warehouse in Alton, Illinois. Stout and muscular with a round face and intense dark eyes, Lovejoy was ready to protect a printing press that had arrived the previous night for his abolitionist newspaper, the *Alton Observer*. It was his fourth press. The first had been destroyed by a white mob in St. Louis, where auctioning human beings was common. Lovejoy had written in his *St. Louis Observer* about the torture endured by Black people, alluded to the frequent rapes committed by enslavers, and insisted slavery was "repugnant to the very first principles of liberty."[18] This was too much for slavery supporters. A committee of leading citizens passed a resolution stating that freedom of speech didn't give people the right "to freely discuss the question of slavery, either orally or through the medium of the press."[19] When a judge (with the appropriate name of Luke E. Lawless) encouraged a grand jury not to indict vigilantes who had lynched a Black man, Lovejoy sharply criticized him. A gang responded by breaking into the *Observer*'s offices and throwing Lovejoy's printing equipment into the Mississippi River.

Lovejoy moved across the Mississippi to Alton, where he thought he'd be safer. He wasn't. Like much of southern Illinois, Alton had many slavery sympathizers. When Lovejoy's new printing press arrived, a gang demolished it. Still, Lovejoy persisted. He bought a third press, published antislavery editorials, organized antislavery talks, and called for a statewide antislavery convention. The white citizens of Alton were livid, and another mob destroyed the third printing press. By then Lovejoy was a national hero to abolitionists, whose donations paid for a replacement press. The day after it arrived, about twenty armed abolitionists joined Lovejoy in front of the warehouse to protect it. They heard shouts from about two hundred approaching men, who hurled stones at the defenders and shot at the building. Lovejoy and his supporters fired back, killing one of the attackers. The mob put a ladder against the warehouse, and a man climbed up to set its roof on fire. As Lovejoy ran out to try to stop the blaze, he was shot five times. He died within minutes.[20]

No one was ever convicted of killing Lovejoy, but his death emboldened the antislavery movement. Former president John Quincy Adams wrote that the editor's killing was "a shock as of an earthquake throughout the continent."[21] Although most of the nation still supported slavery and thought of abolitionists as reckless, many newspapers, preachers, and mass meetings denounced the murder. By the late 1830s, more than a million copies of antislavery pamphlets and newspapers had been distributed. The power of the abolitionist press to spread ideas was proven in 1851 when the *National Era* began serializing a new novel by Harriet Beecher Stowe about slavery's cruelty. It was so popular that it was published in book form as *Uncle Tom's Cabin*, which sold two million copies within a decade, increasing the pressure to end slavery.[22]

A tall, gangly twenty-eight-year-old state representative named Abraham Lincoln was one of the few Illinois politicians who condemned Lovejoy's murder. He denounced mobs that "burn churches, ravage and rob provision stores, throw printing-presses into rivers, shoot editors, and hang and burn obnoxious persons at pleasure."[23] Lincoln at this time was far from an abolitionist, but his law partner, William Herndon, became committed to the antislavery cause because of Lovejoy's death. Herndon corresponded with abolitionist Wendell Phillips and kept copies of *The Liberator* and other antislavery newspapers in their office, reading passages aloud to Lincoln.[24]

Lincoln often contradicted himself when it came to slavery. He despised it as a moral abomination, supported emancipation sometime in the distant future, and donated money for people escaping the South on the Underground Railroad. He was one of only six Illinois legislators to vote against a resolution claiming that "the right of property in slaves, is sacred to the slave-holding States by the Federal Constitution." Yet he carried many of the racist ideas held by nearly every white person of his era. He told "darky" jokes, doubted the intellectual ability of Black people, and opposed allowing them to vote or serve on juries. He thought abolitionists were self-righteous radicals who "would shiver into fragments the Union of these States; tear to tatters its now venerated constitution; and even burn the last copy of the Bible, rather than slavery should continue a single hour."[25]

As a politician, Lincoln constantly searched for compromises. After voters sent him to Congress in 1846, he opposed expanding slavery into new states or territories gained during the Mexican-American War. At the same time, he tolerated slavery in the South because he believed the Constitution and the nation's preservation required it. Lincoln supported the cruel Fugitive Slave Act and thought it would be best for everyone if all Black people in America were sent away to colonize Africa. "What I would most desire," Lincoln said in an 1858 speech, "would be the separation of the white and black races."[26]

By then Lincoln was a star of the new Republican Party, which formed in 1854. (The old Republican Party of Jefferson and Madison had splintered earlier in the century.) To boost his political career, Lincoln knew he needed the press, which had changed dramatically since the century's start. The introduction of cheap paper and steam-powered printing presses meant newspapers could be mass produced at an affordable cost for the expanding and increasingly literate middle class. The telegraph's invention in 1844 enabled news to be delivered instantly, and the growth of railroads and canals allowed publications to be distributed in bulk around the country. The days of waiting a week for information to arrive on horseback were over. News about slavery and the rising opposition to it could spread easily.[27]

Lincoln wooed journalists wherever he found them. His law partner Herndon observed that his friend "never overlooked a newspaper man who had it in his power to say a good or bad thing of him."[28] Because newspapers in the middle of the 1800s were still often closely aligned with political parties, Lincoln enjoyed plenty of partisan support from Republican newspapers. When he ran for U.S. Senate in 1858, he shared campaign intelligence with *Chicago Tribune* editor Joseph Medill and made the newspaper's offices his unofficial Chicago headquarters. The *Tribune* wasn't bashful about backing him, claiming that the "fresh, vigorous" Lincoln "never speaks that he does not bring forward something new."[29] Although Lincoln lost the Senate race to Stephen Douglas, Medill and other leading Republican editors eagerly backed him for president two years later. When Lincoln spoke in New York City in February 1860, William Cullen Bryant, the editor of the *New York Evening Post*, was on stage with him. So was influential *New York Tribune* editor Horace Greeley, whose newspaper called Lincoln "one of Nature's orators" and declared that no one "ever before made such an impression on his first appeal to a New York audience."[30] The *New York Tribune, Detroit Tribune, Albany Evening Journal,* and *Chicago Tribune* printed and distributed copies of the speech. Before the 1860 Republican convention in Chicago, Medill took charge of promoting Lincoln with articles and editorials. This boost by the antislavery press helped Lincoln clinch the Republican nomination.[31]

Lincoln expected that the general election would be close and wanted the support of abolitionist publications. At Lincoln's suggestion, Herndon traveled east and met with antislavery editors including Garrison and Phillips. When Herndon returned to Springfield, he told Lincoln their opinions, which were hardly enthusiastic. Garrison's *Liberator* called Lincoln "the slave-hound of Illinois" because he had supported a fugitive slave law for Washington DC in return for the eventual abolition of slavery in the U.S. capital.[32] But Garrison and other abolitionist editors warmed toward Lincoln as the campaign continued. *The Liberator* observed that the Republican Party "speaks and so acts as to cause the slave-traffickers to gnash their teeth, and the entire body of Southern ruffians to desire to administer lynch law to all who are connected with it."[33] In his new publication, *Douglass' Monthly*, Frederick Douglass described Lincoln as "a man of unblemished private character" with "great firmness of will."[34]

Lincoln won the 1860 election with just 40 percent of the popular vote but triumphed in the electoral college over three other candidates. The abolitionist press had no illusions that the new president planned to end slavery anytime soon. But most were cautiously optimistic about the first president to have a relationship with antislavery leaders, and Herndon continued his back-channel outreach toward them. "For fifty years the country has taken the law from the lips of an exacting, haughty and imperious slave oligarchy," Douglass wrote in *Douglass' Monthly*. "The masters of slaves have been the masters of the Republic. . . . LINCOLN'S selection has vitiated their authority, and broken their power. It has taught the North its strength, and shown the South its weakness."[35]

Southern leaders recognized the growing vulnerability of their slave-labor economy and responded drastically. In January 1861 troops loyal to South Carolina began blockading the federal garrison at Fort Sumter. In February the states of the deep South proclaimed the founding of the Confederate States of America, where slavery could endure forever. *Douglass' Monthly* described it as a "thick atmosphere of treason." Douglass insisted "the contest must now be decided, and decided forever, which of the two, Freedom or Slavery, shall give law to this Republic."[36]

The threat of war hung in the air along with clouds of yellow dust from Washington's dirt streets on March 4, 1861, as Lincoln rode in the presidential carriage to his inauguration ceremony. Squads of cavalry guarded the route to the Capitol to prevent an assassination by Confederate insurrectionists. After reaching the speakers' platform, Lincoln removed his stovepipe silk hat and began speaking with his clear, high-pitched voice. Emphasizing compromise with the South, he vowed to keep the Union together while endorsing the Fugitive Slave Act and supporting a constitutional amendment that would allow slavery to last forever. Lincoln promised he had "no purpose, directly or indirectly, to interfere with the institution of slavery in the States where it exists."[37]

The abolitionist press was outraged by the new president's words. It correctly predicted that attempts at compromise with the South were futile. Douglass said Lincoln's message of appeasement was immoral. "This denial of all feeling against slavery, at such a time and in such circumstances, is wholly discreditable to the head and heart of MR. LINCOLN," Douglass wrote in his *Monthly*.[38] Newspapers that backed the opposition Democrats weren't any happier with Lincoln. The *New York Herald* encouraged overthrowing the president and accused him of leading the country into "an abyss of ruin."[39]

It was the South, however, that started the descent into the abyss. Confederate forces fired cannons at Fort Sumter on April 12 and seized it the next day. The Civil War had begun. The abolitionist press rejoiced that the conflict might finally lead to slavery's end. In their role as advocates for justice, they pressured Lincoln during the war to provide emancipation through a constitutional amendment, protect freedom seekers from the South, allow Black volunteers to enlist in the Union army, and give full rights to Black people throughout the country.[40] By the war's end, they would achieve three of those four goals.

At first the abolitionists muted any criticism of Lincoln, hoping he would use the war to end slavery, but they were soon disappointed. Trying to bolster white public opinion in support of the conflict, Lincoln emphasized that its purpose wasn't emancipation. He also promised that

Union troops would capture and return enslaved people fleeing captivity. *The Independent*, the country's most popular religious publication and a leading abolitionist voice, called the seizure of freedom seekers a "disgrace." Douglass denounced the president as "the most dangerous advocate of slave-hunting and slave-catching in the land."[41] Garrison called Lincoln "a man of a very small calibre."[42]

Although Garrison and Douglass were frustrated, the abolitionist press helped spread opposition to slavery through the North as the war continued. "Never has there been a time when Abolitionists were as much respected as at present," antislavery editor William Goodell wrote in December 1861.[43] The president was paying attention. At the start of 1862, an antislavery lecture series was held in Washington. Lincoln attended some of the talks and invited a few of the speakers to the White House. It was the first time any president had spoken in depth with abolitionist leaders. As they encouraged him to end slavery, Lincoln listened respectfully while answering evasively. In March Lincoln invited Wendell Phillips to meet with him. A month later it was Goodell who visited the White House. Lincoln made clear he'd been reading what the abolitionists were writing, leaving Goodell encouraged that the president was moving in the right direction.[44]

That same spring, Lincoln made his first tentative moves against slavery. He asked Congress to fund compensation for enslavers in the border states who freed their captives, and he signed a bill abolishing slavery in the District of Columbia. For the first time in its history, the federal government had ended slavery where it once existed. The *National Anti-Slavery Standard* praised Lincoln for showing himself as "a resolute and a wise man." But the abolitionists' approval didn't last long. People escaping from slavery continued to be captured behind Union lines, and Lincoln revoked a general's order freeing enslaved people in Florida, Georgia, and South Carolina. When abolitionists visited the White House to urge Lincoln to issue an emancipation proclamation, he rejected the plan as unrealistic.[45]

In August 1862 five Black ministers were excited to meet with Lincoln, hoping he might have some positive news about ending slavery. They were bitterly disappointed when he told them that white and Black Americans "suffer" from each other's company and "should be separated." He suggested the ministers give up their homes in the United States and lead an effort to send freed slaves to colonize parts of Central America. The Black press immediately denounced Lincoln's plan; Douglass called it "silly and ridiculous." He criticized Lincoln for the racism inherent in the idea of pushing Black Americans to leave the country. The president, Douglass wrote in his *Monthly*, "is quite a genuine representative of American prejudice and negro hatred and far more concerned for the preservation of slavery, and the favor of the Border Slave States, than for any sentiment of magnanimity or principle of justice and humanity." Anna Dickinson was even blunter, calling Lincoln "an Ass . . . for the Slave Power to ride."[46]

Six days after Lincoln's meeting with the ministers, Greeley wrote a scathing editorial in the *New York Tribune* headlined "The Prayer of 20 Millions." The famous editor denounced Lincoln's reluctance to move faster to end slavery. Instead of helping people escaping slavery, Greeley said, Union forces were returning them to captivity or sometimes murdering them. Lincoln responded that he had other priorities. "My paramount object in this struggle is to save the Union, and is *not* either to save or destroy slavery," the president said. *New York Tribune* managing editor Sydney Howard Gay wrote Lincoln warning of increasing public frustration with his half measures. Lincoln invited Gay to the White House, where the editor encouraged the president to move forward with emancipation.[47]

Gay, Greeley, and Douglass didn't know Lincoln was secretly planning in the summer of 1862 to take a bold step: drafting an Emancipation Proclamation. It declared that enslaved Black people living in the Confederacy would be "forever" free. Lincoln also decided to allow Black volunteers to enlist in the Union's military. During the war's early months, he worried that enlistment of Black soldiers would erode white voters' support for the conflict. But through most of 1862, the war went terribly for the North. Battles were lost, deaths mounted, popular support dwindled, and enlistment numbers fell. The Union's dire straits and pressure from the abolitionists pushed Lincoln to change his mind in favor of emancipation and Black enlistment. He decided, however, to delay proclaiming his decision until after the North had a battlefield victory. He wanted the proclamation to be seen as a sign of strength rather than desperation.[48]

It took a couple of agonizing months, but finally the Union claimed a victory at the Battle of Antietam. Five days later, on September 22, 1862, Lincoln issued a preliminary Emancipation Proclamation. If the secessionist states didn't return to the Union by January 1, he declared, slavery in the Confederacy would be abolished. In addition, the federal government would work toward gradual emancipation in the four slave states—Missouri, Kentucky, Maryland, and Delaware—that weren't in the Confederacy. Less than two years after Lincoln insisted he wouldn't abolish slavery where it already existed, the abolitionist press had pushed the president to make a drastic change: the U.S. government was now committed to ending more than 240 years of human bondage in North America. Douglass called the preliminary proclamation a "moral bombshell" that would shake the country onto a new, more hopeful path. "The Star Spangled banner is now the harbinger of Liberty," he wrote in *Douglass' Monthly*.[49]

The abolitionist press continued its campaign to make the proclamation official. Some of Lincoln's generals and cabinet members tried to persuade him not to release it, and Democrats opposed to emancipation gained congressional seats in the November 1862 election. But abolitionist writers, editors, and speakers kept up their pressure, and Lincoln didn't back away from his promise. On the first day of 1863, he made the Emancipation Proclamation final. Although it didn't immediately emancipate anyone in territory controlled by the Confederacy, Lincoln knew that a Union victory would mean the end of slavery for millions.[50] *Douglass' Monthly* declared that the Proclamation was "the greatest event of our nation's history."[51]

In the summer of 1863, Douglass went to Washington to lobby the government to recruit more Black troops and to treat them fairly once they enlisted. He was upset that Lincoln allowed white soldiers to be paid thirteen dollars a month while Black troops received only ten dollars minus three dollars for clothing costs. For Douglass, it was significant that he was able to travel as far south as Washington, past the state of Maryland where he had been enslaved as a child, into a city that until recently had allowed humans to be kept as property.[52]

The famous writer and orator went to talk with Lincoln at the White House fully expecting to be kept waiting in the crowded stairway for hours. But within a couple of minutes after sending in his card to announce his arrival, a messenger ushered him past the many waiting white men, at least one of whom snarled "n——" at him. Lincoln was lying on a couch reading, his lengthy legs seemingly stretched into every part of the room. As Douglass entered, the president stood up and shook his hand. "Mr. Douglass," he said, "I know you; I have read about you, and [Secretary of State William] Seward has told me about you." It was an amazing moment: a president was boasting that he had read the words of a Black abolitionist writer.[53]

The crafty politician and the abolitionist editor made strong impressions on each other. Lincoln was eager to justify to Douglass why he had moved slowly on emancipation and better treatment of Black soldiers. He wanted to make sure public opinion would support the measures, the president said. Douglass chided the president for vacillating on granting full emancipation. Lincoln responded, "Mr. Douglass, I do not think the charge can be sustained; I do not think it can be shown that when I have once taken a position, I have ever retreated from it." Douglass left the meeting stirred by Lincoln's "sincerity, with his devotion to his country, and with his determination to save it at all hazards."[54]

Douglass, the best-known Black journalist in America, continued to champion significant social and political changes that eventually became reality. Congress finally approved equal pay for Black troops in the summer of 1864, and Lincoln stopped publicly supporting colonization. Still, Douglass knew more needed to be done. He pushed for full citizenship and voting rights for Black Americans to counter rampant discrimination in education, jobs, public transportation, and nearly every other aspect of life. He argued that "the work of the American Anti-Slavery Society will not have been completed until the black men of the South, and the black men of the North, shall have been admitted, fully and completely, into the body politic of America."[55]

The pressure for change increased with the approach of the 1864 presidential election. To discourage abolitionist editors and other antislavery leaders from backing a third party, Lincoln gave them more attention. One of those was Garrison. *The Liberator* editor, who vehemently condemned Lincoln's early inaction, was now praising the president's recent achievements: the Emancipation Proclamation, the acceptance of Black troops in the Union army, and the abolishment of slavery in U.S. territories and the District of Columbia. Lincoln had brought abolitionism into the political mainstream, Garrison said. "We believe that he is thoroughly devoting his best energies to the overthrow of traitors and the restoration of the Union to its former integrity, and that he will extirpate slavery, root and branch," *The Liberator* explained.[56]

Once considered an extremist who was shunned by most politicians including Lincoln, Garrison was greeted with loud cheers at the Republican-backed "National Union Convention" in Baltimore. The convention unanimously nominated Lincoln and endorsed a platform developed by *New York Times* editor Henry Raymond that included a universal emancipation amendment to the Constitution. Lincoln's party had come a long way from its refusal four years earlier to make the end of slavery part of its platform.[57]

Lincoln had shunned abolitionists for most of his political life, but now he couldn't get enough of them. A day after the convention, he invited Garrison to meet privately at the White House. By then the war had taken its toll on Lincoln. His eyes were ringed with dark circles and his lean, muscular body was becoming gaunt and hunched over, but he still managed to chuckle as they spoke for an hour. "Mr. President, from the hour that you issued the Emancipation Proclamation, and showed your purpose to stand by it, I have given you my hearty support and confidence," Garrison said. Lincoln replied that he could use all of the support the abolitionists could provide and hoped their petition drive for the constitutional amendment banning slavery would be successful. Impressed with the president's candor, the crusading abolitionist editor left the meeting ready to campaign enthusiastically for him.[58]

Lincoln continued to curry favor from the abolitionist press for his campaign. Ignoring taunts from Democrats that presidents shouldn't be friendly with Black men, Lincoln invited Douglass back to the White House in the summer of 1864. He knew Douglass was denouncing him for not doing enough to let Black citizens vote, to stop mistreatment of Black troops, or to make defeated Confederate states reform their racist systems. During their conversation, Lincoln shared a letter he had drafted to counter criticism from some northern whites that he was allowing the war to continue in order to end slavery. Lincoln's draft letter pledged to "not make the abolition of slavery an absolute prior condition to the reestablishment of the Union." The president asked Douglass whether he should make his statement public. "Certainly not," Douglass replied. "It would be taken as a complete surrender of your anti-slavery policy, and do you serious damage." Lincoln followed the editor's advice and never sent the letter.[59]

Following their conversation, Lincoln observed that Douglass had become "one of the most meritorious men in America." Douglass said of Lincoln, "He treated me as a man; he did not let me feel for a moment that there was any difference in the color of our skins." A day or two later, Lincoln sent an invitation for Douglass to join him for tea. The editor sent his regrets that he was too busy.[60] This polite exchange might seem unremarkable today. In 1864 it was a profound change from the time when U.S. presidents used Black Americans for slave labor rather than inviting them for tea. The ideas promoted by the abolitionist press, once kept to the margins of political discussion, now had a home in the White House. Douglass recommended that "every man who wishes well to the slave and to the country should at once rally with all the warmth and earnestness of his nature to the support of Abraham Lincoln."[61]

Lincoln won a second term in 1864 with 55 percent of the vote, carrying all but three states.[62] "Every loyal vote was an anti-slavery vote," Garrison said. The nation now had a mandate, he wrote in *The Liberator*, to pass the Thirteenth Amendment abolishing slavery, which had already passed the Senate. The abolitionist press promoted petition drives to push the House to approve it by the necessary two-thirds majority. Still sounding like a biblical prophet, Garrison wrote that anyone who continued to support slavery "shall be smitten to the dust by an outraged public sentiment."[63] Lincoln listened to the growing public sentiment supporting abolition. He encouraged the House to approve the Thirteenth Amendment and promised to stop anyone who had been freed by the Emancipation Proclamation from ever being enslaved again. After years of saying that slavery should be left alone in Union states, he now supported immediate freedom for all enslaved Americans.[64]

The House gallery was packed with Black and white spectators on January 31, 1865, in anticipation of the Thirteenth Amendment's approval. When it passed with two votes to spare, representatives waved their hats in the air while onlookers hugged, shouted, and applauded. One Black witness was so excited that he found a nearby room where he could dance with joy. The Thirteenth Amendment became law later that year after being passed by the necessary twenty-seven states.. It was "the greatest and most important event in the history of congressional legislation," Garrison's *Liberator* declared.[65]

Lincoln had become a hero of the abolitionist movement. Black Americans comprised at least half the crowd during his powerful second inaugural address when he blamed slavery for causing the Civil War. God, he suggested, was punishing white citizens for their treatment of Black people. The war must be fought to its conclusion, he said, "if God wills that it continue until all the wealth piled by the bondsman's two hundred and fifty years of unrequited toil shall be sunk, and until every drop of blood drawn with the lash shall be paid by another drawn with the sword."[66]

Douglass watched the inauguration and decided to attend the White House reception afterward, something no Black man had ever before dared to do. As he and a friend approached, two policemen started to hustle them away, claiming they could "admit no persons of color," Douglass recalled. Thinking quickly, he asked passersby to tell Lincoln that "Frederick Douglass is being detained by officers at the door." Within moments, he was being ushered into the crowded East Room. When Lincoln saw him, the abolitionist remembered, "his countenance lighted up, and he said in a voice that was heard all around: 'Here comes my friend Douglass.'"

The two men chatted. One, enslaved at birth, had risked his life for nearly a quarter of a century to advocate for emancipation. The other, who once believed the government shouldn't end slavery, had used his power to do more to free Black Americans than any white person in the country's history. "Douglass, I saw you in the crowd to-day listening to my inaugural address," Lincoln said. "There is no man's opinion that I value more than yours: What do you think of it?'" Douglass encouraged Lincoln to visit with other guests, but Lincoln insisted on hearing the answer. "Mr. Lincoln, it was a sacred effort," Douglass replied. The two friends parted. It would be the last time they saw each other.[67]

In his final days, Lincoln often praised the abolitionists. As he visited freed territory in Virginia, a Union officer thanked him "for his great deliverance of the slaves." Lincoln responded that "the anti-slavery people of the country and the army have done it all." After General Robert E. Lee surrendered his Confederate army at Appomattox Court House, Lincoln suggested that Garrison and other abolitionist editors be invited to join the victory celebration.[68] But Lincoln didn't completely please the abolitionist press. In his final speech, he said he supported giving the vote to Black troops who fought for the Union and other "very intelligent" African Americans. Abolitionists were frustrated that the president didn't favor voting rights for all Black people. Douglass feared, quite rightly, that without voting rights for everyone, the fight for all other rights would be crushed. Still, the abolitionists recognized it was the first time any president had publicly supported giving any Black Americans the right to vote.[69]

John Wilkes Booth, a mentally unstable white actor brimming with grievances over the Confederate loss, stood enraged among the crowd outside the White House listening to Lincoln's last speech. Some of Lincoln's most ferocious opponents had argued in the press that assassination was a legitimate response to the president's reelection. The *Argus* of Greensburg, Pennsylvania, suggested either Lincoln's "defeat or his death is an indispensable condition to an honorable peace." The *Richmond Dispatch* insisted that "to slay a tyrant is no more assassination than war is murder." Booth agreed; he shot Lincoln at Ford's Theatre on April 14, 1865.[70] The president died the next day, which released torrents of grief through much of the country and halted any efforts he might have made to guarantee rights for the millions released from slavery. In a traditional sign of mourning, abolitionist editors printed thick black lines around their announcements of Lincoln's death. The assassination, *The Liberator* observed, "has bowed down the Nation with bitter sorrow and lamentation, to an extent so general and deep that none born in the present century can remember the like."[71]

An exhausted Garrison, believing his antislavery work was done, stopped publishing *The Liberator* later that year. Struggling with debt, Douglass had already finished printing his *Monthly*. Only a few abolitionist publications remained as America faced the challenge of making the Thirteenth Amendment's promises of freedom a reality.[72] The abolitionist journalists had helped make emancipation the nation's official policy but couldn't prevent the rise of lynching, the exploitation of sharecropping, the evils of convict leasing, the enactment of Jim Crow segregation laws, the mass incarceration of Black Americans, and other vestiges of slavery.

For most of his life, Lincoln considered these abolitionists to be dangerous fanatics who threatened to tear the country apart. He refused to meet with them, share a podium with them, or join any of their societies. Meanwhile, he supported the acceptance of slavery where it already existed, the Fugitive Slave Law, and the sending of Black Americans to foreign colonies. As Douglass noted eleven years after Lincoln's death, he "was ready and willing at any time during the first years of his administration to deny, postpone and sacrifice the rights of humanity in the colored people to promote the welfare of the white people of this country."[73]

And yet, once he reached the White House, Lincoln was willing to change his mind as he absorbed new information and witnessed the suffering of war. He began corresponding with abolitionist editors and other antislavery activists, then meeting with them, and finally acting on some of the ideas promoted by their publications, at first haltingly and then firmly.[74] To be sure, many different forces influenced Lincoln's actions, but it's doubtful he would have proclaimed emancipation if not for the abolitionist press raising public awareness and pressuring him. In future years this kind of advocacy journalism—when the press argues for a cause—similarly helped the suffragette, civil rights, gay rights, and other social movements persuade presidents and other leaders to make important policy changes.

There was another significant and more troubling aspect of Lincoln's relationship with the press: his curtailment of First Amendment rights. His administration shut down newspapers, confiscated printing presses, prevented some newspapers from being mailed, took control of telegraph wires to censor information, and allowed the military to arrest some reporters and prevent others from covering battles. In Missouri and Indiana alone, nearly 150 newspapers were suppressed. Lincoln justified this assault on the press by arguing it was needed to win the war and preserve the Union.[75]

Lincoln's censorship and suppression of newspapers set a dangerous precedent. When the Civil War ended, press freedoms were restored, but it wasn't the last time the U.S. government restricted the press. A little more than a half century later, a president who spent part of his childhood in the Confederacy faced another terrible war. In response, he put into place methods of intimidating the press and manipulating the public that other presidents have continued to use.

3

Woodrow Wilson, Presidential Propaganda, and the Suppression of the Press

Federal agents barged into the offices of the *Milwaukee Leader* on an October morning in 1917. That same day Postmaster General Albert Burleson revoked the socialist newspaper's second-class mailing privileges, preventing thousands of subscribers outside of Milwaukee from getting copies. Burleson also banned the *Leader* from using the mail to receive reports from correspondents, letters to the editor, and payments from advertisers. The newspaper's readership quickly dropped, and its advertising plummeted, causing it to lose an estimated $120,000 in one year.

The *Leader*'s crime? Criticizing U.S. involvement in World War I. It didn't help that its publisher, Victor Berger, a German immigrant with a thick mustache, thin glasses, and lively sense of humor, was the only socialist in Congress at the time. An ardent believer in democracy, the charismatic and energetic Berger opposed the war, condemned the draft, and argued for free speech against the "hysterical froth of jingo rhetoric." He wrote that young men were being used as cannon fodder while a small group of plutocrats profited from the war. His *Leader* ran the slogan "Starve the War and Feed America."

President Woodrow Wilson's second term was a dangerous time to be a dissident. As Wilson led the American war effort, his administration clamped down on freedom of the press to muzzle any opposition to sending American troops to fight overseas. A wave of repression swept the nation, and journalists with German accents or nonconforming political views were immediately suspected of treason.[1] Federal prosecutors indicted Berger and four other socialist editors and leaders in February 1918 under the harsh Espionage and Trading with the Enemy Acts passed by Congress the previous year. In January 1919 a jury convicted Berger, and he was sentenced to twenty years in federal prison. Finally in 1921, more than two years after the war was over, the Supreme Court overturned Berger's conviction on technical grounds.[2]

Berger was hardly the only member of the press or public attacked by the Wilson administration during World War I. By the end of the war in 1918, the Justice Department had prosecuted nearly 2,200 people under the Espionage and Sedition Acts, convicting more than 1,050. The defendants included journalists as well as labor leaders, pacifists, socialists, anarchists, German Americans, and Irish Americans. These prosecutions were part of a sweeping expansion of presidential power during Wilson's administration that included censoring the press, intimidating dissenters, and surveilling citizens. As Wilson rallied America to the cause of making the world safe for democracy, he significantly limited freedom at home.[3]

Stoking a climate of fear, Wilson created a model for questioning the patriotism of dissenting journalists and aggressively restricting the media in the name of national security. In the words of Wilson biographer A. Scott Berg, no previous president had "ever suppressed free speech to so great an extent in order to realize his principles."[4] His administration was also the first to deploy mass propaganda techniques, inflating the image of the president as the personification of the nation's government.[5] Many of the methods used by Wilson have been employed by other presidents eager to strengthen their authority, especially in times of crisis.

Woodrow Wilson had a rapid rise to the presidency. Deeply religious and a bit of a loner, he grew up in Georgia during the Civil War. His father, a Presbyterian minister, was an ardent supporter of slavery, and

Wilson inherited his racism as well as a tendency to think he knew God's will. The first president with a PhD, Wilson spent most of his career in the rarified air of Princeton University as a professor and then the school's president. With a large, jutting jaw and glinting eyes, he was a charismatic speaker. Sensing that Wilson would appeal to voters, New Jersey's Democratic Party bosses helped him become governor in 1910. His intellect, confidence, and golden tongue made him a political star, and the Democrats chose him as their presidential nominee two years later. He won with 42 percent of the popular vote in a three-way race against incumbent William Howard Taft and former president Teddy Roosevelt, who ran as the Progressive Party candidate.[6]

When it came to his relationship with the press, Wilson suffered in comparison to Roosevelt, who was admired by reporters for his jovial and energetic personality. Toward the end of the 1800s, more journalists began covering the White House on a full-time basis, and Roosevelt courted them to shape public opinion in his favor. He renovated the White House to include a room with telephones for reporters and often hosted informal gatherings with them. Taft tried to replicate Roosevelt's openness by hosting once-a-week sessions with Washington correspondents. But he considered the correctness of his policies to be obvious, and he didn't push himself to explain them to the public through the press. Soon the Washington press corps was pining for Roosevelt's transparency and personal touch.[7]

As Wilson prepared for his own presidency, he was determined to have a strong rapport with the press. After all, his grandfather had been a newspaper publisher in Ohio. The author of a dozen books about history and political science, Wilson understood the importance of positive publicity in shaping public opinion. He often collaborated with the press when he was New Jersey's governor, working with journalists to mobilize people to support his policies. "I, for my part, believe there ought to be no place where anything can be done that everybody does not know about," Wilson proclaimed as he campaigned in 1912. "Secrecy means impropriety."[8]

But Wilson's personality didn't lend itself to working cooperatively with the aggressive Washington reporters. Sometimes friendly in private conversations, he was often haughty in public settings. He had a hard time relating to the rough-and-tumble Washington press corps, most of whom didn't have a college degree, much less a PhD like he did. "Wilson had never met their kind at Princeton and didn't quite know what to make of them," historian George Juergens observed. "Part of the reason he and the press clashed is that they were strangers to one another."[9] As a result, his relationship with journalists was often chilly and even combative. Wilson bristled when reporters asked him questions that probed beyond what he wanted them to write, and he resented how his complex ideas were often reduced to sensationalized headlines and simplistic articles. A group of sympathetic reporters advised him during the 1912 campaign to counter his aloof image by opening up more. "I'd do what you advise if I could," Wilson replied. "But it's not my nature."[10]

Wilson's pride increasingly got in the way of developing a productive relationship with the press. Once, as he waited to learn whether he had won the Democratic presidential nomination, a reporter asked how he was handling the mountains of mail he was receiving. He replied that he felt like a frog stuck in a well who "every time he jumped up one foot, he fell back two." Wilson was offended when a headline in a New York newspaper the next day stated, "Wilson Feels like a Frog." According to Ray Stannard Baker, a popular journalist who was friends with the candidate, the incident intensified Wilson's distrust of journalists. "From this time onward he was never quite free with groups of correspondents," Baker said.[11] Wilson especially disliked articles about his wife and daughters, whom he thought should be protected from reporters' prying. This dislike turned to fury in 1914 when the press covered the illness of his first wife, Ellen, who died later that year from kidney disease.[12]

It didn't help that reporters thought Wilson was deceptive, using the brilliance of his words to mask the reality of what was happening. The mistrust deepened before his first inauguration when he insisted that he hadn't decided yet who his secretary of state would be. He claimed that stories speculating he had picked William Jennings Bryan were false when in fact he had already chosen Bryan. He lied to reporters again when he told them he was going to a nonpolitical dinner when he actually spent the evening in meetings about his future cabinet. Wilson appeared pleased by his successful deception, but reporters who had written inaccurate stories as a result were not amused. By the time Wilson took office in 1913, Juergens noted, he "was thoroughly disillusioned with the press, and the press thoroughly disillusioned with Woodrow Wilson."[13]

Wilson, however, couldn't escape an increasingly vigorous Washington press corps. With radio still in its infancy, people received nearly all of their news from print journalists. Newspapers were at their peak with more than 2,200 dailies and 14,000 weeklies clambering for stories. Magazines had boosted their circulation through hard-hitting "muckraking" articles by Baker, Upton Sinclair, Ida Tarbell, Lincoln Steffens, and other well-known writers who investigated society's ills and political corruption. As literacy soared, the U.S. public became better informed and more active politically, making the shaping of mass opinion increasingly important for politicians.[14]

Throughout Wilson's first term, his ability to inspire audiences through his soaring eloquence garnered positive news coverage despite his uneasy relationship with the Washington press corps. Soon after his inauguration in 1913, he took advantage of that persuasiveness when he delivered a speech to a joint session of Congress—the first president to do so since John Adams in 1797. He arrived at a House chamber teeming with legislators, cabinet members, and international diplomats eager to hear the president's words. He smiled with ease and calmed the applause. In a deep and smooth voice, he began to carefully read his short, well-crafted speech about tariff reform. His nine-minute talk was a big hit among congressmen and journalists, earning positive front-page coverage in newspapers across the country. Even the conservative *Chicago Tribune* noted Wilson's "dignity and impressiveness." He continued to use these formal talks to Congress to gain maximum publicity without answering questions from pesky reporters.[15]

Wilson resisted the warm bantering with reporters that Roosevelt had used successfully to promote his policies. Wilson thought journalists should serve primarily as stenographers who conveyed the official announcements of his administration. Leaking information to the press was terrible, he insisted, even though he did so himself. The best and most patriotic way to determine the truth, Wilson told a group of editors in 1915, was to ask the proper government authority. He didn't understand that many journalists had bitter experiences of seeking information from officials and then later learning they had been told a bundle of lies.[16]

Although his own relationship with the press was awkward, Wilson effectively molded coverage through two trusted intermediaries: Col. Edward M. House and Joseph Tumulty. House was a wealthy political adviser to several Texas governors before befriending Wilson and serving as his faithful counselor. "Mr. House is my second personality," Wilson once told a friend. "His thoughts and mine are one."[17] House often dined with writers and editors, feeding them slices of information favorable to Wilson along with the meal. When publications supportive of Wilson faced financial problems, House helped them find money to stay afloat. In return, journalists took suggestions from the colonel about story ideas, shared information about upcoming articles, and once even agreed to kill a story at House's request.[18]

Tumulty, who had been Wilson's secretary during his tenure as New Jersey's governor, managed the White House for the new president. The garrulous Tumulty was popular with reporters. He met with them every morning, answered their phone calls at any hour of the day or night, scheduled interviews with the president, and orchestrated news leaks. The press corps appreciated that he was always open to them and understood what information made for good headlines. In an era before there was an official position of press secretary, Tumulty served that role.[19]

With Tumulty's help, Wilson introduced a new tradition to the White House: press conferences. At the start of his first term, he held them every Tuesday and Thursday. For the first one on March 15, 1913, about one hundred reporters filled the Oval Office. But the press conference didn't start well. "There was a pause, a cool silence, and presently someone volunteered a tentative question," reporter Edward Lowry recalled. "It was answered crisply, politely, and in the fewest words. A pleasant time was not had by all."[20]

Nearly two hundred reporters crowded into the second press conference, which was moved to the larger East Room, but the results were even worse. Wilson urged the journalists "to go into partnership with me, that you lend me your assistance as nobody else can" so that together they could "make true gold here that will go out from Washington."[21] But the reporters did not see their job as siding with the president, and they didn't like being lectured to as if Wilson were their professor and they were dimwitted students. "It was appalling," reporter Oliver P. Newman later wrote. "[Wilson] utterly failed to get across to these men anything except that this was very distasteful to him, and they, on their part, resented it very, very seriously. They came out of the conference cursing, almost indignant."[22]

After this stumbling start, the press conferences continued to go badly. Wilson could be witty at times, but his aloofness and tendency to pontificate annoyed reporters. The death of his wife, Ellen, put Wilson into a deep depression for several months, leaving him even less willing to chat with reporters whose questions he believed were often ignorant, petty, and much too personal. Soon the number of correspondents attending the press conferences dwindled to about twenty. Wilson kept holding them twice a week for the first twenty-one months of his administration but then reduced them to once a week and less often after that. Following his reelection in 1916, he held only four for the rest of his presidency.[23] Despite Wilson's dislike of press conferences, however, all of the presidents who followed him continued the practice.

Wilson's awkward press conferences and chilly relationship with many reporters didn't stop him from receiving mostly positive coverage. The country was growing more prosperous, and he succeeded in getting popular laws passed. His legislative achievements were significant: a progressive income tax system, child labor protections, an eight-hour workday for railroad workers, reduced tariffs on imports, stronger anti-trust laws, the establishment of the Federal Reserve Board to protect the country from financial panics, and the creation of the Federal Trade Commission to safeguard consumers.[24]

But not all was quiet on the domestic front. The nation's more than two hundred Black newspapers frequently criticized Wilson for his racist policies. He refused to condemn widespread lynchings of Black Americans, imposed Jim Crow laws on Washington DC, and reduced the number of Black federal workers. The 126 Black newspapers of the National Negro Press Association petitioned Wilson to stop this deepening segregation, but he ignored their plea. As was true with all previous presidents, no Black reporters were allowed to cover the White House.[25]

While Wilson wanted to focus on domestic issues, the horrors of World War I began to command his attention. Americans watched in dismay as the bloody stalemate in Europe took the lives of 140,000 Germans and 240,000 British and French soldiers in the spring of 1915. Wilson called for calm and argued that the United States should remain neutral in the war, but Irish American and German American newspapers accused him of favoring the British and French. The *Gaelic American* and *Irish World* called Wilson an "Anglophile even before he became president" and his policies "blatantly pro-British."[26] The German-language newspapers—there were 537 of them in the United States in 1914 as part of a thriving ethnic press—were especially unhappy. One of them, *The Fatherland,* vowed "to place the German side of this unhappy quarrel fairly and squarely before the American people." Its editor, however, was soon caught conspiring with the German embassy in a sweeping propaganda and spying campaign, casting doubt on the motives of other critics of U.S. policy.[27]

In May 1915 German submarines torpedoed the *Lusitania*, a British ocean liner, resulting in the deaths of 128 Americans and more than a thousand others. Wilson avoided commenting about the attack at first in a futile effort to calm the public's anger. He instead spent the weekend playing golf, working in his office, and going to church. The public and the press didn't share Wilson's calm as angry editors described the *Lusitania*'s sinking as a "massacre," "slaughter," and "foul deed of enormous barbarity." When Germany sank another British ship in August 1915, killing forty-four passengers, Wilson knew a tougher stand was needed. The great orator decided to launch a speaking tour across the country to prove his ability to handle the foreign crisis. He preached the need for neutrality coupled with preparedness as large crowds cheered him and newspapers applauded his "forceful and earnest" remarks.[28]

During his reelection campaign in 1916 against Republican Charles Evan Hughes, a former New York governor and Supreme Court justice, Wilson put aside his disdain for the press. He courted individual journalists as Tumulty arranged for sympathetic profiles by renowned writers Ida Tarbell and Ray Stannard Baker. But Wilson had to overcome opposition from the German American, Irish American, and Black press as well as Republican newspapers that accused him of "ineptitude," "ignorance," and "too-patient" diplomacy. "When the sword is at our throat, he will write a little note," the *Chicago Tribune* sneered.[29]

A few publications circulated nasty rumors about Wilson. They said he once had an extramarital affair, fathered a child out of wedlock, and was even responsible for his wife's death by pushing her down a White House flight of stairs. It wouldn't be the last time a president was falsely accused of murder. Ultimately, Wilson gained press support in two crucial states, California and Ohio, where he personally courted newspaper editors. Thanks to a 3,806-vote victory in California, he narrowly won reelection by twenty-three electoral votes.[30]

Wilson campaigned using the slogan "He Kept Us out of War," but pressure to join the conflict mounted as he began his second term. German submarines sank three unarmed U.S. merchant ships in March 1917. The White House also learned from a decoded secret telegram that German diplomats were trying to entice Mexico to join a military alliance against the United Sates. The administration leaked the contents of the telegram to the Associated Press, and the next day headlines around the country trumpeted the news. "Germany is in need of the worst licking she will ever get," the *Daily Traveler* of Arkansas City, Kansas, declared.[31] On April 2 Wilson reluctantly appeared before Congress to declare war on Germany. "The world must be made safe for democracy," he said. Afterward, most newspapers filled their pages with praise for Wilson and enthusiasm for America's entry into the war.[32]

In his scholarly writings, Wilson had compared Lincoln to a dictator for his restrictions on civil liberties during the Civil War. Now Wilson was ready to curtail constitutional rights further than Lincoln ever had and seize additional authority as America prepared to send troops to Europe. The U.S. Navy took control of all commercial wireless stations, amateur radio operators were told to take apart their equipment, and the government seized telephone, telegraph, and cable lines. "It is absolutely necessary that unquestionable powers shall be placed in my hands," Wilson told a congressional delegation.[33]

When the war started, the Allied powers banned reporters from going near the front, afraid they might be spies or inadvertently reveal vital secrets. Some journalists who snuck close to the battle lines were arrested and threatened with execution. But as the war progressed, government and military leaders realized that news, if managed well, could be used as a public relations tool to support the war. "In this war, I consider a trained newspaperman worth a regiment of cavalry," declared General John Pershing, head of the American forces in Europe. "If he is in a position to serve his country with the typewriter and does not, he is lacking in his duty."[34]

Wilson agreed. He believed in the need for a "total war" that used all of America's resources to achieve victory. For the first time, mass advertising and a full-scale marketing campaign to rouse public opinion would be a major part of the nation's military strategy. Wilson needed Americans to buy war bonds and take jobs in crucial industries. Most of all he wanted them to join the army and fight overseas against an enemy who hadn't directly attacked the United States. Before the war, the U.S. Army was so small that it could fit inside a large football stadium. Now Wilson needed to quickly organize an immense fighting force. When people in some parts of the country resisted the military draft he had approved, Wilson decided extra measures were necessary to persuade Americans to enthusiastically support the war.[35]

Wilson launched a massive propaganda and censorship campaign. He created the Committee on Public Information (CPI) under the direction of George Creel, the former editor of the *Rocky Mountain News* in Denver. Friendly and self-confident, Creel endorsed Wilson's idealistic notion that the war could make the world a better, more democratic place. He envisioned the CPI as a "great publicity bureau" that would inform "every man, woman, and child in the United States, so that they might understand that it was a just war, a holy war, and a war in self-defense." Sometimes the CPI spread factual information; other times it shared inaccurate propaganda. For example, the CPI's *Official Bulletin* falsely boasted that hundreds of American planes had been sent to Europe. It also put out a press release saying that navy ships had courageously vanquished several German submarines in a running battle across the Atlantic. In fact, a single submarine may or may not have been sunk in a minor skirmish.[36]

The CPI's propaganda included promoting the president as a unifying commander in chief around whom the country should rally during this wartime crisis. Ray Stannard Baker, Ida Tarbell, and about one hundred other writers agreed to produce articles for newspapers describing the war as a democratic crusade. Posters were printed of ape-like Germans kidnapping Lady Liberty, while renowned illustrator Charles Dana Gibson mobilized artists to create advertisements to support the military. Publicists distributed seventy-five million pamphlets denouncing the brutality of German troops and describing America's noble war aims. Creel called these posters and pamphlets "paper bullets."[37]

Government propaganda reached into Americans' daily lives like it never had before. Teachers received biweekly newspapers that offered tips on how they could incorporate Wilson's policies into their lesson plans. Thousands of volunteers, known as "four-minute men" for their brief speeches, gave an estimated one million talks in churches, factories, schools, clubs, and movie theaters. Exhibits of machine guns, bombs, and other weapons traveled to state fairs around the country to promote the military. Boy Scouts distributed millions of copies of Wilson's speeches to people's homes. Taking advantage of the new movie industry's rising popularity, the CPI produced three feature films. One of them portrayed a German "Hun" raping nurses and throwing a baby out a window. Hollywood producers, who needed to make sure the government didn't cut off their supply of petroleum-based film, voluntarily allowed Creel's staff to edit their scripts.[38]

Wilson and Creel agreed that controlling the news should be part of the war effort. "If a censor is to be appointed, I want to be it," Creel said. At his urging, nearly all publications acquiesced to voluntary censorship. After all, most publishers and journalists didn't want to challenge the country's patriotic fervor or be branded as traitors. When some of the president's top aides suggested he appoint a group of reporters to advise Creel so that he didn't go overboard with censorship, Wilson responded that he didn't believe Creel was making any mistakes. The journalists, the president said, "are a difficult lot to live with." As he depended more on Creel and the CPI, Wilson relied less on Tumulty, who ended his daily briefings for reporters, further insulating the White House from the press.[39]

Several mainstream newspapers—the *Milwaukee Sentinel, St. Louis Democrat, Chicago Tribune*, and *Baltimore Sun*—questioned news reports about the war and criticized Wilson's military policies. Most, however, embraced Wilson's goals once America entered the war. William Allen White, a well-known progressive writer who edited the *Emporia Gazette* in Kansas, argued that the nation needed to work together for an all-out victory. "Having gone into the fight we must wage it so that the world will know that our entrance has counted," White wrote. "We must hit and hit hard and hit as quickly as we can."[40]

Publications serving marginalized communities were less enthusiastic. *The Suffragist*, the leading newspaper in support of women's voting rights, was deeply critical of Wilson. It accused "Kaiser Wilson" of failing to show leadership on behalf of women gaining access to the ballot. Black newspapers noted that Wilson did nothing to prevent white mobs in East St. Louis from killing thirty-nine Black people and burning down entire neighborhoods in 1917. Black editors protested the glaringly unfair treatment of African American troops, especially after the army court-martialed and hanged thirteen Black soldiers who had brawled with white civilians in Houston. The Black press highlighted the contradiction of Americans fighting for democracy abroad but not working toward equality at home.[41]

Wilson believed any criticism that weakened the odds of winning the war was dangerous. In the spring of 1917, he pushed for passage of an espionage law that would give the administration strong censorship powers. Disloyalty must be met "with a firm hand of stern repression," he argued. Censorship, he added, was "absolutely necessary to the public safety."[42] His proposed espionage bill received a barrage of criticism. "The people of this country will not consent to gag law," the *New Haven Times-Leader* warned. "Because he fears that some newspaper may not be loyal and discreet, President Wilson asks that all newspapers be gagged and commanded by dictators named by himself."[43]

The Espionage Act gave the government immense new powers to censor the press. Congress cut some of its harshest provisions before passing the law, but it still gave the postmaster general broad powers to restrict materials "advocating or urging treason, insurrection, or forcible resistance to any law of the United States." It also made it illegal to interfere with the military through "insubordination, disloyalty, mutiny, refusal of duty," or the obstruction of military enlistment and recruitment. Those who broke the law could be tossed in prison for up to twenty years. Although Wilson didn't think the Espionage Act was strong enough at stifling what he considered to be treacherous opinions, he ultimately signed it into law.[44]

The White House won additional control over communications when Congress passed the Trading with the Enemy Act in October 1917. This law allowed the president to order the censorship of "communications by mail, cable, radio, or other means of transmission passing between the United States and any foreign country he may from time to time specify" and to punish anyone who violated these restrictions.[45] Six days after the bill's passage, Wilson created a Censorship Board that allowed Creel to coordinate his work with the Post Office and the Navy and War Departments. Foreign language publications were required to submit copies to the board for review. If the publications were deemed insufficiently loyal, the Post Office could remove them from the mail, the War Board could restrict their supply of paper, or the Justice Department could prosecute them. As a result of the Espionage and Trading with the Enemy Acts, many publications censored themselves out of fear or shut down entirely. For example, by the end of the decade most German language newspapers in the United States had stopped publishing.[46]

By the spring of 1918, the situation in Europe looked dire as Germany was able to shift most of its troops to the Western Front after Russia dropped out of the war following the Bolshevik Revolution. A secret military study warned that labor organizers, anti-war religious groups, philanthropic "slackers," anarchists, and Black people all posed threats to wartime mobilization. When the radical Industrial Workers of the

World union called for strikes that would harm the nation's war-making capacity, Wilson decided that the Espionage and Trading with the Enemy Acts weren't strong enough. He argued that "precautions should be taken" to protect the nation against possible treason or disloyalty while American troops were fighting and dying overseas.[47]

Wilson and Congress were ready to assault the First Amendment. More than a century after Thomas Jefferson let the country's original draconian sedition law expire, Congress passed a series of amendments in May 1918 that became known as the new Sedition Act. Wilson readily signed it. This Sedition Act made it illegal to say, write, or publish anything that contained "disloyal, profane, scurrilous, or abusive language about the form of government of the United States."[48] Any indication of disrespect against the American flag, Constitution, government, or military was banned. The Post Office was allowed to stop the mailing of materials opposing the war or the draft, and it could prevent publications from receiving mail of their own. People convicted of violating the Sedition Act could be imprisoned for twenty years and fined up to $10,000. As Berg noted in his Wilson biography, "America entered a period of repression as egregious as any in American history."[49]

Wilson's administration didn't hesitate to use the Espionage, Sedition, and Trading with the Enemy Acts to criminalize dissent. Attorney General Thomas W. Gregory warned that war critics shouldn't expect any mercy from "an outraged people and an avenging government."[50] Movie producer Robert Goldstein was sentenced to ten years in prison for creating a film, *Spirit of '76*, that portrayed brutality by British troops during the American Revolution. The judge ruled that the movie might "make us a little slack in our loyalty to Great Britain."[51] After Frank Shaffer of Everett, Washington, wrote a book suggesting that "war itself is wrong," he was convicted under the Espionage Act and sentenced to two and a half years in prison. The Rev. Clarence Waldron received fifteen years for distributing a pamphlet that urged Christians not to fight in the war. Anarchist leader Emma Goldman also was arrested after writing that it was "imperative for every liberty-loving person to voice a fiery protest against the participation of this country in the European mass murder."[52]

Postmaster General Albert Burleson used the laws to stomp on press freedoms. He interpreted them to mean that publications couldn't "say that this Government got in the war wrong, that it is in it for the wrong purposes, or anything that will impugn the motives of the Government for going into the war. They can not say that this Government is the tool of Wall Street or the munitions-makers. That kind of thing makes for insubordination in the Army and Navy and breeds a spirit of disloyalty through the country."[53]

Burleson directed local postmasters to send him newspapers they thought looked suspicious. His office then used the Espionage Act to halt the mailing of Berger's *Milwaukee Leader* and other left-leaning publications including *Appeal to Reason* and the *Jewish Daily Forward*. After *The Masses* magazine published critical articles and cartoons, seven of its employees were indicted for conspiracy, and it was forced out of business. The *New York Call* was excluded from the mail after publishing an article with the headline "Bankers Hope to Use Soldiers Back from War to Cut Wages." The *Jeffersonian* of Thomson, Georgia, was similarly banned for suggesting that soldiers sent to Europe were almost certain to die.[54]

Even Wilson thought Burleson sometimes went too far. Distribution of the liberal *Nation* magazine, which had been publishing since 1865, was temporarily halted before Wilson reversed the decision. He questioned the prosecution of the *Milwaukee Leader* and said that he considered some of the editors of *The Masses* to be "well-intentioned people." Still, Wilson did little to stop Burleson. When Herbert Croly, founder of the *New Republic*, warned that moderates thought the suppression of dissent was becoming dangerous, Wilson assured him that Burleson "sought to act in a very just and conciliatory manner."[55]

Wilson led the country to new levels of fear, repression, and intolerance. His authoritarian approach toward dissent soon seeped into nearly every American city, town, and hamlet. Thousands of "Councils of Defense" were created to sniff out disloyalty and, in some cases, crush political opponents. The Justice Department formed the American Protective League, a group of 250,000 volunteers who were allowed to spy on civilians, read private letters, examine medical records, and harass anti-war newspapers. Other groups around the country persuaded local governments to ban the teaching of German in schools and the publishing of German-language newspapers. Encouraged by Wilson's denunciations of the war's critics, vigilante gangs attacked dissenters and ransacked their homes. In Collinsville, Illinois, a mob lynched a man suspected of being sympathetic to the Germans.[56] A few brave dissenters spoke out against the mob violence and the administration's repressive policies. Max Eastman, *The Masses'* editor, wrote to Wilson, "Is there not grave danger to our civil liberties in these hundreds of thousands of armed men, if in the name of patriotism they are allowed with impunity to degenerate into gangs of marauders?"[57]

But Wilson had the courts on his side when it came to limiting freedom of speech and the press. Few judicial precedents protecting First Amendment rights existed at the time, and some judges believed that civil liberties were for proper citizens, not dissenters and radicals. In March 1919 the Supreme Court backed the government in four Espionage Act cases, including the conviction of Eugene Debs, the socialist leader who had won nearly a million votes when he ran for president in 1912. Debs had been sentenced to ten years in prison for criticizing the government's prosecution of people opposed to the draft and for telling workers they were "fit for something better than slavery and cannon fodder."[58]

In November 1919 the Supreme Court decided in *Abrams v. United States* to uphold the conviction of a group of Jewish immigrants for distributing leaflets that protested the sending of U.S. troops to Russia. But Justices Oliver Wendell Holmes and Louis D. Brandeis dissented. Holmes argued that the defendants had as much right to publish their views "as the Government has to publish the Constitution of the United States." Over the next couple of decades, the court gradually shifted toward the opinion of Brandeis and Holmes that free speech and a free press should be protected, even in times of crisis. The repression of the Wilson years thus eventually led to legal rulings that would help defend the press when it clashed with future presidents.[59]

Germany signed an armistice on November 11, 1918, ending a war that had taken the lives of more than eight million people, including at least 115,000 Americans. Wilson was hailed as democracy's champion. He was the most powerful man in the world, possessing more global influence than any previous president. Throughout much of the United States and in many other countries, he was revered for his ideals as well as his ability to swiftly develop a massive and victorious fighting machine.[60] The *New York Times* praised Wilson for his eloquence and the clarity of his moral vision. "The impartial judgment of history will accord to him a high place among the forces that have now prevailed over the false and outworn doctrine of autocratic government irresponsibly controlling vast military power," the *Times* said. "He has become a great leader."[61]

Less than four weeks after the armistice's signing, Wilson headed to France to oversee peace negotiations, becoming the first president to leave the United States while in office. Most newspapers applauded this bold diplomatic move. Simeon Strunsky of the *New York Evening Post* called the president's voyage the most important trip across the ocean since Columbus sailed to America. As Wilson's ship steamed out of New York harbor, crowds saluted him with horns, sirens, and showers of confetti. When he arrived in France, he was greeted with a banner reading, "Hail the Champion of the Rights of Men." Two million people lined the streets of Paris to cheer him with chants of "Long Live Wilson."[62]

Journalists, however, were soon disillusioned with Wilson. Six hundred of them gathered in Paris to cover the president and the leaders of Britain, France, and Italy as they convened what was expected to be the greatest peace conference in history. Forever mistrustful of the press, the president worried that one bad story could overturn the fragile negotiations. Influenced by Wilson, the delegations from the Allied powers decided to bar reporters from their sessions and prohibit their staffs from discussing conference topics with journalists. Reporters complained bitterly that the president's vow to create "open covenants of peace, openly arrived at" was a hollow promise. They argued that the public could not weigh the benefits of a peace agreement if they weren't informed about it; headlines in American newspapers referred to "gag orders." Journalists submitted a petition and threatened to go home unless they could cover the important events. The leaders of the four Great Powers compromised and allowed their staffs to share limited information with the press and permitted a few reporters to attend some of the sessions on behalf of their colleagues.[63]

Out of the ashes of the war, Wilson was determined to create a League of Nations that could settle international disputes and avoid future devastating conflicts. But he couldn't use the magic of his oratory from across the ocean to persuade Americans to support the League because technology didn't yet exist allowing him to do so. He needed the press even though he did not realize it. Stubborn as usual, Wilson spurned reporters' requests to explain his thinking. Instead, he shared his perspective only through Ray Stannard Baker, who had become the Peace Commission's press representative. Rebuffed by the president, the newsmen relied on rumors and tidbits of information from less reliable sources. Even as the negotiators finalized the peace treaty to be signed at the palace of Versailles, Wilson tried to keep the full text from the press. "The newspaper men, for the most part eager to support the American position, were not permitted to know even semiofficially what the American position was," complained William Allen White, the famous editor who had been a strong Wilson supporter. "It is not surprising that under this state of facts they began to lose confidence in American leadership."[64]

By rebuffing the press, Wilson contributed to his greatest political disaster. When he returned to the United States in July 1919 to lobby the Senate to ratify the Treaty of Versailles, an uneasy public—kept in the dark during the Paris negotiations—was uncertain about supporting it. Republicans, who had won majorities in both houses of Congress during the 1918 midterm elections, argued against ratifying the treaty. They didn't like that its proposed League of Nations would obligate members to respond militarily to other countries' aggression. They were also eager to strike a political blow against Wilson. Some Republicans and newspaper publishers said they would back the treaty if it were amended, but a stubborn, exhausted Wilson refused to compromise, and opposition grew.[65]

To rally public support, Wilson launched a grueling, eight-thousand-mile speaking tour by train, planning to visit every state west of the Mississippi. He once again summoned his masterful oratory, giving forty speeches in twenty-one days that shared his idealistic vision of a world where nations cooperate rather than fight. "There is one thing that the American people always rise to and extend their hand to, and that is the truth of justice and of liberty and of peace," he proclaimed in Pueblo, Colorado.[66] It was his last speech. On the night of September 25, 1919, near Wichita, Kansas, Wilson had what was probably a stroke, one of several he likely endured over the years. The president was rushed back to Washington where he suffered a cerebral thrombosis—a blood clot in the artery leading to the brain—that nearly took his life. It paralyzed the left side of his body and left him too weak to lobby for the treaty's passage.

Wilson's disdain for the press and Congress, along with his failing health, doomed his efforts to pass the treaty. In a final effort to control information, his closest aides and his second wife, Edith, hid the president's debilitated condition from reporters and the public, saying that he was suffering from digestive problems and nervous exhaustion. Rumors spread that Wilson had fallen into a coma, gone insane, or died as he remained in almost complete isolation. He gradually became strong enough to review some documents and meet on occasion with his cabinet and congressional leaders, but Edith Wilson, his close aide Tumulty, and Wilson's doctor made many crucial decisions for him. Meanwhile some journalists, whose animosity toward the president had only grown over the years, cooperated with Wilson's opponents to bash the treaty. His cherished goal of the United States joining the League of Nations was crushed in November 1919 when the Senate refused to ratify the treaty. The League eventually sputtered into existence too weak to act decisively without the participation of the world's mightiest country.[67]

While a debilitated Wilson finished his second term, the repressiveness of the war years continued into peacetime. Following the Russian Revolution, a "red scare" swept the United States. Vigilante mobs assaulted labor activists, white gangs attacked Black veterans who were demanding equal rights, the government rounded up and deported immigrants suspected of being leftists, and court cases against dissident journalists such as Victor Berger continued. The worst of the attacks on a free press finally ended when Republican Warren Harding was elected in 1920 to replace Wilson, and fears roused by the war began to recede.[68]

During his presidency, Wilson set a strong precedent for future presidents to deploy the full power of the federal government to hide information, use propaganda, and suppress journalism in times of war and, increasingly, in times of peace. While he led the United States to victory in the fighting, Wilson made the country less safe for democracy. The Espionage Act he approved remains on the books, and recent presidents, especially Barack Obama and Donald Trump, have used it against the press. The reading of emails and the scrutiny of private phone calls by the National Security Agency during George W. Bush's administration resemble the reading of telegrams by the U.S. military during Wilson's presidency. Other presidents including Trump have used the tools of mass marketing and press intimidation just as George Creel and the CPI did.[69]

Historians speculate that if radio broadcasts had been common during Wilson's drive to ratify the peace treaty, he could have skipped his last, desperate train trip. Instead he could have spoken over the airwaves to persuade millions of Americans to support joining the League of Nations. But radio only reached small audiences until the last few months of his presidency when KDKA in Pittsburgh began broadcasting regularly scheduled programs and covered Harding's 1920 victory. It would take just a dozen more years until Franklin Delano Roosevelt was able to use the power of the new technology to successfully circumvent the press and transform the way presidents communicate with the American people.[70]

4

Franklin Delano Roosevelt and
the Power of New Media

A parade two miles long greeted Franklin Delano Roosevelt when he
came to Chicago in October 1936 for his presidential reelection campaign. As he rode from the train station through the city, hundreds of
thousands cheered from the sidewalks, excited to see his well-known
face with its wide smile, broad forehead, and prominent chin. The
police said it was the biggest crowd they'd ever seen. When the president
arrived at the Chicago Stadium to give his seventh speech of the day,
supporters filled each of the twenty-six thousand seats, crammed the
aisles, and swarmed the sidewalks outside.

The throng inside "gave him an almost hysterical welcome that
lasted several minutes as he walked onto the stage of Chicago's huge
stadium," the Associated Press reported. Sweating under a bright spotlight, Roosevelt—affectionately known as FDR—reminded the crowd
and the millions listening on radio that he'd accepted the Democratic
presidential nomination on the same stage four years earlier. In those
dark days of 1932, factories were failing, the stock market was plunging,
and banks were closing. Now, he said, factories "sing the song of industry, markets hum with bustling movement; banks are secure; ships and
trains are running full." The audience roared its approval.[1]

But the next day's *Chicago Tribune* wasn't impressed with the president's visit. After all, *Tribune* publisher Col. Robert McCormick—he

insisted on keeping the "Colonel" before his name after serving in World War I—was a diehard Roosevelt foe. Using one leaflet as evidence, the *Tribune* insisted that the cheering crowds consisted mostly of union members ordered by their "fat Bosses" to attend against their will. "It was an experience with the methods of Hitler and Mussolini," a *Tribune* editorial thundered, comparing the democratically elected president to the two dictators who were menacing Europe.[2] The unwilling participants were so angered by the experience, the *Tribune* claimed, that they threw their Roosevelt campaign buttons to the ground all along the presidential parade route. As proof, a *Tribune* photo showed a man picking up the discarded buttons. There was a problem with this account of events, however. The rival *Chicago Times* revealed that the buttons had actually been spread along the route by a *Tribune* photographer.[3] The *Tribune* had been caught falsifying the news to fit its ideological perspective.

McCormick's *Tribune* wasn't the only publication opposing Roosevelt. Only 36 percent of newspapers endorsed him in 1936 compared with 57 percent for his opponent, Governor Alf Landon of Kansas.[4] The mighty Hearst newspaper chain vehemently denounced most of Roosevelt's policies. So did *Time*, the dominant news magazine of the day. But FDR had found a way to use new technology to get around the opposition from these titans of the press. Soon after he arrived in the White House, he sat down in front of a microphone and forever changed the way presidents communicate with the American people.

For generations the only national politician whom most Americans ever heard was their local congressman if they happened to encounter him in person. Presidents relied primarily on the written word—usually filtered through the perspective of newspaper and magazine editors—to reach the public. FDR changed that. He used the newfangled medium of radio to speak directly to nearly the entire nation. Now the vast majority of citizens could hear the president's voice and listen to his policies without journalists serving as gatekeepers of the news.

Roosevelt successfully used radio to convey the idea that he was the one who truly understood and represented the common people as they faced the crises of the Great Depression and World War II. Because no one in Congress could attract the same kind of audience, the balance of power in Washington shifted toward the executive branch.[5] Future presidents tried to follow Roosevelt's example of using the latest technology to go around the gatekeepers of traditional media. Some, such as John F. Kennedy and Ronald Reagan with television, and Barack Obama and Donald Trump with social media, succeeded at getting their messages out. Others, such as Richard Nixon, never got the hang of it.

FDR was an unlikely populist. A fifth cousin of Theodore Roosevelt, he was born wealthy with an annual trust fund income worth $2 million in 2020 dollars. After graduating from Harvard, he began his political career as a New York state senator in 1910 before becoming assistant secretary of the navy in the Wilson administration. Smart, tenacious, and charismatic, he became a rising star in the Democratic Party. He ran for vice president in 1920 but was crushed in the landslide that made Warren Harding president.[6]

The following year, at age thirty-nine, Roosevelt was stricken with polio. His legs were paralyzed, and from then on he needed iron braces to stand. But along with his family and staff, he maintained a myth that he had almost completely recovered from his paralysis. Writers and photographers respected FDR's requests not to depict him in his wheelchair or struggling to walk. Most Americans had no idea how much the polio had crippled him.[7] It was a deception that could only work in an era before television when reporters gave more deference to presidents.

Projecting himself as a vigorous leader, Roosevelt was elected New York's governor in 1928. From the start he knew how to create events that would garner positive media coverage. He went on frequent trips around the state inspecting hospitals, canals, and schools, giving writers and photographers abundant material to fill their publications' pages. FDR also allowed reporters to meet with him almost daily. With his big grin, easy laugh, and warm voice, he quickly put them at ease. "In less than five minutes I felt that he might be an old friend," journalist Earle Looker said of his first meeting with the governor.[8]

When Roosevelt ran for president in 1932, he courted the rich owners who dominated the media, which was increasingly concentrated into broadcast networks, newspaper chains, and large magazine companies. The media mogul who most worried Roosevelt was William Randolph Hearst. Biographer John Tebbel described Hearst as the "ringmaster of the largest journalistic show on earth."[9] His empire reached twenty million readers through his thirty newspapers. He also owned *Cosmopolitan*, *Harper's Bazaar*, and five other magazines along with two movie companies, eight radio stations, and the International News Service.[10]

As the 1932 Democratic convention drew near, Hearst was ready to play kingmaker because of his heavy influence over the California, Texas, and Illinois delegations. He told his editors to start beating the drums for his own candidate, Speaker of the House John Nance Garner of Texas. His newspapers ran front-page editorials ridiculing Roosevelt and calling him an internationalist, considered a dirty word after the carnage of World War I. To please Hearst, Roosevelt issued a statement claiming he no longer favored entry into the League of Nations. The publishing tycoon savored FDR's humiliation. "Hearst's cohorts here are having the time of their lives raucously laughing at the manner in which their chief brought the Governor of New York to his knees," one of Roosevelt's friends observed. "They boast that from now on Roosevelt is at Hearst's mercy."[11]

Roosevelt couldn't win a majority on any of the convention's first three rounds of voting. Chances were growing that the convention could turn to a dark horse candidate. In desperation, Roosevelt's team asked Boston financier Joseph P. Kennedy to reach out to Hearst. Kennedy persuaded the newspaper baron that if Roosevelt didn't win on the next ballot, a candidate he liked even less probably would. Hearst agreed to tell Garner to release his delegates to Roosevelt in return for becoming the vice-presidential candidate. Garner followed Hearst's orders, and Roosevelt won the nomination on the next ballot. The publisher had flexed his power.[12]

With Hearst finally in his corner, Roosevelt could focus on persuading the public that he was the best candidate to end the Depression that was battering the economy. Fifteen million people—a third of all workers—were unemployed. Hungry people scavenged through trash bins for a morsel to eat. Homeowners were facing foreclosure, struggling farms were being abandoned, and banks were collapsing. The gloomy incumbent, Herbert Hoover, was overwhelmingly unpopular. Roosevelt trounced him, winning all but six states and cruising to a 472 to 59 electoral college victory.[13]

In his first hundred days as president, Roosevelt took action at a breathtaking pace never before seen in Washington, pushing fifteen major bills through Congress. His "New Deal" created the Federal Deposit Insurance Corporation to protect bank deposits, the Federal Emergency Relief Administration to assist the unemployed, and the Tennessee Valley Authority to provide electricity and flood control. The National Industrial Recovery Act encouraged factory production. The Civilian Conservation Corps and the Civil Works and Public Works Administrations employed millions of people. The Farm Credit Administration helped struggling farmers save their mortgages, the Commodity Credit Corporation bought their surplus crops, and the Agricultural Adjustment Administration boosted their income. These first days were "a tornado of activity," *New York Times* White House correspondent Charles Hurd observed.[14]

Roosevelt handled the press deftly, especially compared with Hoover. For his press conferences, Hoover required reporters to submit questions in advance and then picked which ones to answer. By the end of his only term, he refused to answer any questions whatsoever at his rare press conferences, turning them into angry monologues. Hoover's relationship with the press, reporter Paul Anderson observed, "reached a state of unpleasantness without parallel during the present century."[15] In contrast, Roosevelt understood how to work with journalists. As an undergraduate, he had edited the *Harvard Crimson* newspaper, where he developed an appreciation for reporters' deadlines. In the 1920s he wrote regular columns for newspapers near his New York hometown and his Georgia vacation home. FDR was "the best newspaperman who has ever been President of the United States," columnist Heywood Broun wrote.[16]

Borrowing strategies from the growing public relations industry, the Roosevelt administration fed reporters a steady diet of favorable information. Press Secretary Stephen Early briefed them each morning with story ideas they might use that day. If FDR himself wasn't doing something newsworthy, one of his aides, his cabinet members, or his activist wife, Eleanor, surely would be. By the end of Roosevelt's first year, publicists in government agencies produced about one thousand press releases a month for Washington correspondents to use. Early supplied the government's own "feature stories" for the more than six thousand daily and weekly newspapers that couldn't afford their own Washington reporter.[17] The press was covering FDR extensively, but sometimes as more of a lapdog than a watchdog.

The administration's best public relations agent was Roosevelt himself. When he held his first presidential press conference four days after his inauguration, FDR began by shaking hands with the approximately one hundred reporters who squeezed into the Oval Office. Holding his cigarette holder at a jaunty angle, he greeted many of them by their first names. Roosevelt then conducted the press conference like a conversation, charming the usually cynical Washington press corps. At the end they applauded the president for the first time in anybody's memory. The *Baltimore Sun*'s Henry Hyde, one of the oldest reporters around, called it "the most amazing performance the White House has ever seen."[18]

Roosevelt held press conferences nearly twice a week, double the pace of Hoover during his final year in office. When FDR was ready to meet the press, he'd ring a buzzer on his desk. A secretary informed the White House usher, who clapped his hands twice. The waiting reporters then rushed into the Oval Office. Roosevelt sometimes jokingly began, "I don't have any particular news."[19] He then made announcements, answered thirty-two questions on average, and bantered with the journalists for the next twenty or thirty minutes. The president, columnist Mark Sullivan said, "could recite the Polish alphabet and it would be accepted as an eloquent plea for disarmament."[20]

The frequent press conferences allowed the administration to set the agenda for what the press covered and quickly respond to events before any negative news overwhelmed FDR's message. The reporters respected FDR's judgment to such an extent that one of them once asked him, "Mr. President, if you were going to write a story today for the morning papers, what would you write?"[21] It helped that Roosevelt liked most of the White House press corps, understood the challenges of their jobs, and knew how to joke with them. At the start of one press conference, he showed off a saber he'd received. "Are you going to cut off a few heads this morning?" one of the reporters asked. In response FDR teased that they better "be good this morning." When a reporter later asked a tricky question about monetary policy, Roosevelt replied, "Give me that sword" as the newsmen laughed.[22] Few other presidents have enjoyed that kind of relaxed rapport with reporters.

FDR's strongest ally in cultivating journalists was Eleanor. She earned positive coverage by holding her own press conferences with female reporters who had been shunned by previous administrations. She also won acclaim in the press for her efforts to help people living in poverty. The First Lady wrote a popular monthly column for *Woman's Home Companion* and added a daily newspaper column in 1935 and her own radio broadcast in 1937. She and Franklin hosted annual parties for the Washington press corps with dancing, plenty of beer, and a midnight supper. Full-time White House reporters were allowed to use the Executive Mansion's tennis courts and swimming pool, sometimes joining the president in the water. Their children could play in the White House sand box. A few journalists were invited to Sunday night suppers where Eleanor would scramble eggs for them. She once even knitted blankets for the newborn twins of a reporter. "With Roosevelt, this is the only time that I had the feeling that I was welcome here at the White House," one veteran reporter said.[23]

One group of journalists, however, was not welcomed. Reporters for Black newspapers began requesting permission to attend presidential press conferences in 1933. Press Secretary Early refused to accredit any of them to cover the White House, and Roosevelt did nothing to intervene. He was more interested in placating powerful white congressmen and voters from the South who wanted to maintain strict segregation. He also likely didn't want to answer questions about his poor record on civil rights. New Deal programs including the Civilian Conservation Corps and Tennessee Valley Authority practiced racial discrimination when it came to housing their workers. The Federal Housing Administration's mortgage insurance program excluded Black Americans while helping millions of white people. FDR also refused to back a 1933 anti-lynching bill. He did increase the overall number of Black federal employees, quietly ending Wilson's segregation of the government's workforce. But it wasn't until 1944 that Roosevelt and Early allowed a Black reporter, Harry McAlpin of the *Atlanta Daily World*, to attend a presidential press conference.[24] This long-running lack of diversity made a difference in what stories were reported from the White House.

Roosevelt remained friendly with most reporters who covered him, but he complained bitterly that their bosses were unfair to him. He insisted that 85 to 90 percent of American newspapers opposed him because they were owned by greedy, unpatriotic reactionaries determined to stop his economic reforms. In reality, the press was more evenly divided. A 1935 survey of publishers found that 29 percent claimed to be Republicans or Independent-Republicans, 27 percent said they were Democrats or Independent-Democrats, and 44 percent identified as independents. An analysis of nine critical events during Roosevelt's presidency concluded that the unfavorable coverage only slightly exceeded the favorable coverage.[25]

Still, Roosevelt was convinced that some of the most powerful media owners opposed him, which was true. One of them was Henry Luce, who cofounded *Time* in 1923. During FDR's presidency, *Time* was the most influential magazine in the country, as newspapers often echoed its weekly take on the news. Luce's company also produced the successful radio program *March of Time* and published *Fortune*. In 1936 it added the popular *Life* magazine.

The son of Presbyterian missionaries, Luce believed God was always guiding him as he sought to shape the world with his conservative ideas. After initially praising Roosevelt, Luce began criticizing the New Deal, accusing FDR of unfair attacks on businesses and other institutions. In 1935 he ordered his staff to publish an article in *Fortune* with the headline "The Case against Roosevelt." It claimed FDR had "opened a door through which a dictator could easily pass." *Time* opposed Roosevelt in all three of his reelection campaigns.[26]

Roosevelt's most ardent foe in the press was the *Chicago Tribune*'s Colonel McCormick. The grandson of Lincoln's friend Joseph Medill, McCormick ruled the largest newspaper in the Midwest with an iron fist. Shy with people, McCormick was pugnacious in print, vehemently questioning the decency, patriotism, and common sense of anyone who disagreed with him. During the administration's first weeks, he supported Roosevelt, particularly his promise to cut budgets. But within six months, the Colonel grew alarmed that Roosevelt was swiftly expanding government spending. He argued that FDR's National Recovery Administration, which created newspaper employment regulations, threatened freedom of the press.[27]

McCormick turned against the president with a vengeance. "Apprehensions that we are drifting into a dictatorship like that of Mussolini and of Hitler, that the independent authority of congress is doomed to be snuffed out like that of the Italian parliament and the German reichstag, are beginning to reverberate in the national capital," a front-page *Tribune* article claimed. Roosevelt responded at a press conference that McCormick was "seeing things under the bed." The reporters laughed; the Colonel seethed.[28]

A 1936 poll of the Washington press corps ranked the *Tribune* as having the second "least fair and reliable" coverage. First place went to William Randolph Hearst's newspapers. During the early months of Roosevelt's administration, Hearst didn't criticize the president.[29] But that changed when Roosevelt called for higher income taxes on the wealthy, which the newspaper kingpin said was "essentially Communism." From then on, Hearst was at war with FDR.[30] In 1935 the publisher instructed his editors to replace "New Deal" with "Raw Deal" to describe White House policies.[31]

Roosevelt wanted to counter McCormick, Hearst, Luce, and other powerful publishers. One way he did so was to take advantage of the new medium of movie newsreels. Using the advanced technology of sound on film, five newsreel companies distributed dramatically edited news summaries to theaters around the country. The forty-three million Americans who went to the movies every week could now see and hear their president on the screen at their local theater. To get the nation's biggest celebrity—Roosevelt—in their films, newsreel makers were willing to let the White House shape his image. There he was on the screen meeting with world leaders, catching fish, and playing with his grandchildren. "We soon discovered that in Franklin Delano Roosevelt we had the greatest single attraction," one movie house owner said.[32]

Roosevelt took even greater advantage of another technology whose popularity was rapidly rising: radio. He had come of age politically at the same time radio listening was becoming widespread. Between 1927 and 1934, the share of homes with radio climbed from 24 percent to 65 percent. The number of people listening was much higher as relatives and friends gathered together to listen to their favorite comedians, singers, dramas, and sporting events along with the news. By the mid-1930s, Americans listened on average to four hours of radio a day.[33]

Roosevelt wasn't the first president to use radio. Wilson tried, but the technology was so primitive that the handful of listeners could only hear a few words through the static. Harding was uncomfortable using the microphones during his occasional broadcasts and sounded awkward. Coolidge often aired his speeches, but the networks still didn't have large audiences; his radio addresses reached only about fifty thousand people total in the first eight months of 1927. Hoover delivered his broadcast speeches in a dry, monotonous manner rather than adjusting his words and voice for radio. In contrast, Roosevelt had an instinct for radio. When he was governor, New York's Democratic Party bought an hour of airtime each month featuring FDR talking to the public as if they were good friends chatting about common concerns. In 1929 he held the first of what would become known as fireside chats, usually scheduled on Sunday nights when the audiences were largest.[34]

A week after he became president, Roosevelt asked the networks—NBC and CBS—to give him airtime on Sunday evening for his first radio address as president. He wanted to explain why he had ordered that all banks be closed as he prepared a bill to prevent more of them from failing. The networks didn't dare refuse the chief executive's request. "The President wants to come into your home and sit at your fireside for a little fireside chat," Robert Trout of CBS said to start the broadcast for the estimated sixty million listeners, half the nation's population.[35]

Then it was Roosevelt's turn. "My friends," he began with a firm, warm voice. It didn't sound like a typical speech. Instead, FDR resembled a kind uncle sharing his wise thoughts to each listener personally. "I want to tell you what has been done in the last few days, and why it was done, and what the next steps are going to be," he said.[36] Speaking clearly and using words that the public could understand, he explained the reasons for the banking crisis. He reassured people that everything possible was being done to avoid Americans losing their savings when banks opened again the next day. He praised them for their "fortitude and good temper" as they dealt with the inconvenience of closed banks.[37]

The public loved it, flooding the White House with appreciative telegrams. On Monday Americans showed their renewed faith in the banking system by making more deposits than withdrawals. Stock prices jumped 15 percent, and the dollar's value climbed.[38] The *Wall Street Journal* lauded Roosevelt for safely reopening the banks, getting Congress to take action, and giving the nation confidence. "For an explanation of the incredible change which has come over the face of things here in the United States in a single week," the *Journal* said, "we must look to the fact that the new Administration in Washington has superbly risen to the occasion." Humorist Will Rogers joked that FDR had explained the situation so clearly that even bankers understood it.[39]

Through the firesides, FDR created a personal bond with voters like no other politician before him. For the first time, a president could communicate with the entire nation at once without having to worry how journalists might frame his words. Knowing that each fireside would be more memorable if there were fewer of them, he averaged about two and a half per year during his presidency. The firesides became national events as people gathered to hear him in crowded apartments and desolate farmhouses, stately homes and neighborhood bars.[40]

The fireside chats sounded spontaneous, but they went through multiple drafts. Roosevelt, who read eleven newspapers a day, kept a file of clippings and letters to generate ideas. Cabinet members and aides submitted their own suggested topics. FDR dictated parts of each address to his speechwriters, usually after a lively cocktail hour and sometimes as late as 2 a.m. A team then polished the drafts before FDR edited them some more. By the time the talks were ready, FDR often had them nearly memorized. About twenty minutes before each broadcast, an aide pushed Roosevelt in his wheelchair into a first-floor White House room. About thirty invited friends and public officials sat on folding chairs crammed closely together. Puffing on a cigarette, the president chatted with the guests and announcers as network engineers tested the equipment. And then as 10:30 p.m. approached, the room would grow silent. FDR put out his cigarette, took a sip of water, and greeted Americans as "My friends."[41]

The firesides proved so popular that radio stations unaffiliated with the networks clamored to carry the addresses too, which the administration was happy to arrange. The networks had their own good reasons to carry the firesides and other pro-administration content. Unlike print publications, radio stations were regulated by the government to ensure transmitting frequencies didn't interfere with each other. The government's regulatory power gave the networks a strong interest in staying on the president's good side. Hiring people with close ties to the administration didn't hurt. NBC named Early's brother-in-law as its Washington news commentator. CBS chose a college classmate of FDR's as its Washington bureau chief.[42]

Roosevelt wasn't the only savvy user of radio for political purposes. Charles Coughlin, a demagogue known as "the radio priest," reached an estimated thirty million or more people with his broadcasts in the 1930s. At first, Coughlin backed Roosevelt. He spoke at the 1932 Democratic convention and told listeners that "the New Deal is Christ's Deal." But the priest became increasingly erratic and anti-Semitic. When Coughlin realized that FDR wasn't embracing his ideas, he turned against the president, calling him a liar who was moving toward "the form of government formed by Stalin, Mussolini, and Hitler."[43] He now insisted that the New Deal was a "Jew deal." After Coughlin refused to restrain his language, CBS decided not to renew his contract. Ever defiant, Coughlin created an ad-hoc network of more than thirty radio stations around the country to carry his harangues. The stations finally stopped carrying his broadcasts at the end of the 1930s when he became openly pro-Nazi.[44] Coughlin's rantings set an example for current broadcast hosts and other media partisans who spread toxic conspiracy theories and demonize political opponents.

Coughlin was part of a conservative backlash against Roosevelt as the economy continued to struggle. Even though more than two million people found jobs in 1934, the unemployment rate was still over 21 percent. McCormick's *Chicago Tribune* was one of the leading critics. A *Tribune* editorial argued that the "Democratic party has ceased to be an American political party and the government it supports has ceased to be an American government." A *Tribune* article recounted the wild accusations of an Indiana school administrator who said he overheard Roosevelt aides at a dinner party making "communistic plannings and utterances."[45]

In June 1934 Roosevelt responded to the criticisms by the *Tribune*, Coughlin, and others with one of his strongest fireside chats. He queried the public directly about his performance. "Are you better off than you were last year?" he asked. "Are your debts less burdensome? Is your bank account more secure? Are your working conditions better?" He also wanted the American people to decide whether he was too powerful. "Answer this question also out of the facts of your own life," he said. "Have you lost any of your rights or liberty or constitutional freedom of action or choice?"[46]

Roosevelt's media mastery helped Democrats gain a dozen seats in the House and ten more in the Senate in the 1934 midterm elections. The GOP had never held a lower percentage of seats. William Allen White, the legendary Kansas editor, suggested that Roosevelt had been "all but crowned by the people."[47] FDR followed the victory with more New Deal legislation. He won approval from Congress for launching Social Security. The Works Progress Administration put three million people to work building hospitals, schools, roads, and parks. Roosevelt also signed the Wagner Labor Relations Act, giving workers the right to bargain collectively, much to the fury of some media tycoons such as McCormick.[48]

Roosevelt won the 1936 Democratic nomination by acclamation. When he arrived in Philadelphia to give his acceptance speech, a packed stadium of a hundred thousand fans cheered. FDR slowly climbed a ramp to the stage, his right hand holding a cane, his left hand gripping the arm of his son James. Aides screened the struggling president from the crowd's view. As he neared the top, a rivet broke in one of his leg braces, and Roosevelt toppled to the ground. James grabbed his father, dropping the folder holding the unbound pages of FDR's speech that he'd been carrying under his arm. FDR's aides gathered around him to block the scene from the view of the crowd as James quickly picked up the scattered pages. Shielded by a wall of people, FDR was then carried by his elbows to the podium.

Putting all of his weight on the leg with the remaining functional brace, grasping the lectern for support as his knuckles turned white, sweating profusely in the muggy air, Roosevelt grinned broadly. "My friends," he began while looking down at his speech. It was then that he realized the pages were out of order from when they had dropped to the ground. Still, he kept talking about the New Deal's accomplishments as the hand that wasn't grasping the podium put the sheets in order. He transitioned smoothly to his printed words. "This generation of Americans has a rendezvous with destiny," he declared in what became one of his most inspiring speeches. Most in the crowd never knew FDR had fallen. Nor did the millions listening on radio or those reading newspapers the next day. The few reporters who witnessed Roosevelt's collapse kept his secret, preserving their unspoken agreement to respect the president's dignity.[49]

The Republican nominee in 1936 was Alf Landon, the sincere yet dull governor of Kansas. Hearst promoted him, directing his *Cosmopolitan* and *Good Housekeeping* magazines to run favorable profiles. McCormick's *Chicago Tribune* was even more partisan. Instead of a photo of FDR after he won the nomination, a front-page *Tribune* cartoon portrayed him with a Hitler mustache and swastika proclaiming, "I like this role best."[50] Almost all of the newspaper's coverage was devoted to positive stories about Landon, often on the front page. Because Roosevelt dominated radio, the Colonel explained, it was only fair for Landon to dominate the newspapers. When the *Tribune* did mention Roosevelt, it insinuated that he not only sympathized with Hitler but also with communism. "Moscow Orders U.S. Reds to Back Roosevelt," one headline declared for a story that was later thoroughly discredited.[51] The newspaper also tried to connect FDR's campaign to prostitutes and gamblers in a story headlined "Roosevelt Area in Wisconsin Is Hotbed of Vice."[52]

McCormick donated to the Landon campaign and was sure the Kansas governor would win by a big margin. He didn't. Roosevelt took over 60 percent of the popular vote and won more electoral votes—523 compared to 8 for Landon—than any presidential candidate before him.

FDR's Democrats were victorious in other races too, gaining a 331–89 majority in the U.S. House and an enormous 76–16 edge in the Senate. Wallowing in conspiracy theories, the *Tribune* blamed Roosevelt's historic win on "the workingmen and the Socialists and communists and other radically minded groups."[53]

Encouraged by the overwhelming victory, Roosevelt started his second term brimming with confidence. Then he went too far. Frustrated that elderly members of the Supreme Court had ruled against some New Deal programs, FDR proposed a plan giving him the authority to appoint six new justices. The press almost unanimously excoriated the attempted power grab. "President Roosevelt has brought forward a proposal which, if enacted into law, would end the American state as it has existed throughout the long years of its life," the *New York Herald Tribune* exclaimed.[54] Frank Gannett, the owner of a growing chain of newspapers, founded a group to fight FDR's plans for the court and the economy. Walter Lippmann, one of the most prominent American newspaper columnists of the era, accused Roosevelt of engaging in a "subtly legalized coup d'etat."[55] Hearing the criticism from the press and public, the Senate gave FDR a humiliating defeat, voting down his court plan 70 to 20.[56]

Meanwhile, the economy was deteriorating again. Five million people lost their jobs between September 1937 and April 1938, and the stock market plummeted. Eleanor "Cissy" Patterson, the *Washington Times-Herald* publisher and McCormick's sister, penned a front-page "open letter" to Roosevelt. The government's policies, she insisted, were responsible for nervousness about the economy. "You said once, with eternal truth, that the only thing to fear is fear itself," Patterson wrote. "With due respect, you should concede the obvious: This fear is fear of you." Hearst agreed. He quickly wired an order to the editors of all Hearst newspapers: "CHIEF INSTRUCTS PAPERS TO PRINT THE ELEANOR PATTERSON LETTER."[57]

Roosevelt used a fireside chat to counter these criticisms and try to restore public confidence in his leadership. "I propose to sail ahead," he told his listeners. "I feel sure that your hopes and your help are with me."[58] He asked Congress for $3.4 billion for housing, farm subsidies, and other building projects. The stimulus worked. By the end of the year, the economy regained half of what it had lost. But enthusiasm for the New Deal was waning. William Allen White wrote in his column that FDR had lost much of his power and was now only "a crippled leader of the Democratic party."[59] Indeed, Roosevelt's Democrats were walloped in the 1938 midterm elections, losing seventy-two seats in the U.S. House and seven in the Senate.[60] FDR's fireside chats and popularity with reporters weren't enough to ease voters' concerns about the enduring economic crisis.

While Roosevelt struggled at home, trouble brewed overseas. Italy attacked Ethiopia in 1935, Japan invaded China in 1937, and Hitler's Nazis were terrorizing Jews, homosexuals, and other minority groups. Just two decades after World War I, FDR began preparing Americans for possible involvement in another foreign conflict. "Innocent peoples and nations are being cruelly sacrificed to a greed for power and supremacy which is devoid of all sense of justice and humane consideration," he warned in an October 1937 speech. Most of the press praised the speech, but conservative publications—long supportive of U.S. isolationism—condemned it.[61] "We believe the American people are at present firmly opposed to the sending of a single American boy over any sea for any purpose no matter how altruistically the case may be presented," a *Wall Street Journal* editorial argued.[62]

This concern for protecting lives didn't extend to saving Jewish refugees trying to flee Nazi persecution. Roosevelt failed to push Congress to lift strict immigration quotas, which could have saved thousands, perhaps millions, of lives. His inaction reflected the anti-Semitism pervasive in the State Department and the anti-immigration stance held by most newspapers. Even as Hitler's violence escalated, some publications favored raising immigration barriers. The *Jackson Citizen Patriot* in Michigan argued in favor of "the customary bars against undesirable aliens."[63] The *New York Times* suggested that the terror Jews faced in Germany wasn't anything unusual for Europe. The United States, it insisted, could no longer give "unlimited refuge to the victims of political and religious persecution."[64] Even when smaller publications such as the *Jewish Frontier, Nation,* and *New Republic* began carrying stories about the Holocaust, the mainstream press downplayed reports of the genocide during the rest of Roosevelt's presidency.[65] It was a terrible moral failure by both the press and the president.

German forces blitzed across Poland on September 1, 1939, starting World War II. Two days later Roosevelt used the power of a fireside chat to nudge America away from its deep isolationism. "This nation will remain a neutral nation," he promised, "but I cannot ask that every American remain neutral in thought as well." By then more Americans were getting their news from radio than from newspapers.[66] They trusted the familiar voices of newscasters who told them the situation in Europe was dire, building support for Roosevelt's policy of aiding Britain and later the Soviet Union against Germany's attacks.

One of the voices Americans trusted most belonged to Edward R. Murrow, a young, charismatic CBS broadcaster who in 1938 launched live reporting via radio from the capitals of Europe. Thanks to improved technology, Americans could hear for the first time the news from Europe as it happened. Murrow was stationed in London when Germany began bombing England. Living on coffee, cigarettes, and occasional meals, he roamed the city's streets and air raid shelters describing scenes of devastation. On the night of September 21, 1940, Murrow climbed to the top of the BBC's roof to make a remarkable broadcast as German planes strafed the city. His live report began at 3:45 a.m. London time to make sure he would be heard during prime time in the United States. "This is London," Murrow began, bringing his listeners to the scene with a phrase he made famous. He described with his calm voice "the sound of guns off in the distance very faintly, like someone kicking a tub." For most listeners, it was the first time they had heard the sounds of war. When he told of searchlights "in the light of a three-quarter moon," his U.S. audience could see that same moon and knew they shared a bond with the British people.[67]

Haggard from lack of sleep, Murrow returned to the rooftops again and again, swaying public opinion with each broadcast. His live reporting was just what Roosevelt needed to shake the country out of its neutrality. When the German bombing began, only 16 percent of Americans supported giving the British more help. The vehement isolationism of McCormick, Hearst, Patterson, and other top publishers had dominated the public's viewpoint. But after a few weeks of Murrow's broadcasts, a majority of Americans backed giving Britain more aid.[68]

Roosevelt used his own media savvy to help the British. When FDR was visiting Pennsylvania in 1940, one of his aides approached the accompanying reporters with a pile of press releases. They announced an agreement allowing the United States to send fifty destroyers to Britain in return for bases in the Western Hemisphere. It was one of the biggest stories of the year, and the traveling journalists needed to transmit it as rapidly as possible. But they were in a small hamlet far removed from any telephones. Anxious to meet their deadlines, they had to wait until FDR's train reached the next town to sprint to the nearest phones and call their editors with the news. There was no chance to get comments from the deal's opponents. "The stories flashed from the next stop to American newspapers and around the world," Charles Hurd of the *New York Times* later wrote, "were precisely the facts announced by the president, in the manner he wished and told in his words."[69]

The war had reached a crisis point in the Atlantic by the time Roosevelt started his unprecedented third term after crushing Republican Wendell Willkie in the 1940 election. With devastating effectiveness, hundreds of German U-boats were sinking ships delivering vital aid to America's European allies. FDR faced the challenge of providing more assistance without losing congressional or public support.[70] During a press conference in April 1941, he used his wit to deflect tough questions from reporters about the extent of U.S. operations in the Atlantic.

"Mr. President, can you tell us the difference between a patrol and a convoy?" one reporter asked.

"You know the difference between a cow and a horse?" the president responded.

"Yes, I know the difference," the reporter replied.

"All right, there is just as much difference," FDR concluded firmly without making his policy any clearer.[71]

On December 7, 1941, Americans were stunned to hear news flashes on the radio that Japan had bombed the Pearl Harbor naval base. Any doubts whether the United States would go to war were instantly erased. After conferring with cabinet members, congressional leaders, and top military brass, Roosevelt met late that night with Edward R. Murrow, who was home on a break from London. Over sandwiches and beer, the two most famous voices on American radio discussed the war. FDR detailed the way U.S. forces had been caught unprepared by the Japanese. Planes were demolished without even taking off. "By God, on the ground!" the president said, pounding the table. Roosevelt, who usually made clear to reporters what information they could use, never said the conversation was off the record. Back at his hotel, Murrow paced the floor deciding whether to report the information FDR had just given him about how ill-prepared the military was to defend Pearl Harbor. "It would be the biggest story of my life," he told his wife. But he decided not to use it. Reflecting a rare level of trust between presidents and journalists, Murrow believed Roosevelt had meant to keep the conversation confidential.[72]

The next day Roosevelt, in an address to Congress broadcast on national radio, described the devastating attack as "a date which will live in infamy." He asked Congress to declare war on Japan. The following night he gave a fireside chat warning of the shared sacrifices that must be made. "We are now in this war," FDR told the nation. "We are all in it—all the way." He commanded journalists not to spread false rumors about the war: "To all newspapers and radio stations—all those who reach the eyes and ears of the American people—I say this: You have a most grave responsibility to the Nation now and for the duration of this war."[73]

Following the Pearl Harbor attack, Japan won a series of battles: the Philippines, Guam, Wake Island, Java Sea, Malaysia, Singapore, and Burma. To counter growing public despair, Roosevelt turned to radio again to assure Americans that the Allies would ultimately win. Before giving an extraordinary fireside in February 1942, he asked the press to alert listeners they should have world maps in front of them as he spoke. He then skillfully guided his audience around the maps, pointing out military challenges as well as the strategic power of the United States and its allies. "We are daily increasing our strength," FDR confidently said. "Soon, we and not our enemies will have the offensive; we, not they, will win the final battles; and we, not they, will make the final peace."[74]

One of Roosevelt's strategies to win the war was managing the press. He borrowed techniques used by Wilson during World War I but applied them with a lighter touch, confident that most if not all U.S. journalists would patriotically support the country during the wartime crisis. Information from combat zones was restricted, domestic news was put under a highly effective voluntary censorship program, and the government reviewed publications to see if they revealed secrets to the enemy. Six publications had their second-class mailing permits revoked for violating the rules. This number was far fewer than the hundred or so that were restricted under Wilson.[75]

The press escaped the kind of harsh clampdown employed by Adams, Lincoln, and Wilson. Only once did Roosevelt's administration pursue charges under the 1917 Espionage Act. In June 1942 the *Chicago Tribune* published an article correctly implying that the U.S. military had cracked a Japanese secret code. At first an enraged Roosevelt wanted marines to occupy the *Tribune*'s offices but instead settled on prosecuting the newspaper on charges of violating the Espionage Act. When the case went to a grand jury, however, the navy refused to reveal that the code had actually been broken. With this crucial evidence missing, the grand jury declined to indict the *Tribune*.[76]

By the spring of 1944, Roosevelt's health was deteriorating from congestive heart failure, but he and his doctors kept the truth from the public. FDR still remained remarkably productive, plotting military strategy as the Allies turned the war's tide, laying the foundation for the United Nations, and setting in motion the atomic bomb's development. He also launched his election campaign against Thomas Dewey, the Republican governor of New York, for a record fourth term. Roosevelt continued using press conferences and radio speeches to explain his policies and convey his confidence. He flubbed a broadcast only once. In August 1944 the president gave a speech in Bremerton, Washington, that he hadn't crafted with his usual care. Exhausted from a long trip, he suffered chest pains as he spoke from a ship as it swayed in heavy winds. Somehow, FDR made it through to the end, but he rambled and sounded weak to the national audience listening at home. One aide called it "a dismal failure."[77]

Roosevelt recovered sufficiently to campaign vigorously in the days leading up to the November election. After the Bremerton disaster, journalists said an upcoming nationally broadcast speech would be critical for determining whether he was ready to serve another term. "Has he still got it?" *Time* magazine asked. He did that evening. Listeners heard FDR give a carefully prepared and brilliantly delivered talk in which he denounced Republicans and deftly deflected their attacks that he was no longer fit to be president. "Well, here we are together again—after four years—and what years they have been," he told his audience. "You know, I am actually four years older, which is a fact that seems to annoy some people." The crowd roared with laughter. *Time*, which had become more supportive of Roosevelt during the war, reported that the president "was like a veteran virtuoso playing a piece he has loved for years, who fingers his way through it with a delicate fire, a perfection of timing and tone, and an assurance that no young player, no matter how gifted, can equal."[78]

For the fourth time, Roosevelt won a landslide presidential election, taking thirty-six of forty-eight states. But at his inauguration, he appeared pale and gaunt. His health was failing. After a grueling trip to Yalta in the Soviet Union to meet with Churchill and Stalin, Roosevelt went to his Georgia vacation cottage to recuperate. In the early afternoon of April 12, 1945, he died at age sixty-three of a cerebral hemorrhage.[79]

Roosevelt had led the United States out of the Great Depression and to the verge of victory in World War II. Along the way, he changed government's role in American life like no president before him. Social security, the minimum wage, unemployment insurance, farm price supports, a ban on child labor, the Securities and Exchange Commission, and the Federal Deposit Insurance Corporation were introduced by his administration.[80] Roosevelt couldn't have accomplished this much and won four presidential elections by massive margins without impressive press management skills. His willingness to meet frequently with reporters and ability to develop friendly relationships with many of them helped him shape how Americans viewed his presidency. His strategy of using new media—in his case radio and newsreels—to reach the public directly would be copied by other presidents.

Roosevelt was the first president to appear on television, allowing himself to be recorded as he spoke at the 1939 World's Fair. After its development was delayed by World War II, television took off in the postwar years. FDR's successor, Harry Truman, agreed to appear on TV in 1947 as he launched a food relief effort for Europe. The broadcast began by accidentally showing the rear end of an NBC newsman as he adjusted the president's tie. The show went downhill from there. Truman looked uncomfortable, staring down at his typewritten words as he flipped the pages. But he became more comfortable in later broadcasts as he learned to read from cue cards. During his second term, Truman asked that all of his major speeches be televised.[81]

In early 1952 Edward R. Murrow, now a CBS television star, interviewed World War II hero General Dwight Eisenhower for a documentary.

Eisenhower was terrible. He mumbled, his sentences were convoluted, and he wouldn't look into the camera. Murrow told Eisenhower that if he wanted to be president—everyone knew the general was considering a run—he should adjust to the new medium. Eisenhower did. He simplified his sentences, agreed to put on makeup for the camera, and learned to tilt his head so the lights wouldn't emphasize his baldness.[82]

After winning the election that year, Eisenhower was determined to become the television president. Like Roosevelt, he didn't trust the press to fairly convey his policies and wanted to use the latest technology to reach the public directly. "To hell with slanted reporters," Eisenhower press secretary James Hagerty wrote in his diary. "We'll go directly to the people who can hear exactly what [the] President said without reading warped and slanted stories."[83] Using television was the smart way to do it. During Eisenhower's first term, TV surpassed radio for the size of its U.S. audience in the evening hours. During his second term, the percentage of American families with a television set climbed past 80 percent.[84]

It would take two World War II veterans—John Kennedy and Richard Nixon—to fully harness the power of television for their presidencies. Unlike Truman and Eisenhower, who had to work at looking good on TV, Kennedy was a natural. Handsome, witty, and graceful, he appeared at ease in front of the cameras. He held his press conferences live on TV, increasing their drama and the attention they received. JFK made the White House his stage, looking straight at whichever camera was filming him so viewers felt like he was speaking directly to them. Just as FDR mastered radio for political communication, Kennedy mastered television. "When we don't have to go through you bastards," he told Newsweek's Washington bureau chief Ben Bradlee, "we can really get our story to the American people."[85]

Nixon also went to great lengths to use television to his advantage. It helped propel him to the White House and win a second term in a landslide. But when it mattered most during the greatest crisis of his presidency, television couldn't save him. Instead, his intense hostility toward journalists contributed to his downfall.

5 Richard Nixon and the Making of Enemies

In the fall of 1972, former FBI agent Alfred C. Baldwin III was hiding, and Jack Nelson was knocking on doors determined to find him. Baldwin didn't want to be interviewed by journalists such as Nelson about his role in the break-in that June at the Democratic National Committee headquarters at the Watergate complex. But he stood little chance of avoiding Nelson. A wiry and energetic investigative reporter for the *Los Angeles Times*, Nelson had earned the nickname "Scoop" from his admirers for his ability to get big stories before other journalists. The people he investigated were less fond of Nelson, calling him "a skunk, a little bastard, a lying son of a bitch, a hatchet man." Nelson had already won a Pulitzer Prize for revealing widespread abuses at a Georgia mental health hospital where nurses sometimes performed major surgeries instead of doctors. He also did a major investigation in 1968 revealing that police and National Guardsmen in South Carolina had shot Black student protesters in the back, killing three and wounding more than two dozen others. It was stories like these that led Nelson's former editor to describe him as "the toughest, hardest-charging, finest reporter I've known in my 40 years in the business."[1]

Sure enough, Nelson tracked Baldwin from Washington DC to New Haven, Connecticut, where he was lying low. Using his persuasive skills as a reporter, Nelson got Baldwin to start talking. Five hours later, the ex-FBI man finished divulging startling details about the Watergate break-in: how former CIA agent James McCord recruited him to work on President Richard Nixon's reelection campaign, how he listened to illegal wiretaps placed at the Democratic headquarters, how he delivered tapes of the conversations to Nixon's campaign, and how he served as a lookout as McCord and four other burglars broke back into the Democratic offices to place new wiretaps. The burglars had been arrested, starting a chain of events that led to a constitutional crisis and ultimately Nixon's resignation.

Based on the Baldwin interviews, the *Los Angeles Times* ran a blockbuster story by Nelson and Ronald J. Ostrow in October 1972. For the first time, an eyewitness was giving the public details of the connection between the burglary and the Nixon campaign.[2] It was one of many examples of aggressive reporting that helped expose the crime spree and presidential abuse of power known as Watergate. Bob Woodward and Carl Bernstein of the *Washington Post* became the most famous of these journalists, but they were hardly the only ones. In addition to Nelson and Ostrow, syndicated columnist Jack Anderson, Seymour Hersh of the *New York Times*, Sandy Smith of *Time* magazine, Jack White of the *Providence Journal-Bulletin*, and CBS News produced important stories on the misdeeds of Nixon and his men. To be sure, the press had investigated corruption in previous administrations. But none of those investigations had as much impact as the Watergate reporting, which transformed the way presidents are covered. A never-ending search for scandals and deep distrust of presidential motivations would come to permeate Washington reporting.

Nixon's relationship with the press was fundamentally different from that of his predecessors. Most if not all presidents before him had complained about their coverage and did what they could to manage and manipulate it. But Nixon made assaulting the media and casting journalists as enemies of the American people a central strategy of his administration. He and his top aides entered the White House determined to curb the influence of the Washington press corps. They demonized the media as a powerful institution that was out of touch with average Americans and dangerous to democracy.[3] Nixon's lies and his attacks on journalism contributed to Watergate and his eventual disgrace. However, his war against the press outlived him, spreading through American politics and reaching new heights during Trump's presidency.

Nixon had a longstanding loathing for the press.[4] A hardscrabble childhood left him with deep scars of grievance against those who he thought looked down on him: the rich, the popular, or anyone else he considered part of a snobby elite, including journalists. Ironically, Nixon enjoyed strong support from the mostly conservative local newspapers when he first ran for Congress in 1946 as a Republican in a district on the outskirts of Los Angeles. The editor of his hometown paper was a local GOP official who backed Nixon. So did the region's biggest newspaper, the *Los Angeles Times*, helping him to an upset victory.[5]

Once in Congress, Nixon quickly gained the attention of reporters. His tenacious investigation of Alger Hiss, a State Department official accused of being a Soviet spy, attracted front-page headlines and national fame. *Reader's Digest*, the most popular magazine in America at the time, lauded Nixon. The *Washington Post* wrote that the "handsome freshman congressman" was "outstanding."[6] *Time* and *Life* magazines were also big fans. But it was the negative coverage of his role in the Hiss case that he remembered. "I was subjected to an utterly unprincipled and vicious smear campaign," he complained.[7]

After Eisenhower picked him as his running mate in 1952, Nixon showed his skill with the new medium of television. Nixon attracted the largest TV audience ever up to that point when he made a speech defending payments he'd received from wealthy supporters. Playing to the audience's emotions, he vowed to never give up a dog named Checkers that a supporter had given his family. The "Checkers" speech was a hit. Two million people sent favorable telegrams to the Republican National Committee, convincing Eisenhower to keep Nixon on the ticket. Nixon turned a corner with the Checkers speech. He realized he could reach voters directly through television and mostly ignore the print reporters he disdained. "They're the enemy," he told his campaign workers. "We don't need them."[8]

Nixon's Checkers triumph made him overconfident for his first televised debate with John F. Kennedy as the two vied for the presidency in 1960. Nixon did little to prepare and appeared pale, sweaty, and awkward in a suit that was too big for him and with cheap makeup that didn't quite cover his five-o'clock shadow. When he narrowly lost the election, he was sure the Kennedys and their fellow Democrats had stolen it, and he bitterly blamed the media for showcasing JFK's charm.[9]

Nixon's hatred for the press grew after he lost the 1962 California gubernatorial election. Humiliated, he held a news conference the next morning. Even though most large California newspapers had endorsed him, and the *Los Angeles Times* let him write his own column, Nixon accused journalists of giving him "the shaft" and being delighted that he'd lost. "You won't have Nixon to kick around anymore, because, gentlemen, this is my last press conference," he promised.[10]

But it was far from Nixon's last press conference. Six years later he ran for president again and changed the way elections are won. Led by advertising executive H. R. "Bob" Haldeman, his campaign veered from the traditional politics of shaking as many hands as possible and making long speeches full of detailed policy plans. Instead, it packaged the candidate in commercials that played to voters' emotions. Nixon hired a young talk-show producer named Roger Ailes as a consultant. Ailes, who later founded Fox News, advised the campaign to film Nixon holding question-and-answer sessions that appeared spontaneous but featured handpicked audiences with no reporters allowed.[11] This kind of packaged event, novel at the time, would become commonly used by presidents and other politicians.

Nixon won the presidency in 1968, but his insecurities remained. He and his top aides believed they were under siege and the country was unraveling. Protests against the Vietnam War intensified on college campuses and in cities large and small. In October 1969 clouds of tear gas filled Washington's streets as police and anti-war demonstrators clashed. Buses were parked around the White House to protect the president and his aides against possible assaults. To combat this disorder and keep Nixon in charge during dangerous times, the president and his men thought any means were justified—including attacking and spying on journalists.[12]

Even though Lyndon Johnson had been savaged by the press about the Vietnam War during his last years in office, Nixon was sure reporters had a unique dislike for him. Four weeks into his presidency, an aide observed that he was receiving "excellent" press so far. "You don't understand," Nixon replied, "they are waiting to destroy us."[13] To be sure, Nixon received tough press as every president did. The editorial pages of the *New York Times* and *Washington Post* could be especially critical. *Post* cartoonist Herbert Block, known as Herblock, was merciless, drawing Nixon with beady eyes, thick brows, hunched shoulders, and a nose that looked like a ski slope. Still, Nixon received plenty of favorable coverage at the start of his presidency. One study found that he was the subject of more positive stories in magazines during his first six months in office than any other president since Teddy Roosevelt. He had more opportunities to appear on prime-time television during his first eighteen months as president than Eisenhower, Kennedy, and Johnson did combined during their first eighteen months. The *New York Times* called one of his first news conferences a "tour de force."[14]

Nixon claimed not to care about his press coverage, but in reality he was obsessed by it. He started his days by reading a summary of news stories, making notes in the margins about how he wanted his staff to respond and ordering them to punish reporters whose stories he didn't like. He recommended that his aides treat journalists with "the courteous, cool contempt which has been my policy over the last few years."[15] As Nixon's presidency continued, his tactics grew uglier. For potential blackmail purposes, he ordered Haldeman, who had become his chief of staff, to ask the FBI for "a rundown on the homosexuals known and suspected in the Washington press corps."[16]

Despite his animosity toward journalists, Nixon became a pioneer in press relations by creating a new office of White House Communications. Its job was to choreograph all of the administration's contacts with the media to enhance the president's image and sell his policies. Every morning Nixon and his top aides decided on a "line of the day" that they wanted to dominate the nightly news broadcasts. The communications office issued a flurry of news releases on the topic and got cabinet members to appear on talk shows. It also arranged interviews with the president by local journalists around the country who usually asked easier questions than the seasoned Washington press corps. In the words of longtime White House correspondent Helen Thomas, "news management was relentless."[17]

In their quest to control the news, Nixon and National Security Adviser Henry Kissinger leaked information to the press, but they became irate when others did it. After the *New York Times* reported in May 1969 that American planes were secretly bombing Cambodia, Nixon demanded that his aides plug the flow of information. "Have them get off their tails and find out what's going on and figure out how to stop it," he commanded. In response, they wiretapped the phones of thirteen administration aides plus four journalists from the *New York Times*, *Washington Post*, *London Sunday Times*, and CBS. When columnist Joseph Kraft wrote critically of the administration, a White House aide was sent to plant a bugging device in his home. "The illegal snooping train left the station in early 1969," Nixon speechwriter William Safire later wrote, "and could not be recalled."[18]

In addition to spying on journalists, Nixon used resentment toward them as a political weapon. Haldeman advised him that the press could be "a useful enemy" to be hated in the public's mind like crime, drugs, and communism.[19] Nixon encouraged his aides to denounce journalists whenever possible. "It is very important," Nixon wrote in a memo, "that the media be effectively discredited."[20] His White House worked at eroding journalists' credibility by accusing them of acting against the best interests of the country and not telling the public the truth. "In all the world of 'us against them,' the press was the quintessential 'them,'" Safire explained. To make it seem like journalists were part of a dangerous institution, Nixon's men promoted the use of the term "media" to replace "the press." According to Safire, Nixon preferred "media" because it "had a manipulative, Madison Avenue, all-encompassing connotation, and the press hated it."[21]

Nixon's hardball tactics made it nearly inevitable that a showdown would occur between his administration and aggressive journalists who increasingly distrusted him. It began after Nixon gave a highly anticipated primetime address in November 1969 about the Vietnam War. Rather than announce any new policies, he appealed to the "great silent majority of Americans" to rally around him. He thought the speech was great; the network commentators who went on air afterward disagreed. Eric Sevareid of CBS News said it didn't include anything "of a substantial nature or a dramatic nature that is new."[22]

Nixon was furious. Ten days after the Vietnam speech, he sent Vice President Spiro Agnew to Des Moines, Iowa, to deliver a scathing denunciation of broadcasters that Nixon had edited. Agnew assailed the journalists of CBS, NBC, and ABC as "a tiny, enclosed fraternity of privileged men elected by no one and enjoying a monopoly sanctioned and licensed by Government." Most of their views, he said, "do not— and I repeat, not—represent the views of America." The vice president urged the public to write and call to complain about the power of this "small and unelected elite." He questioned whether the networks would have the fairness to cover his speech when in fact all three networks were broadcasting it live.[23]

Nixon loved Agnew's speech. "This really flicks the scab off, doesn't it?" he said as he finished reading it.[24] The networks reacted with disbelief. CBS vice president Frank Stanton described it as an "unprecedented attempt by the Vice President of the United States to intimidate a news medium which depends for its existence upon government licenses."[25]

Agnew wasn't done, however. He gave a follow-up speech in Montgomery, Alabama, this time accusing the *New York Times, Washington Post,* and other large newspapers of having "grown fat and irresponsible." Agnew claimed he didn't "seek to intimidate the press," but that was clearly his purpose.[26] The public attack against journalists set the stage for future battles between presidents and the press.

Nixon was reading the *New York Times* on a Sunday morning in June 1971 when his mood suddenly darkened. He had looked forward to reading about his daughter Tricia's wedding the previous day. But right next to photographs of the wedding was a story about a secret forty-seven-volume Defense Department history of the Vietnam War known as the Pentagon Papers. The study described how presidential administrations from Truman to Johnson had deceived Americans about the war. It didn't matter to Nixon that the Pentagon Papers dealt with the years before he became president. He didn't care that Secretary of Defense Melvin Laird estimated 98 percent of the report could be declassified without harm. Egged on by Kissinger, he was itching for a brawl with the press to preserve his ability to conduct foreign policy in secret.[27]

In a dangerous challenge to the notion of a free press, Nixon's Justice Department got a court order to stop the *Times* from printing the Pentagon Papers. It was the first time the federal government had turned to the courts to block a newspaper from publishing something. When the *Washington Post* started printing its own Pentagon Paper excerpts, the administration got a restraining order against it too. Same thing with the *Boston Globe* and *St. Louis Post-Dispatch.* Finally, in a decision that humiliated Nixon, the Supreme Court ruled that he couldn't prevent publication of the Pentagon Papers. The president had picked a public battle with the press and lost.[28]

An enraged Nixon was determined to stop further leaks. "I don't give a damn how it is done, do whatever has to be done to stop these leaks and prevent further unauthorized disclosures," he ordered. "I don't want excuses. I want results. I want it done, whatever the cost."[29] He also demanded revenge on Daniel Ellsberg, a former Defense Department consultant who had leaked the Pentagon Papers. To fulfill Nixon's orders, a White House team—known as "the plumbers"–was formed to plug leaks and engage in clandestine operations. Two of the plumbers, E. Howard Hunt and G. Gordon Liddy, enlisted three Cuban exiles with CIA connections to break into the office of Ellsberg's psychiatrist in Los Angeles. Their goal: find dirt on Ellsberg to discredit him. Over Labor Day weekend in 1971, the three exiles snuck into the doctor's office while Hunt and Liddy kept watch. The burglars pried open filing cabinets and scattered papers around the floor as they searched for information, but they found nothing useful. When a judge later learned about the burglary, he dismissed all charges against Ellsberg.[30] Instead of harming the whistleblower, Nixon's bungling crew had helped him avoid prison.

Ellsberg wasn't the only person Nixon wanted to wound. Some of Nixon's top aides created an "Enemies List," the purpose of which was to use "the available federal machinery to screw our political enemies." Nixon wholeheartedly endorsed the effort. "I want it done," he told his aides. "I want a list of people."[31] The eventual list of more than 230 names included politicians, celebrities, academics, labor leaders, businessmen, fifty-six journalists, and three entire news organizations—the *New York Times*, *Washington Post*, and *St. Louis Post-Dispatch*.[32]

The Enemies List wasn't just for idle threats. Nixon ordered Haldeman and John Ehrlichman, his chief domestic adviser, to use government agencies such as the FBI and IRS to investigate his opponents. "Pound these people," he said.[33] And pound them they did. Haldeman used the list to select targets for IRS audits including reporter Robert Greene of *Newsday*, who had investigated the financial deals of Nixon's friend Charles B. "Bebe" Rebozo. Liberal columnist Mary McGrory was audited three years in a row for donations she made to an orphan's home. At Nixon's direction the FBI did a background investigation on CBS reporter Daniel Schorr. The White House ludicrously pretended it was interested in hiring Schorr, but in private Nixon was calling him a "son-of-a-bitch."[34]

Nixon's dislike of Schorr was topped by his hatred for investigative reporter Jack Anderson, whose column ran in nearly a thousand newspapers around the country. During Nixon's first term, Anderson wrote exposés that repeatedly embarrassed the president: the CIA's sabotage of the democratically elected government of Chile, Nixon's secret support of Pakistan during a bloody war with India, and the administration's help fixing an antitrust case against International Telephone & Telegraph in return for the company's $400,000 in campaign donations. "I would like to get him," the president told his staff, "get Anderson discredited."[35] Nixon's men tried feeding false documents to the columnist, sending two men to work undercover in his office to find embarrassing information, and planting negative stories about Anderson with other reporters, but none of those moves worked.

The administration was getting desperate. After meeting with Nixon in March 1972, Special Counsel Charles Colson summoned plumber Howard Hunt. Colson told him they needed to "stop Anderson at all costs" and that Hunt was "authorized to do whatever was necessary."[36] Hunt contacted fellow plumber Gordon Liddy, who had once volunteered "to rub people out" and now worked for Nixon's reelection campaign. Hunt also recruited a retired CIA doctor who had worked on the attempted assassination of Cuban dictator Fidel Castro. Hunt, Liddy, and the doctor met to discuss ways to murder Anderson: ramming his car as he drove, sneaking poison into his medicine cabinet, or putting hallucinogens on his steering wheel to seep into his bloodstream and cause a fatal collision. There's no direct evidence that Nixon ordered Anderson's assassination, but historian Mark Feldstein concludes that Colson had a pattern of taking orders from the president to commit illegal activities and was unlikely to have devised such a plot on his own.

Finally, Hunt and Liddy decided the surest way to kill Anderson would be through a fake mugging. Liddy volunteered to do the hit himself because he believed Anderson was "one of those mutant strains of columnist" who endangered U.S. security. Hunt sent a memo to the White House outlining the options, but a few days later he informed

Liddy that the administration had decided the assassination would be "unproductive" at that time. Besides, Liddy and Hunt had a new mission: spying on the Democratic National Committee's headquarters at the Watergate office complex.[37]

The Watergate plot was hatched as part of a wider effort to damage the Democrats as Nixon began his 1972 reelection campaign. He had achieved a string of impressive accomplishments during his first term: historic trips to the Soviet Union and China, a nuclear weapons reduction agreement with the Soviets, the creation of the Environmental Protection Agency and the Consumer Product Safety Commission, the signing of clean air and water laws, and the withdrawal of most U.S. troops from Vietnam. The economy was improving after a rough patch earlier in his term. The press had covered all of these achievements, and in hindsight it seems obvious that Nixon would cruise to victory in November. But Nixon was terrified of being humiliated again as he had been in 1960 and 1962. In his mind, one way to increase his odds of victory was to gather as much intelligence as possible on the Democrats' plans.

And so Attorney General John Mitchell—soon to become Nixon's campaign director—sat puffing a pipe in his Justice Department office one January morning in 1972 as Liddy presented a series of flip charts. Liddy proposed an elaborate scheme: drug and kidnap anti-Nixon protest leaders and hide them in Mexico for the duration of the GOP summer convention; have planes follow the flights of Democratic candidates and intercept their communications; hire prostitutes to lure and then blackmail Democratic officials during their Miami convention; and sabotage the air conditioning in the hall where the Democrats were holding their convention and watch the delegates wilt in the Florida heat. The whole plan could be done for $1 million, Liddy promised.[38]

Mitchell, the nation's top law enforcement officer, didn't say there was no way the campaign would get involved in such illegal actions. He didn't order Liddy's arrest for plotting a series of crimes. Instead he merely responded, "Well, Gordon, that's all very intriguing, but not quite what I had in mind." He sent Liddy back to the drawing board to come up with a cheaper version. Liddy returned a week later with a $250,000 plan that focused on surveillance of the Democrats. Mitchell, Presidential Counsel John Dean, and Deputy Campaign Director Jeb Stuart Magruder later pointed fingers at each other as to who actually approved the revised plan. Regardless of who gave the order, it went into effect. Liddy recruited a team that included Hunt, the former FBI man Alfred Baldwin III, campaign security chief James McCord, two of the burglars who had broken into the office of Ellsberg's psychiatrist, and two other exiles from Cuba.[39]

Throughout the spring Liddy's team displayed remarkable ineptitude. They twice tried to break into the headquarters of the likely Democratic nominee, George McGovern. They failed. They attempted to sneak into the Democratic headquarters at the Watergate office complex but got locked in a banquet room instead. They tried again the next night, but the locksmith in the group couldn't figure out how to open the door to the offices. Finally, during Memorial Day weekend, they successfully snuck into the headquarters. They photographed documents, hid a microphone in a smoke detector, and put wiretaps on two phones. But after they left, they realized that one of the taps didn't work and the other one mostly picked up office gossip.

Hearing that Mitchell was annoyed by their failures, the bumbling spy team tried again. As Hunt and Liddy supervised from a safe distance, McCord and the four other burglars broke back into the Democrats' office in the early morning of Saturday, June 17, 1972. As they planted new bugging equipment and photographed more documents, Baldwin watched from across the street. They were sloppy, however, and a security guard notified police of suspicious activity. The five burglars were arrested, while Liddy, Hunt, and Baldwin escaped, at least for a while.[40]

Reporters competed to cover the break-in, treating it as a local crime story rather than a national political one. The Associated Press got the biggest scoop, reporting that McCord was the Nixon campaign's security coordinator. Three days after the arrest, Bob Woodward and E. J.

Bachinski of the *Washington Post* linked Watergate to the White House for the first time, revealing that address books found on the burglars listed Hunt's name and home telephone number. Police also found a personal check written by Hunt among the burglars' possessions.[41]

Nixon and his aides began working feverishly to block the FBI's investigation of the crime and minimize its press coverage. They were terrified that the Watergate arrests would lead to the discovery of the rest of what Mitchell called "the White House horrors." Two days after the burglary was discovered, Press Secretary Ronald Ziegler refused to comment on what he called "a third-rate burglary attempt."[42] Nixon began lying immediately to the public, insisting that "the White House has had no involvement whatever in this particular incident."[43]

Other presidents had lied—most recently Johnson about the Vietnam War, Kennedy about the CIA's Bay of Pigs invasion of Cuba, and Eisenhower about a U-2 spy plane shot down over the Soviet Union. What was different this time was Nixon using executive branch officials to deceive the public for his own personal political purposes, starting a pattern that some of his successors would follow. Nixon and his men called it "stonewalling," and it worked at first. During a televised press conference soon after the break-in, reporters didn't ask Nixon any questions about Watergate.[44] In the minds of most journalists, the possibility that the White House could be connected to a burglary seemed absurd. CBS White House correspondent Dan Rather thought the story would fade like "a puff of talcum powder."[45] *Time* described the burglary "as an odd, Bondian episode greeted with amused stupefaction in Washington."[46] At the end of July, *Time* reported that $100,000 used to pay for the bugging equipment had been traced to Nixon's campaign. But this juicy information was buried in the middle of an article on page thirty-six of the magazine and received little notice.[47]

A week later, however, a front-page *New York Times* story reported that money found on the Watergate burglars had been suspiciously deposited in one of their bank accounts by a Mexico City lawyer.[48] The *Post*'s Carl Bernstein and Bob Woodward jumped on the story.

The next day they revealed that $25,000 in the burglar's account could be traced to Maurice Stans, the Nixon campaign's finance chief.[49] This astonishing story persuaded the *Post's* top editors to create a team to investigate Watergate full-time. City editor Barry Sussman, who was adept at pulling together the many strands of the complex scandal, was put in charge. Bernstein and Woodward, who had shown more zeal for covering Watergate than anyone else, were assigned to the team.

Woodward and Bernstein both came of age in the tumultuous 1960s. Like many of their peers, they were more willing to challenge authority than previous generations of journalists. Woodward, twenty-nine, was a Yale graduate and navy veteran. At the time of the burglary, he had worked at the *Post* for only nine months but was a rising star, impressing his editors with his hustle as he made front-page headlines with stories about health violations at fancy restaurants. Bernstein described Woodward as someone who "is prone to complete his homework before it is due or even assigned."[50]

Bernstein, twenty-eight, was more likely to lose his homework but still ace the exam. A college dropout, he was known as a street-smart reporter and a good writer when motivated. He was often in his editors' doghouse because he missed deadlines and did sloppy work on stories he cared less about. Bernstein once rented a car to work on a story, parked it, and then promptly forgot about it until the bills started showing up at the *Post's* offices. But after he began working on the Watergate story, Bernstein impressed everyone with his determination. To interview some of the Watergate defendants, he once jumped in the backseat of a taxi, sprawling on their laps as it pulled away from the courthouse after a hearing.[51]

Around the time that Jack Nelson of the *Los Angeles Times* was tracking down Baldwin, Woodward and Bernstein began one of the most remarkable runs of investigative stories in American journalism history. On September 17, 1972, they publicly connected Watergate for the first time to top Nixon aides. Their story described how assistants to Mitchell were among the fifteen people with access to a "secret fund of more than $300,000 earmarked for sensitive projects" including the Watergate bugging.[52] The next day they wrote that two top campaign aides had withdrawn more than $50,000 from the secret fund to pay for spying on Democrats.[53] Two days later they detailed how two other Nixon aides went on a document-destruction binge after the Watergate break-in was discovered.[54] Then they learned that Mitchell, while attorney general, controlled the secret fund used to spy on Democrats. When Bernstein called him late at night to comment on the story, Mitchell responded with a threat against the *Post*'s publisher, Katharine Graham: "Katie Graham's gonna get her tit caught in a big fat wringer if that's published."[55] But the *Post* did publish the story, and the one who ended up in a wringer was Mitchell, who eventually went to prison.

Bernstein and Woodward published another sensational story on October 10, revealing that the Nixon campaign had paid a young lawyer, Donald Segretti, to organize a group dedicated to disrupting the campaigns of leading Democrats. The sabotage activities included swiping confidential files, planting provocateurs at the Democratic convention, and leaking false information to the press. The article described how a Nixon aide forged a letter to the editor published two weeks before the crucial New Hampshire primary claiming that leading Democratic contender Edmund Muskie had slurred people of French Canadian descent. The alleged insult hurt Muskie in New Hampshire, which has a large French Canadian population, causing him to lose momentum. He eventually lost the nomination to McGovern, who Nixon considered a much weaker opponent. Five days later, Woodward and Bernstein tied Segretti's sabotage to the heart of the White House, revealing that he reported directly to Nixon's appointments secretary.[56]

Then Woodward and Bernstein blundered. They wrote that Haldeman, Nixon's closest aide, was one of the five people in charge of the secret campaign fund. That part of the story was true, but Woodward and Bernstein mistakenly reported that former campaign treasurer Hugh Sloan had told the Watergate grand jury about it. Sloan had indeed testified before the grand jury but hadn't been asked about Haldeman's control of the fund. Nixon's team gleefully pounced on the mistake. Ziegler devoted a half hour of his daily briefing to denouncing the *Post*, calling the article a "blatant effort at character assassination" and "shoddy and shabby journalism." But *Post* executive editor Ben Bradlee refused to back down. When other news outlets asked him whether the newspaper would issue a retraction, he responded, "We stand by our story."[57]

Bernstein and Woodward weren't the only reporters investigating Watergate in the summer and fall of 1972. Jack Nelson and Ron Ostrow of the *Los Angeles Times* and Sandy Smith at *Time* were too. Smith remained mostly unknown because his magazine didn't put reporters' names on their stories, but he had some important scoops: Liddy and Hunt had worked for the secret "plumbers" unit in the White House, a top Haldeman aide had helped hire Segretti to lead the sabotage efforts, and Watergate burglar Bernard Barker had paid nine other men to attack Daniel Ellsberg at a rally in Washington.[58]

But most of the press wasn't digging deeply into Watergate. White House correspondents tended to cover events in a pack, focusing on press briefings, interviews with officials, and other daily stories rather than investigative work. Out of 433 reporters in the Washington press corps, fewer than 15 covered Watergate with any persistence, and some of them only briefly. A survey of five hundred political columns written between the break-in and the November election found that less than 5 percent focused on Watergate.[59] Aside from its story about the Mexico City bank account, the *New York Times* barely investigated Watergate because Kissinger assured its Washington bureau that the crime didn't involve Nixon's top men.[60] The *Chicago Tribune* didn't have a Watergate story on its front page until twelve weeks after the burglary.[61] The favorite word used to describe Watergate during this time was "caper," as if it were a comedic movie. As a result, much of the public didn't take it seriously. A Gallup poll in October 1972 found that only 48 percent of Americans even recognized the word "Watergate."[62]

This lack of awareness was partly due to the television networks, whose nightly newscasts carried only short stories about Watergate if at all. This changed dramatically when the CBS *Evening News* devoted fifteen minutes of its twenty-two-minute broadcast to Watergate eleven days before the election. "Watergate has escalated into charges of a high-level campaign of political sabotage and espionage apparently unparalleled in American history," anchorman Walter Cronkite began. Using photos and diagrams, CBS wove together the various strands that Bernstein, Woodward, Nelson, Smith, and others had reported. With the popular Cronkite telling the story, the sordid details of Watergate reached a national audience for the first time. Four nights later, CBS followed up with an eight-minute story digging into the money behind Watergate. It was supposed to be longer, but Colson—Nixon's hatchet man—threatened to have the Federal Communications Commission make life difficult for CBS if it didn't shorten the segment. The network's executives backed down and trimmed the story.[63]

Colson's intimidation of CBS was part of the Nixon team's successful cover-up of Watergate before the election. Evidence was destroyed, witnesses bullied, and hush money paid to the burglars. When prosecutors announced indictments on September 15, they included the five burglars plus Liddy and Hunt but no higher officials at the White House or reelection campaign. The indictments focused on the burglary and wiretapping at Democratic headquarters; they didn't mention any other crimes by the White House or Nixon campaign.[64]

The president was ready to seek revenge against the press for investigating him. The day the indictments were announced, Nixon met with Haldeman and White House Counsel John Dean, congratulated them on the cover-up's success, and plotted retribution against the *Post* for its reporting. "The main thing is the *Post* is going to have damnable, damnable problems out of this one," he vowed.[65] Soon afterward, friends of Nixon and Agnew took the rare step of challenging the license renewals for two Florida television stations owned by the *Post*. The *Post* eventually kept the licenses, but the challenges hurt the company's bottom line. Prices of its stock fell from $38 a share to $28 during the first two weeks after the challenges, and the company spent more than $1 million defending itself. Graham said she lay awake many nights worrying about her newspaper's future. "The very existence of The Post was at stake," she remembered. "I'd lived with White House anger before, but I had never seen anything remotely like the kind of fury and heat I was feeling targeted at us now."[66]

While Nixon complained about the *Post* and other news outlets, the press was actually tougher on McGovern, "savaging him mercilessly" in Safire's words.[67] The Nixon campaign's strategy of sabotaging the candidacy of Edmund Muskie had worked; McGovern was a weaker opponent. Before the November election, 71 percent of newspapers endorsed Nixon, and only 5 percent backed McGovern, while the rest remained neutral. Nixon cruised to a landslide victory, winning 61 percent of the popular vote and forty-nine states.[68]

Despite Nixon's big win, the Watergate story didn't disappear. Tired of being scooped by the *Post*, the *New York Times* assigned star investigative reporter Seymour Hersh to cover Watergate after the election. Hersh didn't waste any time getting a big story: Nixon's men were paying the Watergate burglars at least $400 a month in hush money as they headed to trial. It was the first of many big Watergate stories Hersh wrote for the *Times*. Forty of them made the front page during one seventy-three-day stretch in the first half of 1973.[69]

As the press dug deeper into Watergate, the White House's stonewalling started crumbling. During hearings to confirm interim FBI director L. Patrick Gray as the agency's permanent boss, he admitted that his agency had been sharing copies of its Watergate reports with the White House and discussing the scope of its investigation with Nixon aides Dean and Ehrlichman. He later shared documents that showed the president's personal lawyer had given money to Segretti to disrupt Democratic campaigns. The *New York Daily News* then reported that Gray had burned evidence from Hunt's safe at the direction of

Ehrlichman and Dean. Even more stunning than Gray's revelations was a letter Judge John Sirica received as he prepared to sentence the Watergate burglars. James McCord wrote that White House officials had pressured the defendants to commit perjury about the roles played by the Nixon campaign and administration in their crimes. Dean, seeing that the cover-up was collapsing, started cooperating with prosecutors and feeding them evidence.[70]

Ever since the Watergate burglars were caught, Nixon's men had denied and belittled reporters' stories that top White House and campaign officials were involved. During the fall of 1972, Ziegler claimed Woodward and Bernstein's articles were "based on hearsay, character assassination, innuendo, guilt by association." A campaign spokesman described the *Post*'s sources as "a fountain of misinformation." But as evidence of the cover-up mounted, Ziegler said toward the end of April 1973 that all of his previous statements about Watergate were "inoperative." On May 1, he apologized to Woodward and Bernstein. "I think we'd all have to say mistakes were made," the press secretary admitted. The next week, the *Post*'s Watergate work earned journalism's highest honor, the Pulitzer Prize for public service.[71]

The scandal had become a full-fledged crisis for Nixon and the country as story after story reported on crimes committed by people close to the president. The Senate Select Committee on Presidential Campaign Activities, better known as the Ervin Committee, started holding televised hearings on Watergate. Americans could now watch witnesses as they testified about the administration's law breaking, and they learned that Nixon had secretly taped his Oval Office conversations.

By late spring 1973, journalists who had previously ignored Watergate were swarming all over the story. John Osborne, the national correspondent of the *New Republic*, compared their newfound zeal to "dogs who have scented blood and are running the fox right down to his death."[72] In their desire to beat the competition, some journalists rushed error-filled stories into print and on the air. ABC's Sam Donaldson wrongly implicated a White House aide in a campaign sabotage plot. CBS incorrectly accused a Maryland bank owned by a Nixon aide's brother of money laundering. And the Associated Press wrongly placed John Ehrlichman at a meeting where the cover-up was discussed.[73]

The flood of Watergate stories infuriated Nixon. At an August 1973 news conference, twenty of twenty-one questions had to do with Watergate, wiretapping, the break-in of Ellsberg's psychiatrist's office, or a growing investigation of corruption by Vice President Agnew, who was forced to resign less than two months later. Nixon lashed out at the press, suggesting that liberal journalists wanted to overturn the results of the 1972 election through Watergate. "After all, I know that most of the members of the press corps were not enthusiastic—and I understand that—about either my election in '68 or '72," he said, forgetting that the vast majority of newspapers had endorsed him.[74]

Investigative reporting continued to damage Nixon. Jack White of the *Providence Journal and Evening Bulletin* revealed that the president paid only $793 in taxes in 1970 and $878 in 1971. That equaled what a family making about $8,000 a year normally would have paid; the president's salary was $200,000. The Nixons had also received more than $130,000 in tax refunds over the same period. As a result of the investigation, White earned a Pulitzer Prize, the Nixons had to pay $476,000 in back taxes, and a new tradition began of presidential candidates divulging their tax returns. It lasted until Trump refused to provide his returns in 2016 and again in 2020.[75]

Nixon's support in the press further diminished following events known as the Saturday Night Massacre. On October 20 the president ordered Attorney General Elliot Richardson to fire Special Prosecutor Archibald Cox because he insisted on subpoenaing White House tapes that contained Watergate discussions. Richardson refused and resigned. Deputy Attorney General William Ruckelshaus did the same. Finally, Solicitor General Robert Bork agreed to fire Cox. As the dramatic events unfolded on television, much of the public responded with outrage. So did the press. The *Boston Globe, Atlanta Constitution, New York Times,*

Denver Post, Detroit News, Honolulu Star-Bulletin, Salt Lake Tribune, and *Time* called for the president's impeachment or resignation.[76] A president's "integrity and trustworthiness are perhaps the most important facts about him to his country and to the world," *Time* declared in its first editorial in the magazine's fifty-year history. "And these Nixon has destroyed."[77]

It wasn't just the press that was pressuring Nixon. Congress, the courts, and new special prosecutor Leon Jaworski continued to insist that he allow them to hear the tapes. Finally, on April 30, 1974, the White House released more than twelve-hundred pages of edited transcripts. Nearly fifty newspapers published them, National Public Radio read them on air, and a paperback version sold three million copies in a week. They exposed a foul-mouthed president seeking vengeance upon his opponents and plotting with his staff to derail the Watergate investigation. "The President should resign," concluded the *Omaha World-Herald*, which endorsed Nixon each of the three times he had run for president. The *Los Angeles Times*, which had backed him since his first congressional campaign, said it was time for impeachment. The conservative Hearst newspaper chain told readers it had "never heard anything as ruthless, deplorable and ethically indefensible as the talk on those White House tapes."[78]

The bad news continued for Nixon. In May the House Judiciary Committee started impeachment hearings. On July 24 the U.S. Supreme Court ruled 8–0 that he must release all of the subpoenaed White House tapes, not just edited transcripts of some of them. Three days later, the Judiciary Committee voted 27–11 for an article of impeachment charging Nixon with obstructing justice. Over the next three days, the committee passed two more articles of impeachment and sent them to the full House of Representatives. On August 5 Nixon finally released the rest of the subpoenaed tapes. They included what became known as "the smoking gun" conversation: Nixon telling aides to start the Watergate cover-up by asking the CIA to block the FBI's investigation. Nixon's remaining Republican support in Congress melted.

On August 9, 1974, Nixon became the first president in U.S. history to resign. Although Nixon's successor, Gerald Ford, pardoned him, more than twenty of his men—including top aides Haldeman, Mitchell, Ehrlichman, Colson, and Dean—were convicted of Watergate-related crimes.[79]

Thanks to their Watergate work, Woodward and Bernstein became celebrities. Their book *All the President's Men* was a best seller, and the movie version became a box office hit. *All the President's Men* created a legend that two young swashbuckling reporters single-handedly ended the rule of a corrupt president. But Bernstein, Woodward, and Graham agreed they were far from the only ones to contribute to the demise of Nixon's presidency. The FBI and prosecutors developed the evidence against the Watergate defendants that the press then reported. Acting Associate FBI Director W. Mark Felt served as an anonymous source—made famous in *All the President's Men* with the nickname "Deep Throat"—who confirmed for Woodward and Bernstein they were on the right track with their investigation. Judge Sirica, the grand jury, the Ervin Committee, the House Judiciary Committee, the Supreme Court, and special prosecutors Cox and Jaworski all played essential parts. And the evidence heard on the White House tapes put the nail in Nixon's political coffin.[80]

And yet Nixon might have survived his second term if journalists such as Nelson, Woodward, Bernstein, Smith, and Hersh—along with insiders leaking them information—hadn't kept the Watergate story alive. Their revelations pushed Congress and the courts to keep asking questions about what really happened. Without the work of the journalists, Nixon's cover-up, which worked for more than eight months, may well have lasted much longer. At the start of 1973, prosecutors showed no sign that they had plans to indict anyone beyond the original seven defendants ensnared in the Watergate burglary. In fact, the FBI was sharing its confidential reports with Dean, who was in charge of the cover-up. Assistant Attorney General Henry Petersen, who oversaw the investigation, consulted with Nixon as often as twice a day. In private, Nixon bragged that he had Petersen "on a short leash."[81] If the misdeeds of Nixon's campaign and White House weren't continuously appearing on front pages and eventually the evening news, it's doubtful whether Congress, Judge Sirica, and the special prosecutors would have acted as forcefully as they did. The media's impact during Watergate is seen best through the fearful reactions of Nixon and his aides, who schemed constantly to block and intimidate the journalists who were investigating them.[82]

Nixon's own anger toward the press planted the seeds of his ultimate disgrace. His irate reaction to headlines about the secret bombing of Cambodia and the publication of the Pentagon Papers led to the formation of the plumbers with all their criminality and ineptitude. His command to "do whatever has to be done" to stop leaks and similar orders encouraged an attitude among his aides that ethical and legal lines could be crossed. His decision to wiretap journalists set the stage for planting bugs in the Democratic headquarters. And his desire to smear Daniel Ellsberg led the plumbers to break into his psychiatrist's office, providing a practice run for the Watergate burglary that led to Nixon's ruin.

As respect for Nixon fell, the credibility of the press grew, at least for a few years. Investigative reporting peaked during the rest of the 1970s as newly emboldened journalists became more willing than ever to challenge powerful leaders and institutions. Newspapers, magazines, and television stations added investigative teams, and CBS's *60 Minutes* strengthened its muckraking while it climbed to the top of the ratings.[83] Journalists formed a new organization, Investigative Reporters and Editors, to help with their digging. Presidents were scrutinized more than ever as journalists looked for the next scandal to expose.

At the same time, Nixon's strategy of casting the press as an enemy didn't die with the end of his presidency. Conservative leaders and groups nourished the belief that the press is a powerful and dangerous institution that can't be trusted, just as Agnew said it was. Donald

Trump made the idea a centerpiece of his presidency with disastrous consequences for the nation.

Nixon's creation of a White House communications office to coordinate every aspect of his public persona was an innovation that also lasted. Nixon's own weaknesses, however, doomed his communications efforts. The two presidents who followed him, Gerald Ford and Jimmy Carter, also struggled to use the media to establish themselves as leaders who could handle America's troubles as an emboldened press corps challenged them on every front. It took Ronald Reagan to show how to master White House communications and tame an increasingly aggressive press.

6 Ronald Reagan and the Taming of the Press

President Ronald Reagan strode to the podium in the Grand Ballroom of New York City's Plaza Hotel on a December evening in 1985. Wearing a black tuxedo, he still possessed the rugged good looks that made him a movie star. His body looked strong and trim, his hair showed few flecks of gray despite his seventy-five years, and his face was ruddy with good health after a Thanksgiving holiday spent riding horses and cutting brush at his California ranch. Reagan had every reason to look confident. Public approval ratings had soared past 80 percent for his performance less than three weeks earlier at a historic summit with Soviet leader Mikhail Gorbachev. The previous year he had won his second landslide presidential election.

Approximately seven hundred guests were at the Plaza for the thirtieth anniversary gala of the *National Review* magazine. When Reagan spoke with his smooth baritone, they applauded rapturously every few sentences. These were his people, and he was their champion. The festivities attracted conservative VIPs such as CIA Director William Casey and syndicated columnist George F. Will. Luminaries from the media establishment, so often derided as "liberal" by Reagan and the *National Review*, were also there, including former NBC anchorman John Chancellor and *60 Minutes* star Mike Wallace.[1]

It was a night of triumph for Reagan, *National Review* editor William F. Buckley Jr., and the conservative movement. Buckley, the president declared, "changed our country, indeed our century." Reagan said he'd been reading Buckley's magazine since its early days. "*National Review* is to the offices of the West Wing of the White House what *People* magazine is to your dentist's waiting room," he told the celebrants to loud laughter. The president joked that when Buckley was asked what job he would want in his Republican administration, the editor responded "ventriloquist."[2] Indeed, Reagan personified the postwar conservative movement whose voice Buckley helped create.

Reagan's rise to the presidency in 1980 culminated the efforts of a generation of conservative media activists.[3] Following World War II, magazines such as *National Review* and *Human Events*, rightwing radio stations, Christian broadcasters, and conservative publishing houses promoted a growing movement that challenged Roosevelt's New Deal, big-government consensus. Nixon had courted these conservatives, but they were just one of the factions within the GOP during his presidency. He felt free to ignore them when he occasionally made moves that were anathema to the right, such as creating the Environmental Protection Agency and holding summits with the leaders of communist China and the Soviet Union. In contrast, Reagan made deep conservatism the core of the GOP and carried the once fringe movement into the mainstream.

Reagan also perfected the art of White House communications that Nixon failed to master. Reagan's media skills allowed his administration to rebound from three crises that might have sunk other presidencies: an assassination attempt that nearly ended his life, a sharp economic downturn, and the Iran-Contra scandal. His ability to project an image of strength and good humor tilted the balance of power between presidents and the press back toward the White House after the Watergate debacle and the weaknesses of the Ford and Carter administrations. In addition, he diluted broadcast regulations, allowing the proliferation of opinionated news channels and the rise of partisan radio hosts such as

Rush Limbaugh. This change shook the media landscape so forcefully that we are still feeling its aftershocks.

The ideological grandfather of Limbaugh, Fox News, and other conservative media outlets was born in 1944 when a small group met in Chicago. Their mission: launch a weekly newsletter, *Human Events*. They included FDR's archenemy Colonel McCormick of the *Chicago Tribune*, aviation hero and Nazi sympathizer Charles Lindbergh, and ex–*New York Times* correspondent Frank Hanighen. They hated the New Deal's legacy of big government and business regulations. They criticized U.S. involvement in negotiations that led to the creation of the United Nations a year later. And they argued that mainstream journalism couldn't be trusted because it was too liberal. At the time, these ideas were considered extreme, but the conservative press would help popularize them.[4]

The first four-page issue of *Human Events* was compiled in Hanighen's bedroom. The publication struggled at first with only 120 subscribers. (An actor named Ronald Reagan eventually became one, declaring it his "favorite newspaper.") But it was backed by wealthy people including Texas oil millionaires and Pierre S. du Pont, former president of General Motors and his family's chemical and weapons company. Despite its powerful, wealthy supporters, *Human Events* portrayed itself as an underdog whose aggrieved readers were treated unfairly by liberal elites. It promised to accurately report facts through "eyes that are BIASED in favor of limited constitutional government, local self-government, private enterprise, and individual freedom."[5] In other words, it wasn't going to pretend to be impartial.

In the 1950s the small conservative media world welcomed young William F. Buckley Jr., a rich, pugnacious, and erudite writer who founded the *National Review*. His magazine attacked the "decadent, lukewarm mood of indifference which permeates our Liberal press."[6] Like many others in the conservative media, Buckley defended Senator Joseph McCarthy's wild accusations that many liberals were secretly communists. Buckley and other rightwing leaders adamantly opposed the civil rights movement, which they accused of being communist inspired. He made the repugnant argument that the "advanced race" of white people of the South should take "such measures as are necessary to prevail, politically and culturally."[7] *National Review* lost millions of dollars in its early years but stayed afloat thanks to the wealth of Buckley and his friends. Additional conservative publications—*Public Interest, Conservative Digest, American Spectator, Weekly Standard,* and others—eventually followed. Buckley expanded his reach with *Firing Line,* a television interview show that PBS began airing in 1971.[8]

Ronald Reagan was paying attention to *National Review, Human Events,* and other conservative media. As a young man in Illinois, he had supported Democrats because his father found a job through FDR's Works Progress Administration during the height of the Depression. Reagan listened to Roosevelt's fireside chats and marveled at the president's ability to use his words to inspire the nation. After graduating from tiny Eureka College in 1932, Reagan worked as a sports announcer at an Iowa radio station. He took bits of information received by telegram and skillfully re-created Chicago Cubs baseball games with his imagination and dramatic voice. When his radio station finally began broadcasting the actual games, listeners complained. They preferred hearing Reagan's inventive descriptions of the action.[9]

Reagan visited Hollywood in 1937 and took a screen test. He aced it and went on to appear in fifty-three films. Some of the traits that later made him a successful politician—his wisecracking sense of humor, reliability, and ability to memorize lines—made him a favorite of directors. Other performers liked Reagan too, electing him to seven terms as president of the Screen Actors Guild. When his movie career faded, he found new life as host of *General Electric Theater,* the top television show on Sunday nights.[10] He became a regular on the lecture circuit, making thousands of speeches on behalf of General Electric and the actors union. Like Roosevelt, Reagan skillfully used everyday language to reach his audiences. "You have the ability of putting complicated technical ideas into words everyone can understand," Richard Nixon once told him. Influenced by his deeply conservative father-in-law and the wealthy circles in which he socialized, Reagan had switched by then from FDR Democrat to hardline Republican.[11]

Reagan went from Hollywood celebrity to political star in 1964 when he gave a nationally televised speech supporting Republican presidential candidate Barry Goldwater. Reagan spoke apocalyptically about America's battle with communism and a tyrannical federal government. "We'll preserve for our children this, the last best hope of man on earth," he said, "or we'll sentence them to take the last step into a thousand years of darkness."[12] The speech inspired, by some estimates, millions of dollars in campaign donations to Goldwater. The Republican National Committee rebroadcast it twice nationally, and Goldwater supporters arranged for it to be aired hundreds of times on local stations. Reagan's reputation as "The Great Communicator" was born.[13]

In 1966 Reagan ran for governor of California. Political experts didn't give him much of a chance of beating incumbent Pat Brown. Reagan was just an actor, after all. He was more conservative than most voters and freely admitted he didn't know much about government. But the experts underestimated Reagan as they did throughout his political career. "What I noticed was that everyone seemed to like him, the reporters included," journalist and Reagan biographer Lou Cannon observed. Reagan trounced Brown by a million votes.[14]

During his two terms as governor, Reagan railed against taxes, government bureaucrats, welfare recipients, and especially student demonstrators. At a time of national upheaval—burning cities, protests against the Vietnam War, the rise of the feminist movement—Reagan offered a rosy vision of a traditional America. He personally confronted jeering student protesters and sent in the National Guard and state highway patrol to confront campus rebels "at the point of a bayonet."[15] Using skills honed from his decades in front of the camera, he looked strong and reasonable on TV, at least to many Americans who resented the young activists. He gained national attention, appearing on the network news for eight straight evenings during his second month as governor.[16]

Reagan ran for president in 1976, narrowly losing a brutal Republican nomination battle to Gerald Ford. Four years later he won the nomination. For his acceptance speech at the 1980 GOP convention in Detroit, his advance team led news crews through underground rooms and hallways of the vast arena to a prime vantage spot. When they arrived at a locked door, it was opened for photographers and TV cameramen only. Print reporters were locked out. "We started pounding on the doors, but we didn't get in," one *Time* magazine journalist remembered. "They don't give a damn about the print people. They were only interested in getting the cameras up there."[17] It gave the press a taste of what Reagan's media strategy would be as president.

In the 1980 general election, Reagan campaigned on a platform that *Human Events, National Review*, and others in the conservative press had promoted for years, including lower taxes, more military spending, and less money for social services. In their debate a week before the election, incumbent Jimmy Carter criticized Reagan as a dangerous extremist who didn't care about the suffering of many Americans. Toward the end of the debate, Carter attempted one more attack. Reagan responded, "There you go again," with a big smile, shaking his head like a patient parent who just caught a child telling a fib. The audience laughed, and Reagan was on the way to a huge victory, winning 489 electoral votes to 49 for Carter.[18] It was a triumph not only for Reagan but also for Buckley and other conservative media activists who finally had their own man in the White House after decades in the political wilderness.

By the time Reagan entered the White House, the DC press corps had become part of the Washington establishment. Unlike the rough-and-tumble working-class reporters of the previous generation, many journalists now had college degrees, earned good salaries, and thought of themselves as polished professionals. They hobnobbed with the rich and powerful at cocktail parties and Gridiron Club dinners. The Carters disdained this kind of schmoozing, but not the Reagans. They succeeded in building cordial relationships with the city's elites, including journalists. "Jimmy Carter you felt sorry for, but he was aloof and hard to get to know," Susan Zirinsky of CBS News said. "But Reagan always made you laugh."[19]

The press was justly criticized for hyping a series of mini-scandals during the Carter presidency, adding "gate" to their names to make them sound as serious as Watergate. There was "Peanutgate" about Carter's Georgia farm, "Billygate" about his brother's business deals in Libya, and "Lancegate" about bank transactions by one of his closest aides.[20] Once Reagan took office, journalists—whom conservatives had accused of being too liberal for decades—bent over backward to show how fair they could be to a Republican. "We've been kinder to President Reagan than any President that I can remember since I've been at the *Post*," Executive Editor Ben Bradlee said in 1984.[21] Michael Deaver, Reagan's deputy chief of staff, agreed. "Most of all, after Johnson, Nixon, and Carter, the press did not want to be accused of destroying another president," Deaver said.[22]

The owlish looking Deaver, whose training was in public relations, excelled at making Reagan look good. Fiercely loyal, he had worked with Reagan since he was governor and knew what made him shine and what made him stumble. Deaver understood that television was how most Americans now got their news, replacing political parties as the primary means for achieving power. He demonstrated his image-making skills when Reagan delivered his inaugural address. For the first time, the speech was given from the west side of the Capitol so Reagan could face the National Mall with its inspiring vista of monuments. His words were written with television visuals in mind, a tactic that seems obvious now but was groundbreaking then. His staff gave the networks a copy of the speech the day before so they could plan their camera angles. As a result, when Reagan mentioned Washington, Jefferson, Lincoln, and the heroes buried at Arlington National Cemetery, viewers could see stirring images of each memorial. Even as Reagan spoke of the nation's economic crisis, Americans could feel uplifted by patriotism and hope.[23]

Deaver became the producer of the daily TV show known as the Reagan presidency, making each presidential appearance a skillfully scripted performance. When Reagan gave his first State of the Union address, he introduced the country to Lenny Skutnik as "the spirit of American heroism at its finest." Two weeks earlier Skutnik had jumped into the frigid Potomac River to save a woman from drowning after an airplane crash. Even though the majority of Congress consisted of Democrats opposed to Reagan's policies, they gave a standing ovation as the television audience saw Skutnik in the gallery next to a beaming First Lady Nancy Reagan. From then on, State of the Union addresses have regularly featured people whom speechwriters referred to as "heroes in the balcony." Journalists playfully called them "Skutniks."[24]

Wherever Reagan traveled, Deaver and his team visited the location in advance to identify places that offered the strongest images for photo opportunities. To highlight positive news about housing starts, they sent Reagan to Texas to make the announcement surrounded by construction workers in hard hats in front of a new housing development. Before Reagan visited the demilitarized zone between South and North Korea, they marked the exact spots in the ground where he should stand looking through field glasses toward the communist regime. "When he didn't stand on his toe mark he was signaled by one of the advance men to move over into the sunshine," Andrea Mitchell of NBC recalled. The dramatic image was featured on evening newscasts and newspaper front pages.[25]

Without Reagan's talents, Deaver's tactics wouldn't have worked. The president was a professional actor who understood his role and played it to near perfection. He delivered his speeches with soothing optimism, much like Roosevelt's firesides. He spoke of values such as peace, patriotism, family, neighborhood, and hard work. And he inspired audiences as he described America "as God's shining city on a hill," a beacon of liberty for the rest of mankind.[26] Most effective of all was

Reagan's sense of humor. At the start of his first State of the Union, he made fun of his own age, which was seventy at the time. He began by citing a passage from President Washington's first State of the Union. "For our friends in the press, who place a high premium on accuracy, let me say: I did not actually hear George Washington say that," Reagan said to gales of laughter.[27]

Along with the humor came serious policy changes. In his first year, Reagan proposed reducing income taxes, with most of the savings going to the top earners, while cutting money for social services. These "Reaganomics" policies received mixed reviews as critics highlighted the millions of people who would be hurt by the budget cuts. "Blacks Will Suffer from Reaganomics," read a headline in the *Philadelphia Tribune*. "Thorns Have Begun to Appear in Reagan's Economic Garden," the *New York Times* reported. After two months in office, Reagan's disapproval rating in the Gallup poll jumped 11 points. Conservative columnists Rowland Evans and Robert Novak declared, "The Honeymoon Is Definitely Over."[28]

But it wasn't. On March 30, 1981, Reagan was shot after giving a speech at a Washington hotel. A .22-caliber bullet punctured his left lung and stopped three inches from his heart. Reagan's press secretary, Jim Brady, was severely wounded with a bullet lodged in his brain; he would need a wheelchair for the rest of his life. A Secret Service agent and a DC policeman were also hurt. As Reagan was wheeled into emergency surgery, he began with the jokes. "I hope you are all Republicans," he told the doctors. "I'd like to do that scene again—starting at the hotel," he wrote in a note to his nurses.[29]

Reagan's courage and good humor following the assassination attempt attracted widespread sympathy and admiration. "The remarkable acceptance of at least the first six years of his presidency and the astounding personal popularity Reagan was to enjoy began to take shape that day," Deaver recalled.[30] The press understandably took it easy on the seventy-year-old president as he recovered. Less than four weeks after the attempt on his life, a friendly interview with Reagan about the shooting was splashed across front pages throughout the country. His approval ratings in some surveys climbed to the highest of any president in the history of polling.[31]

Reagan parlayed this personal admiration into support for Reaganomics. He persuaded Congress to pass his first budget with hardly any revisions. It cut taxes and increased military spending, while slashing spending on job training, housing, school lunches, and food stamps. "Not since the first six months of Franklin Roosevelt's Administration has any president done so much of such magnitude so quickly to change the economic direction of the nation," *Time* observed.[32] The editors of Buckley's *National Review* were ecstatic, calling Reagan's budget "magical."[33] For decades they had promoted their policies to no avail. Reagan made them law.

On a beautiful sunny day in March 1982, reporters stood in a clump on the White House lawn as the Reagans walked to the Marine One helicopter for a trip to Camp David. The journalists screamed questions about the troubled U.S. economy and Reagan's policies in Central America, but they could barely be heard as the pilot ran the helicopter's engine at full throttle as directed by the president's aides. Reagan looked dignified, answering some questions that he liked and ignoring others as reporters competed to be heard beneath the helicopter's roar. Nancy Reagan stood behind him, smiling as if patiently waiting for unruly children to calm down.[34]

Similar scenes happened repeatedly during Reagan's presidency, making the press seem rude and desperate. After the White House press corps yelled questions at him following a Rose Garden ceremony for teachers, some of the guests shouted back angrily at the reporters for "taking away the joy" of the occasion.[35] Whenever reporters battled for Reagan's attention, the aggressive, high-decibel Sam Donaldson of ABC often won the prize of a presidential answer. Donaldson "forever shouts at the President above the noise of the waiting helicopter, and the President forever turns and cups his hand quizzically," Lance Morrow of *Time* observed. "The ceremony almost never yields any news, only the ritual impression that 1) Donaldson is a loud, obnoxious reporter; and 2) the President is a nice guy with a crinkling smile who would be happy to oblige even the cretins of the press, if it weren't for that darned helicopter."[36]

These scenes were part of the carefully crafted White House communications strategy. Deaver, Chief of Staff James Baker, and White House Communications Director David Gergen expertly managed the news about Reagan without engaging in the kind of open warfare that Nixon did. They knew, for example, that the TV networks wanted at least one White House story for each evening newscast. Every day they made sure to suggest a positive story with strong visuals for the cameras. This reduced the odds that reporters would spend time digging for their own investigative scoops. As Deaver explained it, "We fed them and they ate it every day."[37]

Protecting the president from tough questions was at the heart of the communications strategy. It was no accident that Reagan held fewer news conferences than any president since Calvin Coolidge. Spontaneous interactions between the president and the press were also discouraged. Using the assassination attempt as an excuse, Reagan's aides had the Secret Service block journalists from getting near Reagan in situations where he might not look or sound his best. "I would see Jimmy Carter almost every working day of his presidency," Sam Donaldson said. "With Reagan, cameras always get in. It's reporters they don't want there."[38] In the ultimate irony, when Reagan made a 1983 speech in Japan extolling freedom of the press, reporters were prevented from covering it.[39]

One reason Reagan's staff shielded him from reporters was his embarrassing habit of not telling the truth. He exaggerated frequently, often forgot basic facts, and sometimes completely made up stories. Reagan once famously said that trees cause 80 percent of air pollution, which is far from accurate. On the campaign trail, he deepened racial stereotypes by giving the example of a Black "Welfare Queen" convicted of defrauding the government of $150,000; in reality she had pled guilty to only $8,000 of fraud. Most welfare recipients were white, but that didn't fit Reagan's narrative. He also often told the dramatic story of a World War II pilot who won a Medal of Honor for sacrificing his life to comfort an injured crewman as their damaged B-17 bomber plummeted to earth. The story came from a movie, not real life. Was Reagan intentionally lying? Perhaps not. People close to him claimed that once he believed something, he believed it with all his heart, no matter what contrary evidence was presented.[40]

Reagan often got away with these falsehoods. Journalists eventually stopped challenging them, partly because readers and viewers complained reporters were being mean to the likeable president, and partly because he did it so often it hardly seemed like news anymore. "I mean, for a long time we were writing practically every week a little box on what he said that wasn't true," explained Merrill Sheils, *Newsweek*'s national news editor at the time. "We ultimately just couldn't stand doing it week after week after week because it seemed sort of unfair."[41] Because mistakes seemed to slide right off him, Reagan earned the nickname "The Teflon President" after the nonstick coating on cookware. "I think a lot of the Teflon came because the press was holding back," Gergen said. "I don't think they wanted to go after him that toughly."[42] It was a trait his successors wished they had, as journalists became more aggressive at identifying lies.

Reagan couldn't completely avoid negative news. As unemployment soared, the federal deficit skyrocketed, and America fell into its worst economic slump since the Depression, Reagan's approval ratings plunged to 35 percent in January 1983. In the midst of the economic crisis, Reagan protested that the press was portraying him as a Scrooge because of his budget cuts. "Is it news that some fella out in South Succotash some place has just been laid off, that he should be interviewed nationwide?" Reagan complained in an interview.[43] CBS anchorman Dan Rather said the White House objected repeatedly when the network ran multiple stories about the unemployment rate hovering over 10 percent. The administration's complaints were "designed to have us think twice" about similar stories in the future, Rather said.[44]

Deaver knew that no matter what negative words journalists said about Reagan, viewers would remember positive images of him on their screens. The same day that the president called for ending corporate income taxes, Deaver scheduled him to spend time drinking a beer and shaking hands at an Irish bar in Boston. Even as NBC's Chris Wallace said the tax plan "will only fuel the charge that Mr. Reagan cares most about the rich," the visuals in his story showed a bar full of working-class men cheering their smiling president. "It may sound cynical," Deaver told journalist Mark Hertsgaard, "but you can do a lot of things cutting programs, but a picture of an Irish president in an Irish pub at two o'clock in the afternoon raising his glass with a bunch of blue-collar workers and an Irish priest—that will last you for a long time."[45]

The administration used all of its news management skills in October 1983 after 241 Americans died in a terrorist bombing at a U.S. military barracks in Lebanon. Reagan was roundly criticized for not doing more to prevent the attack. But two days later attention shifted from the carnage in Lebanon when the United States invaded the island of Grenada, the tiniest country in the Western Hemisphere. The administration said between eight hundred and one thousand U.S. citizens in Grenada were in grave danger from a new communist government supported by Cuba. Some Americans on the island, however, said the danger didn't seem so severe. The U.S. military kept reporters away from Grenada so they couldn't try to verify the claims until the battle's third day. The administration distributed its own bloodless videos of the military intervention, exaggerated the number of Cuban and Grenadian troops, and falsely claimed there were no civilian casualties during the invasion.[46] It was a template of image over reality that other presidents would try to use.

The press complained about the news blackout of the fighting in Grenada, noting that Cubans were getting more accurate information than Americans. "It is another irony of this anti-communist administration that Oct. 27 was one of the few times in history when citizens of a communist country knew more about what was going on than

Americans did," Lou Cannon wrote in the *Washington Post*. But the public wasn't bothered by the press restrictions. Americans were just happy to win a war, no matter how small, after the humiliation of Vietnam. Finally a president seemed to be in command of events.[47] In the aftermath of the Grenada invasion, Reagan's approval ratings climbed to the highest they'd been in two years.[48]

By 1984 Reagan was cruising toward an easy reelection victory. As *Newsweek* put it, much of the public believed Reagan personified "America as it imagined itself to be—the bearer of the traditional Main Street values of family and neighborhood, of thrift, industry and charity instead of government intervention where self-reliance failed." To avoid potential gaffes, his staff made sure he didn't hold any press conferences between the end of July and the November election.[49]

But Reagan stumbled through the first debate on October 7 against his Democratic opponent, former vice president Walter Mondale. Reagan's answers rambled, and his poll numbers dropped. A front-page *Wall Street Journal* headline asked, "Is Oldest U.S. President Now Showing His Age?"[50] Reagan's aides invited Roger Ailes, Nixon's former TV consultant, to the White House for advice. Ailes told Reagan not to worry about memorizing information for the next debate. Instead, he urged the president to prepare an answer in case he was asked about his age. When the question was indeed raised, Reagan was ready. "I will not make age an issue of this campaign," he replied with a deadpan expression. "I am not going to exploit, for political purposes, my opponent's youth and inexperience." Everyone laughed, including the fifty-six-year-old Mondale.[51] Once again Reagan's humor saved him. He won the debate and the election, taking 59 percent of the popular vote and carrying forty-nine states.[52]

In his second term, Reagan earned the crowning achievement of his presidency—a better relationship with the Soviet Union that led to nuclear weapons cuts. He had already overseen the largest boost in military spending during peacetime in U.S. history. Reagan's aggressive military policy brought the United States and Soviets closer to the brink of a nuclear war during his first term, but the relationship thawed after Mikhail Gorbachev became the new, reformist Soviet leader in 1985.[53] Gorbachev was desperate to reduce military spending by stopping the arms race. He reached out to Reagan, and the two of them held four summits. During a 1987 summit in Washington, they signed a treaty eliminating short-range and intermediate-range nuclear missiles. It was the first time the Soviets and Americans had ever agreed to reduce nuclear weapons. The summits garnered nearly unanimous acclaim for Reagan in the press. "A Clear Success," the *Daily Advocate* of Stamford, Connecticut, said. "Reagan Wins Bipartisan Praise for Talks," declared the *Evening Post* of Charleston, South Carolina. "Summit 'First Step' Toward Peace," the *Fort Worth Star-Telegram* predicted.[54]

The second term also brought the greatest crisis of Reagan's presidency. It began in October 1986 when Nicaraguan troops shot down a CIA-chartered airplane. It was full of weapons being delivered to the Contras, a rebel group trying to overthrow the socialist Nicaraguan government, even though Congress had banned such military aid. At first Reagan and others in his administration falsely denied in the press that the plane had any ties to the U.S. government. But the scheme unraveled when a surviving crew member admitted that it was supplying the Contras.[55]

The next month *Ash-Shiraa*, a Lebanese magazine, broke startling news: a former U.S. official had gone on a secret mission to trade weapons to Iran in return for the release of seven U.S. hostages held by an Iranian-backed militia. Within a day, Iranians confirmed the report and said the official was Reagan's former national security adviser, Robert McFarlane. The trade violated Reagan's stated policy of not trading arms for hostages and his vow "never to negotiate with terrorists." Two years earlier, the administration had identified the Iranians as state sponsors of terrorism. U.S. law prohibited giving Iran weapons unless the president notified Congress of a reason to do so. Reagan hadn't done that.[56]

The White House issued a stream of lies in a desperate attempt to contain the damage in the press. Reagan insisted "no foundation" existed for the article in the Lebanese magazine. The arms were sent, he said, to encourage Iran to become more moderate, not to trade for hostages. In his diary Reagan complained, "The media looks like it's trying to create another Watergate." But his diary made clear he knew more than a year earlier that anti-aircraft and anti-tank weapons were being traded for hostages.[57]

To escape the mess, Reagan gave a televised address on November 13, 1986. These big speeches had always worked for him before. He began by belittling reporters' sources for their stories. He claimed that press reports of his government using "weapons to Iran as ransom payment for the release of American hostages" were "rumors" and "utterly false."[58] But it was the president's speech that was inaccurate, and polls showed most Americans didn't believe him. Reagan's television magic wasn't strong enough this time to get him out of the crisis.[59]

At a press conference six days later, Reagan again insisted the administration had done nothing wrong. His face looked older, paler, and more perplexed than it had just one year earlier during the *National Review* gala. There was none of the famous Reagan swagger as reporters aggressively challenged him. Sam Donaldson asked why the administration was pressuring U.S. allies to embargo Iran while the U.S. was secretly selling it weapons. "How can you justify this duplicity?" Donaldson wondered. Reagan responded haltingly that the embargo still existed. His answers to questions from Chris Wallace of NBC sounded befuddled as he meandered into a comment about Danish ships. Once again his remarks were full of mistruths: the deal was only meant to improve relations with moderates in Iran, Israel wasn't involved in the weapons swap (it was), and only a thousand anti-tank missiles had been sent (the real number was more than twice as many). Instead of admitting a mistake, Reagan accused the media of screwing up the deal. "I believe and have reason to believe that we would have had all five of them [hostages] by this weekend had it not been for the attendant confusion that arose here in the reporting room," he said.[60] Like other presidents caught in scandals, he found blaming the press to be convenient.

On the morning of November 25, Reagan spoke to reporters again. He announced the resignation of National Security Adviser John Poindexter and Lt. Col. Oliver North, a National Security Council staffer. Reagan said the arms deal had "serious issues of propriety" but blamed his staff for not previously informing him. He spoke for just four minutes, refusing to answer questions and looking less genial than usual. Then Attorney General Edwin Meese III took the podium. He admitted the trading of weapons to Iran had indeed taken place and that up to thirty million dollars of the money received had been diverted to support the Nicaraguan Contras. Sending the money to the Contras rather than returning it to the U.S. Treasury violated U.S. law. The White House press corps immediately knew this was a big deal. "Reporters were dashing for phones, the flush of a great story on their faces," Eleanor Randolph of the *Washington Post* observed. "In stark contrast, Reagan's press staff sat watching the newscasts in what some veterans described as a state of total gloom, 'at absolute rock bottom.'"[61]

The Iran-Contra scandal, as it came to be known, dominated the news from Washington for the next year. An independent counsel began investigating, and Congress held three months of televised hearings. Under pressure, Reagan appointed a three-man mission led by former GOP senator John Tower of Texas to study what went wrong. Polls showed Reagan's public approval sliding from 63 percent in October 1986 to 45 percent in March 1987 despite a strong economy. The president had convinced himself it wasn't an arms-for-hostages deal when in reality it was. He couldn't understand why people didn't believe him when they had trusted him for so many years on other matters.[62]

Like Nixon's staff during Watergate, members of Reagan's administration engaged in an extensive cover-up. Meese distributed a memo dictating that "blame must be put at NSC's door—rogue operation, going on without President's knowledge or sanction." It wasn't true, but Reagan's line of defense had been set, and everyone was expected to follow it.[63] CIA Director William Casey and National Security Adviser Poindexter made deceptive and inaccurate statements to Congress about the weapons sent to Iran. Poindexter and McFarlane created a false chronology of events, and Poindexter and North destroyed evidence. North's secretary stuffed incriminating documents down her blouse and in her boots to smuggle them out of the White House. Vice President George H. W. Bush, Secretary of State George Shultz, and Defense Secretary Caspar Weinberger withheld evidence for years. In contrast to Nixon's aides, Reagan's people effectively shielded him from impeachment charges.[64]

The press covered Iran-Contra intensely at first. In the first three months of the scandal, the *New York Times* and *Washington Post* combined had more than a thousand stories about it. Most of them weren't favorable to Reagan. But reporters couldn't puncture the code of secrecy protecting the president.[65] His new spokesman, Marlin Fitzwater, later observed that the "issues in Iran-Contra were complex and the sequence of 'who talked to who, and when?' were impossible to follow." Gallup's president said Americans were disturbed by Iran-Contra but also tired of the saturated news coverage.[66]

On March 19, 1987, Reagan held his first televised news conference since his disastrous one four months earlier. The stakes were high. The Tower Commission had just issued its Iran-Contra report, and it wasn't pretty. It concluded that Reagan had done nothing illegal but was uninformed, disengaged, and easily swayed by his staff. If Reagan stumbled during the press conference, the last two years of his presidency would be severely weakened. The president needed, Marlin Fitzwater said, to appear "still tall in the saddle."[67]

The press was on edge too. The previous day White House reporters had experienced a bizarre verbal attack that foreshadowed the kind of hostility journalists would face in future years for questioning presidents. Republican senator Alan Simpson of Wyoming, a loyal Reagan ally, had shouted at them for their "irrational" and "lurid fascination" with Iran-Contra. He accused them of doing a "sadistic little disservice" to the country for questioning Reagan during a photo opportunity. "You're asking him things because you know he's off balance and you'd like to stick it in his gazoo," he snarled, contorting his face, his hands mimicking the claws of a wild beast. "Here's the way you look as you go, 'Mr. President! Mr. President!'"[68]

With tension in the air, Reagan strode into the East Room for the news conference, his back straight and his head held high, making a confident entrance as he'd done hundreds of times before. Reporters were ready to grill the president, but this time he was well prepared. His staff had compiled twenty single-spaced pages worth of possible questions for him to practice answering. Reagan had rehearsed his responses for four hours with staff members playing the roles of reporters. Once Reagan was comfortable with an answer, he memorized it, almost as if he had pressed an internal record button.

As expected, the reporters repeatedly pressed Reagan about the specifics of what he knew and when he knew it. But the president refused to get bogged down in the details and firmly stuck with his prepared answers. His swagger was back. When it was over, reporters, photographers, and cameramen surged toward Reagan, hoping to get at least one unscripted response before he was gone. They didn't succeed, and he left the room smiling. "I think his performance was first-rate," said NBC's Chris Wallace.[69] *Baltimore Sun* television critic Bill Carter noted that Reagan made no major mistakes, while the press—more docile than usual—failed to clarify the complexities of his role in Iran-Contra. "Indeed," Carter said, "it seemed as if the TV press was extremely conscious of the possibility that they might start to appear cruel and unfair to this venerable, popular man."[70]

The watchdog press had been tamed, and Reagan survived the crisis. Congress continued its Iran-Contra hearings, and the independent counsel's investigation lasted six more years. They both found that Reagan was responsible for a White House atmosphere where laws were ignored, but they concluded he hadn't acted criminally.[71] Despite his administration sending weapons to a U.S. enemy, violating congressional bans, and destroying evidence, the public—and much of the press—accepted that Reagan had only good intentions in wanting to get the hostages released.

Reagan's approval ratings climbed back to 53 percent by the end of his second term. Most Americans applauded his successful summits with Gorbachev and a strong economy that created more than eighteen million new jobs. Although he had vowed to cut deficits, the national debt tripled to $1.86 trillion on his watch. But the public was willing to look past the massive borrowing as the good times rolled. Reagan could end his presidency with the positive image that he and his staff worked so hard to project. A White House communications strategy that emphasized photo ops and minimized time spent answering reporters' questions had proven effective.[72]

The day before Reagan's March 19 press conference on Iran-Contra, his handpicked chairman of the Federal Communications Commission, Mark Fowler, testified before the Senate Commerce, Science and Transportation subcommittee. Fowler, a thin man with big glasses and even bigger ambitions, opposed regulations as a matter of free-market principle. He was trying to persuade the senators to abolish the rules of the Fairness Doctrine, which required TV and radio stations to give time to differing viewpoints. If he succeeded, television and media coverage of presidents, other politicians, and policy issues would be transformed.

The FCC had rarely enforced the Fairness Doctrine from its introduction in 1949 through the start of the 1960s. While liberals made little effort to develop partisan programming on local radio stations, conservative radio shows spread. Often in the guise of religious broadcasts that eluded regulators, these shows typically opposed the civil rights movement, social welfare programs, and liberalism in all its forms.[73] A 1963 study found that corporations and other conservative funders were spending between $15 million and $25 million a year bankrolling broadcasts on more than a thousand stations across America. The radio show of the Rev. Carl McIntire, who trafficked in racist and anti-Semitic conspiracy theories, was heard on more than six hundred stations. Billionaire oil tycoon H. L. Hunt sponsored a show on more than five hundred stations. Hunt advocated, among other things, that "the more taxes you pay the more votes you [should] get." Alarmed by the growth of these shows, the FCC under Kennedy and Johnson aggressively responded to complaints of biased broadcasts. By the early 1970s, the number of highly conservative broadcasts had dwindled.[74]

The Reagan administration was determined to reverse this trend for radio and the even more powerful medium of television. Fowler pushed for weaker regulations, arguing that television "is just another appliance—it's a toaster with pictures." When he first proposed scuttling the Fairness Doctrine early in Reagan's presidency, he was belittled as being naive. The *Washington Post* reported that "a number of communications lawyers are raising questions about Fowler's political savvy, wondering why the chairman is spending such a large part of his time on a cause that is clearly not about to go very far any time soon."[75]

But it did go far. After Congress passed a bill protecting the Fairness Doctrine, Reagan vetoed the legislation. Congress wasn't able to override the veto, putting the Fairness Doctrine in the hands of Fowler's FCC, which killed it in August 1987. The regulation that had encouraged objective broadcast journalism was dead.[76] "This decision is not a free speech decision," media critic Tom Shales wrote. "It is a bought-and-paid-for speech decision. It aims to protect broadcasting companies still further from the public they are supposed to serve."[77] The door was opened wide for radio stations and TV channels that no longer needed to try to be fair or balanced. America would enter an age of increasingly polarized media that resembled the era of John Adams except this time partisan opinions could be shared with millions of people in an instant.

A year after Reagan's FCC shredded the Fairness Doctrine, a conservative Sacramento talk radio host named Rush Limbaugh hit the national airwaves. Limbaugh was a college dropout who began his disc jockeying career more interested in playing music than talking politics. But he gradually realized the appeal of being politically provocative. He verbally pummeled liberals, whom he derided as the "arts and croissants crowd." He delighted in being cruel and offensive. "One of the things I want to do before I die," Limbaugh announced, "is conduct the homeless Olympics." He called feminists "feminazis." He made racist comments. He mocked people dying from AIDS.[78]

Through most of the twentieth century, the mass news media generally portrayed political leaders as reasonable, well-meaning human beings even as journalists challenged them on specific issues and hunted for examples of corruption. To be sure, there were some publications and radio stations that were bitterly partisan, but network television and most large newspapers and magazines attempted to share a range of viewpoints and usually assumed that presidents and other leaders were decent, patriotic people. That all changed with Limbaugh.

Limbaugh made claims that eventually became gospel in the conservative movement. Supporters of abortion rights do so because "there's a lot of money being made on abortions." Liberals support social programs, he said, "to use the plight of the poor to advance their goal of dominating society." And global warming is "a scientific fraud" perpetrated by "the environmental wacko crowd."[79] In Limbaugh's world, there was only right and wrong, and he was always right while anyone who disagreed with him was delusional or evil and quite likely un-American.

Soon Limbaugh turned into a media juggernaut as talk radio became America's favorite format on the airwaves by the mid-1990s, more popular than sports or any kind of music. Older audiences—the people who voted most—especially liked it. New satellite technology meant hosts such as Limbaugh could easily be heard around the country. Improved phone lines allowed listeners across the nation to join in the conversation. Limbaugh offered a snarky and often vicious version of the deep conservatism that *Human Events* and *National Review* had introduced to postwar American. But instead of a few thousand readers, he reached millions of people every week.[80]

Limbaugh spawned many right-wing imitators on talk radio, cable television, and eventually the internet. Their influence continued to strengthen into the next century, making politics more bitterly partisan as they gained power within the Republican Party and tormented Democratic presidents and any GOP leader who didn't agree with them. Nearly three decades after the end of the Fairness Doctrine, Limbaugh and other conservative media stars would help bring to power a president who was in their image and then encourage his efforts to overturn the results of the 2020 election and incite an insurrection.

7   Bill Clinton and the Scandalized Press

Matt Drudge smirked as he looked down at the cream of the Washington press corps who had come to hear him speak in June 1998. He had good reason to feel pleased with himself and scornful toward the journalists gathered at the posh National Press Club. Drudge, a self-described loner with no newsroom experience, had scooped them all on the biggest story of Bill Clinton's presidency thanks to his tenacity, computer skills, and willingness to upend the standards of mainstream journalism. Less than five months earlier, he posted on his *Drudge Report* website that *Newsweek* magazine was sitting on a story that President Bill Clinton had an affair with a young White House intern. The scandal escalated as the rest of the press tried to catch up with Drudge. Now the president faced the biggest crisis of his career and the possibility of impeachment for committing perjury about the affair.

Drudge told the National Press Club members that he had been an aimless young adult working in the CBS gift shop in Los Angeles when his father bought him a computer in 1994. He found a home on the internet and created the *Drudge Report*, a website that shared rumors, linked to news from other sites, and posted Drudge's own stories (which were sometimes based on things he found in the trash cans at his CBS job). He ran the *Drudge Report* by himself out of his apartment, he said, "petting the cat and watching the wires."[1]

Drudge liked to wear a brown fedora to project the persona of an old-fashioned journalist. In contrast to actual journalists, he spent little time trying to verify what he published. Like the millions of other Americans sharing stories online, Drudge had no editors pestering him to check the information he posted. Sometimes it proved accurate, sometimes it didn't. "I don't listen to anybody," Drudge boasted. But people paid attention to him. America Online, then a dominant force on the internet, hired Drudge, allowing his site to be seen by millions. "Every citizen can be a reporter, can take on the powers that be," Drudge explained to the journalists at the National Press Club. "I guess this changes everything," he added. He was right.[2]

Drudge began his speech by recalling how he sometimes used to walk by the *Washington Post*'s offices while growing up in the DC area. He'd look up longingly, wanting to work there someday but feeling sure the powerful newspaper would never hire a middle-class kid like him. He ended his talk by saying the previous night he'd once again walked by the *Post*'s building. This time he didn't look up wistfully. "This time I laughed," he said, expressing his disdain for journalism's establishment. "Let the future begin." The assembled journalists had few smiles on their faces as they grudgingly applauded.[3]

As Drudge made abundantly clear, journalism was transformed in the 1990s. Online media, cable news, and talk radio changed the profession's norms, opening the door to more sensationalism and a nearly constant quest for White House scandals. The heightened competition to attract bigger audiences put pressure on reporters to come up with something to report every hour of every day. Journalism and entertainment became increasingly intertwined as more news shows took on the traits of tabloid journalism with its emphasis on rumors and the private lives of public figures. Political partisans in the media weaponized news in an effort to wound their political rivals and get rich. These forces nearly toppled the Clinton administration. The upheaval in the press, much of it driven by new technology and well-funded ideologues, would continue to shape the fates of presidents who followed Clinton.

Bill Clinton had a commanding presence. He stood six feet two inches tall with a thick head of hair, chubby cheeks, and a wide grin. He disarmed people with his warm Arkansas drawl and big laugh, but he possessed a steely determination and a quick temper. A Rhodes scholar and Yale Law School graduate, the restless Clinton was always eager to meet new people, read more books, and climb higher in politics.

Arkansas voters elected him in 1978 to become the nation's youngest governor at age thirty-two. During his dozen years running the state, he developed a reputation as a reform-minded centrist who was friendly with business interests but also championed the state's poorest people. He won more money to pay teachers but also demanded stricter standardized testing. He pushed through work requirements for welfare recipients while also providing them with more childcare and job opportunities.[4] No matter the issue, he seemed to find a way to split the difference between competing sides.

In 1988 Clinton finally had the moment in the spotlight he craved—giving the nominating speech on primetime TV for Massachusetts governor Michael Dukakis at the Democratic National Convention. But the speech was disastrously long, the crowd hissed, and ABC switched to a movie out of sheer boredom. Instead of a political star, Clinton became a national punchline. On *The Tonight Show Starring Johnny Carson*, the host joked that Clinton had been approved as a sleeping aid. But the young governor recovered brilliantly. He went on *The Tonight Show*, playing the saxophone and trading quips with Carson. The audience—bigger than the one for his convention speech—loved it. Clinton had adeptly used entertainment media to connect with the public. He survived what seemed like political doom, an ability he would call on repeatedly.[5]

Clinton was a natural politician who loved shaking hands with voters and talking about issues until well after midnight. In 1992 he became the first baby boomer to win the Democratic nomination, using his youthful charisma to appeal to young voters. Clinton appeared on the popular *Arsenio Hall Show*, donning sunglasses and playing Elvis Presley's

"Heartbreak Hotel" on saxophone to a dancing, cheering crowd.[6] As he did on *The Tonight Show*, he was using non-news media to show the world that he wasn't confined by the old rules. For Clinton, politics and entertainment mixed easily together.

Journalists, however, weren't always impressed. Clinton kept running into controversy as he developed a reputation among the press corps for often skirting the outer edges of the truth. He said he'd smoked marijuana but raised eyebrows when he claimed he "didn't inhale." The *Wall Street Journal* revealed that he misled the public about how he avoided being drafted during the Vietnam War. The tabloid *Star* newspaper reported that he had a long-running extramarital affair; Clinton then lied about it on *60 Minutes*. Years earlier, the *Pine Bluff Commercial* newspaper in Arkansas gave him the nickname "Slick Willie." It stuck.[7]

Concerns about his trustworthiness weren't enough to stop Clinton. His Republican opponent, incumbent George H. W. Bush, had lost popularity after a recession led to rising unemployment. In a three-way race that included Texas billionaire Ross Perot running as an independent, Clinton won thirty-two states and an impressive 370 electoral votes to 168 for Bush. But Clinton earned only 43 percent of the popular vote, a less-than-overwhelming mandate as he began his presidency.[8]

As a candidate and then as president, Clinton thought reporters were obsessed with grilling him about petty details in an effort to catch him in a mistake.[9] He complained that the press in the post-Watergate era was overly cynical and fixated on political process—who was up and who was down—rather than the substance of policies. In return, many Washington correspondents saw the Clinton team as brash, inexperienced interlopers who couldn't keep their stories straight. After twelve years of covering Republicans in the White House, journalists were determined to show they could be equally tough on a Democrat.[10] "In short order," *Washington Post* reporter John F. Harris observed in his Clinton biography, "there was a low-grade war under way between the Clinton White House and the veteran White House reporters who covered it."[11]

The administration stumbled out of the gate. After four months, Clinton's job approval rating had dropped to 36 percent, the lowest for any president during a similar period since polls began tracking presidential popularity during the Truman administration. Compared to Reagan's efficient first-term team, Clinton's staff was a mess during its early months, and its relationship with the press suffered. Many top aides were chosen at the last minute, and their responsibilities weren't always clear. Both Press Secretary Dee Dee Myers and Communications Director George Stephanopoulos gave daily briefings to reporters, creating inconsistency and confusion. It wasn't until the end of his first year that Clinton began receiving a weekly memo summarizing communications strategy and press events for the week ahead.[12]

The White House press corps grew frustrated. Journalists traveling with Clinton griped that arrangements for the press pool were chaotic, making it hard for them to file their stories. Back in Washington, reporters found that one of the few opportunities to ask the president a question was to chase after him when he went on unannounced jogs. "Every time he would run by us on a jog," Mark Knoller of CBS Radio recalled, "we'd shout a question and, in between huffs and puffs, he'd give us a one- or two- or three-word answer."[13]

During the 1992 campaign, Jeff Gerth of the *New York Times* began investigating a money-losing Arkansas land deal. Gerth discovered that in the 1970s, the Clintons invested $203,000 in the Whitewater Development Corporation at the suggestion of their friends James and Susan McDougal. James McDougal also bought and defrauded a small Arkansas bank named Madison Guaranty Savings and Loan. Some Madison money was used to subsidize the failing Whitewater and pay off Clinton campaign debts. Clinton was suspected of using his power as governor to reduce government scrutiny of McDougal's dealings. After Madison went belly up, it cost taxpayers $60 million to bail it out.

Whitewater was a murky tale of sweetheart deals, shredded documents, and sordid Arkansas politics. When Gerth questioned him about it,

Clinton was evasive, spurring the reporter to dig deeper. Gerth's first Whitewater story appeared on the front page of the *Times* in March 1992 at the height of the Democratic presidential primaries.[14] It didn't make a big splash at first, but he and other journalists continued to investigate the Clintons' Arkansas years. Like a leaky faucet, suspicious details kept dripping into the news through most of Clinton's presidency. For the first time, the national press corps was intensely investigating not only what a president did after he entered the White House, but also what he and his wife had done before they came to Washington. The administration objected that the stories distorted the facts.[15] No one could prove the Clintons had broken any laws, but it sure didn't look good. "Could it be that a suspicious set of mores has been carried from Arkansas to the White House?" the conservative *Wall Street Journal* asked in an editorial full of innuendo but scant evidence of wrongdoing.[16]

The press uncovered more Clinton controversies, attaching a "gate" suffix to each as if it were the next Watergate. There was "Coptergate" about the use of military helicopters by White House staff. "Filegate" occurred when Clinton aides were discovered to suspiciously have FBI files in their possession. The wheeling and dealing of his wife, Hillary Rodham Clinton, that turned a $1,000 investment in cattle futures into nearly $100,000 was dubbed "Cattlegate." And "Travelgate" occurred when the Clintons suddenly fired seven members of the White House travel staff, replacing them with a firm that had ties with one of their close friends. Travelgate especially irked White House reporters who liked the way the fired employees had treated them.[17]

Each new scandal raised more questions about the Clintons' integrity and competence. Their tendency toward secrecy made matters worse. "Whitewater has been the worst of it," a *Newsweek* article said. "From the start, aides pleaded with the Clintons to come clean—to release all relevant documents, answer all questions. They didn't. They have, instead, sulked and blamed Republicans and the press for blowing things out of proportion." Later in the article, *Newsweek* reluctantly admitted, "There still isn't a hint of criminality here."[18] But the hunt for scandals continued, and the burgeoning rightwing media were determined to use them to destroy Clinton's presidency.

During the 1992 campaign, President Bush had invited Rush Limbaugh to meet at the White House and spend a night in the Lincoln Bedroom. Bush was hoping for stronger support from the radio host in order to attract conservative voters. In a surprising twist of protocol, the desperate president even carried Limbaugh's luggage into the White House.

Bush understood that Limbaugh had become the undisputed king of conservative media. Building on his radio success, he launched the syndicated *Rush Limbaugh Show* on TV in 1992. It aired on 185 stations reaching 95 percent of the country. Limbaugh also published two best-selling books. The *National Review* put a picture of him on its cover and named him "The Leader of the Opposition." Conservative commentator William Bennett called Limbaugh "the most consequential person in political life at the moment." Ronald Reagan joined the chorus of praise. "Now that I've retired from active politics, I don't mind that you have become the Number One voice for conservatism in our Country," he wrote Limbaugh.[19]

Limbaugh viciously attacked the Clintons after they entered the White House, reveling in brutal name-calling that unfortunately became common in some media circles. Just like Colonel McCormick's *Chicago Tribune* comparing FDR to Hitler, Limbaugh called Vice President Al Gore an "environmental fascist."[20] He told his audience a crude, sexist joke that involved a naked Hillary Clinton folding laundry for him. On his TV show, he showed a photo of the Clintons' thirteen-year-old daughter Chelsea and asked, "Did you know there's a White House dog?" Limbaugh nurtured a sense of grievance among his audience that liberal media and political elites unfairly discriminated against conservatives. He made this complaint despite making millions of dollars through the media. It also ignored the fact that Republicans Reagan and Bush had just enjoyed twelve uninterrupted years in the White House.[21]

Limbaugh begat a new generation of right-wing radio hosts whose words were full of fury and disdain toward Democrats—especially the Clintons—and anyone else they didn't like. Gordon Liddy, who spent four years in prison for organizing the Watergate burglary, got his own show in 1992. Liddy celebrated the idea of political violence, once boasting that he used images of the Clintons for target practice.[22]

Extremism and outrageousness could now help a pundit rocket to fame and fortune. Ann Coulter, an MSNBC commentator and *Human Events* columnist, accused liberals of being treasonous and godless. She called Hillary Clinton "white trash" and Washington socialite Pamela Harriman a "whore." Rather than shunning Coulter, the mainstream media spotlighted her. Universal Press Syndicate and *George* magazine gave Coulter her own columns, the *New York Times* and *Newsday* profiled her, and *Today*, *Hardball*, and other broadcast shows welcomed her as a guest. By one estimate, Coulter parlayed her extremist views into a net worth of $10 million.[23]

The 1996 Telecommunications Act, signed by Clinton, also accelerated the growth of conservative media. The law loosened regulations on media corporations and allowed them to further consolidate. Clear Channel Communications, for example, aggressively expanded and owned 10 percent of U.S. radio stations by the end of Clinton's presidency. In addition to music, Clear Channel filled the airwaves with conservative talk radio including Limbaugh's show.[24]

Conservative media also got a big financial boost from reclusive billionaire Richard Mellon Scaife, who inherited a fortune from his great-grandfather's banking empire. Scaife gave millions of dollars to the libertarian *Reason* magazine, the conservative watchdog group Accuracy in Media, and the neoconservative *National Interest*, *Public Interest*, and *Commentary* publications. Scaife hated the mainstream press. When a reporter for the *Columbia Journalism Review* asked him about his generosity toward conservative causes, he called her a "fucking Communist."[25]

Scaife was at the heart of right-wing media efforts to spread conspiracy theories about the Clintons. When Deputy White House Counsel Vince Foster, a close Clinton friend, committed suicide, Scaife hired freelance journalist Christopher Ruddy to investigate. Ruddy falsely speculated that Foster was killed because he knew too much about Whitewater. Additional investigations by law enforcement and Special Counsel Robert Fiske concluded Foster's death was indeed a suicide, but right-wing media spread the awful lie that the Clintons had their friend murdered. The *American Spectator* said "foul play cannot be ruled out."[26] Limbaugh told listeners about "claims that Vince Foster was murdered in an apartment owned by Hillary Clinton." The *New York Post*, owned by conservative billionaire Rupert Murdoch's News Corp, began putting quotation marks around "suicide" when it wrote about Foster's death. Mainstream news outlets such as the *Washington Post*, *60 Minutes*, and *Newsweek* ran stories about the spread of the conspiracy theories, which only served to publicize them further.[27]

Scaife's most successful investment in damaging the Clintons came when he donated $2.4 million to the *American Spectator* magazine's "Arkansas Project." Its goal: find dirt on the Clintons buried in their past. The *Spectator* hired conservative writer David Brock, who penned a story headlined "His Cheatin' Heart" alleging that Bill Clinton had used Arkansas state troopers to arrange and then cover up his sexual liaisons.[28] Brock later recanted the story, writing that none of the "trooper allegations that could be independently checked turned out to be true." But in the meantime the *American Spectator*'s circulation tripled, and Brock's "Troopergate" claims against Clinton attracted widespread media attention. Rush Limbaugh devoted an entire three-hour episode to Brock's story. CNN featured the allegations at the top of one of its newscasts.[29] The *Los Angeles Times* published its own investigation.[30]

"Troopergate was described as tasteless and irrelevant," Brock noted in his book *Blinded by the Right*, "but it was allowed to enter the media ether as if it were true."[31] It also led to legal and political problems for Clinton. A former Arkansas state employee named Paula Jones held a press conference in 1994 announcing she was one of the women in Brock's Troopergate story. Jones said that in 1991 troopers escorted her to a Little Rock hotel room where Clinton made unwanted sexual advances. At first the mainstream press mostly disregarded the allegations. Reporters didn't want to describe the lurid details and were suspicious that Jones's press conference was sponsored by the Conservative Political Action Conference. Clinton furiously denied the accusations, and many of the men who dominated journalism tended not to take sexual harassment allegations seriously. But once Jones sued the president for $700,000, her case gained more attention.[32] It would continue to shadow Clinton's presidency.

The Jones case, Foster's suicide, Whitewater, Travelgate, and all the other scandals took their toll on Clinton's popularity. So did political and policy failures. At the start of his first term, he pushed to allow gay people to serve openly in the military, but Pentagon leaders and conservative members of Congress objected. Clinton backed down. He withdrew several nominations to his administration after they met resistance. He introduced a comprehensive health-care bill to reduce soaring costs and provide health insurance for the first time to every American. Hillary Clinton had led the effort to draft the complex bill, which was supposed to be the crown jewel of Clinton's policies, but it flopped. The insurance industry lobbied furiously against it, potential allies in Congress were incensed they weren't consulted, and talk radio hosts rallied their listeners to oppose it. Congress didn't even vote on the bill.[33]

Republicans successfully made the policy failures and scandals into campaign issues for the 1994 midterm elections. In a stinging repudiation of Clinton, the GOP swept the midterms, picking up an incredible fifty-four seats in the House and eight in the Senate. It gave Republicans control over both houses of Congress for the first time in forty years. Limbaugh was credited with helping rouse the GOP base to vote in force. One Republican congressman put a pin on Limbaugh's lapel that read "Majority Maker."[34]

Clinton blamed the press for many of his problems. At one strategy meeting with his staff, he shouted about journalists treating him with "the drip, drip, drip of this innuendo, of lies and defamation and slander and totally concocted, fictitious stories, one after the other after the other," according to Bob Woodward's book *Shadow*.[35] Clinton knew he needed to improve his relationship with the press and began inviting journalists to the White House for lunch, dinner, and movies. Clinton became more disciplined about what he told the press, no longer giving impromptu, unprepared interviews at the end of his jogs. "Gone are the days where you bring in a few reporters to sit around the desk in the Oval Office and chitchat them up and that's your communications strategy," Deputy Chief of Staff John Podesta said.[36]

Clinton also continued to adeptly use entertainment programs, local newscasts, and talk shows to avoid the Washington press corps and reach the public more directly. He went on MTV and answered a question about his underwear preferences ("usually briefs").[37] He appeared on Don Imus's popular radio program and Larry King's cable talk show. "Larry King liberated me by giving me to the American public directly," Clinton later said. The lack of formality during some of these media appearances appalled some longtime journalists; many in the public were delighted with the president's casualness and ability to entertain.[38]

As he launched his 1996 reelection campaign, Clinton began getting more attention in the press for achieving some of his goals. Congress narrowly passed his economic plan, which reduced deficits while expanding tax credits for low-income workers. Economists credited Clinton's plan for helping lead the country to greater prosperity. He signed the North American Free Trade Agreement, creating the world's largest free-trade zone. He produced a peace plan to end the bloody wars in the Balkans. He won bipartisan support in Congress for a bill that mandated life sentences for people convicted of three or more crimes and provided billions of dollars to hire more police and build more prisons. (It has since been widely condemned for introducing an era of mass incarceration, especially for people of color.)[39]

Clinton's popularity rose, and he won an easy reelection victory over Republican senator Bob Dole of Kansas.[40] Clinton became the first

Democratic president to serve two full terms since Franklin Roosevelt. But sweeping changes in the media contributed to making his second term even more challenging than his first.

Roger Ailes was furious. The former consultant for Richard Nixon, Ronald Reagan, and George H. W. Bush had been running America's Talking, an NBC cable channel, when in late 1995 the network pulled the plug on it. Its replacement: a new collaboration with Microsoft named MSNBC. Ailes wasn't put in charge of MSNBC, and he left NBC in a huff. Within a month Ailes had a deal with conservative billionaire Rupert Murdoch, who already controlled dozens of newspapers and television stations around the world. Together they launched Fox News in 1996 to rival MSNBC and CNN, which led the cable news ratings. Using "fair and balanced" as Fox News's motto, Ailes and Murdoch insisted their new network wouldn't be biased but just give conservatives an equal voice. For its October 1996 debut, it had as a guest one of the strongest conservative voices of all—Rush Limbaugh.[41]

Fox News's first star was Bill O'Reilly, who came over from the tabloid news show *Inside Edition*. While CNN stuck with traditionally reported stories and MSNBC searched for an identity, O'Reilly copied Limbaugh's style and emphasized partisanship and personality. "I'm looking for emotion," O'Reilly said. "That's number one."[42] Although he went to private school and earned a master's degree from Harvard, he claimed to be from the working class. He condemned government, Hollywood, and "media barons" (although not the media baron who paid his ample salary). O'Reilly didn't waste any time attacking the Clintons. On his first episode, he rehashed the Travelgate controversy, calling the Clintons' conduct "outrageous." O'Reilly's formula of bashing liberals and projecting conservative grievances worked. By the end of Clinton's presidency, he had climbed to the top of the cable news ratings and become the model for future Fox hosts.[43]

Fox News, CNN, and MSNBC relentlessly hunted for content to help fill twenty-four hours of airtime every day for the more than 60 percent of U.S. homes that had cable TV by the start of Clinton's first term. "Congress, with its 535 wrangling lawmakers and endless speechifying and molasses-like deliberations, made for terrible television," *Washington Post* media reporter Howard Kurtz noted.[44] In contrast, the presidency was dramatic. The rapidly growing cable audience could watch nearly everything the president did in public and hear about many of the things he did in private. There was Clinton shaking hands with well-wishers. There he was going for another jog and then stopping for a hamburger. There was a pundit discussing the latest White House rumor. The administration struggled to respond to the avalanche of coverage. As Clinton's aides would discuss how to react to a story, they often looked up and saw CNN's Wolf Blitzer on the screen, recalled Mike McCurry, Clinton's second press secretary. Blitzer would be talking about some new development "based on God knows who he had talked to, beginning to shape the story that you were still trying to think through," McCurry said.[45]

Cable TV wasn't the only media innovation transforming news coverage. The World Wide Web allowed anyone with access to a computer, an internet connection, and a few dollars to launch their own online publication. Between 1995 and 1996, the number of people using the web tripled from ten million to thirty million. The Clinton administration joined the action, unveiling the whitehouse.gov site. New websites—many of them focused on politics—popped up faster than anyone could count.[46] One of them, the *Drudge Report*, nearly ended the Clinton presidency.

By early 1998, investigative reporter Michael Isikoff had uncovered a huge scandal: President Clinton lied under oath about an affair with twenty-four-year-old former White House intern Monica Lewinsky. The tenacious Isikoff had been investigating Paula Jones's sexual harassment allegations against Clinton, first for the *Washington Post*, then for *Newsweek*. Isikoff figured if Clinton was lying about Jones, he might be deceiving the public about other matters.[47] In the past the press had kept silent about politicians' sex lives. That changed after Gary Hart, the frontrunner in the 1988 Democratic presidential primaries, brazenly challenged reporters to prove rumors he was having an extramarital affair. The *Miami Herald* did, and the resulting story torpedoed Hart's campaign.[48]

Isikoff learned of Clinton's affair from Linda Tripp, a Clinton critic who befriended Lewinsky after the young woman was transferred to the Pentagon. Betraying her friend, Tripp secretly taped Lewinsky as she shared intimate details of the affair and Clinton's efforts to hide it. Tripp then shared the recordings with conservative activists, Jones's lawyers, and Isikoff. She also gave the tapes to Kenneth Starr, a veteran of the Reagan and Bush Justice Departments who had been appointed as an independent counsel to investigate Whitewater. Starr never did find any Whitewater crimes, but in his zeal to corner Clinton, he expanded the scope of the investigation to include Jones's allegations, which led him to Lewinsky.[49]

On January 17, 1998, Clinton sat down for a six-hour deposition with Jones's lawyers, who asked about his relationship with Lewinsky. It was a trap. "I have never had sexual relations with Monica Lewinsky," Clinton insisted, not realizing Jones's attorneys had Tripp's tapes.[50] Thanks to Tripp and leaks from Starr's office, Isikoff knew many of these facts. But his *Newsweek* editors decided to hold his story until they could confirm more details and make sure it wouldn't compromise Starr's investigation. Accusing the president of having an affair with a young intern and obstructing justice was a big deal, and *Newsweek* wanted to preserve its reputation as one of the country's two leading news magazines. One editor told Isikoff that sometimes "it's just not worth being first."[51]

But a version of the story did run—in the *Drudge Report*—courtesy of a tip from one of Tripp's advisers. On Sunday morning, January 18, 1998, Isikoff opened his computer to find a "World Exclusive Blockbuster Report" by Matt Drudge. "At the last minute, at 6 p.m. on Saturday evening, Newsweek magazine killed a story that was destined to shake official Washington to its foundation: A White House intern carried on a sexual affair with the President of the United States!" Drudge's story said.[52]

Newsweek was scooped by an inexperienced internet renegade. Drudge continued posting updates, including one saying that Lewinsky kept a "garment with Clinton's dried semen."[53] A turning point had been reached where online journalists—and anyone else on the web—could drive the news cycle. Now the rest of the press had to scramble to catch up on the biggest scandal of the decade. The *Washington Post* followed with a Lewinsky story on Tuesday night, then ABC News radio and the *Los Angeles Times*. They said Starr was investigating whether Clinton told Lewinsky to lie about the affair to Jones's lawyers. Four days later *Newsweek* finally posted Isikoff's version of the story on its America Online site.

A media frenzy ensued as journalists chased the swirl of rumors, hoping not to be beaten on a big revelation as Isikoff had been. "The story detonated in the media with Watergate-like intensity," Howard Kurtz of the *Washington Post* observed.[54] CNN, Fox News, and MSNBC carried a live news briefing by Press Secretary Mike McCurry when he desperately tried to fend off reporters' questions about the scandal. ABC, CBS, and NBC cut into their programming to show Clinton being interviewed on PBS. The *Dallas Morning News* rushed to post an update on the scandal in the middle of the night and then was forced to take it down the next morning when it proved incorrect.

Some journalists remained wary of posting on the web. They understood the risks of publishing hurried stories and realized the internet drained advertising dollars away from their publications and broadcasts. WashingtonPost.com editor Leslie Walker called it the "Internet swamp of instant news." But mainstream outlets really had no choice but to wade into that swamp if they wanted to compete for the biggest story of the year if not the decade. Traffic on some of their sites doubled as the scandal intensified. CNN solemnly informed its audience, "Internet news is here to stay."[55]

The war of words between Clinton and his detractors escalated online, on air, and in print. Starr's office eagerly leaked damaging information about the president. Clinton's aides offered their own leaks protecting the president and attacking Starr. Because of the growth of the internet and cable news, leakers increased their odds of finding a journalist who would report their information, no matter how shaky it was. Media scholars Bill Kovach and Tom Rosenstiel found that less than one percent of statements in the press about the Clinton-Lewinsky scandal relied on two or more named sources, 40 percent were based on one anonymous source, and 41 percent weren't factual reporting at all.[56]

Clinton's initial response to the scandal was to be evasive and, if that didn't work, to lie. Three days after Drudge's initial story appeared, Clinton sat down for a previously scheduled interview with Jim Lehrer of PBS's *NewsHour*. The president brought in his dog, Buddy, to distract the cameras, but Lehrer didn't waste time before asking tough questions about Clinton's interactions with Lewinsky. "There is no improper relationship," Clinton answered, looking straight into the camera. When people noted afterward that Clinton had used the present tense in his denials, he switched to past tense for an interview later that day. "The relationship was not sexual," he told *Roll Call*'s Morton Kondracke.[57]

The next morning Clinton defended himself more aggressively in a televised statement with his wife by his side. "I want you to listen to me," he commanded, jabbing his finger at the TV cameras and pounding his fist on the lectern. "I'm going to say this again. I did not have sexual relations with that woman—Miss Lewinsky. . . . These allegations are false. And I need to go back to work for the American people." Done with his lying, at least for the moment, he stalked away without taking questions.[58]

Clinton's denials didn't impress the Washington press corps, many of whom warned that his political death was imminent. "Mr. Clinton, if he's not telling the truth and the evidence shows that, will resign, perhaps this week," Sam Donaldson predicted. Each detail of the case became the latest breaking news. Because of the scandal's sensational details, White House coverage began to resemble a tabloid entertainment show. MSNBC was nicknamed the "all-Monica channel" for its wall-to-wall coverage.[59]

The spring and summer were filled with more damaging news for Clinton. Under pressure from Starr, Lewinsky agreed to cooperate with the investigation and appeared before a grand jury. Clinton was also forced to testify as were many of his aides, friends, and Secret Service agents who might have witnessed his interactions with Lewinsky. The president's DNA was collected to see if it matched the stain on Lewinsky's dress. In August Clinton went on national television to finally admit that he'd had "an inappropriate" relationship with Lewinsky. He later agreed to pay Jones $850,000 to settle her lawsuit without admitting any wrongdoing.[60]

Conservative journalists gleefully piled on. The Clinton presidency, columnist George F. Will said, "is as dead, deader really, than Woodrow Wilson's was after he had a stroke." Limbaugh excitedly read updates by Drudge to his listeners. Ann Coulter made the case for impeaching Clinton with words that now seem prophetic in light of Trump's presidency: "It is essentially impossible to have democracy if elected leaders do not tell the truth, everyone knows they do not tell the truth, and no one cares. Presidents who by their deceit spread such cynicism actually do commit 'offenses that subvert the system of government.'"[61]

There was a disconnect, however, between what the pundits were saying and what most Americans were thinking. Clinton's revamped communications team successfully focused attention on the accelerating economy that was leading to the first federal budget surplus since 1960. They found events where Clinton could demonstrate he was dealing with issues that mattered to the public. "Each day the president could be seen speaking to groups, discussing his policy initiatives, and generally engaged in government business," presidential scholar Martha Joynt Kumar explained. As a result, Clinton's approval ratings climbed.[62]

On September 9, 1998, Starr gave his final report and thirty-six boxes of evidence to the House of Representatives. The GOP majority on the

Judiciary Committee voted to release nearly all of it to the public. They posted 119,059 words of Starr's report on the web, thinking it would permanently crush Clinton's reputation. Sections of it read like a cheap pornographic novel, and the public lapped up the tawdry details, setting a new record for internet traffic. Broadcast journalists read portions of it on air, skipping over the most salacious parts. Although the public was riveted by the report, Clinton's popularity persisted.[63]

The House Republicans then released a video of Clinton testifying to the grand jury. When it aired nationally, the president's lawyers worried it would crush his remaining support. The opposite happened. With the camera trained tightly on his face, Clinton looked beleaguered yet sounded reasonable as Starr's prosecutors interrogated him about intimate details of his affair with Lewinsky. "Even I felt sorry for him," one GOP consultant told the *Washington Post*. "It was like the Gestapo."[64]

The *Philadelphia Tribune* observed that the "intent of releasing the videotape seemed to be to sour Clinton's image even more, but it might prove to have a reverse effect."[65] It did. Republicans had high hopes of gaining congressional seats in the 1998 midterm elections by emphasizing the Lewinsky scandal. Most pundits agreed that Democrats would take a beating from voters. On the election night of November 3, an aide showed Clinton how to do a new trick: using a computer to check the returns. The president nervously clicked on CNN's website for updates. As the night wore on, he and his staff grew more excited. The Democrats held their own in the Senate and added five seats in the House. It was the first time since FDR's first term that a president's party had gained House seats in a midterm election. Despite all of the attention in the press, the scandal hadn't hurt Clinton with voters.[66]

The growing sensationalism in the press took its toll on Republican leadership, however. In September 1998, the online magazine *Salon* revealed that Representative Henry Hyde, a leader of the GOP effort to impeach Clinton, had committed adultery thirty years previously. *Salon* was criticized heavily for reporting on a politician's long-ago affair, but the rest of the press felt obliged to report the story too. Other leaders of the GOP impeachment drive were soon caught in their own hypocrisy. Three days after the midterm election, Clinton nemesis Newt Gingrich announced he was resigning as Speaker of the House. Gingrich later admitted he had committed adultery at the same time he was railing against Clinton's morality. The man chosen to replace Gingrich as speaker, Robert Livingston, also resigned after he learned the pornographic magazine *Hustler* was preparing to reveal his own multiple adulterous affairs.[67] Media sensationalism had reached the point that a magazine sold in adult bookstores could help determine the nation's leadership.

But Republicans still held a majority in Congress, which they used to approve two articles of impeachment against Clinton on December 19, 1998. One was for committing perjury, the other for encouraging witnesses to conceal evidence and not testify truthfully.[68] Clinton joined Andrew Johnson as the only presidents to be impeached, and he now faced a Senate trial. If two-thirds of the Senate voted to convict, Clinton would be booted from office. But on the same day as the House's impeachment vote, a Gallup poll showed Clinton enjoyed a 73 percent job approval rating, the highest of his two terms so far and one of the highest for any president over the previous three decades. The appetite for forcing Clinton out of office was shrinking. At the end of the Senate trial on February 12, 1999, ten Republicans joined all forty-five Democratic senators to defeat the first article of impeachment. The second article was defeated 50–50 with five Republicans voting with the Democrats. Most White House reporters said they were relieved the saga was over so they could pay more attention to other issues, but not Brit Hume of Fox News. "This story has been good to Fox News Channel in general," he said.[69] Hume understood that scandals could be excellent for the news business.

Clinton had dodged the crisis of the Lewinsky scandal and survived the closest scrutiny of a president by the press since Nixon was forced to resign. Media forces unleashed during Clinton's presidency—growing sensationalism, the spread of online media, and the rise of intensely partisan publications, radio shows, and cable news channels—would continue to vex future presidents. The nation's next leader, however, would find a way to manipulate the press, at least temporarily, when he faced his first great crisis.

8

George W. Bush and the War on Truth

At least fifty TV stations around the country aired good news about Medicare in the winter of 2004. "Karen Ryan helps sort through the details," the TV anchors promised as they introduced a story about changes in prescription drug benefits. During the ninety-second segment, viewers could see President George W. Bush receive a standing ovation as he signed a new Medicare bill. They could hear Bush administration officials promote the bill's benefits. And they could watch smiling senior citizens get their prescriptions. The new law "simply offers people with Medicare ways to make their health coverage more affordable," Ryan assured her audience. The segment ended with a typical broadcast signoff: "In Washington, I'm Karen Ryan reporting."

But Ryan wasn't really a reporter. Instead, she was a public relations specialist hired by the U.S. Department of Health and Human Services who read a script prepared by the Bush administration to make the president look good. What unsuspecting viewers had seen was a simulated story, known as a video news release, using actors and fake reporters designed to fool the public by pretending to be journalism. Corporations and nonprofits had used video news releases for several years. Now taxpayers were paying for their own government's propaganda—fake news that just happened to be airing as Bush launched his reelection campaign.[1]

For her efforts, Ryan received a "Falsie Award" at the end of the year from the Center for Media and Democracy, but she was hardly the only fake reporter.[2] During the Bush presidency, the Department of Education, Census Bureau, State Department, Transportation Security Administration, and Office of National Drug Control Policy all produced video news releases. In one of them, an actor playing a patient tells a pharmacist that Bush's Medicare policy "sounds like a good idea." The pharmacist replies, "A very good idea." The Government Accountability Office concluded that these video news releases violated a law prohibiting the creation of domestic propaganda not approved by Congress.[3]

The blurring of truth—what comedian Stephen Colbert called "truthiness"—was a hallmark of the Bush presidency, and all too often journalists were his accomplices.[4] Politicians using public relations techniques to manipulate the media was certainly nothing new. And since its earliest days, the American press has at times spread government propaganda for its own partisan or financial reasons. The editors who backed John Adams and the newspapers that carried Woodrow Wilson's wartime hype were more than eager to do so. But Bush's White House took deceiving the press and the American people to depths not seen previously. Many journalists, intimidated by Bush's popularity following the 9/11 terrorist attacks against the United States, responded by acting more like lapdogs than watchdogs. The result was two disastrous wars that cost more than a hundred thousand lives and trillions of dollars. It also eroded Americans' confidence in mainstream journalism's ability to tell them the truth, making it easier for disinformation to flourish in the coming years.

George W. Bush came to the presidency wary of the press. His father, President George H. W. Bush, had made a point of being accessible to journalists. He held an average of nearly three news conferences per month, more than every president since Truman. But when the elder Bush lost his reelection bid to Clinton in 1992, both father and son blamed the press as being largely responsible. They had some good reasons. For example, there was the *Newsweek* cover with the headline "Fighting the 'Wimp Factor'" over a photo of the elder Bush.[5] News reports mocked him for not knowing what a grocery store scanner was even though the story wasn't accurate. After the election, the bitter former president said that Americans "know today that the media has become too adversarial, too intrusive into personal lives, and at times, too arrogant."[6]

His son agreed. Nicknamed "Dubya" for the Texas pronunciation of his middle initial, George W. Bush was known for his garrulousness and irreverent humor. He grew up in Midland, Texas, best known for its oil rigs and dust, but attended the elite Phillips Academy boarding school in Massachusetts. Despite mediocre grades, his family's connections got him into Yale, where he was known as an indifferent student but determined partier. In his own words, he was a "boozy kid."[7]

Bush earned an MBA from Harvard Business School before settling back in Midland, running unsuccessfully for Congress, and owning a series of struggling oil ventures. In the mid-1980s, he became an evangelical Christian and gave up alcohol. After working on his father's winning 1988 presidential campaign, he led a group of investors who bought the Texas Rangers baseball team. Although he distrusted the press, Bush knew how to turn on the charm and quickly developed a reputation as being friendly and accessible. "When you are around George," *Fort Worth Star-Telegram* sports columnist Jim Reeves observed, "he has a way of making you feel comfortable and that you and he have been friends for a long, long time."[8]

Bush parlayed the team's popularity into a victorious run for Texas governor in 1994. He easily won reelection four years later and immediately began preparing to run for president in 2000. Bush earned the Republican nomination and faced Democrat Al Gore, Clinton's vice president, in the general election. Despite his wealth and Ivy League pedigree, he campaigned for president as a folksy Texan. He walked with a swagger and talked with a twang. He was playful with reporters and made fun of his own frequent verbal gaffes such as saying that

Americans were struggling to "put food on the family." During his last flight before the election, he got on the plane's public-address system and joked, "Last chance for malaprops."[9]

The race was neck and neck. On election night it dissolved into media-fueled confusion that turned into a constitutional crisis. It was clear Gore had captured the popular vote, but the electoral college was undecided. It all came down to Florida, and news outlets gave shifting accounts of who had won the state. By the next morning, Bush held a narrow lead of fewer than 2,000 votes out of 5.8 million cast in Florida, requiring a recount under state law. A bruising thirty-six-day legal, political, and public relations battle ensued over which votes should be recounted. Both sides tried desperately to spin the press. Gore argued that all the ballots in question should be recounted. Bush's aides said an accurate count of the disputed ballots was futile and would rob him of the victory that most networks had declared on election night. The process of deciding who would become president had broken down. Finally, five weeks after the election, the Supreme Court decided 5–4 to stop the recount, giving the presidency to Bush. All of the justices who ruled in favor of Bush had been appointed by Republican presidents, angering Democrats who thought the court had played politics. Still, Gore conceded the next day and called Bush to congratulate him.[10]

Although his victory was disputed, Bush began his presidency with an ambitious agenda. He approved an 8.6 percent increase in Pentagon spending during his first year, and the military budget continued to soar through the rest of his presidency. Working with Democrats, he succeeded in passing the No Child Left Behind Act that boosted education spending for impoverished schools while placing greater emphasis on standardized tests. During his first months in office, he also got a $1.35 trillion tax cut through Congress that lowered top rates for the biggest earners. Two years later he pushed through another round of reduced taxes with most of the benefits going to the richest Americans.[11]

Bush had no previous governing experience in Washington, but he had the help of Vice President Dick Cheney, a former Wyoming congressman who had served in Republican administrations dating back to Nixon's. Cheney spoke in a bland, soft monotone, but his words were forceful. Showing self-doubt wasn't his style, and he quickly became the most powerful vice president in history. Cheney believed in secrecy as a way to strengthen the presidency.[12] When he created an energy task force, for instance, he refused to release the names of its members to the press. Bush embraced secrecy too. Soon after he took office, sixty-eight thousand pages of records from Reagan's presidency—when Bush's father was vice president—were due to be released. Bush ruled they should stay sealed.[13]

Bush was determined to avoid the unruliness of the Clinton administration. Using his Harvard Business School training, he brought corporate discipline to the White House. Bill Keller of the *New York Times* described it as a "secretive, country-club executive style."[14] Compared with other presidencies, the Bush White House had little infighting. As a result, there were few information leaks, much to the chagrin of the White House press corps. "Washington correspondents live off leaks," *Chicago Tribune* syndicated columnist Clarence Page explained. "They are the mother's milk of Washington journalism. In the Bush years, we are running the risk of dying of thirst."[15]

To handle the press, Bush's communications guru Karen Hughes and political adviser Karl Rove (nicknamed "Bush's Brain") developed a plan to devote each week to a different theme. Borrowing a tactic from the Reagan administration, Hughes made sure all of Bush's staff stuck to the message to discourage the press from covering other topics. With the Bush White House, "you only need to make one phone call, and you've heard everyone's story," Michael Barone of *U.S. News & World Report* said.[16] Like Clinton's staff, Bush's communications team prioritized media outlets that don't typically cover Washington, making them less likely to ask tough questions and more likely to feature Bush's lighter side. His staff invited reporters from *Field and Stream*, *Runner's World*, and other outdoor magazines to interview Bush for what one aide called the "hook and bullet crowd." Writers for *Bicycling* and *Sports Illustrated* spent time with the president at his Texas ranch.[17]

Bush's team came up with an ingenious way to attract people who don't usually follow politics to the White House website: the "Barney Cam," which followed the adventures of Bush's dog. Viewers could watch the adorable Scottish terrier romping around the Executive Mansion and attending the White House Christmas party. The Barney Cam became an internet hit, getting six million views in one month. One of the most popular videos featured Barney biting a Reuters White House correspondent. People who visited the White House website to watch the Barney Cam then often checked out other information favorable to Bush.[18]

In Bush's eyes, the press was just another special interest group pleading for attention rather than an important check on government power. He remained friendly toward individual reporters but disdained their profession, repeating the longtime conservative refrain that journalists were biased toward liberals. During his first year in office, he held nineteen news conferences, half as many as Clinton did during his first year. Knowing that the president wasn't much of a TV news watcher and usually only read the sports sections of newspapers, a reporter once asked him, "How do you then know what the public thinks?" Bush responded, "You're making a huge assumption—that you represent what the public thinks." It was a taunt that stung Washington journalists.[19]

Cooperating with the White House press corps wasn't a priority for the administration. Chief of Staff Andrew Card and other Bush aides took pride in not returning reporters' phone calls. "Our job is not to make your job easy," Card told journalists. The president of the White House Correspondents Association sent Card a letter in December 2002 complaining that Bush hadn't answered a single question from a White House reporter in the past two weeks. Card never bothered to respond. Another administration official told reporter Ron Suskind that people such as journalists who were obsessed with facts were part of "the reality-based community." It was an ominous statement that foreshadowed the Trump administration's disregard for accuracy.[20]

The White House's contempt for Washington reporters was on display when Bush held a state dinner during his first year for Mexican president Vicente Fox. As guests danced, watched fireworks, and dined on upscale Tex-Mex cuisine, reporters weren't allowed to observe any portions of the event or talk to anyone in attendance as they had with previous presidents. The administration regarded the reporters like "mosquitos at a nudist colony," Roxanne Roberts of the *Washington Post* complained.[21]

Six days after the state dinner for Fox, complaints about press access suddenly seemed trivial. On the morning of September 11, 2001, Bush was reading to children in a Florida classroom when he learned that airplanes hijacked by Al Qaeda terrorists had crashed into the twin towers of the World Trade Center in New York City, destroying them. A third plane flew into the Pentagon, and a fourth slammed into a Pennsylvania field before it could hit its likely target of the White House or U.S. Capitol. Nearly three thousand people died, and the nation was in crisis.[22]

Bush was rightfully accused of having ignored warnings that terrorists were preparing to attack the United States. Al Qaeda and its leader Osama bin Laden were mentioned forty times in daily briefings given to Bush in the months before 9/11. An August 6 memo titled "Bin Laden Determined to Strike in US" warned that the FBI had found "patterns of suspicious activity in this country consistent with preparations for hijackings or other types of attacks." But Bush had put no new security measures in place.[23]

The administration tried desperately to spin his poor performance at protecting the country by preparing "Setting the Record Straight" talking points. Showing he was resolute and in charge became essential. Three days after the attack, the president went to Ground Zero where the World Trade Centers had been destroyed. As rescue workers chanted

"U.S.A., U.S.A.!" Bush shouted through a bullhorn, "The rest of the world hears you, and the people who knocked these buildings down will hear all of us soon!"[24] Viewers watching on television loved Bush's forceful response. According to a Gallup poll, his public approval rating soared from 51 percent just before 9/11 to 90 percent ten days afterward.[25]

In response to the attacks, Bush ordered U.S. forces to attack Afghanistan on October 7, 2001. They led a global coalition seeking to overthrow the Taliban government, which had harbored bin Laden and other Al Qaeda members. The U.S. forces enjoyed initial success, driving the Taliban out of the capital of Kabul in less than six weeks and helping install a new Afghan government by December 22. But they didn't capture bin Laden, and the Taliban continued to control large parts of the country. At first, four out of every five Americans supported the invasion, but public support soon weakened.[26] The war lasted nearly twenty years until Joe Biden withdrew all American troops, the U.S.-backed Afghan government collapsed, and the Taliban came back to power in the summer of 2021. By then the war had cost the lives of more than 6,000 U.S. troops and contractors and at least 160,000 Afghans.[27]

As American troops fought in Afghanistan, Bush turned his attention toward overthrowing the government of Iraqi dictator Saddam Hussein. Bush, Cheney, and other top administration officials were certain Hussein posed a unique threat to the United States. They argued that overthrowing him would be easy and lead to a new era of peace and democracy in the Middle East. Bush privately vowed to kick Hussein's "sorry motherfucking ass all over the Middle East."[28]

Bush's aides showed the press scraps of intelligence bolstering their case for war while leaving out information that challenged White House assumptions. Much of what they told reporters wasn't true. Bush, Cheney, Secretary of Defense Donald Rumsfeld, and five other top administration officials made 935 false statements about Iraq in the two years following 9/11. The administration meanwhile muffled the voices of intelligence analysts and career government officials who doubted Hussein posed much of a threat to the United States or suggested Bush and his aides were cherry-picking the evidence they shared.[29]

National Security Adviser Condoleezza Rice, for instance, told PBS's *NewsHour* that Iraq was training Al Qaeda on how to develop chemical weapons, a claim intelligence analysts questioned. A grim-looking Cheney went on *Meet the Press* to suggest that Hussein had aided the 9/11 terrorists. He told host Tim Russert that "it's been pretty well confirmed" that one of the hijackers had met in Prague with an Iraqi intelligence service officer. In reality, the CIA and FBI had already found that the meeting probably never took place. Still, Russert bought Cheney's claim. "If they're harboring terrorists," Russert asked, "why not go in and get them?"[30]

Russert's comments reflected widespread willingness among the mainstream press to accept Bush's case for attacking Iraq. Journalists rallied around the president just as they had when America entered the two world wars. "George Bush is the president, he makes the decisions, and, you know, as just one American, he wants me to line up, just tell me where," CBS anchorman Dan Rather said.[31] The Washington press corps felt renewed urgency as DC became a wartime capital once again. Instead of writing about Monica Lewinsky's semen-stained dress, they were reporting on matters of life and death. "Not since Watergate have journalists felt such a strong sense of mission and responsibility," veteran Washington reporter Ted Gup observed.[32]

At the *New York Times*, Executive Editor Howell Raines was determined to beat the newspaper's competitors with its coverage of the terrorist attacks and their aftermath. "There was a sense of patriotism, and you felt it in every question from every editor and copy editor," reporter Carlotta Gall recalled. "I remember a foreign-desk editor telling me, 'Remember where we are—we can smell the debris from 9/11.'"[33] To lead the *Times'* reporting on Bush's preparations for invading Iraq, Raines chose Judith Miller, who had written a best-selling book about Hussein and won a Pulitzer Prize for her past coverage of Al Qaeda. Miller was known for her strong sources within the administration, but some colleagues warned that she often used unverified information fed to her by top officials. Raines's choice proved to be disastrous.

Miller and other reporters at the *Times* relied heavily on Ahmad Chalabi, a rich Iraqi exile and convicted embezzler with close ties to American conservatives. Chalabi dreamed of becoming the country's leader if Hussein was overthrown. Chalabi introduced *Times* reporters to his exile friends, who buttressed his false claims that Hussein was developing weapons of mass destruction. The *Times* also interviewed U.S. officials who were relying on the same misinformation from Chalabi. The *Times* then printed that it had multiple sources saying Hussein posed a dire threat to the United States when in reality the other sources were repeating what Chalabi had told them.[34]

In December 2001 Miller flew to Thailand to interview an Iraqi defector at the recommendation of Chalabi's group, the Iraqi National Congress. The interview led to an alarming story on the *Times*' front page. "An Iraqi defector who described himself as a civil engineer said he personally worked on renovations of secret facilities for biological, chemical and nuclear weapons in underground wells, private villas and under the Saddam Hussein Hospital in Iraq as recently as a year ago," Miller wrote. Thirty-one paragraphs later, she admitted that "American intelligence officials have long had cause to be skeptical of such defectors." In the third-to-last paragraph, Miller added, "There was no means to independently verify" the defector's allegations. But the implication was clear: Hussein was developing weapons of mass destruction that endangered the United States. Miller didn't investigate enough to discover that the defector had failed a CIA lie detector test and that U.S. intelligence agencies concluded he had made up his story.[35]

Miller's misleading reporting gave Bush ammunition to make his case for invading Iraq, but she wasn't alone in relying on Chalabi. The Associated Press, CNN, NPR, *60 Minutes*, Fox News, *Atlantic Monthly*, *Time*, *Vanity Fair*, *New Yorker*, *National Review*, *Newsweek*, *Washington Times*, and other media outlets used information provided by his Iraqi National Congress in late 2001 and early 2002. Its lobbyists and lawyers, for example, promoted the story of an exiled Iraqi military captain who claimed to have worked at a training camp for terrorists. A front-page *New York Times* story, a *Washington Post* column, and a PBS *Frontline* report cited what the captain said. His claims were false and rejected by U.S. intelligence agencies, but lazy reporting allowed them to be trumpeted by leading news outlets.

The administration's manipulation of the press accelerated starting in the late summer of 2002. Top Bush aides including Rove, Hughes, and Rice began meeting weekly in the Situation Room. Their goal: create a marketing campaign to persuade the public that intervention in Iraq was necessary.[36] They had immediate success with a front-page *New York Times* story cowritten by Miller and national security reporter Michael R. Gordon. "In the last 14 months, Iraq has sought to buy thousands of specially designed aluminum tubes, which American officials believe were intended as components of centrifuges to enrich uranium," Miller and Gordon reported. The frightening story relied on unnamed administration sources and an anonymous Iraqi defector. Not until the fifteenth paragraph did it mention sources who criticized the White House's arguments.[37]

The critics were right. Only one CIA analyst believed the aluminum tubes were being used to enrich uranium. Others in the intelligence community had concluded they were just tubes. But the morning that Gordon and Miller's story appeared, Cheney used it during a *Meet the Press* appearance to bolster the case for going to war. Meanwhile, Rumsfeld gave a terrifying warning on CBS's *Face the Nation*: "Imagine a September 11 with weapons of mass destruction." Rice appeared on CNN to argue that Iraq posed a mortal threat to America. "We don't want the smoking gun to be a mushroom cloud," Rice said, employing a vivid phrase that had also been used in Gordon and Miller's article. The moderators of these shows did little to challenge the arguments made by Rice, Rumsfeld, and Cheney.[38]

The administration was spreading misinformation, and the press was failing to counter it. The next day the International Atomic Energy

Agency's former weapons inspector, David Albright, called Miller to tell her most scientists didn't believe the aluminum tubes were being used to develop nuclear weapons. She and Gordon did mention the debate among experts about the tubes in the middle of a story later that week. But it ran on page thirteen and still insisted that intelligence agencies were "unanimous" that the tubes were for nuclear centrifuges, which was untrue.[39]

On the first anniversary of the 9/11 attacks, Bush stood on Ellis Island to address the nation. Remembering those who died in the attacks and quoting scripture, he hinted that Hussein might be America's next target. "We will not allow any terrorist or tyrant to threaten civilization with weapons of mass murder," the president declared. As he spoke, the television audience could see the Statue of Liberty bathed in light behind him. Observing how Bush's team staged the event, Michael Deaver marveled at their use of imagery to make the president appear resolute during a crisis just as he had once done as Reagan's communications wizard. "They've taken it to an art form," Deaver said. The press coverage the next day eagerly quoted Bush while describing his actions and emotions. Not much attention was given to counterarguments that perhaps Iraq wasn't much of a danger to Americans.[40] Such was the power of the presidency.

The White House's pro-war marketing campaign dominated news coverage. From August 2002 to March 2003, the *Washington Post* put 140 stories on its front page emphasizing the administration's case for war. The headlines included "Bush Cites Urgent Iraqi Threat," "Bush Tells Troops: Prepare for War," and "War Cabinet Argues for Iraq Attack." The *Post*'s reporters wrote some stories challenging the administration's claims, but editors buried them on inside pages. Reporter Walter Pincus, for example, wrote a story exposing weaknesses in the administration's case that Hussein had weapons of mass destruction. It appeared on page seventeen. "There was an attitude among editors: Look, we're going to war, why do we even worry about all this contrary stuff?" Pentagon reporter Thomas Ricks said. The *Post*, criticized for years as hopelessly liberal by conservatives, editorially endorsed Bush's invasion plans.[41]

The poor performance by the *Post*, *Times*, and other news outlets reflected a longtime tendency among journalists to report something as true if top officials said it was, especially in matters of national security. The president, with his large communications staff and cameras recording his every public move, has a unique power to amplify his message. It's easier to accept his narrative than to investigate alternatives. In the first months after the Watergate burglary, for example, only Bernstein and Woodward consistently probed the Nixon administration's cover-up in the face of vehement White House denials. Likewise, in the months leading up to the Iraq War, few reporters probed deeply to determine how strong Bush's arguments for an invasion really were. Woodward, one of the *Post*'s assistant managing editors at the time, later admitted that he and other journalists took part in a "groupthink" approach. They didn't want to look silly, he said, if weapons of mass destruction were actually found in Iraq.[42]

In contrast, the Knight Ridder newspaper chain's Washington bureau energetically investigated Bush's case for war. Knight Ridder reporters checked with other sources and found cracks in the administration's evidence. As a result, they wrote a series of articles in late 2002 with headlines such as "Lack of Hard Evidence of Iraqi Weapons Worries Top U.S. Officials," "Some in Bush Administration Have Misgivings about Iraq Policy," and "Iraq Has Been Unable to Get Materials Needed for Nuclear Bomb, Experts Say." But Knight Ridder's newspapers were located primarily in cities far from Washington and received scant attention from people in power.[43]

And then there was Helen Thomas, the veteran White House reporter who was working for Hearst News Service at the time. At a May 1, 2002, press briefing, she peppered Press Secretary Ari Fleischer with questions about speculation that Bush wanted to invade Iraq. "What is the president's rationale for invading Iraq?" she asked. When Fleischer answered that the people in Iraq would be better off without Hussein, Thomas interjected, "A lot of people would be better off in a lot of places." When Fleischer repeated that Iraq would be better off without Hussein, Thomas retorted, "That's not a reason."[44]

But Thomas's questions and Knight Ridder's articles couldn't overcome the administration's pro-war propaganda campaign that was abetted by most of the press. Out of 267 Americans—most of them current or former administration or Pentagon officials—interviewed on network news shows during a two-week span, only one, U.S. senator Ted Kennedy, questioned the wisdom of going to war.[45] In October 2002 the Senate and House voted overwhelmingly with bipartisan support to authorize Bush to use the military "as he determines to be necessary" against Iraq. Just over five months later, U.S. and allied forces invaded Iraq. Within nineteen days, they reached Baghdad and Hussein's government collapsed.[46]

On May 1, 2003, Bush landed a fighter jet on a U.S. aircraft carrier off the coast of California. Wearing combat boots and a flight suit, he posed with smiling sailors before giving a speech declaring "major combat operations have ended" in Iraq. The late afternoon Pacific sun gave Bush's face a warm glow as television cameras recorded the event. Behind him his staff had hung a banner boasting "Mission Accomplished." It was a perfectly produced photo op, and all the television networks used images from Bush's swashbuckling performance at the top of their evening newscasts.[47]

Unfortunately, the banner didn't match reality because the mission was far from over. For a White House that relied heavily on images to convey its message, the use of the banner backfired badly. The "Mission Accomplished" statement haunted Bush for the rest of his presidency. American troops were stuck in Iraq for nearly nine years, costing taxpayers more than $2 trillion as determined insurgents continued to battle. The fighting killed at least 180,000 Iraqi civilians (with many others dying from war-related hunger and disease) and more than 4,400 American troops. Meanwhile, the search for weapons of mass destruction in Iraq came up empty. Bush finally admitted in September 2003 that there was no evidence connecting Hussein to 9/11. As the administration's case for war collapsed, *Newsweek* featured a cover story with the headline "Bush's $87 Billion Mess." A *Time* cover showed Bush on the flight deck with the headline "Mission Not Accomplished."[48]

Journalists also began criticizing their own performance during the lead-up to the war. "I think the press was muzzled and I think the press self-muzzled," CNN's Christiane Amanpour said in the fall of 2003. The *Times* published an extraordinary mea culpa the following spring about its failures. "Articles based on dire claims about Iraq tended to get prominent display, while follow-up articles that called the original ones into question were sometimes buried," *Times* editors admitted. "In some cases, there was no follow-up at all."[49] Katie Couric, who was a host on NBC's *Today* at the start of the invasion and later anchored the CBS *Evening News*, called the media's coverage of the war's lead-up "one of the most embarrassing chapters in American journalism."[50]

As the situation in Iraq deteriorated, however, the reporting got tougher. In the spring of 2004, *60 Minutes II* aired a deeply disturbing story about torture and other abuse by U.S. troops at Abu Ghraib, a U.S. detention center in Iraq. The following week, the *New Yorker*'s Seymour Hersh—a journalism legend who had exposed U.S. massacres during the Vietnam War and uncovered the payment of hush money to the Watergate burglars—provided more horrifying details. Hersh described how prisoners at Abu Ghraib had been subjected to "sadistic, blatant, and wanton criminal abuses."[51] The torture at Abu Ghraib was widely condemned in the rest of the press. "How could American men and women treat Iraqi prisoners with such cruelty—and then laugh at their humiliation?" *New York Times* columnist Anthony Lewis asked. He answered his own question by putting the responsibility squarely on Bush. "Again and again, over these last years, President Bush has made clear his view that law must bend to what he regards as necessity."[52]

The Abu Ghraib story broke as the 2004 presidential election was heating up. To take on Bush, the Democrats thought they had a strong candidate for a country fighting two wars and fearing another terrorist attack. Their nominee, Senator John Kerry of Massachusetts, had won Bronze, Silver, and Purple Heart medals for heroism while commanding a gunboat during the Vietnam War. Kerry left the Democratic convention leading Bush in the polls, but he was soon hit by a barrage of unfriendly media fire.

A week after the Democratic convention, Fox News's Sean Hannity previewed the first in a series of brutal advertisements against Kerry. The commercials were produced by Swift Boat Veterans for Truth, a group connected with GOP operatives and donors. They claimed Kerry had not legitimately earned the medals he was given and had "betrayed" and "dishonored" the United States because he denounced the Vietnam War after returning home.[53] Journalists and fact-checkers investigated and found that the evidence used by the Swift Boat Veterans was shaky. Many veterans were shown in the commercial denouncing Kerry and implying they had firsthand knowledge of his actions, but only one had actually served under him. Other veterans who had served with Kerry continued to extol his bravery. The advertisements were discussed on news shows and spread online, giving them further credence among the public. Within a few weeks, Kerry had lost his lead in the polls, and his campaign became a casualty in the war on truth.[54]

The weakening of broadcast regulations allowed the Swift Boat allegations to spread wider. They were promoted by the Sinclair Broadcast Group, whose top executives contributed to Bush's campaign and the GOP. Thanks to the 1996 Telecommunications Act, Sinclair had become one of the nation's largest local television owners, with sixty-two stations reaching about a quarter of U.S. homes. David Smith, Sinclair's chairman, got his start in media by making television transmitters and reproducing pornographic movies. He took over his father's group of three television stations in the early 1980s and expanded it rapidly. After Bush became president, Sinclair—with no Fairness Doctrine to worry about—began producing conservative news segments for its stations to run. Two weeks before the 2004 election, Sinclair ran portions of a documentary connected with the Swift Boat Veterans. Sinclair also ordered its reporters to produce stories about the documentary, which questioned Kerry's patriotism. It then fired its Washington bureau chief after he called the film "biased political propaganda."[55]

As the 2004 election neared, Bush's own military service during the Vietnam War was questioned. CBS's *60 Minutes II* aired a story in September describing how he enlisted in the Texas Air National Guard in 1968 with the help of his father's politically connected friends despite weak grades on his pilot aptitude test. Serving in the Texas unit protected him from being drafted and sent to fight in Vietnam. *60 Minutes II* accused Bush of ignoring orders to get a physical and using political connections to "sugar coat" the service he was supposed to provide the National Guard. The story, narrated by veteran anchor Dan Rather, relied on memos supposedly taken from the files of the deceased commander of Bush's unit.[56]

Rather and *60 Minutes II* didn't count on the power of bloggers to challenge the mainstream media. The new medium of blogging had soared in popularity since it developed in the late 1990s. Blogs allowed people to easily create their own websites, update them constantly, link to other sites, and allow viewers to comment, generating giant online conversations. By the end of 2004, eight million Americans had blogs that shared everything from recipes to political opinions. Twelve thousand more were being launched every day.[57]

Often openly partisan like the press in the nation's early days, bloggers were putting politicians under constant scrutiny. One of them was Charles Johnson, a Los Angeles musician who thought the *60 Minutes II* investigation seemed fishy. He noticed that the story featured memos about Bush's military service with typefaces that could be produced on Microsoft Word, which didn't exist during his National Guard stint. Johnson immediately posted his doubts on his conservative *Little Green Footballs* blog. Johnson's followers then posted their own analysis of the *60 Minutes II* story.

Meanwhile, a reader with the username TankerKC posted on the *Free Republic* blog that the style of the memos didn't resemble the ones he'd seen in the air force. "The documents CBS used are FRAUDS!!!!!!!!"

TankerKC declared three minutes later. Other bloggers jumped into the fray. Soon mainstream media outlets were covering the story, and CBS had to admit it couldn't verify the authenticity of the memos. An independent review panel later concluded that *60 Minutes II* committed "countless misstatements and omissions" in reporting the story. The producer was fired, Rather retired a year early, and three other people who worked on the investigation were asked to leave CBS. The reporting debacle, dubbed "Rathergate" and "Memogate," damaged the reputation of CBS News and the mainstream media, or as Little Green Footballs and other blogs called it, "the lamestream media."[58]

Thanks to the bloggers, Bush's reputation survived the National Guard story. Although polls showed that 51 percent of Americans thought the Iraq War was a mistake, he narrowly won reelection over Kerry with 50.7 percent of the vote.[59]

Bush began his second term with grand plans of prevailing in Iraq and Afghanistan, spreading democracy around the world, reforming the immigration system, and revamping Social Security by adding personal retirement accounts. But things went downhill quickly. Although Bush attracted plenty of media coverage for his Social Security plan, it was wildly unpopular, and the GOP congressional leadership never brought it to a vote. Immigration reform met similar opposition and died in Congress. And there were few signs the two wars would end. In Iraq more than seventy-five Americans were being killed and more than four hundred wounded every month in 2005. Head shots of the dead Americans regularly appeared in newspapers and on TV newscasts.

The bad news overwhelmed Bush's communications team. They excelled at producing detailed strategies for issues he wanted to emphasize, but they stumbled badly when they had to respond quickly to unexpected events.[60] At no time did the president's image in the press look worse than in the terrible aftermath of Hurricane Katrina, whose winds slammed into Mississippi, Alabama, and Louisiana on August 29, 2005. Flood waters smashed through levees that were supposed to protect New Orleans, inundating about 80 percent of the city. The news showed horrifying images of residents pleading to be rescued from rooftops, dead bodies floating through the streets, and hungry, sick, and miserable people stuck inside the sweltering New Orleans Convention Center and Superdome.[61]

Bush was wrapping up a twenty-nine-day vacation at his Texas ranch and a visit to San Diego for a political speech. Despite pleas for help, he gave the hurricane and floods little attention at first, and the federal government was slow to send people and resources to the Gulf Coast. When he flew back to Washington two days after the storm hit, the White House released a photo of Bush looking down at the damage from Air Force One, far removed from the human suffering. For many, it symbolized presidential indifference as people—most of them poor and Black—suffered and died while local officials begged for more assistance. In the words of reporter April Ryan, "the storm of storms had hit and the Bush administration was laid bare and exposed as hundreds of people were dying after the levy break in New Orleans."[62]

Because of his disdain for the press, Bush failed to understand that journalists could inform not only the public but also the government about what was happening in the world. Katrina struck New Orleans on a Monday. Bush's aides later admitted that the president, who wasn't a regular newspaper reader or TV news watcher, didn't realize the extent of the horror until Thursday night when he was given a DVD showing news coverage of the catastrophe. Michael Brown, the director of the Federal Emergency Management Agency (FEMA), said during a CNN interview that he had been unaware until Thursday of the unimaginable suffering in the Superdome and Convention Center even though TV news had been covering it for four days. "Don't you guys watch television?" ABC's Ted Koppel asked Brown in another interview. "Don't you guys listen to the radio?"[63]

As Bush finally flew to the Gulf Coast that Friday, the reporters on board peppered Press Secretary Scott McClellan with questions. "People are dying from lack of food and water," one reporter said. "Not only are they waiting to be rescued, but they're waiting for food and water and they're not getting it. So—why is the president not more angry about that?" McClellan replied tepidly, "He's not pleased with the results."[64] While touring the devastation that day with reporters by his side, Bush told Brown, "Brownie, you're doing a heck of a job!"[65] Like "Mission Accomplished," it was a phrase that returned to haunt Bush. As the press noted, Brown wasn't doing a good job.

In the following days, the administration scrambled to defend itself against accusations that it responded too slowly to the crisis, which caused more than 1,800 deaths and wrecked more than three hundred thousand homes. The White House continued to support Brown's leadership of FEMA despite press revelations that he had inflated his résumé when he was appointed to lead the agency. The press office released talking points lauding the federal response to Katrina and responded to criticism that Bush had cut the budget for the Army Corps of Engineers, which was responsible for flood control.[66]

But the talking points couldn't stop the surge of negative coverage. Bush was never able to regain momentum for his presidency after Katrina. In addition to his bungled response to the hurricane, the press continued to report on the devastation in Iraq and the faulty claims that Bush used to justify the invasion.[67] The hesitancy to challenge his policies in the aftermath of 9/11 had faded. In November 2005 the *Washington Post* published a story by investigative reporter Dana Priest revealing that the CIA was operating secret "black site" prisons in eight foreign countries. In those prisons people suspected of terrorism—none of them yet convicted of a crime—were brutally interrogated without the protections of the U.S. legal system.[68]

The next month James Risen and Eric Lichtblau of the *New York Times* revealed that Bush had approved of spying on Americans without a warrant. The National Security Agency's snooping included monitoring emails and international phone calls in the hope of spotting terrorist activity. The *Times* had sat on the story for more than a year because the administration said it might alert would-be terrorists. Critics hammered the newspaper for the delay because it meant voters didn't see the story before the 2004 election.[69]

The *Times*' handling of this story, the reporting failures leading up to the Iraq War, and CBS's mangling of the Bush National Guard investigation contributed to a downward spiral in the press's reputation. The contempt for the media that Nixon and Agnew had shown was now widespread. The percentage of Americans who thought stories in the press were often inaccurate had climbed from 34 percent in 1985 to 53 percent in 2007, according to a Pew Research Center study. Those who thought the press was "immoral" jumped from 13 to 32 percent during the same time.[70]

The Bush administration's negative attitude toward journalists and its disdain for truth telling further weakened the role of the press. It increased the number of documents that were kept secret, delayed responding to requests for records under the Freedom of Information Act, and scrubbed government websites of information previously available to reporters and the public. "The Bush administration will leave the White House with relations between the presidency and the press in shambles," observed the *Washington Post*'s Murrey Marder, who had covered the capital since Harry Truman's time. "No other president has set out so determinedly to discredit the role of the press as a watchdog on the transparency and accountability of government."[71]

As Bush's presidency wound down, he could still point to some significant achievements. He had prevented any major terrorist attacks against the United States following 9/11, passed substantial tax cuts that temporarily stimulated the economy, expanded Medicare prescription drug benefits, and launched a program that saved millions of lives by treating and preventing the spread of AIDS in Africa. On the other hand, U.S. troops were still dying in two wars, he had botched the response to Hurricane Katrina, and the budget surpluses he inherited from Clinton had turned into massive deficits.

Then things got worse as the economy fell into its worst crisis since the Great Depression of the 1930s. An estimated 1.5 million people lost their jobs in the last three months of 2008, the stock market nosedived, more than two million homes went into foreclosure, and banks and the auto industry teetered on the verge of collapse.[72] Bush gave a primetime television address on September 24, 2008, to warn the country that it could be facing a long and painful recession. "There's been a widespread loss of confidence," the president admitted, his face looking haggard and his famous smirk now a grimace. "And major sectors of America's financial system are at risk of shutting down." The speech didn't win many rave reviews in the press. "It took President Bush until Wednesday night to address the American people about the nation's financial crisis," the *New York Times* commented after the speech, "and pretty much all he had to offer was fear itself."[73]

Bush did have a celebratory moment in the White House a week before his second term ended. He hosted a one-hour lunch for a special guest—Rush Limbaugh. Together they enjoyed a three-layer chocolate cake in honor of the radio host's fifty-eighth birthday. The president then gave Limbaugh one final interview.[74] Bush had made time for the conservative star several times before. In 2007 he had given Limbaugh a private interview before smoking cigars, eating dinner, and chatting off-the-record with the radio host. The next day Limbaugh bragged on his show about his influence over the president:

> Limbaugh: You know, people have been asking me, "Well, what did the president tell you last night?" That's not it. "What did I tell the president?" is the correct question.
> Caller: (*Laughing*) So he also recognizes that you're the man running the country?
> Limbaugh: Well, who doesn't? I mean there are certain things that don't need to be said.[75]

Limbaugh may have been joking (that was often his explanation when he said something outrageous), but he and the other titans of conservative radio had real clout. Progressives had nobody with similar power on the air. Bill Clinton had felt comfortable on talk radio, but most Democratic politicians avoided it because they considered its hosts to be thoroughly hostile toward them. In 2004 liberals tried one well-publicized effort, Air America, to counter conservative dominance of the radio airwaves. It flopped, lasting just six years due to inexperienced hosts, weak management, and flimsy funding. The remaining handful of liberal radio shows were often stuck on low-wattage stations with little national reach. In the words of *Variety*'s Brian Lowry, they were "outgunned, and out-shouted, by the right's bigger, older and better-marketed megaphone."[76]

By 2006 all seven of the most popular talk radio shows in the country were hosted by conservatives.[77] Bush invited many of them to his White House Christmas parties. The president's staff put up tents on the White House lawn on three separate occasions to let conservative hosts spend the day interviewing top officials.[78] Bush also held Oval Office meetings with right-wing TV and radio stars such as Sean Hannity (who starred in his own radio and Fox News shows), Laura Ingraham (whose radio show was carried by 250 stations), and Michael Medved (who was heard in 180 markets around the country).[79]

Bush understood that no Republican leader could afford to be on the wrong side of the increasingly powerful kings and queens of conservative media. A Democratic president was about to learn just how damaging they could be to his administration.

9 Barack Obama and the Fragmented Media

President Barack Obama was ready to make a big announcement. Looking squarely at the camera, he acknowledged for the first time that the U.S. military was using drones to kill suspected terrorists overseas. Obama didn't share this important news during a news conference, an interview with a journalist, or a major speech to the nation. Instead, he discussed the top-secret drone program in response to a taped question from "Evan in Brooklyn" on YouTube during a live Google+ Hangout on January 30, 2012.

Sitting in the White House, a smiling Obama held the Google+ virtual conversation with five Americans from Michigan, Texas, Illinois, New Jersey, and California. More than a quarter million other people—including Evan from Brooklyn—submitted questions beforehand. Google+ users then got to vote on which ones the president should answer. In addition to drones, Obama was asked about unemployment, immigration, foreign aid, college affordability, and the plight of small businesses. There were questions about what he planned to do for his wedding anniversary and whether he would do a jig for the audience (he declined). An Obama impersonator even asked the president what he thought of Obama impersonators.

It was the first time the White House had hosted a completely online interview. New social media technology was allowing Americans from a variety of backgrounds to question the president in ways they never had before. But it was far from a perfect example of digital democracy. The White House and Google prescreened questions to avoid the most uncomfortable ones. A marijuana legalization question had earned the most votes, but it was never asked during the Hangout. After watching Obama's Google+ performance, Erik Kain of *Forbes* magazine wrote, "Whether it was a victory for democracy or a savvy PR stunt on the part of Google and the administration is an open question."[1]

Obama of course wasn't the first president to take advantage of technology. FDR used radio to reach the public directly, and Kennedy and Reagan mastered television, but they still needed the cooperation of the broadcast networks to do so. Obama didn't. He (or his staff) just needed to set up his social media accounts. Although Clinton and George W. Bush had occasionally answered questions over the internet, doing so wasn't at the core of their communications strategy.[2] For Obama it was. His administration took the use of digital technology to a new level, projecting a carefully crafted image to millions of people through Facebook, Instagram, Reddit, LinkedIn, Google+, Twitter, MySpace, and YouTube.[3] Social media platforms would come and go (Google+ didn't make it past 2019), but Obama forever changed presidential communications.

Obama—like George W. Bush before him—made it harder for reporters to cover the president. He frequently shunned White House correspondents while his administration tightly restricted information, denied access to photojournalists, and prosecuted more people than ever before for leaking to the press. But as much as Obama tried to control his image by avoiding mainstream journalists, he couldn't escape relentless attacks by conservative talk radio hosts, Fox News, and a bevy of rightwing websites. They weakened his ability to govern, spread false conspiracy theories that continue to infect U.S. politics, and contributed to Donald Trump's election in 2016. The intense and bitter polarization they fueled remained one of the nation's deepest problems as Joe Biden began his presidency.

Obama enjoyed often glowing press coverage during his meteoric rise to the White House. He first gained national notice in 1990 when at age twenty-eight he was selected as the first Black president of the *Harvard Law Review*. Articles in the *New York Times, Los Angeles Times, Chicago Tribune*, and other newspapers offered the now familiar Obama profile: son of a Kenyan father and a white mother from Kansas, a childhood in Hawaii and Indonesia, an undergraduate degree from Columbia University, and a job as a community organizer in some of Chicago's poorest neighborhoods. Obama told reporters he might want to go into politics after Harvard.[4]

Six years later Obama won a seat in the Illinois State Senate, where he championed bills decreasing taxes for low-income residents, expanding children's access to health care, and increasing tax credits for building affordable housing. His early opposition to the Iraq War helped him defeat seven opponents to win the Democratic primary for U.S. Senate in 2004. That summer he gave the keynote address at the Democratic National Convention, where his soaring words of unity electrified the crowd and earned him national acclaim. Even though Bush was reelected that November, Obama routed a weak Republican opponent in the Senate race with more than 70 percent of the vote.[5]

The press was dazzled by the cerebral, skinny young senator with big ears and a bright smile. "Obama has been embraced by a party hungry for new faces, and described by almost everyone who has met him as a rising star," the *New York Times* said five days after the election.[6] *Newsweek* put Obama's picture on its cover. So did *Time* with the headline "Why Barack Obama Could Be Our Next President." Legendary Washington reporter Godfrey Sperling of the *Christian Science Monitor* agreed, suggesting that the Democrats choose the freshman senator as their next presidential nominee.[7]

After fewer than four years in the Senate, Obama ran for president. Despite starting off behind in the polls, he defeated New York senator and former First Lady Hillary Clinton for the Democratic nomination in a close, bitter contest. He then took on Republican Senator John

McCain of Arizona in the general election. As the first African American nominee for a major political party, Obama ran on a theme of hope and change. The campaign's excitement spread through the news media.[8] David Ignatius of the *Washington Post* observed that Obama resembled a rock star more than a typical politician. After one Obama speech, Chris Matthews of MSNBC said he "felt this thrill going up my leg."[9]

The Obama campaign's harnessing of social media set his candidacy apart from other campaigns. Social media hadn't existed a few years earlier, but now Facebook, Twitter, and YouTube were flourishing. My .BarackObama.com had more than two million profiles of volunteers who used the site and its social media channels to raise $30 million, plan two hundred thousand events, and get out the vote. The campaign even had its own iPhone app that supporters could use to encourage friends to vote for Obama. McCain's team couldn't keep up.[10]

As the economy went into a freefall during the last weeks of Bush's presidency, Obama pulled ahead of McCain. Some conservative media commentators desperately tried to portray the Illinois senator as an un-American militant. Fox News anchor E. D. Hill speculated that a fist bump between Obama and his wife, Michelle, was really a "terrorist fist jab."[11] On right-wing radio, the racist taunts weren't subtle. San Francisco radio host Brian Sussman referred to Obama as a "halfrican." Conservative radio star Michael Savage, falsely suggesting that Obama is a Muslim, asked, "Are you going to tell me that Obama, Barack Hussein Obama, is going to take our side should there be some sort of catastrophic attack on America?"[12]

The scare tactics didn't work. Obama was elected with 52.9 percent of the vote and 365 electoral college votes to 173 for McCain. It was the biggest margin for a Democrat in a presidential race since Lyndon Johnson in 1964.[13] Obama's win stirred a sense of idealism among some in the press that hadn't been seen in years. Columnist Maureen Dowd of the *New York Times* wrote two days later that "the Lincoln Memorial might be getting its gleam back" thanks to the "elegant and disciplined" Obama.[14]

Obama's victory was especially sweet for members of the Black press, which had been excluded from covering the White House for most of the nation's history. "As I write this, I fight back tears that are falling down my cheeks," wrote CNN analyst Roland S. Martin, former executive editor of the *Chicago Defender*, the nation's premier Black newspaper for many years. "Now, I can tell my children with certainty, that yes, even you can grow up to be president of the United States. Sen. Barack Obama, thank you. The ancestors thank you. America thanks you."[15]

An estimated two million people poured into Washington to cheer Obama's inauguration. Despite their euphoria, the new president faced an immediate crisis. The country was suffering from its deepest recession in more than seventy years. The American economy lost 3.5 million jobs in 2008 and another 800,000 in January 2009 as Obama took office. The banking system was on the verge of collapse. The U.S. auto industry was facing bankruptcy. People were losing their homes as the housing market crumbled.[16]

Obama had campaigned on the theme of ending partisan gridlock in Washington, but the Republican Party and its media allies weren't interested in cooperating. When asked what his hope was for the Obama presidency, Rush Limbaugh replied, "I hope he fails." The Republican leadership followed Limbaugh's lead. "The single most important thing we want to achieve is for President Obama to be a one-term president," Senate majority leader Mitch McConnell said.[17]

This GOP strategy made any kind of compromise nearly impossible and guaranteed that every policy debate would become intensely polarizing. This became clear when Obama introduced an $800 billion stimulus package to revive the economy that included tax cuts for 95 percent of Americans. Even though Republicans usually championed tax cuts, every GOP member of the House voted against it. The bill passed thanks to support from the Democratic majority. Obama also pushed through loans to banks and the auto industry that kept them from collapsing. The economy still struggled to climb out of the recession. The unemployment rate reached 10 percent in the fall of 2009, and

Obama's approval rating fell below 50 percent after a year in office. For many Americans, Obama's message of hope and change was looking more like despair and stagnation.[18]

Less than two months after Obama's inauguration, reporter Rick Santelli was live on the CNBC financial news network waving his arms in the trading pit of the Chicago Mercantile Exchange. Santelli was railing against Obama's economic policies, in particular a $75 billion plan to help struggling homeowners avoid foreclosures. "How about this, president new administration," Santelli shouted to his viewers, "why don't you put up a website to have people vote on the internet as a referendum to see if we really want to subsidize the losers' mortgages?" Referring to the Boston Tea Party, Santelli vowed to hold a "Chicago Tea Party" to challenge Obama's economic policies. "All you capitalists that wanna show up to Lake Michigan, I'm organizing," he declared.[19]

Santelli's outburst became known as "the rant heard round the world."[20] Within a day, a petition and two websites were created to support his crusade. The *Drudge Report* linked to the video, right-wing bloggers posted it, and conservative activists tweeted about it. Within three days, the video of Santelli's tirade had been seen 1.7 million times, and it became a top story on all the network newscasts. The Tea Party movement was born with the goal of stopping Obama and his policies. To some extent, it was a grassroots effort appealing to older, white, middle-class voters who felt ignored by Washington. But it wasn't all spontaneous. The group was promoted by well-funded conservative organizations such as FreedomWorks, led by former GOP House majority leader Richard Armey.[21]

The biggest Tea Party booster of all was Fox News, whose influence over Republicans continued to rise. With its no-apologies brand of hard-hitting conservatism, Fox had become the most popular cable news channel. Republicans rated the network as their most trusted news outlet as they grew increasingly suspicious of the mainstream press, which Fox hosts repeatedly told them was liberally biased. In what became known as "the Fox News Effect," GOP turnout and vote totals grew in communities after Fox became available.[22] Meanwhile CNN, which had once prided itself on being politically neutral, increasingly appealed to Democrats.[23] MSNBC also tilted toward the left in an effort to compete with Fox's partisan style.[24]

Once Obama entered the White House, Fox News's ratings climbed higher as it shed any pretense of neutrality. Alan Colmes, the network's token liberal, had quit the show he co-hosted with Sean Hannity and wasn't replaced. Roger Ailes gave McCain's outspokenly conservative running mate, Sarah Palin, a $1 million contract to become a Fox commentator. And the day before Obama's inauguration, firebrand talk-radio star Glenn Beck launched his own Fox News show in an afternoon time slot previously reserved for more objective news reporting.[25] "I see this as the Alamo," Beck recalled Ailes saying when Fox hired him. "If I just had somebody who was willing to sit on the other side of the camera until the last shot is fired, we'd be fine."[26]

Beck was an immediate hit, doubling the ratings for his time slot in his first month. He relied on fear and conspiracy theories as he derided Obama's attempts to deal with the financial crisis as "socialism." Beck claimed that Obama was antagonistic to "true American values." Echoing Colonel McCormick's attacks on FDR, Beck compared the president to Hitler and Stalin and hinted that FEMA might be setting up concentration camps. "I think our country is on the verge of disintegration," Beck said.[27] After Obama addressed Congress, Beck asked his viewers, "Did anybody watch the speech last night and have blood just shooting right out of your eyes?"[28]

Beck and the rest of the Fox News crew eagerly endorsed the nascent Tea Party movement and promoted its upcoming Tax Day protests, ignoring the fact that Obama's economic plan included middle-class tax cuts. Beck told his viewers, "You don't want to miss it." Megyn Kelly advised people to go to Fox's website to find Tea Party events near their homes. Sean Hannity reminded his audience, "Anybody can come, it's free."[29] Tea Party organizers didn't need their own public relations team. They had Fox News.

The partisan news channel and the Tea Party blended together. When the political movement's Tax Day protests were held on April 15, 2009, Beck aired his show from a Tea Party rally at the Alamo in Texas. Hannity did the same in Atlanta, as did fellow Fox stars Neil Cavuto in Sacramento and Greta Van Susteren in Washington DC. Once the April protests were over, Beck continued to invite Tea Party organizers onto his show to promote additional events and helped organize a September rally in Washington. Freedom Works, the pro-business Tea Party funder, began using a picture of Beck on its publicity material.[30]

The Tea Party received equally strong support from talk radio. The conservative-leaning Clear Channel (which eventually became iHeartMedia) owned eight hundred stations by the start of Obama's presidency and had just signed Rush Limbaugh to a $400 million, eight-year contract. Limbaugh—still tops in the ratings with twenty million listeners—gleefully went after the new president. When Obama proposed spending more money to tackle climate change, Limbaugh called global warming a "hoax" and claimed that "militant environmentalism" was now the "home of displaced communists after the Berlin Wall came down."[31] Limbaugh's words had influence. When a Gallup poll in June 2009 asked which person speaks for Republicans, first place went to "no one." Second went to Limbaugh.[32]

Conservative talk shows had found a comfy home on AM stations, which needed new content after many music programs migrated to FM, where the sound had less static. At least 90 percent of the political talk shows were conservative with Hannity, Beck, Laura Ingraham, Mark Levin, and many others joining Limbaugh. With a shortage of strong Democratic voices on the air, talk radio along with Fox News became a conservative echo chamber leaning further and further to the right. Like Limbaugh, many of the new generation of conservative media stars came from entertainment rather than journalism backgrounds. Beck, for instance, had been a morning radio shock jock. Forget nuance. Forget moderation or nonpartisanship. None of that sold well on talk radio, cable news, or the internet. Instead, they presented only one side to every issue and only anger—the more vehement the better—toward their political opponents and even moderates. A similar phenomenon occurred on the left with MSNBC and websites such as *Huffington Post.*[33]

Limbaugh, Fox, and other conservative media relentlessly promoted the Tea Party as the last hope of true patriots. "This is God's work," conservative radio host Mike Gallagher told a crowd of about two thousand people—most, if not all of them, white—at a Tea Party gathering in April 2009 in Greenville, South Carolina. Dressed in gray slacks and a dark blazer, the stocky, middle-aged Gallagher didn't have the physical charisma of a successful politician or TV host, but he had a smooth, dramatic voice that made him a star to his legions of fans. When Gallagher mentioned Obama, who had been in office for less than three months, the crowd booed. "We're fed up with Barack Obama!" he shouted as the crowd waved American flags and banners saying, "Hope Obama Fails" and "No to Socialism!" Gallagher promised that "the left" would have to listen to the Tea Partiers. "This is about a love of country," he said. "This is about a love of patriotism. This is what this country was founded on." Gallagher then promoted his book, *Surrounded by Idiots: Fighting Liberal Lunacy in America.*[34]

Thanks to promoters like Gallagher, the loose collection of Tea Party groups gained momentum and began receiving more coverage outside of conservative media circles. CNN highlighted their rallies and sent reporters to travel with a "Tea Party Express" bus tour.[35] The press reported extensively that summer on Tea Party disruptions of congressional town halls where its activists denounced Obama's health-care plan, the Affordable Care Act, which they derided as "Obamacare."[36] Sarah Palin posted on Facebook (the president wasn't the only politician taking advantage of social media) that the Affordable Care Act would give government the power to withhold health care from the elderly and other vulnerable people. "The America I know and love is not one in which my parents or my baby with Down Syndrome will have to stand in front of Obama's 'death panel' so his bureaucrats can decide, based on a subjective judgment of their 'level of productivity in society,' whether they are worthy of health care," Palin wrote. The "death panel" accusation wasn't close to true, and the fact-checking site PolitiFact named Palin's claim its "Lie of the Year" for 2009. But even as her lie was being debunked, GOP politicians repeated the disinformation and news outlets covered it, spreading the conspiracy theory further. During the rest of 2009, news reports mentioned "death panels" more than six thousand times. According to two polls, about 30 percent of the public believed death panels were really in the legislation no matter what the fact-checkers said.[37]

Conservative media, rather than the Republican Party, had become the principal organizer of mass opposition to the president. In the months before the 2010 midterm elections, the Tea Party and their media allies continued to attack the president on Obamacare, his stimulus plan, and the rising federal deficit. With the economy continuing to stumble, Democrats lost sixty seats in the House. Obama called it a "shellacking."[38] About forty members of the new GOP majority in Congress owed their allegiance to the Tea Party and pushed the party further to the right. They had no interest in compromising with Obama or any other Democrat and had enough power to make sure that no other Republicans did either.[39]

Following the midterms, Obama struggled in the polls as the economy recovered at a painfully slow pace. But campaigning for reelection in 2012, he could point to a string of accomplishments: ending the recession, providing affordable health care to more people, bringing a hundred thousand U.S. troops home from Iraq, getting Wall Street reform through Congress, improving vehicle fuel-efficiency standards, and encouraging marriage rights for gay and lesbian couples. Under his leadership U.S. special forces found and killed Osama bin Laden, the mastermind of the 9/11 attacks.[40] Gradually, Obama regained popularity as the economy picked up steam. He won reelection, beating former Massachusetts governor Mitt Romney with 51 percent of the popular vote and 332 electoral votes to 206. The next day Rush Limbaugh warned his listeners, "I think we've lost the country."[41]

Obama was in good humor when he spoke at the annual Gridiron Club dinner seven weeks after his second inauguration. "Some of you have said that I'm ignoring the Washington press corps—that we're too controlling," he told the journalists in the audience. "Well, you know what? You were right. I was wrong, and I want to apologize in a video you can watch exclusively at whitehouse.gov." Obama then promised to answer one question from the journalists that night. The question, he said, was, "Mr. President, will you be taking any questions tonight?" His response: "I will not." The audience laughed, but the joke was on them.[42]

During the 2008 campaign, Obama had chided Bush's fondness for secrecy. "My administration is committed to creating an unprecedented level of openness in Government," Obama promised after being elected.[43] Indeed, his White House made federal spending data, government studies, and the salaries of White House staff readily available online for journalists and the public to see. But on the whole, the Obama administration was less open than its predecessors. It prevented government experts from being questioned by reporters, blackballed journalists it didn't like, and delayed interviews until after reporters' deadlines. Federal officials refused to answer questions about climate change, the handling of hazardous waste, and a new coding system affecting Medicare and Medicaid patients.[44]

Obama himself was often prickly with journalists, growing visibly irritated when asked questions he didn't like. A few days after his first inauguration, he stopped by the White House press room for a friendly visit. But the president became annoyed when one reporter did what journalists are paid to do, which is to ask questions, this time about a lobbyist appointed to a top Pentagon job. "Ahh, see," Obama responded, "I came down here to visit. See this is what happens. I can't end up visiting with you guys and shaking hands if I'm going to get grilled every time I come down here."[45]

Obama's relationship with the White House press corps didn't improve from there. He gave press conferences during his first two years at a slightly slower pace than his two predecessors, but that wasn't the biggest problem. Instead, it was his tendency to make it difficult for journalists to cover his presidency. He held short question-and-answer sessions with reporters at a third of Bush's rate and a fifth of Clinton's. Chinese journalists were once invited into a meeting between Obama and the Chinese premier but not the White House press corps.[46] If frustrated reporters wanted to learn about Obama's words and actions, his staff sometimes referred them to the White House website to watch videos and photos selected by his aides. It was a far cry from the relaxed conversations FDR used to have with journalists. "He's the least transparent of the seven presidents I've covered in terms of how he does his daily business," ABC White House correspondent Ann Compton said.[47]

While reporters struggled to have a chance to talk with Obama, photojournalists had a hard time taking his picture. The White House kept them away from bill signings, Oval Office meetings, and swearing-in ceremonies. It told news outlets that meetings with U.S. House members, human rights activists, and Middle East peace negotiators were private and couldn't be covered, but then the administration released its own photos of the events. "As surely as if they were placing a hand over a journalist's camera lens, officials in this administration are blocking the public from having an independent view of important functions of the Executive Branch of government," thirty-eight news organizations complained to Press Secretary Jay Carney.[48] Carney promised to make changes, but when Obama met with the Dalai Lama in 2014, photojournalists were barred from the meeting. Instead, the White House issued a picture by official staff photographer Pete Souza. The administration's visual version of events, guaranteed to make the president look good, was the only one the public was allowed to see.[49]

This lack of openness extended to government records that journalists and the public were supposed to be able to see under the Freedom of Information Act (FOIA). While publicly insisting it wanted to strengthen

FOIA, the Obama White House worked behind the scenes to sabotage a bill that would have increased access to government records. More Freedom of Information Act lawsuits—422—were filed against the federal government in the 2014 fiscal year than ever before. In the summer of 2014, the leaders of thirty-nine news organizations wrote a scathing letter to Obama. "You recently expressed concern that frustration in the country is breeding cynicism about democratic government," the letter said. "You need look no further than your own administration for a major source of that frustration—politically driven suppression of news and information about federal agencies. We call on you to take a stand to stop the spin and let the sunshine in."[50]

Obama did give lots of interviews—674 of them during his first term, more than triple the number George W. Bush did during his first four years. But the interviews often seemed like lectures rather than the usual give-and-take with reporters. The longer Obama was in office, the more he avoided talking with the Washington press corps. For several years of his presidency, he didn't grant interviews with reporters for the *New York Times*, CBS, *Wall Street Journal, Washington Post, Los Angeles Times, Chicago Tribune,* or *Politico.*

As newspaper and magazine readership declined, Obama's staff believed he could reach more people and be treated more favorably by appearing on entertainment and sports broadcasts rather than talking with print reporters. During his first two years as president, Obama went on non-news shows four times more often than Clinton or the two Bush presidents.[51] Twelve days after his inauguration, Obama sat down with the *Today Show*'s Matt Lauer for an interview before the Super Bowl. Along with questions about the economy and national security, Lauer asked the president about college football, his family's adjustment to White House life, and his predictions for the big game.[52] Obama went on ESPN annually to talk about his NCAA basketball tournament bracket. Like Clinton, he went on MTV. He also appeared on *Entertainment Tonight, The Oprah Winfrey Show, The View,* and late-night comedy shows.[53] The strategy worked. In 2014 the president visited the comedy web series *Between Two Ferns* to trade barbs with host Zach Galifianakis. Using his wry sense of humor, Obama encouraged people to enroll for health insurance under the Affordable Care Act. The video of his *Between Two Ferns* appearance received more than fifty million views, and traffic on the healthcare.gov website soared.[54]

Obama's media strategy included reaching out to audiences rarely represented by the mostly white reporters who typically covered the president. During his 2012 reelection campaign, Obama gave over thirty-five interviews to Black media outlets. His White House also gave more access to the growing Hispanic media than any previous administration. It was the first to have a Latinx media director and hold a bilingual daily press briefing. The president wrote op-eds for Hispanic newspapers and gave more than a dozen interviews to Telemundo, Univision, and other Latinx news outlets.[55] Journalists who had covered the White House for many years could grumble, but Obama had succeeded in finding new ways to reach voters through minority-owned media outlets that had been largely ignored in the past.

Jake Tapper looked grim as he accused the Obama administration of being hypocritical. Glaring at Press Secretary Jay Carney, he asked at a February 2012 news briefing why the administration kept praising the courage of journalists in Syria while it attacked American whistleblowers who gave information to U.S. reporters. Tapper, then with ABC News, noted that Obama officials were using the Espionage Act to try to send the whistleblowers to prison. "You want aggressive journalism abroad," he said. "You just don't want it in the United States."

Carney, stumbling with his words a bit more than usual, refused to discuss the specifics of any of the cases, saying they involved "highly sensitive, classified information."

Tapper didn't relent. "So the truth should come out abroad; it shouldn't come out here?" he asked.

"Well, that's not at all what I'm saying, Jake, and you know it's not. Again I can't [be] specific . . ."

"Well," Tapper interrupted, "that's what the Justice Department is doing."[56]

As Tapper observed, the administration had an alarming zeal for prosecuting whistleblowers. It also spied on journalists and intimidated them to reveal their sources. To go after leakers, Obama dusted off the Espionage Act, created during Wilson's presidency to prevent secrets being given to America's World War I enemies. Obama's Justice Department used the Espionage Act to prosecute eight people, five more than all previous presidents combined. Two other leakers were prosecuted using different laws. David Carr of the *New York Times* noted that most of the cases "seem to have everything to do with administrative secrecy and very little to do with national security."[57]

Thomas Drake, for instance, gave copies of documents to the *Baltimore Sun* revealing that the National Security Agency had wrongly ended a surveillance program in favor of a costlier one with fewer privacy safeguards for Americans. The *Sun*'s story concluded that bureaucratic infighting had "produced a far less capable and rigorous program." In response, Obama's Justice Department charged Drake in 2010 with ten felony counts, including violation of the Espionage Act. His lawyers later proved that most of the information Drake shared had never been classified. Prosecutors dropped all charges in return for Drake pleading guilty to a misdemeanor count of misusing the NSA computer system. Instead of being lauded as a whistleblower, his career was destroyed. The judge said it was "unconscionable" that prosecutors had subjected Drake to "four years of hell."[58] It was a taste of what would happen to whistleblowers during the rest of Obama's presidency and then Trump's.

Obama's Justice Department also indicted CIA officer Jeffrey Sterling in 2010. It accused him of giving *New York Times* reporter James Risen secrets about a failed U.S. attempt to sabotage Iran's nuclear program. In his book *State of War*, Risen described the sabotage program as mismanaged and potentially helpful to Iran. Determined to learn the source of Risen's information, the Justice Department seized years of his emails and telephone records and repeatedly subpoenaed him to testify. Risen refused, vowing to go to prison rather than identify his source. He argued that important stories about government could never be written without confidential sources. Attorney General Eric Holder finally relented and said prosecutors wouldn't force Risen to testify. Sterling, however, was convicted in 2015 and sentenced to three and a half years in prison.[59]

Despite the administration's attempts to stop leaks, the digital revolution was smashing holes in the walls of government secrecy. In 2010 army intelligence analyst Chelsea Manning (then known as Bradley Manning) produced the biggest leak of classified information in U.S. history up to that point. Using a CD labeled as music by Lady Gaga, Manning downloaded a video of U.S. military helicopter crews in Iraq killing civilians, including two journalists for the Reuters news agency. Manning gave the video to the anti-secrecy website WikiLeaks, which posted it. She then copied a half million U.S. Army incident reports, a quarter million State Department cables, and dossiers of terrorism suspects being held at Guantanamo Bay onto a thumb drive and gave them to WikiLeaks. The information included embarrassing information about corrupt U.S. allies and troubling conduct by U.S. forces overseas, including the killing of civilians.[60]

WikiLeaks initially partnered with the *New York Times*, the *Guardian* in Great Britain, and *Der Spiegel* in Germany to publish stories about the leaked information. Some details were edited out of the articles to protect lives. But WikiLeaks also posted unredacted versions of the documents including the names of people in dangerous places overseas who had assisted the United States, putting their lives at risk. Manning was arrested and charged with violating the Espionage Act and twenty-one other offenses. She was sentenced in 2013 to thirty-five years in prison, the longest punishment ever for a leak conviction. Four years later Obama commuted her sentence after Manning twice tried to kill herself in prison.[61]

The Obama administration argued that WikiLeaks shouldn't enjoy the same legal protections as the press. After all, it didn't engage in original reporting or pretend to be objective like traditional journalists. That line of thinking didn't stop the administration from spying in 2013 on the Associated Press, the standard bearer of traditional reporting. To find the source of a story about CIA activity in Yemen, the Justice Department secretly obtained the records for more than twenty phones used by Associated Press journalists. Thousands of calls were tracked. AP president Gary Pruitt called the sweeping seizure of records a "massive and unprecedented intrusion" into newsgathering. He said the administration's message was clear: "If you talk to the press, we're going after you."[62]

Six days later, the *Washington Post* revealed that the Justice Department was also spying on Fox News reporter James Rosen. The government had tracked Rosen's movements and seized his personal email and phone records to determine if a State Department employee was the source for one of his stories. Most disturbingly, the affidavit for the secret subpoena against Rosen said he might be violating the Espionage Act by seeking information as a journalist.[63] In other words, it was equating reporting with spying.

Finally, the Obama administration backed down. Like Wilson during World War I and the Adams administration with the Sedition Act, it had gone too far. After an avalanche of criticism, the Justice Department met with journalism leaders to develop guidelines for when the press should be involved in prosecutions. In a move supported by Obama, Attorney General Holder announced that journalists' email and phone records would only be searched if they were the focus of a criminal investigation for conduct that didn't involve news gathering.[64]

Then the biggest leak of all occurred. The *Guardian* and the *Washington Post* revealed in June 2013 that the administration was collecting emails, phone records, photos, and video chats of millions of Americans as part of the post-9/11 "war on terrorism." The information was gathered about users of Facebook, Google, Apple, YouTube, AOL, and Skype whether they were suspected of doing anything wrong or not. An NSA contractor, Edward Snowden, soon stepped forward as the leaker. He escaped to Russia as Obama castigated him and the Justice Department charged him with violating the Espionage Act. His revelations, however, led to reforms including a requirement that intelligence agencies get a court order before collecting telecommunications data about Americans.[65]

The long series of leak investigations and Espionage Act prosecutions deepened tensions between Obama and the press. A 2013 study by the Committee to Protect Journalists found that the White House was using intimidation to discourage watchdog reporting. Sources were now scared to share information with reporters even on subjects that had nothing to do with national security. "In the Obama administration's Washington," the study said, "government officials are increasingly afraid to talk to the press."[66]

This tension didn't seem to bother Obama. He continued a trend of recent presidents who worried less and less about what reporters, editors, or owners of the mainstream press thought of them. No one in journalism had as much power anymore as William Randolph Hearst, Henry Luce, Edward R. Murrow, or Walter Cronkite once did. Instead, Obama turned increasingly to social media. His administration was the first to have a director of new media and its own social media operation. The White House created Facebook, Instagram, and Flickr accounts full of inspiring photos of the president and his family. The whitehouse.gov site included a daily blog highlighting Obama's actions, a videographer was hired to create YouTube videos, and the administration produced its own webcast, "West Wing Week." Sometimes it contained videos of events that reporters were never told about.[67] The White House was shaping its own stories without any independent vetting by journalists. In the words of one frustrated photojournalist, it was "propaganda by definition."[68]

Twitter was perhaps Obama's most successful media platform. His @POTUS account had twenty-seven million followers, more than the circulation of the largest seventy-five newspapers in the country combined. It was bigger too than the total nightly audiences for the network newscasts. The president's followers could see him posing for a Christmas photo with his family, serving meals to veterans, signing legislation, and smiling with his arm wrapped around Vice President Biden's shoulder.[69]

Obama's opponents, however, knew how to deploy the web and social media too. Just as they did during the 2008 campaign, conservatives portrayed the president as extreme, dangerous, and un-American. They posted conspiracy theories that Obama was friendly with terrorists and practiced socialism. A false yet widespread rumor that Obama had studied at an Islamic seminary in Indonesia began as an anonymous blog post. In a fractured media environment where fewer people paid attention to mainstream news, the conspiracy theories gained traction. A *Time* magazine survey in 2010 found that nearly half of all Republicans believed Obama was a Muslim.[70]

The online venom against Obama resembled what some talk radio hosts were saying. "He has been conducting a civil war on America's institutions from the day he seized power," Michael Savage, the fifth-most popular radio show host in the country, said of Obama. Savage (whose real name is Michael Weiner) added the wild claim that Obama was intentionally infecting Americans with the Ebola virus and should therefore be called "Obola." Rick Wiles insisted on his TruNews radio show that Obama was a "Marxist Muslim jihadist in the White House, planted there many years ago for this very day to bring down the nation."[71]

In April 2013 forty-six radio hosts gathered in a hotel ballroom in the nation's capital. Separated by red velvet curtains, they aired their shows as part of the annual "Hold Their Feet to the Fire" event sponsored by the conservative Federation for American Immigration Reform. Their goal: denounce anyone—Democrat or Republican—who supported comprehensive immigration reform legislation being considered by Congress.[72] After Romney's defeat the previous year, some GOP leaders had decided they could win more Latinx votes by working with Democrats to pass immigration reform. A "Gang of Eight" senators—four Democrats and four Republicans—hammered together a bipartisan bill that would strengthen border security and create a path to citizenship for eleven million undocumented immigrants. Obama backed it. So did George W. Bush, John McCain, and other GOP leaders. But the Tea Partiers didn't. Talk radio, conservative websites, and Fox commentators led the charge against the bill, predicting waves of migrants from Mexico and Central America would overrun the country if the bill passed.[73]

To attract bigger audiences, each host tried to outdo the other with alarmism. Moderate Republicans who backed the immigration legislation were derided as RINOs—"Republicans in name only." Mark Levin, the nation's seventh-most popular radio host, called the bill a "disgusting disgrace" that would lead to more crime.[74] Laura Ingraham said on her radio show that Republicans who supported the immigration bill "are in violation of their oath of office."[75] Anyone who supported the immigration reform bill was prepared "to sell out the country," conservative commentator Ann Coulter said. GOP representatives realized that cooperating with Democrats would provoke the wrath of conservative voters in upcoming primary elections. Republican support for the bill withered, and it died in the House of Representatives.[76] Thanks to right-wing media, any GOP politician who attempted compromise risked political suicide.

Breitbart.com was one of the loudest voices against the immigration bill. Latinx immigrants were raping, pillaging, and drug-dealing their way across the United States because of the corrupt policies of Obama and other liberals, *Breitbart*'s readers were told.[77] The website was founded by Andrew Breitbart, a Los Angeles native with a ruddy face and piercing blue eyes. Breitbart was drifting after college until he started listening to Limbaugh and other radio hosts. He worked on conservative websites such as the *Drudge Report* before launching *Breitbart News* in 2007. Sometimes funny and often vicious, he ardently supported the Tea Party and attacked liberals without remorse. He said Obama's election was a putsch by Democrats. When Democratic Senator Edward Kennedy died, Breitbart called him "a special pile of human excrement." Breitbart eagerly mocked the mainstream press.

"It's not your business model that sucks," he told journalists. "It's you that sucks."[78]

At first most of the journalism world didn't take Breitbart seriously. "He's become known as the guy who yells at people in the halls," said one media critic. "And his sites have little impact."[79] That was wishful thinking because Breitbart excelled at figuring out what material attracted attention. He showed his power when he pushed a false story that Shirley Sherrod, a Black official in Obama's Agriculture Department, had disparaged white farmers in a speech. The Agriculture Department fired Sherrod only to learn her comments had been taken out of context and she really said the opposite of what Breitbart claimed. More than anyone, *New York Times* media critic David Carr observed, Breitbart "turned the Web into an assault rifle."[80]

After Breitbart died in 2012 of a heart attack at age forty-three,[81] Steve Bannon—a former investment banker and movie maker with a fondness for sloppy clothes and white nationalists—took charge of the site. With $10 million in funding from the billionaire Mercer family, *Breitbart* grew in popularity. In addition to Obama, journalists, and immigrants, its favorite targets included Muslims and gay people. Along the way, it became less concerned with verifying what it published as long as it fit Bannon's nationalist narrative. "Truth and veracity weren't his top priority," former *Breitbart* writer Ben Shapiro recalled.[82] It was an attitude that would soon become increasingly common in right-wing media.

One of *Breitbart*'s biggest fans was real-estate developer and reality TV host Donald Trump. Its take-no-prisoners style and focus on hostility toward Mexican and Muslim immigrants proved a good fit for Trump's personality. Known for his glitzy buildings and bankrupt casinos, Trump had flirted with a presidential run against Obama in 2012.[83] He pushed himself into the political discussion by promoting a bogus conspiracy theory that the president had been born in Kenya, not Hawaii, and thus wasn't really American. This "birther" lie against Obama took root within right-wing media, which was eager to spread racist innuendo and outright dishonesty about America's first Black president. *Breitbart* helped spread it as did Limbaugh, the *National Review*, and Fox's Hannity, Beck, and Lou Dobbs. They questioned Obama's citizenship even though he'd already posted a copy of his Hawaiian birth certificate on his website and independent experts had verified its authenticity.[84]

It wasn't just right-wing media that allowed Trump to propagate the birther conspiracy. Mainstream media was complicit too. On *Good Morning America*, Trump said he was a "little skeptical" that Obama was really born in Hawaii. He said something similar on NBC's *Today Show*. "I want him to show his birth certificate," he said on *The View*. "There's something on that birth certificate that he doesn't like." In a taste of things to come, Trump used Twitter to say he had an "extremely credible source" that Obama's birth certificate was a fake. Even though Trump never produced a shred of evidence to support his birther claims, the media continued to cover Trump's false allegations.[85] After all, it was good for ratings.

Obama tried to ignore Trump and the other conspiracists but eventually decided he had to respond. At a news briefing in April 2011, he produced a longform copy of his birth certificate that he had requested from the state of Hawaii to erase any doubts. No other president had ever been forced to do anything similar. That week Congress was considering a budget plan with major repercussions for all Americans, but Obama noted that "the dominant news story wasn't about these huge, monumental choices that we're going to have to make as a nation. It was about my birth certificate." Trump had won the media attention he wanted, and his lie about the president had seeped into the national consciousness. One study found that 94 percent of Americans had heard of the birther conspiracy and nearly a quarter thought it was true.[86]

Obama was ready to put Trump in his place. Three nights after sharing his longform birth certificate, Obama roasted him at the annual White House Correspondents' Association Dinner. Trump was there as a guest of the *Washington Post*, sitting among celebrities, politicians, and luminaries of the media world when Obama began skewering him. "Now I know that he's taken some flak lately, but no one is happier, no one is prouder, to put this birth certificate matter to rest than the Donald," Obama said as the audience chuckled. "And that's because he finally can get back to focusing on the issues that matter. Like did we fake the moon landing."

Trump wasn't smiling as the audience clapped and roared with laughter. "All kidding aside, obviously we all know about your credentials and breadth of experience," Obama continued sarcastically. The president then made fun of Trump's show, *Celebrity Apprentice*, and his choice of which B-list actor to fire in a recent episode. "And these are the kind of decisions that would keep me up at night," Obama added as the audience applauded and laughed. Trump stared straight ahead looking humiliated.[87]

Afterward, most in the media believed that Trump's political dreams had been thoroughly shredded that night. He had been ridiculed. He was embarrassed. And he would get revenge.

10 Donald Trump and the Art of the Lie

Alex Jones was waving his hands around his face and speaking with manic excitement in the Austin, Texas, studio of his *InfoWars* radio and internet video show. His guest that December day in 2015 was one of his heroes, Republican presidential candidate Donald Trump. The production quality was low. The same cheap graphic kept playing behind Jones, and Trump's face appeared washed out because of poor lighting. But the GOP candidate looked happy to be interviewed by the country's leading conspiracy theorist. Jones's *InfoWars* was attracting ten million unique visitors a month, more than mainstream sites such as *Newsweek* and *The Economist*.

Jones's falsehoods were epic. Over the years he had said that the Apollo moon landing was fake, the U.S. government had plotted the 1995 Oklahoma City bombing and the 9/11 attacks, and the Sandy Hook massacre of schoolchildren was a hoax. He told anti-Semitic tales about the "Jewish mafia," which was one reason the Southern Poverty Law Center labeled him a dangerous extremist. Jones's conspiracy theories had netted him a fortune. His radio show was syndicated on more than one hundred stations, and his website was used to hawk precious metals, dietary supplements, and survivalist gear.[1]

Trump was a perfect match for Jones. He too was an expert liar, a wizard at using media to attract large audiences, and a super-spreader of conspiracy theories: that Obama wasn't born in the United States and had won the 2012 election unfairly, that vaccines cause autism, and that China invented the concept of global warming to hurt American manufacturing. Trump got some of his most absurd claims from *InfoWars*.[2]

Jones began the interview by praising Trump. "He is a maverick," Jones said in his gravelly voice. "He's an original. He tells it like it is." Jones called Trump "self-made," ignoring the fact that the real estate developer had inherited hundreds of millions of dollars from his father. Jones also supported Trump's bogus claim that "radical Muslims" in New York and New Jersey cheered as the World Trade Center towers burned during the 9/11 attack. Jones falsely said that Turkey and Germany were making a deal to bring in "millions of radical Islamists." Trump was on "a dangerous mission," Jones added, assuring the candidate that "90 percent" of the *InfoWars* audience supported him.

Trump returned the love. "Your reputation is amazing," Trump told Jones. "I will not let you down."[3] And he didn't. On the campaign trail, Trump repeated some of Jones's wildest claims, sometimes word for word, such as GOP primary opponent Ted Cruz's father being connected to the assassination of John F. Kennedy and Democratic nominee Hillary Clinton being a cofounder of the violent Islamic group ISIS. Jones, for his part, ratcheted up the awful right-wing conspiracy theory produced more than two decades earlier that the Clintons had killed their friend Vince Foster. Jones told his millions of followers that Clinton was "one of the most vicious serial killers the planet has ever seen" who had "personally murdered, and chopped up, and raped" children.[4]

The mainstream press scolded Trump for appearing on Jones's show, but the candidate knew exactly what he was doing. *InfoWars* fans were the type of disaffected Americans who Trump was trying to attract to his campaign. "I think Alex Jones may be the single most important voice in the alternative conservative media," said Roger Stone, a former Nixon campaign operative, Trump adviser, and self-described dirty trickster, who set up the interview.[5]

Political conspiracy theories have percolated through the U.S. press since its beginning. Newspapers falsely accused John Adams of wanting to become king, Woodrow Wilson of killing his first wife, Franklin Roosevelt of being a communist, and the Clintons of killing Vince Foster. Now, thanks to the wonders of mass media and the digital age, Jones and Trump were able to instantly share their whacky yet dangerous theories with millions of people. After Trump won the 2016 election, the ideas of people like Jones that once floated on the fringes of the media entered the White House. Disseminating disinformation (the intentional spreading of false or misleading information)[6] and accusing journalists of plotting against the American people were at the heart of Trump's political strategy.

Unlike Obama's cool aloofness toward journalists, Trump was pure fire, torching the norms of presidential conduct. Trump's presidency was in many ways the presidency of Alex Jones, Rush Limbaugh, Steve Bannon, Fox News commentators, and other right-wing media stars whose belligerent partisanship had been unleashed since the Fairness Doctrine's destruction under Reagan and the rise of the internet and cable television. In contrast, journalists trained in the objective style of the twentieth century—with its emphasis on verification, balance, and neutrality—struggled to adequately cover the Trump phenomenon.[7] Despite instances of powerful and brave reporting, it was often unclear if the press could act as an effective watchdog for democracy as Trump and the nation experienced crisis after crisis: a special counsel investigation of whether Trump's campaign conspired with Russia and the president obstructed justice; Trump's impeachment for using military aid to Ukraine for his own political purpose; the coronavirus pandemic; uprisings across America over racial injustice; devastating natural disasters because of climate change; and a second Trump impeachment for inciting an insurrection against Congress. The growing power of disinformation spread through the media intensified each of these crises.

A genius at self-promotion, Trump eagerly courted the media during his rise to fame as a New York real estate developer. His marriages, divorces, night clubbing, and business feuds provided a feast of juicy items for gossip columnists, celebrity magazines, and tabloid TV shows. Trump himself eagerly fed them the material they craved, pretending to be a public relations agent named "John Barron." He frequently exaggerated or completely made things up. His Trump Tower, for instance, was advertised as having sixty-eight floors. It only had fifty-eight. Trump made a big splash in 1989 when he took out full-page advertisements in four New York newspapers calling for the return of the death penalty in the case of five Black and Latino teens accused of raping a white jogger. DNA evidence cleared the teens, but Trump never admitted he was wrong or apologized.[8]

Even though Trump's businesses went in and out of bankruptcy, he became a favorite character for movies and TV shows that needed an instantly recognizable symbol of wealth. He played himself on television shows such as *Days of Our Lives*, *The Fresh Prince of Bel-Air*, *Spin City*, and *Sex and the City* and in movies including *Home Alone 2*. Trump's fame skyrocketed when NBC made him the centerpiece of *The Apprentice* starting in 2004. It was supposed to be a reality show, but it was built on the fiction that Trump was a successful businessman. In actuality, Trump's core businesses lost nearly $90 million the previous year. Every episode, however, featured Trump in sleek limousines and plush boardrooms. *The Apprentice* ran for fourteen seasons, attracting twenty million viewers a week at its peak.[9]

Starting in 2011, the *Fox & Friends* morning show aired a "Mondays with Trump" segment every week. He recapped the previous week's *Apprentice* episode and shared his political observations with the Fox News audience. Trump spread his racist "birther" conspiracy theory against Obama on the show, claiming Obama's "family doesn't even know what hospital he was born in!" It wasn't true, but Fox's viewers didn't know that. Trump realized he could lie on television with impunity.[10]

When Trump announced he was running for president in June of 2015, most of the mainstream press treated his candidacy more as comic entertainment than as a realistic bid to win the White House. His casinos had failed, Trump Shuttle had failed, Trump Steaks had failed, Trump University had failed, *Trump Magazine* had failed, and Trump Vodka had failed, so it was hard for journalists to believe that Trump the Candidate would succeed.[11] But he understood television, he grasped the power of social media, and he tapped into the frustrations of people who didn't think political and media elites served their interests.

Trump had already mastered Twitter, attracting more than four million followers and averaging a dozen tweets a day by 2015. He'd have his staff print copies of his most popular tweets, which he examined to determine what content worked best. He saw that the most incendiary tweets got the most retweets. Subjects like immigration that aroused anger were sure-fire winners. Even more than radio for FDR and TV for JFK, who needed the networks to approve their requests for airtime, Trump could deploy Twitter to reach the public directly, bypassing the gatekeepers of the press.[12]

Throughout the campaign, Trump used *Breitbart* as one of his main news sources, absorbing its nationalist, anti-immigrant message. With Bannon's encouragement, one of Trump's first trips as a candidate was to the Texas-Mexico border, where he railed against illegal immigration. It worked. By the end of his Texas trip, Trump was ahead of the sixteen other Republican candidates in polls of GOP primary voters. When Trump's campaign was in the doldrums after he captured the Republican nomination, he made Bannon its chairman. "Darkness is good," Bannon counseled Trump during the campaign. "Don't let up."[13]

In one of his earlier careers, Bannon had invested in multiplayer online games such as *World of Warcraft*. He saw that message boards related to online gaming were attracting a stunning 1.5 billion page views each month. Bannon realized he could attract these gamers to *Breitbart* and the Reddit, 4chan, and 8chan message boards, whose loose rules made them homes of the growing alt-right, white nationalist movement. "These guys, these rootless white males, had monster power," Bannon told journalist Joshua Green. They used their firepower for Trump, spreading memes that glorified him, conspiracy theories aimed at Clinton, and violent and often anti-Semitic threats targeting journalists they didn't like.[14]

Trump's campaign milked conspiracy theories for all they were worth. His surrogates spread a rumor that Clinton was dying of a severe illness. Political adviser Roger Stone falsely told people that Clinton had been carried off stage with an oxygen mask after her first debate with Trump. Other stories circulated that 20 percent of the money for Clinton's campaign came from the Saudi royal family and that Republican rival Jeb Bush had "close Nazi ties."[15] Journalists and Trump's opponents didn't know what to do. If they responded, they just gave the conspiracy theories more attention. If they tried to ignore them, the disinformation spread unanswered.[16]

Edgar Maddison Welch, a twenty-six-year-old North Carolina man, didn't ignore the conspiracy theories. In December 2016 he drove to Washington DC, stopped at a pizza parlor named Comet Ping Pong, and fired an AR-15 assault-style rifle inside. His reason? He'd seen posts on social media claiming Comet Ping Pong had a basement dungeon filled with children who had been kidnapped as part of a sex trafficking ring tied to Hillary Clinton, and he was there to free them. Welch didn't find any captured children there. In fact, Comet Ping Pong didn't even have a basement, but that hadn't stopped the "Pizzagate" conspiracy theory from metastasizing on right-wing media such as *InfoWars* and One America News Network, a cable channel launched in 2013. Nearly half of all Trump supporters, according to opinion polls, believed there was some truth behind Pizzagate.[17] Four years later, a majority of Trump's backers would believe in an even bigger conspiracy.

WorldPoliticus.com had a big scoop in 2016 that spread through Facebook: Hillary Clinton was going to be indicted for crimes related to an email scandal. The story received more than 140,000 shares, comments, and reactions. But Clinton wasn't being indicted. *BuzzFeed* reporters discovered that WorldPoliticus.com was run by a young man in Macedonia. His phony site was one of at least 140 run by young people in a small Macedonian town. They raked in Facebook advertising dollars by posting sensational stories appealing to Trump supporters.[18]

The algorithms used by social media companies favored these types of controversial posts, making it easy for disinformation and divisive content from hucksters, partisan trolls, and hostile foreign governments to go viral. A Knight Foundation study found more than 6.6 million tweets during the month before the 2016 election linked to conspiracy and fake news sites. During the three months prior to the election, the twenty most popular false stories on social media were shared more often than the twenty most popular stories based on fact-checked reporting.[19]

Social media intensified political polarization. Users tended to cluster in homogenized groups and share posts that reinforced their existing views, ignoring those that came from opposing perspectives. A study by Harvard and MIT researchers of 1.25 million stories shared online through Twitter and Facebook before the 2016 election found that *Breitbart* was at the heart of a right-wing media ecosystem that included Fox News, *InfoWars*, and *Gateway Pundit*. The hardcore left had its own sites, but they linked more often to mainstream news media.[20]

Fox News gave Trump almost constant coverage for most of the campaign, broadcasting his rallies from start to finish. So did CNN. Trump's outrageous statements played particularly well on cable news channels, which were always looking for new controversies to boost ratings and profits. Sometimes CNN just showed an empty lectern before a rally as a chyron promised "DONALD TRUMP EXPECTED TO SPEAK ANY MINUTE."[21] During one stretch of the primary season, he received nearly three times more media attention than Clinton even though she was locked in her own primary battle. Overall, Trump received an estimated $5.6 billion worth of free media publicity for his presidential run.[22] His rallies were spectacles, his speeches were unpredictable, and the GOP debates were like gladiator fights. "It may not be good for America, but it's damn good for CBS," the network's CEO, Les Moonves, said in early 2016. "The money's rolling in and this is fun . . . this is going to be a very good year for us . . . bring it on, Donald. Keep going."[23]

Despite the free publicity, Trump complained about his media coverage and looked for ways to damage the press. Like Nixon before him, he found the media to be a useful enemy. CBS reporter Lesley Stahl asked Trump why he persistently attacked the press. "You know why I do it?" Trump responded. "I do it to discredit you all and demean you all, so when you write negative stories about me no one will believe you."[24] At various times Trump's campaign blocked the *Des Moines Register, Politico,* Univision, *Huffington Post,* and *Daily Beast* from covering him because he didn't like one or more of their stories. Trump specifically targeted the *Washington Post,* which was investigating him intensely. "If I become president, oh, do they have problems," he promised, using language eerily similar to Nixon's during the height of Watergate, except Nixon made his threats in private while Trump made his publicly.[25]

Trump triumphed in 2016, enjoying one of the greatest presidential election upsets in U.S. history. Clinton won 2.9 million more votes, but Trump led by a combined 79,646 in Michigan, Pennsylvania, and Wisconsin, giving him an Electoral College victory of 304 to 227. Much of the mainstream press was in shock. "Can't believe what I'm seeing," one reporter told Bannon. On MSNBC, the anchors seemed nearly speechless. In the *InfoWars* studio, Alex Jones and Roger Stone drank champagne together.[26]

Any illusions Trump would have a functional relationship with the press were smashed the day after his inauguration. He gave a speech at CIA headquarters where he bragged about the size of his inauguration crowd. He then pointed to the reporters in the back and said, "They are among the most dishonest human beings on Earth."[27] Press Secretary Sean Spicer continued the theme that evening at his first briefing. Looking agitated, he berated journalists for reporting that fewer people attended Trump's inauguration than Obama's. "This was the largest audience to ever witness an inauguration, period—both in person and around the globe," Spicer insisted. Shaking his finger at the White House press corps, he called the reporting on the inauguration "shameful and wrong." A quick look at photographs of the two events and ridership data for DC's Metro system made clear he was mistaken. Spicer ended his first briefing by refusing to take questions and leaving the room as quickly as possible.[28]

Spicer's tirade against the press was part of a broader Trump strategy, journalist Ezra Klein wrote in *Vox*. The exact size of Trump's inaugural crowd wasn't important. But it was important that Trump and Spicer insisted on lying about it and lashing out against anyone who disagreed. "The Trump administration is creating a baseline expectation among its loyalists that they can't trust anything said by the media," Klein observed.[29] That weekend top Trump aide Kellyanne Conway told NBC's Chuck Todd he was being "overly dramatic" to challenge Spicer's blatant disregard for accuracy. Spicer was simply giving "alternative facts," she said. Those "alternative facts" would come to symbolize the Trump administration's relationship with the truth.[30]

Trump wasn't the first president to lie, of course. Johnson lied about the Vietnam War. Nixon lied about Watergate. Reagan exaggerated about people on welfare. Clinton lied about sex. Other presidents avoided questions and spun the news to try to make themselves look good, but they usually did what they could to avoid accusations of outright dishonesty. Not Trump, who took presidential lying to a whole new level. By the end of his presidency, he had made more than 30,000 false or misleading statements, according to the *Washington Post*'s Fact Checker team. His lies reached a peak of 503 the day before the 2020 election.[31] It was a pernicious effort to overwhelm the factual basis of reality necessary for democracy to function.

At first, most journalists didn't know how to handle Trump's contempt for the truth and fretted about calling his statements falsehoods. Reporters for mainstream news outlets had been trained not to call people liars because it was nearly impossible to know someone's intent when they said something wrong. But Trump repeated mistruths even after he had been corrected, and eventually the falsehoods became too many and too blatant to ignore. Toward the end of the 2016 campaign, the *New York Times* took the significant step of labeling Trump's bogus claims as lies. His false statements became so common that CNN and MSNBC added fact-checking chyrons on the bottom of the screen when he and Vice President Mike Pence spoke. "PENCE DENIES TRUMP SAID THINGS HE SAID," one of them read.[32]

Trump's lies often hinted at dark yet unproven conspiracies against him. "A lot of people are saying," Trump would suggest as if that equaled some sort of proof.[33] In addition to calling news "fake," he repeatedly accused journalists of committing treason.[34] He suggested that the Justice Department—led by people he appointed—was engaged in a "coup" against him. "No president—indeed, no national official—has resorted to accusations of conspiracy so instinctively, so frequently, and with such brio as Donald Trump," Russell Muirhead and Nancy L. Rosenblum noted in their book *A Lot of People Are Saying: The New Conspiracism and the Assault on Democracy*.[35]

Trump's favorite tool for spreading conspiracy theories and attacking the press was Twitter. He could say whatever he wanted, no matter how outrageous, to his more than eighty million followers without having it edited by the press.[36] In February 2017 he tweeted, "The FAKE NEWS media (failing @nytimes, @NBCNews, @ABC, @CBS, @CNN) is not my enemy, it is the enemy of the American People!" Trump's use of "enemy of the people" had an ugly history. Robespierre used it during the French Revolution's reign of terror to justify chopping off the heads of those who disagreed with him. The Nazis, Lenin, Stalin, and Mao used it too.[37] Trump's repeated use of the phrase to describe the press— twenty-one times on Twitter in 2019 alone—influenced his supporters. One third of respondents, including 51 percent of Republicans, agreed in a 2019 poll that the media are "the enemy of the people."[38]

Any journalist who challenged Trump was likely to be insulted or threatened in return. He attacked MSNBC host Mika Brzezinski as "low IQ Crazy Mika" who was "bleeding badly from a face-lift."[39]

Female reporters of color seemed to especially trigger Trump. When Abby Phillip of CNN asked him a reasonable question about whether he wanted to rein in the investigation of his campaign's ties to Russia, Trump grew irate. "What a stupid question that is. What a stupid question," Trump repeated himself, shaking his finger at Phillip. "But I watch you a lot, you ask a lot of stupid questions," he added before walking away from her.[40] He told Yamiche Alcindor of PBS to not ask "threatening" questions. He called April Ryan of the American Urban Radio Networks "a loser" and "nasty." He also used "nasty" to describe a question by CBS's Weijia Jiang.[41]

A week after a gunman killed five employees of the *Capital Gazette* newspaper in Annapolis, Maryland, in June 2018, Trump went to Montana for a rally to incite more hatred against the press. Journalists are "bad people" he declared as the packed crowd cheered and laughed. "They're so damn dishonest," he said, pointing to the reporters kept in a pen at the back of the room. "I don't mean all of them, because some of the finest people I know are journalists. Really. Hard to believe when I say that. I hate to say it, but I have to say. But 75 percent of those people are downright dishonest. Downright dishonest. They're fake!"[42]

"Fake news" was Trump's favorite way to describe reporting he didn't like, using the term 273 times in 2019 alone.[43] Emboldened authoritarian rulers in other countries copied his rhetoric as part of crackdowns on journalists in their own countries. More than fifty foreign leaders including Nicolás Maduro of Venezuela, Rodrigo Duterte of the Philippines, and Recep Tayyip Erdogan in Turkey used allegations of "fake news" to justify anti-press actions. At least 250 journalists were jailed around the world by the end of 2019; more than 30 of them were accused of producing "fake news."[44] Saudi Arabia's crown prince, Mohammed bin Salman, approved the murder of *Washington Post* columnist Jamal Khashoggi. Trump continued to pursue a cozy relationship with bin Salman and called him a good ally.[45]

In Trump's world, violence against journalism was celebrated. He retweeted a doctored image of him pummeling someone whose face was replaced by a CNN logo.[46] After a Montana congressional candidate slammed a journalist to the ground, Trump said any "guy that can do a body slam, he's my guy."[47] As Trump's verbal assaults against journalists increased, so did the frequency of violent threats against them. "You're the enemy of the people, and we're going to kill every fucking one of you," a California man told the *Boston Globe*; police later found twenty guns in his house. The Los Angeles bureau of the Associated Press received a similar menacing message. MSNBC anchor Katy Tur received a death threat with "MAGA" (the initials of Trump's Make America Great Again slogan) at the end of it. When inoperable pipe bombs were sent to CNN's New York office, a man called its Atlanta headquarters to warn, "I'm going to gun you down." A Coast Guard lieutenant was caught stockpiling weapons to use against CNN and MSNBC employees. *Chicago Tribune* columnist Rex Huppke was told, "You're going to look awfully stupid trying to keyboard with two broken arms."[48] The threats weren't empty words. At least twenty-four U.S. journalists were attacked physically in 2018.[49]

In some ways, Trump's political agenda was similar to those of Ronald Reagan, George W. Bush, and other Republican presidents before him. He boosted military spending. He slashed environmental regulations. He got a big tax cut through Congress that mostly benefited corporations and the wealthy. And he worked with Republicans in the Senate to approve more than 225 conservative federal judges, including Supreme Court justices Neil Gorsuch, Brett Kavanaugh, and Amy Coney Barrett.[50]

But despite Republicans holding both houses of Congress during his first two years in office, he failed to fulfill many of his campaign pledges. His vow to repeal Obamacare fizzled once it became clear the GOP had no alternative to offer. Instead of eliminating the national debt, it soared to more than $27 trillion. Trump's pledge to rebuild America's infrastructure went nowhere. And he couldn't get Mexico to pay for his biggest campaign promise of all, to build a massive border wall. His ban on travel from seven countries with Muslim majorities, policies separating immigrant children from their parents and putting them in cages, and other controversial actions and statements led to widespread protests and contributed to negative news coverage.[51]

Constant White House chaos didn't help. During Trump's term, he cycled through four chiefs of staff, five deputy chiefs of staff, four national security advisers, and six communications directors. The turnover rate among his cabinet members and top aides was higher than for any president since at least Reagan.[52] The disarray included his press office; Trump switched press secretaries once per year on average. Under other presidents, press secretaries had sparred with reporters, spun the news, and sometimes avoided the truth, but they fulfilled their basic job of providing information that reporters could convey to the public. Even Ron Ziegler, Nixon's press secretary, apologized when evidence showed his previous statements about Watergate were wrong. But in Trump's White House, press secretaries served a completely different purpose: to show disdain and hostility toward the press in a way that pleased their boss. The truth was a casualty. "Spicer was the first White House press secretary I encountered who habitually said things that were simply untrue," wrote ABC's Jonathan Karl, who had worked with a dozen previous press secretaries.[53]

As the administration's tensions with the press grew, the number of formal briefings dwindled. Trump's second press secretary, Sarah Huckabee Sanders, didn't hold any briefings during her last three months on the job. Following Sanders's precedent, press secretary #3, Stephanie Grisham, didn't give any briefings during her nine months in charge of the press office. Grisham said it was Trump's decision that she shouldn't hold briefings. "He's so accessible, so right now I think that that's good enough," she said.[54]

After 417 days without a White House press secretary giving an official briefing, press secretary #4, Kayleigh McEnany, held her first one on May 1, 2020. "I will never lie to you," she promised. She then lied. She claimed Special Counsel Robert Mueller's report gave Trump a "complete and total exoneration." She gave inflated numbers for the cost of Mueller's investigation. She misquoted an FBI agent's comments about former national security adviser Michael Flynn. She even got one of Trump's tweets wrong.[55] After that first briefing, McEnany's performance further deteriorated as she avoided answering basic questions, denied things that Trump had said, and frequently insulted reporters. She gave only forty-one formal press briefings while appearing as a guest on Fox News weekday shows more than ninety times (and no appearances on CNN or MSNBC).[56]

Trump's battles with the press included trying to limit which reporters could cover him. His administration restricted *New York Times*, *Los Angeles Times*, *BuzzFeed*, *Politico*, and *Washington Post* journalists from reporting at the White House at various times.[57] During one highly contentious news conference in 2018, CNN reporter Jim Acosta repeatedly insisted on asking Trump a follow-up question and held on to the microphone as an intern tried to grab it away. Trump called Acosta "a rude, terrible person" and CNN an "enemy of the people." The administration revoked Acosta's White House press credentials. Trump's Justice Department argued that "no journalist has a First Amendment right to enter the White House," meaning presidents could pick and choose who got to cover them doing the people's business. CNN sued. Nine days later a U.S. district court judge ruled that the White House had violated Acosta's constitutional rights and should immediately restore his press pass.[58]

The administration found other ways to block reporters from doing their jobs. Official schedules, White House visitor logs, and information on climate change, Obamacare, domestic violence, and LGBTQ issues disappeared from the government's websites. Response times to Freedom of Information Act requests, already sluggish under Obama and Bush, became slower. The number of FOIA lawsuits filed in federal courts to get the government to release information reached eighty per month by the last months of Trump's term, more than double the rate at the end of Obama's presidency.[59]

The effort to suppress information included pursuing whistleblowers with greater zeal than did Obama. In fewer than three years, the Trump administration indicted nine people for disseminating or publishing leaks, six times using the Espionage Act. A National Security Administration contractor was sentenced to more than five years in prison for sharing information about Russian interference in the 2016 election. An FBI agent, a CIA software engineer, a former Senate staffer, and Treasury Department, IRS, and Defense Intelligence Agency analysts were prosecuted for leaking to the press.[60]

Ironically, many of the leaks denounced by Trump came from his own staff. Intense internal rivalries contributed to more leaks from his administration than any other that the Washington press corps could remember. "Everyone is trying to undermine each other," *Washington Post* editor Marty Baron observed. There were leaks about drafts of executive orders, administration strategy, and Trump's phone calls with foreign leaders.[61] Bannon and Conway were two of the biggest culprits. It got so bad that National Security Adviser H. R. McMaster distributed a memo on the importance of guarding against leaks. His memo was promptly leaked to *BuzzFeed*, which published the whole thing.[62]

The so-called invaders were heading toward the United States, dangerous people who would bring crime and disease. At least that was the big news on Fox News and conservative talk radio in the fall of 2018 as a caravan of hungry men, women, and children from Central American headed through Mexico toward the United States. The fears were similar to the ones spread by Federalist newspapers about French and Irish immigrants in the late 1790s and by some politicians and media outlets through the years against each new wave of people arriving in the United States. "This is a foreign invasion, whether they're armed or not," Rush Limbaugh warned. "Some of them, no doubt, are."[63] The drumbeat of dread was orchestrated to motivate Trump's conservative base as the midterm elections approached. It didn't work. Democrats gained forty congressional seats, enough to regain control of the House, a shift that would cause trouble for Trump the following year.[64]

In some ways the media during Trump's presidency resembled the bitterly partisan press at the nation's founding. John Adams enjoyed the unabashed support of the *Gazette of the United States* and other Federalist newspapers, while Thomas Jefferson was wholeheartedly backed by the *Aurora*. Trump enjoyed similar support from Fox News, the Sinclair Broadcast Group, Limbaugh, Jones, *Breitbart*, and an army of other talk radio and social media partisans. They regularly told their fans that most journalists were a bunch of unpatriotic liars. Sean Hannity of Fox joined Trump on stage for a rally ahead of the 2018 midterms. To cheers from the crowd, Hannity pointed to the reporters covering the rally and taunted, "By the way, all those people in the back are fake news."[65] On the left, MSNBC added conservative commentators at the start of Trump's term for greater balance, but hardcore liberal hosts such as Rachel Maddow and Chris Hayes were the ones whose ratings soared. Most of the conservatives were eventually booted.[66] Compromise wasn't good for business; outrage was.

Trump was an avid Fox News viewer. He had the White House furnished with multiple TVs and DVRs so he could watch at all hours. He once bragged that in a single night he watched Lou Dobbs and Elizabeth MacDonald of Fox Business Network, and Hannity, Tucker Carlson, and Laura Ingraham of Fox News. Then Trump watched *Fox & Friends* the next morning.[67] The president regularly tweeted about what had just appeared on Fox, whether it was true or not. For example, soon after it ran an incorrect story that South Africa was taking land from white farmers, Trump repeated it on Twitter. In 2019 he tweeted about content on Fox shows at least 657 times. In contrast, he tweeted about content on other networks 24 times.[68]

Trump depended on conservative media, and they depended on their most loyal audience members, who were staunchly right wing, especially about immigration. When Trump agreed in December 2018 to a budget compromise to keep the government open through the holidays, conservative media pounced because the deal didn't include $5.7 billion for a wall on the Mexican border. Trump should risk a government shutdown, they argued, rather than sign a spending plan without the extra wall money. "NO WALL = SHUT IT DOWN," Pete Hegseth of Fox News tweeted. Trump wilted under the pressure, telling Limbaugh he wouldn't accept the budget compromise after all.[69]

As a result, the government shut down on December 21, leaving its workers without pay right before Christmas. Conservative commentators rejoiced. "Mr. President," Jeanine Pirro said on Fox News, "I understand the pressure that you are under from every side, but the wall at our southern border is a promise that you made, ran on, got elected on, and must keep." But Trump made a huge mistake by listening to the right-wing commentators. The shutdown, the longest in history, was wildly unpopular. His job approval ratings in the Gallup poll fell to 37 percent, tied for the lowest of his presidency. Trump retreated, agreeing to a compromise on January 25 that didn't include the amount he wanted for the wall.[70]

In a White House marked by constant turmoil, Fox's opinions filled a policy-making void, Jane Mayer of the *New Yorker* observed. Fox founder Rupert Murdoch spoke regularly with Trump and the president's son-in-law, Jared Kushner. Hegseth and Dobbs participated in White House meetings. Hannity was nicknamed Trump's "shadow chief of staff" for the advice he gave the president during phone calls at all hours of the day.[71] Fox commentators took top positions in the administration: Ben Carson as secretary of housing and urban development, John Bolton as national security adviser, and K. T. McFarland as deputy national security adviser. When Sanders resigned as press secretary, she accepted a more lucrative job at Fox. So did Hope Hicks, one of Trump's closest aides. Fox Business host Anthony Scaramucci became Trump's communications director for ten tumultuous days and was then fired after a *New Yorker* reporter quoted him giving an obscenity-filled rant about White House colleagues.[72] The former co-president of Fox News, Bill Shine, became Trump's new communications director and deputy chief of staff. Shine continued to get paid by Fox—$3.5 million in both 2018 and 2019—even after he joined the administration. By the end of Trump's term, nearly two dozen people went through the revolving door between Fox and the White House. "It's the closest we've come to having state TV," historian Nicole Hemmer told journalist Jane Mayer.[73]

The close ties with Trump profited Fox. In 2018 the company proposed selling its entertainment divisions to Disney, creating a massive conglomerate that would receive about half of U.S. box office receipts. It was the type of deal that usually receives intense antitrust scrutiny, but the administration approved it without raising concerns. The Murdoch family made more than $2 billion from the transaction.[74]

Fox wasn't the only network favoring Trump. By the start of Trump's presidency, Sinclair was the largest U.S. owner of local TV stations, owning 173 of them in markets ranging from Washington DC to Sioux City, Iowa. Through much of Trump's first term, Sinclair required its local stations to run commentary by Boris Epshteyn, a former Trump aide. The company also ordered all of its anchorpeople to read a statement echoing Trump's criticism of journalists as being purveyors of fake news.[75] The websites of at least twenty Sinclair stations published almost identical stories promoting Trump campaign gear. "Donald Trump's re-election campaign has rolled out new hats as the President aims for another four-year term in 2020," the stories said. They included a link to the Trump campaign store and a photo of the hat.[76] For all of Trump's complaints about liberal press bias, he had powerful media friends on his side.

One of those friends was David Pecker, head of the company that owned the *National Enquirer* gossip tabloid. Three days before the 2016 election, the *Wall Street Journal* reported that Trump had made a secret deal with Pecker to pay $150,000 to former *Playboy* model Karen McDougal for the rights to a story that she had an affair with Trump. Pecker paid McDougal, and the *Enquirer* didn't publish the story in an arrangement known as "catch and kill." The *Journal* wasn't done investigating, however. In January 2018 it revealed that Trump attorney Michael Cohen had paid pornographic movie star Stephanie Clifford, known as Stormy Daniels, to stay quiet about Trump having sex with her soon after his wife, Melania, had given birth to their son. (Fox News reporter Diana Falzone had uncovered the payment to Daniels during the 2016 campaign, but Fox refused to run the story and demoted Falzone.)[77] Trump denied knowing about the $420,000 payment, but he could be heard discussing it in a recording later released by Cohen's lawyer.[78]

The Daniels story was just one example of relentless investigative reporting about Trump and his administration. During the 2016 campaign, the *Washington Post*'s David Fahrenthold reported that Trump used money people donated to his charitable foundation to buy a six-foot-tall portrait of himself and settle lawsuits against his businesses.[79] Less than three weeks later, Fahrenthold revealed a video of Trump lewdly bragging to *Access Hollywood* host Billy Bush about assaulting women.[80] Environmental Protection Agency Director Scott Pruitt resigned after the press disclosed he was engaged in extensive corruption. So did Interior Secretary Ryan Zinke and Health and Human Services Secretary Tom Price.[81] In October 2018 the *New York Times* published a deep investigation of Trump's finances. It disclosed that much of his wealth came from $413 million in today's dollars he inherited from his father and from fraudulent tax schemes.[82]

The first great crisis of Trump's presidency began after the *Washington Post*'s David Ignatius revealed eight days before the inauguration that Trump's incoming national security adviser, Michael Flynn, had talked several times with Russia's ambassador to the United States. Flynn then lied to the FBI and Vice President Mike Pence about the conversations. Trump pressured FBI Director James Comey to drop its probe of Flynn's actions. Trump also wanted Comey to announce that Trump was innocent of wrongdoing regarding Russian interference in the 2016 election. When Comey refused, Trump fired him. Suspicious of Trump's conflicting explanations for the firing, Deputy Attorney General Rod

Rosenstein named former FBI director Robert Mueller III as a special counsel to investigate ties between Trump's campaign and Russia.[83]

As Mueller got to work, the press published investigations at a pace not seen since the days of Watergate. The *Washington Post* disclosed that Trump had shared "highly classified information" with the Russian ambassador and foreign minister.[84] Reuters revealed that Flynn and others in Trump's camp made at least eighteen phone calls and emails to Russian officials during the last seven months of the campaign.[85] The *New York Times* reported that during the 2016 campaign Trump's son Donald Jr., son-in-law Jared Kushner, and campaign chairman Paul Manafort met with a Russian lawyer with Kremlin ties promising to provide dirt on Clinton.[86]

Mueller's team of prosecutors often pursued evidence the press uncovered. True to form, Trump aggressively attacked the investigations, tweeting they were part of a "hoax," "scam," and "WITCH HUNT!"[87] Conservative media helped him. On Fox News, Hannity ran 468 segments attacking the probe, labeling it a potential coup that was just "the tip of the iceberg" of a vast sinister plot hatched by Obama and "the deep state." Jeanine Pirro also painted the investigation as a giant conspiracy against Trump. Never in presidential history, she claimed, had there ever been "as great a crime or as large a stain on our democracy than that committed by a criminal cabal in our FBI and the Department of Justice who think they know better than we who our president should be."[88]

Trump and his media allies, however, couldn't stop the investigation. By the time Mueller's team was done, it had indicted thirty-four people. They included Flynn, former deputy campaign chairman Rick Gates, and campaign adviser George Papadopoulos, who all pleaded guilty. Within a head-spinning hour on August 21, 2018, Manafort was convicted by a jury in the Mueller probe, and Cohen pleaded guilty in the Stormy Daniels case, implicating Trump along the way. "All the President's Crooks" said a headline above a *New York Times* editorial that day, referencing Woodward and Bernstein's Watergate work.[89]

For any other president, having two top associates convicted of felonies and one of them accusing him of committing a crime would have been a knockout punch. But Trump had spent the last three years telling his loyalists not to believe the mainstream press, and the right-wing media made sure to divert attention to other matters. That afternoon Fox News featured a breaking news alert, but it wasn't about the guilt of Cohen and Manafort. Instead, it was about an immigrant accused of murdering an Iowa college student. *Breitbart*'s home page the next day featured three stories about the dangers of immigrants. Meanwhile, radio host Mark Levin declared: "Trump is in the clear."[90]

Trump was also protected by his loyal second attorney general, William Barr, who conducted a master class in how to spin the news. When Mueller finished his report in the spring of 2019, Barr didn't immediately release it. Instead, he issued his own misleading summary declaring that Trump had been cleared. Mueller's investigation didn't find evidence "sufficient to establish that the president committed an obstruction-of-justice offense," Barr wrote.[91] He then delayed releasing the actual report for twenty-five days. Once he finally made it public, the report showed how Russia "interfered in the 2016 presidential election in sweeping and systematic fashion." It said Trump and his campaign welcomed the foreign meddling and listed ten times that Trump might have illegally obstructed justice. Mueller's report stated that while it "does not conclude that the President committed a crime, it also does not exonerate him." But few people read through its 448 pages full of damning details.[92] Trump, his lawyers, and his media acolytes had already successfully constructed a narrative that Mueller cleared Trump of wrongdoing.

The press had ridden the "Russiagate" story hard. The *New York Times*, *Wall Street Journal*, *Washington Post*, *Mother Jones*, *ProPublica*, network newscasts, and other media outlets had already reported large portions of the evidence in the Mueller report. Numerous stories that Trump denounced as "fake news" proved to be true. But because the Mueller Report didn't explicitly say Trump was guilty of any crimes or contain any explosive new revelations, it made less of a splash than it would have if the press hadn't already revealed torrents of information about the allegations.[93] As Michael Schmidt observed in his book *Donald Trump v. The United States*, "It is a great irony that, as with so much else with the way that Trump operates, a cascading chaos dulls the senses, sows confusion, and has the effect of protecting him."[94]

More startling news about Trump emerged in the late summer of 2019. *Politico* reported that the administration had held up $250 million (later proven to be $391 million) in taxpayer-funded military aid Congress had approved to protect Ukraine against a Russian invasion.[95] The *Washington Post* followed up with an editorial denouncing the delay. "Some suspect Mr. Trump is once again catering to [Russian president Vladimir] Putin, who is dedicated to undermining Ukrainian democracy and independence," the *Post* editorial said.[96] According to a whistleblower, the president withheld the aid and delayed offering Ukrainian president Volodymyr Zelensky a coveted White House meeting to pressure him to give Trump dirt about former vice president Biden and his son Hunter. Trump feared Biden could defeat him in the 2020 election.[97]

After an intensive investigation and televised hearings, the House of Representatives passed two articles of impeachment against Trump on December 18, 2019: abuse of power for using the presidency and military spending for his own political purposes, and obstruction of Congress for refusing to release relevant documents and prohibiting White House officials from testifying.[98] He was the third president to ever be impeached.

All of the pro-impeachment votes came from Democrats, who built a thorough legal narrative based on testimony and documents, the kind of case that worked during Watergate. But while the Democrats played chess, the Republicans played rugby. They claimed that the impeachment probe was really a media-fueled hoax. GOP congresspeople repeatedly asked questions about unsubstantiated conspiracy theories regarding a "black ledger." None of it made much sense. Witnesses looked confused and stammered their answers to the bizarre questions, which was the whole point. The confusion made for good video that could easily be turned into viral Facebook posts, talk radio soundbites, and Fox News segments supporting Trump.

Stories attacking the impeachment witnesses circulated on *Breitbart* and other right-wing sites. On Facebook, conspiracy posts from Rush Limbaugh, Glenn Beck, and other conservative commentators outnumbered stories from mainstream publications.[99] After Lt. Col. Alexander Vindman, an Iraq War veteran with a Purple Heart, testified that he heard Trump try to pressure Ukraine to investigate Biden, Fox News's Laura Ingraham suggested Vindman might be a Ukrainian spy because he is an immigrant. QAnon, a group of rabid conspiracy theorists, quickly spread the lie about Vindman to 160,000 Twitter followers.[100]

Anyone who watched most of the hearings heard a cascade of evidence against Trump. But with all of the disinformation circulating through the media, it became difficult for people to follow the complex facts of the case involving a distant country that most Americans knew little about. They were sick of the partisan arguments and exhausted by the constant scandals. In contrast to Watergate, the Trump hearings failed to attract a mass TV audience. Fox News's primetime hosts scorned the ratings, as if those were the true measure of the case's seriousness. "If you're like most Americans, you didn't watch today's impeachment charade," Sean Hannity crowed after one of the hearings.[101]

But it was the Senate impeachment trial that was a charade. Only two Republicans, Mitt Romney of Utah and Susan Collins of Maine, voted with the Democrats to have witnesses testify. The other Republicans, who were the majority, didn't want to hear witnesses, not even Trump's former national security adviser John Bolton. The *New York Times* reported Bolton had written in his forthcoming book that Trump said he was freezing aide to Ukraine until the country investigated Biden. It would have strongly supported the impeachment case, but most Republicans didn't want to hear it.[102] On February 5, 2020, the

Senate voted 52–48 to acquit Trump on the abuse of power charge and 53–47 on the obstruction of Congress charge.[103]

The next day supporters gave Trump a standing ovation as he strode smiling into the White House East Room to the sounds of "Hail to the Chief." For more than an hour, he gave a rambling victory speech accusing Democrats of engaging in an "evil" and "corrupt" conspiracy. "It was all bullshit," the president told his cheering supporters.[104] After enduring the crisis of the impeachment trial, the Mueller probe, and constant investigations by the press, Trump was riding high. His job approval rating climbed to 49 percent in February, tied for the best of his presidency.[105] He was confident he would be reelected that November. And he was sure a deadly virus on which he had been briefed nine days earlier wouldn't get in his way.

11 Donald Trump and the Year of Crises

Trump sat down for a pre–Super Bowl interview on February 2, 2020, at his Mar-a-Lago estate in Florida. Answering questions from his friend Sean Hannity, the president repeated some of his favorite themes. The impeachment and Mueller investigation were a "witch hunt," "hoax," and "lies," he told the Fox News host. "The economy is the best in the history of the country," he insisted, which wasn't true. He made school-yard taunts against potential Democratic opponents in the upcoming presidential election: "Sleepy Joe" Biden, "Little" Michael Bloomberg, Elizabeth "Pocahontas" Warren, and "Crazy Bernie" Sanders.

Hannity then asked Trump about a deadly coronavirus that was spreading around the globe from China. "Disney is closed," Hannity said. "Movie theaters are closed. Hospitals being built. I think we are now up to our eighth case in the United States. How concerned are you?"

"Well, we pretty much shut it down coming in from China," Trump replied. Hannity didn't ask any follow-up questions. Instead, his next question was about the importance of sports.[1]

The coronavirus wasn't shut down, however, and Trump knew it. Five days before the Super Bowl interview with Hannity, National Security Adviser Robert O'Brien warned Trump that the virus was spreading rapidly and could ravage the United States. "This will be the biggest national security threat you face in your presidency," O'Brien told the president, according to Bob Woodward in his book *Rage*.[2] Trump didn't want to admit any vulnerability in an election year and decided to downplay the seriousness of the coronavirus disease, known as COVID-19. On February 27 he predicted the virus is "going to disappear."[3] At a rally in South Carolina the next evening, Trump said coronavirus concerns were a "hoax."[4] On March 11, he gave a primetime address from the Oval Office. "The virus will not have a chance against us," he tried to reassure Americans.[5]

But the news wasn't reassuring. The same day Trump delivered his Oval Office address, the World Health Organization declared COVID-19 a global pandemic.[6] The Dow Jones average tumbled 10 percent the next day, the worst drop in more than thirty years. Dr. Anthony Fauci, the nation's chief epidemiologist, testified that the government had botched testing for the virus. Hospitals struggled with shortages of basic protective equipment.[7] Some governors began ordering schools, stores, and restaurants to close to stop the virus's spread. In contrast, Trump seemed to follow the Tinkerbell strategy from *Peter Pan*—if people just believed enough, the disease would go away.[8] But it didn't. By mid-May, the United States had more confirmed COVID-19 deaths than any other country in the world.[9]

Trump demonized the people who delivered the bad news about COVID-19. "The Fake News Media is doing everything possible to make us look bad," he tweeted. "Sad!"[10] He was angry because journalists were chronicling the White House's disorganized response to the pandemic. Unlike countries that were successfully containing the virus, the United States had no system of free testing, coordinated contact tracing of COVID cases, or mass production and distribution of basic protective gear. The president didn't encourage people to take the most basic of safety precautions. When it came to the all-important COVID-19 prevention method of wearing masks, Trump's message was muddled. "You can do it. You don't have to do it. I'm choosing not to do it," he said. "It's only a recommendation." By the middle of April, more than two thousand Americans a day were dying from COVID-19.[11]

Still craving the media's attention, Trump began holding daily Coronavirus Task Force press briefings with himself as the star. The president used them to make the crisis worse by spreading misinformation and attacking governors and scientific experts who encouraged stronger restrictions to combat the pandemic. At a briefing in April, he dangerously suggested that injecting disinfectant might be a possible cure for the virus.[12] In May he told reporters he was taking the medicine hydroxychloroquine on a daily basis in the belief it could prevent COVID even though medical experts warned that it didn't and could have serious side effects. This was too much for Fox News host Neil Cavuto, who was highly vulnerable to the virus because of underlying health problems. "If you are in a risky population here and you are taking this as a preventive treatment to ward off the virus . . . it will kill you," Cavuto warned about hydroxychloroquine. "I cannot stress enough: This will kill you."[13] Trump was furious. "@FoxNews is no longer the same," the president tweeted. "You have more anti-Trump people, by far, than ever before." Trump also tweeted that Cavuto was "foolish" and an "asshole."[14] Not everyone at Fox was parroting Trump, and it terrified him.

The coronavirus pandemic was just one of the crises that challenged the United States in 2020. There were shuttered businesses and devastating unemployment because of an ailing economy, mass uprisings in the streets because of racial injustice and police brutality, record storms, wildfires, and heat waves because of climate change, and an all-out assault on democratic institutions led by Trump. The president's relationship with the press had never been worse. Just as he did during the Mueller probe and his impeachment, Trump responded to the crises by denying the reality of the news and challenging the legitimacy of the press. He complained he was the victim of vast conspiracies propagated by the media.

Trump could still count on Rush Limbaugh, however. Like both Bush presidents before him, Trump had good reason to genuflect to the conservative star whose show remained the most popular on American talk radio with more than fifteen million listeners. Limbaugh was a dedicated cheerleader for Trump. When the president held a rally before the 2018 midterm elections, Limbaugh joined him. During his State of the Union address in early February 2020, Trump returned the favor, awarding Limbaugh the Presidential Medal of Freedom.[15]

Limbaugh's attacks on institutions of knowledge had become gospel for Trump and much of the GOP. Since 2009 Limbaugh repeatedly told his listeners that the media, science, academia, and government were the "Four Corners of Deceit."[16] In Limbaugh's world the experts from these four institutions were part of a gigantic liberal conspiracy to lie to Americans about global warming, or what he called the "ClimateGate" hoax. "Science has been corrupted," Limbaugh said. "We know the media has been corrupted for a long time. Academia has been corrupted. None of what they do is real. It's all lies!"[17] And who did Limbaugh say Americans should trust instead? Himself, of course. Limbaugh laid the groundwork for Trump and large portions of the public to ignore scientists, journalists, governors, and academic experts who were issuing the direst warnings about COVID-19. In a Pew Research Center survey completed just before the virus began taking its toll, only 20 percent of U.S. conservatives trusted scientists "to do what is right." Among those on the left, it was 62 percent.[18]

Limbaugh assured his listeners in late February that the coronavirus "appears far less deadly" than the flu. When someone who survived a case of COVID called into his show, Limbaugh cited it as proof the virus wasn't especially dangerous. "We have people who are purposely creating a panic here—or trying to—to have a negative impact on the stock market, to maybe have a negative impact on the economy, because they are hoping to have a negative impact on President Trump," Limbaugh said. He then mocked people who were worried about the virus. "Oh, my God, 58 cases! Oh, my God. Oh, my God."[19]

But those fifty-eight cases soon turned into millions of cases.[20] Rather than admit a mistake, Limbaugh suggested Americans should just be tougher. For people living during the Spanish Flu pandemic of 1918–19, he said admiringly, "There was no national policy to deal with it. There was no shutdown. There was just, 'Hey, go outside, get some fresh air, stand in the sun as long as you can, get some vitamin D, feel better.'" Then in a truly bizarre moment, Limbaugh endorsed the methods of the Donner party, a group of travelers who resorted to cannibalism in the 1840s when they got stuck in the mountains during a harsh winter. "If you read the diaries written by the leaders of the Donner party, the only reference to how cold it was was one sentence," Limbaugh said on the air. "They didn't complain about it because there was nothing they could do. They had to adapt. This is what's missing. There seems to be no concept of adaptation."[21]

Limbaugh wasn't the only one in conservative media spreading disinformation about the pandemic and downplaying COVID's danger. Mark Levin did the same thing on his radio show. Alex Jones echoed Trump's rhetoric that fears over the virus were a Democratic hoax. *Breitbart* posted a video on Facebook suggesting that people didn't need to wear masks; it received twenty million views.[22] Fox News promoted coronavirus misinformation more than 13,500 times during 2020, according to one study. The misinformation not only endangered its audience; it reinforced the misguided views of one of its biggest fans—Trump—who in 2020 tweeted at least 475 times while watching Fox.[23] Even as Fox put its own coronavirus precautions in place—deep cleaning its offices, activating a work-from-home plan, and canceling large events with advertisers—some of its most popular commentators insisted the virus wasn't a real threat. Hannity insisted the press and Democrats were scaring people to score political points against Trump. "The apocalypse is imminent and you're going to all die, all of you in the next 48 hours. And it's all President Trump's fault," Hannity sarcastically told his millions of viewers on his February 27 show. "Or at least that's what the media mob and the Democratic extreme radical socialist party would like you to think."[24]

On May 4 an obscure movie maker named Mikki Willis posted *Plandemic*, a twenty-six-minute video, on YouTube. Echoing Limbaugh's

"Four Corners of Deceit" refrain, *Plandemic* claimed the coronavirus was a plot by shadowy elites to gain power over Americans and profit from a vaccination. Although its claims were debunked, it became instantly popular on conspiracy theory sites. Within a week, *Plandemic* had been viewed more than eight million times. Sinclair's TV stations were set to air a favorable interview about *Plandemic* until the network backed down after a wave of complaints.[25]

While conservative media spread disinformation about the pandemic, mainstream news outlets were exposing a White House more concerned with preserving the president's power than helping protect Americans. The *Los Angeles Times* reported that the Trump administration had stopped a program to help scientists around the world detect and prevent pandemic threats. *60 Minutes* aired a devastating report about heroic doctors, nurses, and other health-care workers who didn't have access to basic protective gear as they struggled to treat the flood of COVID patients.[26] The *Washington Post* revealed that the administration had relied for three weeks on an ineffective coronavirus test while scientists grew increasingly alarmed by bureaucratic infighting that delayed adequate testing. The *New York Times* analyzed data to find that Black and Latinx Americans were three times more likely than white people to become infected with the coronavirus.[27] Journalists around the country told heartbreaking stories of victims dying in agony alone in hospitals because the virus prevented family members from being by their side.[28]

Because Trump and his media allies were battling fact-based journalists over the basics of the pandemic's reality, Americans' responses to the crisis depended largely on their news sources. Conservative media consumers were more likely to think the government was exaggerating COVID's dangers and incorrectly believe Vitamin C could cure it, one study found. Those who relied on mainstream outlets such as the Associated Press, *New York Times*, and NBC News had a more accurate picture of COVID's deadliness and a better understanding that basic steps such as washing hands could prevent its spread.[29]

For some people, anger toward the media trumped concern about COVID. Kevin Vesey, a reporter for a Long Island TV station, experienced this hostility in the middle of May when he walked down a sidewalk to cover a rally opposing anti-COVID restrictions. Protesters—only a few wearing masks—screamed phrases that echoed Trump's media taunts. "Go home, you fake news!" one woman yelled. "You are the enemy of the people," a man shouted. "You're disgusting," a woman snarled. Another man gave him the middle finger and said, "Fuck you." Trump loved the confrontation. He tweeted a video of the scene and called the hecklers "Great people!"[30]

Americans had become intensely polarized over how to respond to the virus. Soon confrontations over a different crisis would engulf the United States.

Breonna Taylor, a twenty-six-year-old Black emergency room technician, was asleep in her bed in the early hours of March 13 when a group of men barged into her Louisville apartment and shot her to death. The assailants? Police officers on a botched drug raid.[31]

George Floyd, a forty-six-year-old Black man, was accused on May 25 of using a counterfeit twenty-dollar bill. Minneapolis police handcuffed Floyd and pinned him to the ground. A white police officer jammed his knee into the back of Floyd's neck for more than nine minutes as bystanders begged him to stop. Floyd repeatedly pleaded "I can't breathe" before dying.[32]

Video of Floyd's killing quickly spread through social media, and the country erupted in protests with "Black Lives Matter" as the rallying cry. Pollsters estimated that up to twenty-six million people participated through June in more than five hundred cities and towns, making it the largest protest movement in U.S. history. News broadcasts showed protesters chanting the names of other unarmed Black people killed by police: LaQuan McDonald, Eric Garner, Rekia Boyd, Tamir Rice, Walter Scott, Philando Castile, Tony McDade, Atatiana Jefferson, Alton Sterling, Stephon Clark, Botham Jean—the horrible list went on and on.[33]

The protesters were part of a growing social movement—an organized and sustained effort by people without official power demanding that government make significant changes. Like the abolitionists who pressured Lincoln to end slavery, Black Lives Matter activists skillfully used media to further their cause. Other social movements had also done so to win substantial political victories.[34] Women earned the right to vote. Civil rights activists ended legal segregation. Workers fought for the right to organize unions. The Right to Life movement restricted abortion. Gay and lesbian couples won the right to marry. Environmentalists pushed for cleaner air and water.

For the Black Lives Matter movement, social media played a crucial role like newspapers and pamphlets did for the abolitionists. Activists used Twitter, Facebook, TikTok, Instagram, and other social media to post videos and photos of police violence, announce rallies, spark discussions of systemic racism, and spread their message to the wider public. Black Americans had already harnessed Twitter to raise awareness of issues often ignored by the mainstream press. #YouOkSis publicized the experiences of Black women subject to harassment. #OscarsSoWhite pushed the Academy Awards to be more inclusive. #BlackonCampus shared the experiences of college students subjected to racism.[35]

#BlackLivesMatter first spread after a vigilante killed Trayvon Martin, a Black teenager returning to his Florida home from a store in 2013. When a white police officer killed Michael Brown, a young Black man in Ferguson, Missouri, in 2014, the movement grew. Because of the awareness created by Black Lives Matter, the press became eleven times more likely to cover the deaths of people of color at the hands of police than before Brown's killing. Following the outrage over George Floyd's death, the mainstream media began paying even more attention to police violence and systemic racism. Journalists gave more coverage to the protests and uprisings of 2020 than they had to any since the height of the anti-Vietnam War movement.[36]

Trump was paying attention too. A president's ability to publicize issues and set policy, or at least passively accept change, is vital for the success of U.S. social movements. But unlike Lincoln, Trump didn't have an open mind about social change. Although most Black Lives Matter protests were peaceful, he seized on instances of violence to inflame tensions. He tweeted without evidence that antifa—a small left-wing anti-fascist group—was responsible for the unrest. He retweeted a video posted by a white supremacist organization that falsely blamed Black Lives Matter and antifa for a New York City subway attack. When protesters for racial justice filled the streets, he tweeted, "when the looting starts, the shooting starts," a phrase segregationists had used during 1960s civil rights uprisings.[37]

As the protests grew, Trump continued to bash the press, tweeting that the "Lamestream Media" are "truly bad people with a sick agenda."[38] Growing hostility toward reporters endangered their safety as they did their jobs covering the news. In the two weeks following Floyd's death, there were at least three hundred attacks against journalists including physical assaults, arrests, and damage to equipment. Some of the violence came from protesters, but police committed most of the attacks against the press in an unprecedented wave of violence toward U.S. journalists by those who are supposed to protect the peace. In New York City, officers repeatedly hit reporter Tyler Blint-Welsh even though his hands were in the air and his press badge clearly visible. In Louisville, a police officer shot a pepper ball at TV journalist Kaitlin Rust. In Minneapolis, police pepper-sprayed *Los Angeles Times* photographer Carolyn Cole in the eye, damaging her cornea. Minnesota State Police handcuffed CNN correspondent Omar Jimenez while he reported live on the air.[39] And across Lafayette Square Park from the White House, rampaging officers clubbed Australian reporter Amelia Brace in the back with a baton as they cleared the area of protesters.[40]

In early June Martin Gugino, a seventy-five-year-old peace activist, was protesting Floyd's killing when Buffalo police pushed him to the ground, cracking his head on the sidewalk. Trump got busy on Twitter. "Buffalo protester shoved by Police could be an ANTIFA provocateur," he tweeted as Gugino lay in the hospital, struggling to recover from his head wounds. Trump based his cruel and false tweet on an OAN segment whose "reporter" had also worked for Sputnik, a Kremlin news service. The OAN story was based on an anonymous blog post by someone using the name "Sundance."[41] This was the quality of presidential communications in 2020.

Trump reached a milestone in the spring of 2020: he made his two thousandth negative tweet about the news media since the start of his 2016 campaign. He averaged more than one negative tweet a day about the press and made the attacks central to his reelection campaign.[42] "Our real opponent is not the Democrats, or the dwindling number of Republicans that lost their way and got left behind, our primary opponent is the Fake News Media," he tweeted. "In the history of our Country, they have never been so bad!"[43] In the era of John Adams and Thomas Jefferson, political parties had sponsored newspapers. Now the president was saying the press was an opponent more powerful than political parties.

When Trump gave interviews, they were usually with conservative media. Through July of 2020, he had done ninety-six interviews with Fox News, more than double the combined total for ABC, CBS, NBC, CNN, the *New York Times*, *Washington Post*, and *Wall Street Journal*, according to Mark Knoller of CBS News.[44] Trump's advisers told him if he wanted to win the election, he needed to reach beyond his Fox base. But in the rare instances when Trump agreed to interviews with other journalists, they often went sour. In an interview that aired on HBO in August, reporter Jonathan Swan of *Axios* asked the sort of follow-up questions that the president wasn't used to hearing from Fox hosts. As he stumbled for answers, Trump displayed a lack of basic understanding of the coronavirus pandemic.

"Right now, I think it's under control," Trump told Swan.

"How? 1,000 Americans are dying a day," Swan responded.

"They are dying—that's true. And it is what it is," Trump said without a trace of sorrow.

During the rest of the interview, Trump made a string of outlandish statements about COVID-19. "And there are those that say you can test too much, you do know that," he said.

"Who says that?" Swan asked.

"Oh, just read the manuals," the president responded. "Read the books."

"Manuals?"

"Read the books," Trump insisted. "Read the books."

"What books?" Swan tried again.

The questions stumped Trump. He didn't have answers.[45]

Disinformation continued to spread through social media and some segments of the press during the 2020 campaign. Top contenders for the Democratic nomination were targeted. A hoax spread through the internet claiming that South Bend, Indiana, mayor Pete Buttigieg was accused of sexual assault. A doctored photo falsely showing a racist figurine in Senator Elizabeth Warren's kitchen went viral. After Biden was endorsed by the International Association of Firefighters, Trump retweeted nearly five dozen posts inaccurately saying that no firemen actually backed Biden. The president tweeted his support for QAnon, the conspiracy group that claimed a cult of cannibals and pedophiles connected with Hillary Clinton and other Democrats were killing children and plotting against Trump. It was a more demented, elaborate version of the conspiracy theory that Rush Limbaugh and others in right-wing media spread in the 1990s that the Clintons had killed Vince Foster and other friends. The FBI considered QAnon a terrorist threat, but Trump said, "I've heard these are people that love our country."[46]

For years social media companies resisted calls to restrict false and dangerous content, but then advertisers threatened boycotts, and Congress held antitrust hearings in July 2020.[47] Facebook finally promised to take down posts that sought to suppress voting, incite violence, or spread misinformation about COVID-19. In August Facebook took the significant step of removing a president's post for the first time. The post showed Trump claiming that children are "almost immune" from getting the coronavirus, which was hazardous and wrong.[48] Other social media companies joined the crackdown. The gaming platform Twitch banned Trump's account for hateful content. Twitter announced it would delete or label misleading claims about the election. YouTube deleted content from racists. Reddit banned thousands of hate-filled subreddits, including its biggest pro-Trump forum. As Kevin Roose noted in the *New York Times*, one of the web's mottos had been "move fast and break things"; now some of its leaders were worried about what they had broken.[49]

The crises of 2020 kept coming. In the United States, there were a record-breaking twenty-two natural disasters that caused at least $1 billion in damages each. Fueled by years of drought, wildfires blazed through more than five million acres in the West, an area larger than Connecticut. More than thirty people died.[50] In the Midwest, massive floods destroyed crops, swept through towns, and burst a Michigan dam. More named storms battered the Atlantic and Gulf Coasts than ever before. Glaciers melted. Sea levels rose. By the end of December, 2020 had tied with 2016 for the hottest year ever recorded.[51]

The conservative media denied it was a crisis. Rush Limbaugh once again claimed there was no proof of man-made global warming. Instead he accused "environmentalist wackos" of trying to control Americans' lives. On Fox News, Tucker Carlson said people blaming climate change for the bad weather were just being partisans. *Gateway Pundit* falsely blamed leftist arsonists for starting the wildfires. And Trump refused to acknowledge the impact of global warming. "It'll start getting cooler," he promised.[52]

It was the economy, however, that was getting cooler. Because of the pandemic, the U.S. gross domestic product fell 3.5 percent for the year, the worst drop since 1946. The budget deficit soared to $3.1 trillion in the fiscal year that ended in September, the highest ever and more than five times what it was during Obama's last year in office.[53] Economic disparities widened. The stock market reached record highs by the end of Trump's term, mostly benefiting people with high incomes, while more than nineteen million Americans remained jobless and one in eight adults said they didn't have enough to eat sometime in the past week.[54] Out of all the presidents since World War II, Trump was the only one to leave office with fewer people employed than when he began his term.[55]

Since his days investigating Watergate with Carl Bernstein, Bob Woodward had become the premier chronicler of U.S. presidents. He wrote best-selling books about the administrations of Nixon, Ford, Carter, Reagan, Clinton, both Bushes, and Obama, using inside sources to paint often unflattering portraits of their presidencies. Woodward's first book about Trump, *Fear*, was published in 2018. It described a chaotic administration led by a temperamental president who was a pathological liar. Trump didn't agree to be interviewed for *Fear*.[56] When he heard Woodward was working on a second book about his administration, he decided to cooperate, hoping for a more favorable portrayal. Trump let Woodward interview him an extraordinary eighteen times, sometimes even calling the reporter at home late at night, perhaps thinking he could successfully charm and manipulate the legendary journalist as he had done with New York gossip columnists for many years.[57] It was a colossal miscalculation.

Woodward's second Trump book, *Rage*, was published in September 2020. Woodward detailed a White House COVID response that was deeply mismanaged and mostly concerned with getting Trump reelected. It contained the explosive revelation that Trump knew the virus was highly lethal while he was telling the public the risk was low. "This is deadly stuff," he told Woodward on February 7, admitting he intentionally downplayed the virus's seriousness to avoid panic. Woodward isn't usually the type of journalist to boldly state his opinions in his books, but in *Rage* he did. He criticized Trump for failing to do his homework, listen to experts, craft plans, stay organized, admit mistakes, and speak with a calming voice during a time of crisis. "I can only reach one conclusion," Woodward wrote. "Trump is the wrong man for the job."[58]

Woodward wasn't the only journalist revealing damaging information about Trump that fall. The September issue of *The Atlantic* featured a story by Jeffrey Goldberg reporting that Trump had repeatedly insulted veterans, calling people killed in the line of duty who were buried in military cemeteries "losers" and "suckers."[59] The *New York Times* published a devastating story about eighteen years of Trump's tax returns that he had tried to keep secret. It revealed that Trump had paid only $750 in taxes in both 2016 and 2017. In eleven years, he paid no taxes at all. The story contained other juicy details such as Trump taking deductions for $70,000 in hairstyling costs. "His reports to the I.R.S. portray a businessman who takes in hundreds of millions of dollars a year yet racks up chronic losses that he aggressively employs to avoid paying taxes," the *Times* said. To no one's surprise, Trump called the story "fake news."[60]

One week before the election, a *Washington Post* investigation showed that Trump's businesses had made at least $8.1 million from taxpayers during his presidency. For example, when Japanese prime minister Shinzo Abe met with the president, Trump had him stay at his Mar-a-Lago resort rather than Washington. The resort then billed the U.S. government $16,500 for meals and wine, $13,750 for guest rooms, and $6,000 for flowers.[61]

At the start of Trump's term, Steve Bannon had told the press to "shut up." It didn't. Despite Trump's attacks against them and his torrent of disinformation, journalists followed standard reporting practices to develop sources, gather facts, and verify information about his presidency. As *Washington Post* media critic Margaret Sullivan observed, "The mainstream media, however flawed, has managed to tell us who Trump is."[62]

In the early morning of October 2, the president announced on Twitter that he and First Lady Melania Trump had COVID-19. The White House was less than forthcoming about his condition as his doctor dodged questions from reporters about when Trump got sick, how severe his symptoms were, and whether he'd received supplemental oxygen. It was later disclosed that Trump had needed steroids and his blood oxygen levels had dropped twice, indicating his condition was worse than the White House originally reported. But Trump recovered quickly. After three days in the hospital, he returned to the White House and once again compared COVID to the flu.[63]

The West Wing had become a COVID hotspot with at least thirty-five cases among people connected to the president including Chief of Staff Mark Meadows, top aide Hope Hicks, Press Secretary Kayleigh McEnany, and two of her aides. The president and his staff routinely refused to wear masks near reporters or take other precautions.[64] At least three members of the White House press corps caught the virus. The *Wall Street Journal*, *Washington Post*, and *New York Times* stopped sending reporters to travel with Trump because the risk of infection was too high. For the first time ever, the White House Correspondents' Association had difficulty finding reporters willing to join the pool that covers presidential events. "I felt safer reporting in North Korea," CBS White House correspondent Ben Tracy tweeted, "than I currently do reporting at The White House."[65]

In the last days before the election, Trump barnstormed through key swing states, holding large rallies where many people didn't wear masks even as the pandemic's death toll surged past a quarter million Americans. Trump blamed the press. "With the fake news, everything is COVID, COVID, COVID, COVID," he said at an Omaha rally. The *New York Times* analyzed a speech Trump gave at a Wisconsin rally and found 131 statements that were "either false, misleading, exaggerated, disputed or lacked evidence." They included falsehoods about COVID, taxes, health care, and especially Biden, the Democratic nominee.[66]

Trump made a special point of lying about the upcoming election, trying to engineer a crisis of faith in U.S. democracy so he could remain in power. Back in July he had tweeted that the election should be postponed—in violation of the Constitution—because of unfounded allegations of fraud.[67] He then continually repeated the false claim that Democrats were rigging the voting. Right-wing outlets and social media spread his bogus claims. There were allegations that Biden supporters were collecting illegal votes, destroying ballots of Trump supporters, and preparing to go on a violent rampage to take over polling places. One rumor that unauthorized people were illegally dropping off ballots in Minnesota received nearly a million Facebook shares, likes, or comments. Former Trump aide Michael Anton posted an essay claiming that Democrats and the "deep state" were plotting a coup that included harvesting ballots in swing states. This conspiracy theory was repeated in videos attracting more than six million views. Similar fake coup claims were shared on Tucker Carlson's show.[68]

Trump was copying a technique mastered by the Nazi propaganda ministry: keep repeating a big lie using the power of mass media, and eventually many people will believe it.[69] By the end of September, 65 percent of Republicans were telling pollsters they weren't confident that the election "will be conducted in a fair and equal way." In another survey conducted before the election, 52 percent of respondents who used Fox News as their main news source said voter fraud is a "major problem."[70] In the right-wing media echo chamber, there was little doubt that the election was being rigged in Biden's favor despite the lack of evidence. This belief would have deadly consequences in the weeks ahead.

A presidency like no other ended with an election like no other. Nearly 160 million citizens voted, the most in U.S. history. The vote counting stretched into the wee hours of Tuesday night, November 3, and then into Wednesday, Thursday, Friday, and Saturday. The mainstream press had warned for weeks that it might take days until the winner was known because of the millions of mail-in ballots that GOP lawmakers in some states prevented from being counted ahead of time. Be patient, the news anchors advised their viewers.[71]

Trump wasn't patient. His strategy was to declare victory early based on in-person voting that was likely to favor him, sue to stop the counting of mail-in votes favoring Biden, and take the case if necessary to the Supreme Court, whose balance he had shifted by appointing three conservative justices. The plan was working perfectly early on election night. He was winning the swing states of Florida and North Carolina. Ohio and Texas were safely in his camp after early scares from Biden. He had small but dwindling leads in the key states of Georgia, Michigan, Wisconsin, and Pennsylvania.[72]

At Trump's election night party at the White House, Fox News played on the big screen. When it called Arizona for Biden, the mood quickly soured. Without Arizona, Trump couldn't claim he had the necessary 270 electoral college votes. He was furious and ordered his aides to push Fox to reverse its call. Jared Kushner contacted Rupert Murdoch. Kellyanne Conway complained to Fox anchor Bret Baier. Hope Hicks messaged a former Trump aide who now worked at Fox. And Mark Meadows called Fox's decision desk several times. But its chief, Arnon Mishkin, held firm. The data showed that Biden's lead in Arizona was insurmountable, he insisted. Fox stuck with its Arizona call. During most of his presidency, Trump referred to Fox as "my network," but on this night journalists were running the show, not Hannity, Carlson, and other ideological opinion hosts.

The Associated Press, Univision, *USA Today*, *Wall Street Journal*, NPR, and PBS soon joined Fox in calling Arizona for Biden.[73] Many of the other swing states were too close to call, but that didn't stop Trump from giving a victory speech at 2:20 a.m. "Frankly, we did win this election," he defiantly lied to supporters crowded together in the East Room. Trump insisted fraud was to blame for not making his triumph clearer. He demanded that votes stop being counted in the states where he led and continue to be counted where he was behind.[74]

The press immediately undercut Trump's victory claim. After years of covering him, journalists were prepared for his lies. ABC and MSNBC stopped airing Trump's speech as he descended further into delusional and antidemocratic falsehoods. Chris Wallace on Fox News, Norah O'Donnell on CBS, Savannah Guthrie on NBC, and Jake Tapper on CNN immediately condemned him. "This is an extremely flammable situation, and the president just threw a match on it," Wallace said.[75] When Trump lawyer Rudy Giuliani gave a news conference later that day to spout baseless conspiracy theories, Fox cut away to announce Biden had won Michigan.[76] "Fox is tiptoeing away from Trump like someone at a party edging away from the guy who farted," *Vanity Fair* correspondent Gabriel Sherman tweeted that evening.[77]

That may have been true for Fox's news anchors and reporters, but its popular opinion hosts were still pretending the stench didn't exist. Jeanine Pirro falsely tweeted there was voter fraud "on a national scale."[78] Laura Ingraham insisted Democrats were trying "to destroy the integrity of our election process with this mail-in, day-of-registration efforts, counting after the election's over."[79] Hannity used a trick commonly employed by conspiracy theorists by asking a series of insinuating questions: "Do you trust what happened in this election? Do you believe these election results are accurate? Do you believe this was a free and fair election?"[80] The absence of a factual basis for his questions didn't matter; the goal was to generate distrust in the democratic process. The racism of the Fox hosts bubbled to the surface as they alleged voting shenanigans in cities with large Black and immigrant populations while ignoring the fact that Biden made some of his biggest gains over Hillary Clinton's 2016 totals in suburbs with white majorities.[81]

Trump remained furious that Fox's news desk showed Biden winning and urged his followers to switch to OAN and the extremely conservative Newsmax, which nearly tripled its audience in the three weeks after the election. OAN posted two YouTube videos declaring Trump the winner; they were viewed more than a half million times.[82] Right-wing talk radio hosts repeated the lie that the election was stolen from Trump. Mark Levin encouraged GOP legislators in swing states that went for Biden to ignore the will of voters and give their electoral college votes to Trump instead.[83] There was now a branch of the media that wasn't just liberal, conservative, or neutral; it was authoritarian and devoted to keeping a single man in power.

Election disinformation spread further on social media. A Spanish-language YouTube channel with two million subscribers claimed that hordes of antifa were ready to pillage Washington.[84] By the end of the week, posts using #StoptheSteal—the hashtag preferred by Trump supporters—had received 3.5 million shares, likes, and other Facebook interactions.[85] When Facebook and Twitter began labeling Trump's election claims as untrue, he and many of his fans began using Parler, a social media site partially funded by Rebekah Mercer, who was also a big *Breitbart* backer. Parler made no effort to stop misinformation about the election and allowed racism, anti-Semitism, and conspiracy theories to flourish. One OAN reporter called Parler a "never-ending Trump rally."[86]

On Saturday morning, November 7, Biden's lead in Pennsylvania grew. CNN declared him the state's winner, giving the former vice president enough electoral votes to claim the presidency. The Associated Press and other news outlets quickly followed. "America's 46th President," the Fox News homepage declared over a photo of Biden and his wife, Jill.[87] The front-page headline of the *New York Post*, one of Trump's most loyal backers, simply said, "It's Joe Time."[88]

Biden's margin of victory eventually exceeded seven million votes, but Trump refused to concede.[89] Unlike every other president before him who had lost reelection, Trump was determined to stay in power by overturning the will of the voters. By declaring himself the winner of an election he hadn't won and pressuring others to undermine democracy, he attempted what is known as an *autogolpe*—a Spanish word meaning "self-coup." Autogolpes had often occurred in Latin America and elsewhere around the world when government leaders illegitimately tried to stay in power, but never before in the United States.[90] Unlike authoritarian wannabes in other countries, Trump didn't have the support of military leaders, the courts, or an official state-run media. But he did have loyal right-wing media willing to spread his conspiracy theories.

Trump and his allies unsuccessfully tried to stop the counting of votes in Pennsylvania and the certification of results in Arizona, Nevada, and Michigan. They paid three million dollars for recounts in two Wisconsin counties, which netted Biden eighty-seven more votes. Two Georgia recounts also left Biden as the state's winner. Trump turned to the courts with cases based on minor clerical errors, unsubstantiated poll watcher allegations, and complaints that his allies weren't allowed to observe the vote counting (they were). The court challenges flopped.[91] Judges, some Republicans and others Democrats, rejected Trump's claims more than sixty times.[92] His allegations of massive voter fraud were disproven by his own Department of Homeland Security, which issued a report stating the election "was the most secure in American history." Attorney General William Barr said the Justice Department found no evidence of widespread fraud.[93] *New York Times* reporters called election officials in every state. None reported problems with fraud.[94] The evidence didn't matter to Trump; he had a conspiracy theory to promote. "RIGGED ELECTION!" he tweeted as if using all capital letters and an exclamation mark somehow made it truer. Based on facts being reported by journalists, Twitter slapped warning labels on Trump's false statements: "Some or all of the content shared in this Tweet is disputed and might be misleading about an election or other civic process."[95]

The spirit of antidemocratic revolt swept through right-wing media as commentators tried to keep their audiences engaged by stoking as much outrage as possible. Flirting with treason, Limbaugh told his listeners, "I actually think that we're trending toward secession." When he was roundly criticized for suggesting a civil war, Limbaugh retreated the next day. He used one of Trump's favorite rhetorical tricks by claiming he had only repeated what other people said.[96] Limbaugh was tame compared with radio host Eric Metaxas, whose commentary was carried on 1,400 stations. Metaxas told his listeners, "We need to fight to the death, to the last drop of blood because it's worth it."[97]

Trump's big lie was having an impact. In the two weeks after Biden was declared the victor, Fox News cast doubt on the election results more than 770 times, often encouraging viewers to resist the outcome. Hannity kept promising that a big breakthrough proving Trump won was just around the corner. "Tonight, we are tracking multiple stories, serious allegations of election irregularities all across the country," Hannity said.[98] A majority of Republicans believed these claims. An opinion poll conducted the week of November 13 found that 52 percent of Republicans thought Trump "rightfully won" the election. More than two-thirds of the Republicans surveyed believed the lie that the election was "rigged."[99]

In contrast, most journalists grew increasingly scornful of Trump's failure to concede. On December 2 Trump gave what he promised might be "the most important speech I've ever made." It was full of more unsubstantiated fraud claims. News outlets that gave Trump all the attention he wanted in the 2016 campaign, no matter how far he strayed from the truth, mostly ignored this speech. The Associated Press, known for its neutral reporting, covered the address but couldn't hide its disgust. "Increasingly detached from reality," the AP story began, "President Donald Trump stood before a White House lectern and delivered a forty-six-minute diatribe against the election results that produced a win for Democrat Joe Biden, unspooling one misstatement after another to back his baseless claim that he really won."[100]

Undaunted, Trump's team tried another attempt to hijack the election. Texas's attorney general sued to overturn the results in Michigan, Wisconsin, Georgia, and Pennsylvania. The president, 126 GOP members of the House, and eighteen other Republican attorneys general joined the lawsuit. Trump called the case "the big one"; the *Chicago Tribune*, the longtime bastion of midwestern conservatism, called it an effort "to subvert the vote." The Supreme Court—with six members appointed by Republican presidents, including three by Trump—unanimously rejected the lawsuit on December 11.[101]

Even Richard Nixon had accepted the Supreme Court's decision when it ordered him to turn over the White House tapes that doomed his presidency. But not Trump. He tried to spur an uprising, tweeting through the night and into the next morning while denouncing Republican-appointed members of the Supreme Court, the GOP governors of Georgia and Arizona, and his own attorney general. "WE HAVE JUST BEGUN TO FIGHT!!!" he vowed, encouraging his followers to mass in the streets of Washington.[102]

A few thousand Trump supporters rallied in Washington the afternoon of December 12. Alex Jones, looking scruffier than when he swapped conspiracy theories with Trump five years earlier on *InfoWars*, was there to incite the crowd. "We will never back down to the Satanic pedophile, globalist New World Order and their walking-dead reanimated corpse Joe Biden, and we will never recognize him," Jones said in a deranged speech. He ominously suggested Biden should be removed "one way or the other."[103] That evening members of the Proud Boys, a pro-Trump group known for its racist and anti-Semitic connections, rampaged through the streets, vandalizing Black churches and setting fire to Black Lives Matter banners. Four people were stabbed. In Olympia, Washington, one rioting Trump protester shot a counterprotester.[104] The violence of December 12 was a dress rehearsal for events soon to follow.

Three days later, the first American received a COVID vaccination after an unprecedented effort by scientists backed by the government. It was perhaps the greatest accomplishment of Trump's term. At last there was hope of stopping the pandemic. The United States had twice as many confirmed cases as any other country, and the virus was stealing three thousand American lives every day—more than the U.S. death toll from the bombing of Pearl Harbor, D-Day, or the 9/11 attacks.[105] But instead of putting his energy into making sure the vaccine was distributed as quickly and effectively as possible, or reassuring a doubtful public of its safety, Trump raged about the election. That night he tweeted dozens of election falsehoods. He continued through the next week. And on Christmas Day. And on New Year's Eve.[106] The *Washington*

Post revealed that Trump called Georgia's secretary of state, urging him to "find" enough votes to overturn the results there.[107]

Trump hatched one more reckless plan to maintain his power: He and his allies would pressure Congress to reject the Electoral College results when it met on January 6, 2021. If that failed, they would demand Vice President Pence illegally declare Trump the winner. Trump repeatedly urged his supporters to flock to Washington for another protest that day. "Be there, will be wild!" he tweeted. In another tweet, he exhorted, "Get Smart Republicans. FIGHT!"[108]

Right-wing media fanned the flames of rebellion. On Christmas Day Levin repeated the lie that Democrats had stolen the election, and he urged his viewers to "crush them" and "kick their ass." On January 5 Levin told his radio audience that the certification of votes by Congress would be an act of "tyranny." Glenn Beck told his radio listeners it was time to "go to war" and "rip and claw and rake."[109] On Parler, users plotted ways to avoid police and break into the Capitol. Some talked about bringing guns inside. According to one analysis, the phrase "Storm the Capitol" was mentioned one hundred thousand times on social media in December and early January.[110] The *X22 Report*, a podcast popular in conservative circles, said Trump would need to remove members of Congress so he could serve a second term. The podcast made its warning clear: "We the people, we are the storm, and we're coming to DC."[111]

The U.S. Capitol was attacked on January 6, 2021, not by foreign enemies but by a mob of thousands of Trump supporters. The president and his media partisans had sparked an insurrection. At his "Save America" rally next to the Washington Monument earlier in the day, Trump began his speech, as he so often did, by blaming the media. He claimed television news cameras weren't showing the "hundreds of thousands" of people at the rally, even though there weren't anywhere close to that number present. He encouraged his followers to "fight much harder" and "show strength" against the "bad people" who opposed him. If Congress certified the election that day, the country would have an "illegitimate president," Trump warned. "If you don't fight like hell, you're not going to have a country anymore." He ended by urging the crowd to march to the Capitol, vowing "I'll be there with you." But Trump didn't go with them. Instead, he hid in the White House, tweeting furiously that Pence was betraying him by certifying the election results.[112]

High on disinformation, the pro-Trump mob surged toward the Capitol to find Pence and overthrow Congress. They brought bats, chemical spray, shields, and handcuffs, and they carried Nazi paraphernalia, Confederate flags, and Trump flags as if he were his own nation. "Hang Mike Pence!" some of them shouted while others erected gallows. At about 2 p.m. they broke through police barricades and began rampaging through the Capitol. As the mob smashed windows and doors, Congress stopped debating certification of the Electoral College. Its members frantically hid inside the House chamber and under tables in their offices. The Secret Service rushed Pence to a safe room. The insurrectionists briefly took control of the Senate chamber and tried to crash through doors into the House chamber. About 140 Capitol and DC police officers were injured during the assault, and 4 others committed suicide afterward. Four of the invaders died.[113]

During the attempted autogolpe, Trump's four years of verbal attacks against the press came to life as the raging mob attacked journalists bravely covering the events. Rioters repeated Trump's words that the media were "the enemy of the people." *Washington Post* photographer Amanda Andrade-Rhoades said three people threatened to shoot her. Shouting, "Fuck you!" the mob assaulted Associated Press photographer John Minchillo, punching, shoving, and dragging him until they pushed him over a wall to the ground. A rioter threw *New York Times* photographer Erin Schaff to the ground and smashed her camera. "Murder the Media," was scrawled on a Capitol door.[114]

The news channels that had been covering Congress's certification debate quickly switched to covering the violent insurrection. "We are witnessing an attempt at sedition," CNN's Jake Tapper told viewers.

"There have been some elements of a coup attempt," NBC's Lester Holt said. Even Fox News made clear the treasonous nature of what was occurring. "The mob upended American democracy today as they try to count the Electoral College," Fox reporter Chad Pergram said.[115]

GOP congresspeople cowering in their offices called the White House, begging Trump's aides to get him to ask his supporters to stand down. House GOP leader Kevin McCarthy urged him to tell the mob to stop. But instead of restoring law and order, the president was busy watching the bloody events unfold on TV, enjoying the show. "He was hard to reach, and you know why? Because it was live TV," one Trump adviser later told the *Washington Post*. At 2:30 p.m., Trump's aides got him to tweet, "Please support our Capitol Police and Law Enforcement. They are truly on the side of our Country. Stay peaceful!" He didn't ask the mob to leave the Capitol, stop hunting for Pence, or end the attempt to overthrow Congress. Finally, the president's staff got him to release a video statement. "We love you," he told the violent mob. "You're very special." At last, he told them to "go home in peace."[116] After nearly five hours of deadly chaos, police, the FBI, and National Guard units regained control of the Capitol. The insurrection was over, and the House and Senate were able to reconvene to do their constitutional duty. Just after 3:40 a.m. Washington time, they certified the victory by Biden and Vice President–elect Kamala Harris.[117]

The whitewashing of the day's seditious events began immediately on right-wing media. Trump's loyal Fox News commentators and other conspiracy theorists in right-wing media had blood on their hands, but they either pretended something awful and treasonous didn't just happen or they blamed others. On his show that evening, Carlson blamed Democrats for the violence. "We got to this sad, chaotic day for a reason," Carlson told his audience. "It is not your fault. It is their fault." Soon after the Capitol was clear of insurrectionists, Hannity was once again lying, claiming there was massive election fraud. He announced that the Senate had just resumed its certification debate as he showed GOP senator Josh Hawley of Missouri adamantly defending Trump. In reality, the Senate had resumed about an hour earlier with speeches by Republicans and Democrats denouncing Trump, but that was too much truth for Hannity to share with his audience. Hannity, Ingraham, and Greg Kelly of Newsmax promoted the absurd rumor that the rioters were Black Lives Matter members or antifa protesters in disguise. On Newsmax, one commentator insisted no more than ten people invaded the Capitol, which was clearly false to anyone who watched the events for more than a minute.[118] The next day Rush Limbaugh blamed "Antifa, Democrat-sponsored instigators" and then encouraged more mayhem. "There's a lot of people calling for the end of violence," he told his listeners from the comfort of his Florida studio. "I am glad Sam Adams, Thomas Paine, the actual Tea Party guys, the men at Lexington and Concord didn't feel that way."[119]

In contrast to Limbaugh, most of the press immediately condemned Trump and the insurrection. Norah O'Donnell of CBS News called it a national disgrace. A *Washington Post* editorial demanded Trump's immediate removal, labeling him "a grave threat to U.S. democracy." The *Chicago Tribune* said Pence and the Cabinet should invoke the 25th Amendment to remove Trump because of his unfitness for office. The conservative *Wall Street Journal* called for his resignation. Trump's actions, a *Journal* editorial said on January 7, crossed a constitutional line and were "impeachable."[120]

The majority of the House of Representatives agreed. A week after the insurrection, Trump became the first president in history to be impeached twice. Ten Republicans joined all 222 House Democrats voting to approve a single article charging him with "incitement of insurrection." As Congress voted, thousands of National Guard troops patrolled the Capitol, their weapons ready, to prevent another attack on the U.S. government by the president's supporters. But a month later the Senate acquitted Trump after a short trial. Seven Republicans voted with all fifty Democrats to find him guilty, but the total was far short of the sixty-seven needed to convict. A majority of GOP senators argued that a former president couldn't be impeached, although most constitutional scholars disagreed.[121]

Trump had incited an insurrection and gotten away with it. After the Senate's verdict, he issued a statement: "Our historic, patriotic and beautiful movement to Make America Great Again has only just begun." And then he continued lying about the election.[122]

Donald Trump ended his term with a job approval rating of 29 percent, the lowest of his presidency, according to a Pew Research Center survey. He skipped Biden's and Harris's inauguration, the first president to miss the ceremony in 152 years. Instead, Trump made one last speech to a small crowd before departing Washington for his Mar-a-Lago resort, where he would plot another run for president. "Have a good life," he said before climbing the steps of Air Force One to the sound of the disco hit "Y.M.C.A." As he departed, Fox News still portrayed Trump as a victim. "Regarding the press, he never got a break," Steve Doocy of *Fox & Friends* complained.[123]

But Trump wasn't the true victim. The day before his presidency ended, the U.S. death toll from COVID reached four hundred thousand, more than the number of U.S. troops who died in battle during World War I, World War II, and the Vietnam War combined. An American was dying of COVID every twenty-six seconds. The National Center for Disaster Preparedness estimated that more than half of U.S. COVID deaths could have been avoided, but thanks largely to Trump's inept response and misinformation, the United States performed worse than nearly every other nation. Just 9 countries around the world had higher recorded death rates; more than 160 had lower death rates.[124]

Democracy was also a victim. Trump's attempt to steal the election failed, but he and his media allies succeeded in creating a crisis of distrust in U.S. democratic institutions and in factual knowledge by spreading a cloud of toxic disinformation. By the end of 2020, a disturbing number of Americans believed things that were untrue, an NPR/Ipsos poll found. Nearly half of respondents falsely believed that a majority of Black Lives Matter protests were violent. One in six didn't think humans play a significant role in climate change. The same percentage agreed with QAnon that a "group of Satan-worshipping elites who run a child sex ring are trying to control our politics and media." In a survey conducted the week after Biden's inauguration, two-thirds of Republicans said they didn't think he was legitimately elected.[125]

And yet despite Trump's efforts to misinform the public and overturn the election, the institutions of democracy—including the press—survived the assault, battered but still standing. Democratic and Republican county and state election officials counted ballots and certified the results, ignoring Trump's threats against them. Judges, some appointed by Trump, rejected his spurious legal arguments. State legislatures didn't follow his demands to defy the will of their voters by choosing pro-Trump electors. Congress certified the results. And thousands of journalists reported the truth—that Joe Biden defeated Donald Trump.

When Trump continued to make false claims about the election, Twitter permanently banned him two days after the Capitol insurrection "due to the risk of further incitement of violence." After tweeting more than twenty-five thousand times as president, Trump no longer possessed the digital megaphone he had used for free to reach eighty-eight million followers. Facebook, Instagram, Snapchat, and several other sites also banned him.[126] Meanwhile, Google and Apple removed Parler from their app stores, and Amazon banned it from its Web-hosting service. Within a week, the amount of disinformation about election fraud on social media plummeted 73 percent.[127]

As much as Trump tried to control the media narrative, he no longer could by the end of his presidency. Like Woodrow Wilson, he understood the power of propaganda. Like Franklin Roosevelt, he mastered a young technology to communicate directly to the public. And like John Kennedy, Ronald Reagan, and Barack Obama, he instinctively knew how to attract the cameras. But unlike Wilson, FDR, Kennedy,

Reagan, and Obama, he was incapable of inspiring a nation during a time of crisis. And he certainly didn't have the temperament to build positive relationships with most journalists. He could dominate the news, but he couldn't get most of the press to believe him. In the end, neither did a majority of Americans.

12 Presidents and the Crisis of the Press

Two weeks after the bloody attack against Congress, Joe Biden and Kamala Harris were inaugurated on January 20, 2021. Like the cavalry that guarded Lincoln's inauguration from Confederate insurrectionists, heavily armed National Guard troops ringed the Capitol to protect the ceremony. Because extremists had threatened another assault against the government, some news organizations selected journalists with war-zone experience to cover the event. "We realized that we had the same conversations about what to do during the uprisings in Libya or Cairo," *Intercept* photographer Ron Haviv said, "or fighting in Baghdad or coup attempts here or there."[1]

In his speech Biden alluded to the conspiracy theories circulating in the media that led to the coup attempt. "Recent weeks and months have taught us a painful lesson," Biden said. "There is truth and there are lies. Lies told for power and for profit."[2] But the truth was hard to find on some media outlets following the ceremony. Rush Limbaugh said the idea that Biden legitimately took office was "bogus." Without giving any evidence, Tucker Carlson insisted, "Joe Biden isn't well—Everyone in Washington knows that." OAN pretended the inauguration didn't exist. It skipped the ceremony and Biden's speech, instead running a segment titled "Trump: Legacy of a Patriot."[3]

Once the presidential transfer of power occurred without any more bloodshed, the Washington press corps was ready to cover the new administration. That evening Biden press secretary Jen Psaki spoke to reporters in the White House briefing room. Unlike Sean Spicer's first briefing four years earlier, she didn't lash out at the press. She answered questions calmly. And she told no lies about the size of the inauguration. *Washington Post* media columnist Margaret Sullivan described it as "weirdly normal."[4]

The next day Biden sat at a White House table signing executive orders to address the COVID crisis. As Biden finished, Zeke Miller of the Associated Press asked if the administration's goal of one hundred million Americans being vaccinated in the next hundred days was "high enough." Biden bristled. "Come on, give me a break, man," he responded. "It's a good start, a hundred million." He then walked away without taking any more questions.[5]

The scene was a sign that the new president and the press would be in tension with each other as they had been during every other administration in U.S. history. After all, their goals are fundamentally different. Presidents try to communicate their messages to the American people without interference, attempting to frame their actions and policies in the best ways possible. And reporters are constantly probing for more information, asking questions presidents don't always want to answer, and framing stories based on their own judgments. By the end of Biden's first week in office, PolitiFact had already set up a "Biden Promise Tracker," and the *New York Times* ran a fact check of his statements so far as president.[6] No doubt there will be deeper investigations of the Biden administration as his presidency unfolds. That's the way it should be when journalists cover presidents.

Since the founding of the United States, the relationship between presidents and the press has been inspiring and troubling, fragile and durable, vital and dysfunctional, often all at the same time. As we have seen throughout this book, the following dynamics have shaped the current tense relationship.

Starting with the nation's early years, presidents have frequently attacked, restricted, manipulated, and demonized the press in order to strengthen their own power. The Adams administration used the Sedition Act to jail editors, Lincoln allowed newspapers to be shut down, and Wilson and George W. Bush used misleading propaganda to promote going to war. The Wilson and Obama White Houses sought to intimidate the press through the Espionage Act. Nixon sent Agnew to give speeches describing the press as a treacherous enemy. Trump amplified this dangerous hostility by his glorification of violence against journalists and his characterization of the press as un-American.

While Trump and other leaders menaced journalists, technological advances fragmented the media and enhanced presidents' ability to avoid the White House press corps and communicate directly to the public. Roosevelt used radio, Kennedy and Reagan mastered television, and Obama turned to social media to reach mass audiences without relying on the gatekeepers of the press. Clinton and Obama used TV entertainment and talk shows for the same purpose. Trump deployed Twitter successfully to set his own agenda and often overwhelm the ability of journalists to put his presidency in perspective.

Trump, however, never learned the lesson that presidents who nurture respectful relationships with reporters have more long-term success than those who don't. "Some presidents are reasonably secure in themselves, or in the affection of the voters," former White House reporter James Deakin observed. "As a result, their dealings with the news media, although highly important, do not become an overriding or neurotic preoccupation."[7] Lincoln, FDR, Kennedy, and Reagan had that kind of confidence along with good senses of humor. Adams, Wilson, Nixon, and Trump certainly didn't.

Although sometimes sloppy, partisan, and sensationalistic, journalists have often courageously served the public when covering presidents despite formidable forces trying to stop them. Matthew Lyon went to jail rather than muzzle his criticism of John Adams. Victor Berger went to prison because his newspaper opposed Wilson's war plans. Katharine Graham supported Carl Bernstein and Bob Woodward's investigations of Watergate despite Nixon's attempts to punish the *Washington Post*. Knight Ridder reporters bravely and accurately challenged Bush's misleading rationale for going to war in Iraq. And many journalists continued to question and investigate Trump in the face of furious threats against them.

Sometimes pressure on presidents has come from social movements that have harnessed the media to advocate for dramatic policy changes. The abolitionist press proved this. Frederick Douglass, William Lloyd Garrison, Elijah Lovejoy, and other abolitionist writers spread their descriptions and denunciations of slavery through newspapers and pamphlets that were passed from person to person, eventually influencing Lincoln. Other social movements, such as the long campaign to win voting rights for women, employed similar tactics. The activists of the Black Lives Matter movement, some of them acting as citizen journalists, have used social media to share videos, photographs, firsthand accounts, and other information about police violence. Although most aren't employed by news companies, their deft handling of media allowed their message to reach millions of people, spurring professional journalists to deepen their coverage of the Black Lives Matter cause. Trump mocked the Black Lives Matter movement, but now it is influencing the Biden administration to take steps to reform policing and reduce systemic racism.

Since George Washington's second term, partisans in the media have frequently attacked presidents and other politicians. Writers such as William Duane and James Callender showed how vicious the press could be during the Adams administration. William Randolph Hearst, Henry Luce, Col. Robert McCormick, and Charles Coughlin ferociously attacked Franklin Roosevelt. Partisanship has escalated in recent years following Reagan's destruction of the Fairness Doctrine. Powerful right-wing media—unmatched by anything nearly so strong on the left—intensified the nation's polarization during the Clinton, Bush, Obama, and Trump presidencies. Talk radio hosts, conservative cable channels, and websites such as *InfoWars* spread conspiracy theories and abetted Trump's effort to overturn democracy.

This toxic partisanship has encouraged a growing disregard for the truth by some recent presidents and their media allies, eroding trust in democratic government. Nixon deceived the public about Watergate, Reagan about Iran-Contra, Clinton about his extramarital affairs, and Bush about the Iraq War, to name a few. Trump trampled the truth at a pace that far surpassed his predecessors. As historian Timothy Snyder notes, "Post-truth is pre-fascism, and Trump has been our post-truth president."[8]

The truth about presidents may now be harder to know. The declining economic health of the news business has weakened its ability to hold presidents accountable. One reason the nation has been in crisis is that journalism is in crisis. Squeezed by financial pressures and disrupted by powerful new technologies, U.S. journalism is struggling to survive. The press will need substantial change if it is to effectively report on government, lessen the polarization that threatens democracy, and combat disinformation that denies election results, climate change, and the existence of pandemics.

The rest of this chapter examines journalism's crisis and offers recommendations for what news organizations, government, and the public can do to allow the press to perform its essential role in U.S. democracy. Change is necessary if we want to avoid a perilous descent into authoritarianism.

In the 1920s Colonel McCormick held an international architectural competition to design a grand tower in the heart of Chicago for his powerful *Chicago Tribune*. The resulting building resembled a Gothic cathedral. A soaring monument to the power of the press, it housed the offices of the *Tribune* and its affiliated WGN radio station for nearly a century. Then financial pressures forced the Tribune to abandon its tower in 2018 and move to a nearby office building. Less than three years later, the struggling company announced it would move its newsroom to a windowless space behind its printing plant in an industrial area away from downtown. In early 2021 the *Tribune* and three sister newspapers—the *New York Daily News, Orlando Sentinel,* and *Hartford Courant*—were bought by Alden Global Capital, a hedge fund infamous for slashing reporting jobs at the other newspapers it owns. Within six weeks, Alden had let go or bought out the contracts of at least 10 percent of Tribune Publishing's already diminished newsroom staff.[9]

The *Tribune*'s fall from glory is just one example of the economic pain felt by news companies in recent years. The press's financial crisis has weakened the quality of journalism, including reporting about the presidency. For most of the twentieth century, many newspapers and magazines enjoyed enormous financial success. Some had profit margins of up to 30 percent thanks to hefty advertising revenues; local TV stations often had even bigger profits. Even midsized newspapers could afford to have at least one reporter cover the White House. The broadcast networks, news magazines, and big newspapers had many more. By the end of the twentieth century, thousands of journalists covered Washington.[10]

But then journalism's economic structure started crumbling. Owners of newspapers, which produced the majority of original reporting, recklessly took on massive debt to finance mergers and expansion in the 1990s and early 2000s. They struggled to pay creditors after the recessions in 2001 and 2007–9 led to steep drops in advertising revenue. Some eventually went bankrupt.[11] Meanwhile, the digital revolution drained more money away from legacy news outlets. Only 2 percent of Americans went online regularly for news in 1995. By the end of Trump's term, more than 90 percent of U.S. adults got at least some of their news digitally. Advertisers followed them, and Facebook became the biggest media company in world history.[12]

Facebook, Instagram, Twitter, YouTube, and other social media apps and websites have given people fabulous opportunities to connect with each other and share photos, videos, and information. At the same time, the companies have acted like digital parasites when it comes to news, profiting from content created by news outlets while producing little actual journalism themselves. Google and Facebook alone absorbed three-fifths of all digital advertising revenue by 2018.[13] These changes have devastated U.S. journalism. Between 2004 and 2020, the number of newsroom reporters plummeted more than 60 percent. About 1,800 U.S. communities were left with no local news outlet at all. Then COVID arrived, and advertisers slashed spending even more. During the first three months of the pandemic, an estimated thirty-six thousand U.S. news workers either were furloughed, were laid off, or suffered pay cuts.[14]

The economic distress has weakened White House reporting. The best public affairs journalism is expensive to do. It requires time on the beat to develop sources, find relevant data and documents, and identify trends. Investigative reporting is even costlier because months or even years of reporting are required for in-depth projects. High costs have forced many news outlets to reduce or eliminate their DC bureaus and investigative projects.[15]

Despite journalism's economic turmoil, a few national news outlets still managed to prosper. Ironically, some of the media companies that Trump insisted were failing—and had investigated him the hardest—actually thrived during his presidency. Between 2016 and 2020, both the *New York Times* and *Washington Post* tripled their digital subscribers. Trump was also lucrative for cable news, whose audiences couldn't turn away from the spectacle of his presidency.[16] For the first time, MSNBC's operating revenues climbed above $1 billion in 2019, doubling its total from five years earlier. In 2020 CNN reached more viewers than ever before. And Fox News continued to rule the cable news roost, leading the ratings on most days.[17] But even though a handful of large media companies were succeeding financially, most news organizations still struggled.

To survive, the news media must continually reinvent itself. Fortunately, the past fifteen years have seen the birth of *Axios, Bustle, Grio, The Intercept, Latino USA, Politico, ProPublica, The 19th, Daily Beast, The Root, Vox*, and other news outlets that are primarily or completely digital and produce valuable journalism. More than a third of Americans now listen to podcasts, many of them featuring politics and investigative reporting, at least once a month.[18] Newsrooms will need to accelerate this type of innovation to reach young audiences where they are, whether its TikTok, Reddit, or Twitch today or completely new media platforms tomorrow.

Digital transformation, however, may not be enough to overcome journalism's financial struggles. The press needs an assist from government. George Washington and Congress created the model for this when they decided to give the press a boost in 1792. Recognizing the value of an informed citizenry, they approved the Postal Service Act, allowing newspapers to circulate through the mail at a steep discount. The law greatly enhanced the distribution of news through the mostly rural country. Just as Washington and the other founders did, we should recognize quality journalism as a basic public good that needs support just as education, transit, and the common defense do.[19] It's time once again for the government to look for ways to bolster the press so it depends less on shrinking advertising revenue.

The federal government should pressure Google, Facebook, Twitter, and other social media companies to send more of the profits they make from the work of journalists—including White House reporters—back to the news outlets who produce the content in the first place. Occasionally the companies vow to help. In 2018 Google pledged $300 million to assist news organizations. The following year, Facebook announced it would pay for content appearing in a news tab it was launching.[20] But these efforts were drops in the buckets of revenue that social media companies have siphoned from news outlets.

If the tech giants don't compensate news organizations in a fairer way, Congress can take antitrust action against them or close some of their tax loopholes. It can also pass a law like one introduced in Australia requiring Facebook, Google, and other digital platforms to pay for news content appearing on their platforms. Using a different approach, Maryland's legislature passed a new tax in February 2020 on digital advertising revenue, which will generate an estimated $250 million annually. Some European countries already have a similar tax, and Indiana and Connecticut are considering adding ones of their own.[21] States can allocate some of the tax money to news outlets whose content the digital companies are taking.

The Local Journalism Sustainability Act, introduced to the U.S. House in 2020 and again in 2021 with fifty-three Democratic and Republican cosponsors, is another option. The bill would give Americans a $250 tax credit if they subscribe to local newspapers or donate to nonprofit news organizations. Media companies would get a tax break for employing journalists, and so would small businesses for advertising in local media. News outlets would compete for subscriptions and donations, giving them incentives to produce quality journalism. If the act becomes law, it could provide an estimated $5.5 billion annually to strengthen the press.[22]

The U.S. government currently funds journalism on a smaller scale by contributing to the Corporation for Public Broadcasting. Managed independently of the government, it provides money to 1,500 local television and radio stations along with NPR and PBS. It received $445 million from the federal government in 2020, or about $1.35 per U.S. resident.[23] Would it be worth another $10 per American to support digital, broadcast, and print outlets that provide fact-based journalism to counter the surge of disinformation? I think so.

The *American Thinker* was forced to print an extraordinary retraction in January 2021. Apparently the *Thinker*, a conservative online magazine, hadn't thought carefully before publishing fake allegations that the voting machine company Dominion Voting Systems had conspired to rig the 2020 election for Biden. When Dominion threatened to sue, the *Thinker* admitted it had "relied on discredited sources who have peddled debunked theories. . . . These statements are completely false and have no basis in fact. . . . We also apologize to our readers for abandoning 9 journalistic principles and misrepresenting Dominion's track record and its limited role in tabulating votes for the November 2020 election."[24] Threatened with lawsuits, Fox News and Newsmax were forced to run their own "clarifications" after making similar false allegations against another voting technology company.[25]

Apologies like the *American Thinker's* and clarifications like Fox's and Newsmax's won't be enough to stop the flood of disinformation that has swept through the media. In April 2020 content from the ten most popular COVID misinformation sites received three hundred million views on Facebook; information from ten top health institutions received only seventy million. Facebook had become "a killing field for truth," Shoshana Zuboff of the Harvard Business School observed.[26] A month after Biden's inauguration, more than two-thirds of Republican voters wrongly believed the election had been stolen despite the lack of supporting evidence.[27] Alarmed by the conspiracy theories spreading after the 2020 election, Facebook adjusted its algorithms so users would see more fact-based content from reliable journalism sources. But the change was only temporary because the social media colossus didn't want to hurt its profits.[28]

Facebook and other social media companies should permanently change their algorithms so they no longer propagate disinformation. They also must consistently place warning labels on misleading political posts as they did during the months before the 2020 election. And they ought to shut down accounts—even ones originating in the Oval Office—that frequently spread bogus conspiracy theories. If they don't, Congress can act. Section 230 of the 1996 Communications Decency Act gives technology platforms immunity for the content they distribute, no matter how untrue or damaging. Section 230 can be revoked if the social media titans don't limit the flow of disinformation.[29]

When he was president, Teddy Roosevelt liked to invite a few reporters into a room near the Oval Office to chat as a barber gave him an afternoon shave. With a face full of lather, the president shared news tips, answered questions, and traded jokes. The reporters loved it, and they increased the number of stories they wrote about his administration, frequently with the spin he wanted. Prior to Roosevelt, reporters didn't cover the White House on a regular basis. Roosevelt changed that. By using savvy methods like the shaving visits, Roosevelt promoted himself rather than Congress as the center of national attention.[30] The formerly sleepy White House beat was further awakened as his successors hired press secretaries, added news conferences, produced mountains of press releases, and began making national broadcasts. The two world wars, the New Deal, the Cold War, Watergate, and the post-9/11 battles against terrorists further increased the media's focus on the executive branch.

Now presidents receive nearly constant attention, and that's a problem. The traditional standards of mainstream journalism, which emphasize statements made by top officials, give prominence to nearly every presidential remark. But as journalism historian Perry Parks explains, covering Trump in that manner amplified and normalized lying, name-calling, and the embracing of authoritarianism.[31] Obviously, important presidential policies and statements should be deeply reported and executive branch wrongdoing investigated. But the press doesn't need to cover every presidential tweet and utterance or constantly speculate about behind-the-scenes White House drama.[32]

The day after Sean Spicer spent his first briefing attacking the press for accurately reporting the size of Trump's inauguration crowd, media analyst Jay Rosen had a suggestion: news outlets should send interns rather than their veteran reporters to White House press conferences if nonsense is being spouted.[33] Instead of endlessly discussing the administration's falsehoods, the press could have better covered Trump's presidency by focusing more on climate change, structural racism, widening income inequality, the continuing war in Afghanistan, and the collapsing public health system. Additional attention must also be paid to Congress, federal agencies, and state and local governments, which have received less coverage in recent decades. And if future presidents insist on lying, the press should stop carrying their speeches, interviews, and briefings live so they can be fact-checked before being presented to the public.[34]

BuzzFeed published a shocking story in January 2019: Trump had encouraged his former lawyer Michael Cohen to lie to Congress about the president's business dealings in Russia.[35] If true, the president had broken the law. The next day, MSNBC and CNN mentioned impeaching Trump 179 times, salivating over a possibility many liberals had dreamed of since Trump's inauguration.[36] But Special Counsel Robert Mueller's office quickly refuted the *BuzzFeed* story. It was an example of a news outlet being so eager to publish sensational news that it didn't carefully verify its information. The bad journalism was a gift to Trump, giving him ammunition for his claims that the press was full of "fake news."[37]

Now more than ever, the press needs to be careful not to publish or air flawed stories. Journalists were sloppy too often during Trump's presidency. ABC News's Brian Ross falsely reported in 2017 that Trump had directed Michael Flynn to reach out to Russian officials during the 2016 campaign. Four days later the *Wall Street Journal* and other news outlets erred when they said Mueller's team subpoenaed Deutsche Bank for Trump's business records. A few days afterward CNN incorrectly said Donald Trump Jr. knew ahead of time that WikiLeaks was going to publish stolen documents from the Democratic National Committee.[38]

These mistakes amounted to a tiny percentage of the stories produced about Trump, but they tarnished the reputations of the offending news organization and journalism as a whole. The press needs to double down on accuracy because it can't afford further damage to its image. About six out of every seven Americans think bias exists in news coverage, a Gallup/Knight Foundation study found in 2020. Increasing numbers of people don't trust fact-based journalism at all, making it easier for propaganda to flourish.[39]

The cable news channels have decreased their own original, fact-based reporting, which costs more to do than opinion journalism. Instead, CNN, MSNBC, and Fox News rely heavily on opinionated commentators and endless panels of pundits who are encouraged to be provocative. The cable channels have found greater success appealing to intensely loyal, politically passionate news followers than by trying to capture a mass audience with mixed viewpoints. A 2019 study in the *Journal of Communication* found that people with the most extreme views on the left and right are overrepresented on cable as well as network news shows.[40]

This intense media partisanship exacerbates political polarization. Rather than simply disagree, Americans are now more likely to actively hate people from the other political party and consider them to be "immoral" and "dislikable," a 2020 study found. This polarization makes politicians less willing to compromise,[41] and it enables leaders like Trump with authoritarian instincts to incite violence. Political scientists Steven Levitsky and Daniel Ziblatt have found that "extreme polarization can kill democracies."[42] Indeed, it contributed to the attempted coup of January 2021.

What can be done about media polarization? Ever since the death of the Fairness Doctrine in 1987, broadcast channels haven't been required to present a range of viewpoints. With the exponential growth of cable and digital news, government regulation of content may now be impossible and is likely unwise. But journalism codes of ethics that emphasize fairness and accuracy already exist. They ought to be promoted, and news outlets should be transparent about which ones they use. The outlets that follow these standards could feature a logo signaling to the public that they seek a variety of perspectives and are committed to accuracy. Readers, listeners, and viewers would be able to point out when the standards aren't being followed.

These standards must prioritize greater diversity within journalism. In 1954 reporter Ethel Payne of the *Chicago Defender*—only the second Black woman permitted to cover the White House—asked President

Eisenhower when he was going to ban segregation in interstate travel. It was a question that the white reporters who dominated the press corps hadn't thought to ask even though it was an issue that affected millions of Americans. Payne's exchange with Eisenhower made news around the country.[43]

The press would paint a clearer picture of the presidency—and the United States—if its members came from a broader range of backgrounds. Journalists are less likely to be women, working class, and people of color than the U.S. population as a whole.[44] News organizations must recognize their own racism, sexism, homophobia, and elitism if they are going to truly hold accountable the president and others with power. They should regularly rotate reporters away from covering the president and have them spend time covering the rest of the country to learn about the issues that concern a broad range of Americans the most. They can bring that understanding back to the White House beat and ask questions that are more reflective of the public's needs and less focused on insider politics, just as Ethel Payne did with Eisenhower.

Ultimately, the fate of the relationship between presidents and the press isn't only up to the government, individual journalists, or tech companies. It's up to the American people. Citizens choose their leaders and pick which channels to watch, what publications to read, and whose social media feeds to follow. They have the power to ignore talk radio hosts spewing vitriol, the shouting pundits of the cable news circus, and social media posts spinning wild conspiracy theories. The public can opt instead for fully reported news stories that use verified information. The big challenge, of course, is how to motivate people to do so.

Back in 2006, when social media was in its infancy and political bloggers were gaining prominence, journalist Dan Gillmor made a prediction in his book *We the Media*: "If this goes well, we'll move into a new era of media literacy and what we might call news activism."[45] Gillmor was right about news activism, but media literacy hasn't improved. As rampant disinformation about the coronavirus, climate change, and the 2020 election made abundantly clear, we need to make media literacy a requirement in schools and encourage adults to master it too. Understanding the media that saturate our lives is just as important now as algebra or poetry for navigating the world. We must learn how to separate news from opinion, evaluate the accuracy of information, seek a range of perspectives, recognize the ways algorithms determine what we see online, distinguish between journalism and marketing, and analyze how fear, outrage, and disinformation are used to lure audiences.[46] If Americans can understand how journalism and propaganda work and distinguish one from the other, they are more likely to be informed and discerning citizens who can preserve democracy.

Fortunately, we already have models of how this can work. The Center for News Literacy, the News Literacy Project, and Media Literacy Now provide resources for teachers.[47] At least eighteen U.S. colleges and universities offered media literacy courses in 2020; some have media literacy minors.[48] Senator Amy Klobuchar of Minnesota and seven cosponsors introduced a bill in 2019 that would spend $20 million to promote media literacy education.[49] Passing it would be a good beginning if we are serious about combating disinformation.

Trump was tremendously effective at gaining attention and communicating with his loyal base of supporters. But he never developed the kind of healthy relationship with the press that he needed to serve the majority of Americans. What can Biden and future presidents do to improve the relationship between presidents and the press? No doubt they'll keep trying to spin the news in their favor and deploy technology to send their messages directly to the public without going through reporters. They'll certainly complain that journalists don't always give them the coverage they want. But they should also recognize that a productive relationship with the press can strengthen their presidencies.

For starters, presidents would be smart to make themselves accessible to reporters from a broad range of news outlets. Trump heavily favored Fox News and eventually OAN, relying on them for friendly interviews that rarely included tough questions. By staying in his comfort zone of conservative media, he had a harder time reaching out to the moderate voters that he needed to win reelection. It left him ill-prepared when he encountered tough questioning from less conservative journalists. It didn't expose him to the concerns and perspectives of people outside his political base. And it allowed him to wallow in conspiracy theories without being challenged.

Like Toto in the *Wizard of Oz*, the watchdog press pulled back the curtain on Trump, using story after story to expose a cruel and inept man not up to the job that he claimed to be great at doing. To distract people, he relentlessly assaulted the press, but those attacks boomeranged on him just as similar attacks had on Richard Nixon. Like most people, journalists don't take kindly to being told lies or hearing threats and insults. Trump's aggressive hostility made many journalists more determined than ever to persistently report on his failings.

Wise presidents do not demonize or try to suppress the press. Those who get along with journalists tend to be the ones remembered most favorably by future generations. Lincoln, both Roosevelts, Kennedy, and Reagan had friendly relationships with reporters, and historians usually rank them among the top tier of greatest U.S. presidents.[50] After all, journalists write the first rough drafts of history that start to define each president's legacy. That history will be unlikely to remember Trump kindly, which is a lesson future presidents would do well to remember.

ACKNOWLEDGMENTS

This book began with a handshake. When I was five, my family went on vacation to San Diego, where my dad heard that Republican presidential candidate Richard Nixon was staying at a hotel down the beach. Dad took my brother and me over to Nixon's hotel, and we waited outside until he appeared. We walked over to him, and Nixon graciously shook our hands. Nixon won that 1968 election, and my fascination with the presidency was born. It grew during the lively dinner table conversations my parents, Maxine and Jonathan Marshall, held with my siblings and me about politics and the press (both of them were newspaper editors). I remain forever grateful to them for sparking my love of learning and for their enduring support.

I have been extraordinarily fortunate to enjoy the support of many others while working on this book. My colleagues at Northwestern University's Medill School of Journalism, Media, and Integrated Marketing Communications have been marvelous. Dean Charles Whitaker and Associate Dean Beth Bennett provided encouragement and time to complete my research and writing. So did former dean Brad Hamm and former associate dean Craig LaMay. David Abrahamson has been a wise mentor who helped me to shape the initial idea for this book, and Senior Associate Dean Tim Franklin was generous with his help. Members of Medill Creatives & Researchers United gave useful feedback as I crafted my proposal. Jenna Braunstein offered valuable assistance and a much-appreciated sense of humor. I am lucky to work with such a great group of people.

The students in my classes, particularly those in my Watergate's Legacy & the Press seminar, have inspired me with their scholarship. I'm especially grateful to three amazing students who served as research assistants while I wrote this book. Nirmal Mulaikal gathered essential information for the initial proposal and contributed content for the Wilson chapter. Tina Huang proofread several chapters and helped with a preliminary draft of the Clinton chapter. Gregory Svirnovskiy helped edit the entire manuscript, gathered information for the Trump chapters, and checked endnotes. All three of them provided wise counsel and good company. Hire them if you can.

I am indebted to the many scholars whose wisdom and tireless research have informed this book. I learn constantly from my fellow members of the American Journalism Historians Association and the Association for Education in Journalism and Mass Communication. David Sloan shared with me an extensive bibliography he compiled of books on media history. Ford Risley offered thoughtful feedback on the Lincoln chapter. And Tom Mascaro read through the entire manuscript, giving valuable advice for every chapter. I can't thank them enough.

Other friends and family members generously offered to read chapter drafts and share helpful editing suggestions. I'm indebted to Gail Goldstein, Laurie Goldstein, Art Gunther, Jennifer Lind, Carol Shukur, and Andrew, Justin, Laura, and Zachary Marshall for their insightful feedback and kindness. Don Goldstein, Roberta Luisza Marshall, and Lucinda Marshall provided much-needed wisdom and encouragement throughout the process.

I also deeply appreciate archivists everywhere whose work to digitize their collections made it possible to find a bounty of primary sources despite the travel constraints of a pandemic. I owe a special thanks to Christopher Davidson of the Northwestern University Library, who directed me to many valuable resources.

I can't thank Jane Curran enough for her careful and thorough copy-editing. Michael Mungiello has been a superstar agent; I'm grateful to him and the entire team at InkWell Management for guiding me through this process and finding a home for this book. Michelle Blankenship has been terrific about helping with publicity. Tom Swanson, Taylor Rothgeb, Sara Springsteen, Rosemary Sekora, Tayler Lord, Tish Fobben, Andrea Shahan, and the rest of the staff of Potomac Books and the University of Nebraska Press have been wonderful, and I thank them for bringing this book into the world and for patiently answering my many questions.

Justin, Andrew, and Zachary Marshall encouraged me throughout this process and offered valuable editing tips. Their senses of humor kept me smiling, and they never complained when I disappeared into my basement office for long stretches of writing time. I'm a lucky dad. And thanks most of all to Laurie Goldstein, my best friend, inspiration, and companion in the journey of life. She's also an ace editor who patiently put up with my emotional ups and downs during the writing process. I adore her.

NOTES

INTRODUCTION

1. "New Cases by Day," COVID-19 (Coronavirus Disease) Cases, Data, and Surveillance, Centers for Disease Control and Prevention, accessed December 12, 2020, https://www.cdc.gov/coronavirus/2019-ncov/cases-updates/previouscases.html.

2. "Remarks by President Trump, Vice President Pence, and Members of the Coronavirus Task Force in Press Briefing," White House, March 19, 2020, https://trumpwhitehouse.archives.gov/briefings-statements/remarks-president-trump-vice-president-pence-members-coronavirus-task-force-press-briefing-3/; Oliver Darcy and Jim Acosta, "White House Correspondents Association Removes Far-Right Outlet from Briefing Room Rotation," CNN, April 1, 2020; E. J. Dickson, "How Far Will Chanel Rion Go for Trump?" *Rolling Stone*, September 25, 2020, https://www.rollingstone.com/culture/culture-features/oan-chanel-rion-trump-correspondent-1003975/.

3. "Remarks by President Trump," March 19, 2020; Tom Jones, "A 'Reporter's' Softball, a President's Swing," Poynter, March 20, 2020; Manuel Roig-Franzia and Sarah Ellison, "A History of the Trump War on Media—the Obsession Not Even Coronavirus Could Stop," *Washington Post*, March 29, 2020; "President's Response to Chanel Rion," C-SPAN, March 19, 2020, https://www.c-span.org/video/?c4862397/user-clip-presidents-response-chanel-rion.

4. Margaret Sullivan, "Trump Has Sown Hatred of the Press for Years," *Washington Post*, May 30, 2020; Anne Gearan and Josh Dawsey, "Stephanie Grisham Out as White House Press Secretary," *Washington Post*, April 7, 2020.

5. Tom Gralish, "Scene through the Lens: June 29, 2020," *Philadelphia Inquirer*, June 29, 2020, https://www.inquirer.com/photo/photojournalism-aggession

-black-lives-matter-floyd-journalism-gralish-philadelphia-20200629.html; "Tehran Court Sentences AmadNews Editor Rouhollah Zam to Death," Reporters without Borders, June 30, 2020, https://rsf.org/en/news/tehran -court-sentences-amadnews-editor-rouhollah-zam-death; "Let's Not Allow Beijing to Stifle Press Freedom in Hong Kong," Reporters without Borders, June 30 2020, https://rsf.org/en/news/rsf-lets-not-allow-beijing-stifle-press -freedom-hong-kong; "Opposition Reporter Convicted on Trumped-up Hooliganism Charge," Reporters without Borders, June 25, 2020, https://rsf .org/en/news/opposition-reporter-convicted-trumped-hooliganism-charge.

6. Hindman and Barash, *Disinformation, "Fake News," and Influence Campaigns*; Sheera Frenkel, Kate Conger, and Kevin Roose, "Russia's Disinformation Playbook for Social Media Disinformation Has Gone Global," *New York Times*, January 31, 2019; Ben Collins, "On Reddit, Russian Propagandists Try New Tricks," NBC News, September 25, 2018, https://www.nbcnews.com/tech /tech-news/reddit-russian-propagandists-try-new-tricks-n913131.

7. Michael M. Grynbaum, Sydney Ember, and Charlie Savage, "Trump's Urging That Comey Jail Reporters Denounced as an 'Act of Intimidation,'" *New York Times*, May 18, 2017, A13; Colby Itkowitz, "Trump Threatens Reporter with Prison Time during Interview," *Washington Post*, June 21, 2019; Grace Panetta, "Trump Called Journalists 'Scumbags' Who Should Be 'Executed,' According to John Bolton's New Book," *Business Insider*, June 17, 2020.

I. JOHN ADAMS

1. "Communication," *American Citizen and General Advertiser*, July 1, 1800, 2; *Aurora*, August 4, 1800, cited in Rosenfeld, *American Aurora*, 831; Pasley, *"Tyr- anny of Printers,"* 185–88; Daniel, *Scandal & Civility*, 234, 258–59, 281; Brown, *John Adams and the America Press*, 36; A. C. Clark, *William Duane*, 16, 21, 57; Tagg, *Benjamin Franklin Bache*, 92–95; Phillips, *William Duane*, 2; Sheppard, *Partisan Press*, 42.

2. *Gazette of the United States*, December 2, 1799, 3; Timothy Pickering, letter to John Adams, July 24, 1799, in Adams, *Works of John Adams*, 9:3; Phillips, *William Duane*, 70–75; Daniel, *Scandal & Civility*, 77–80, 261; A. C. Clark, *William Duane*, 21–22; Sheppard, *Partisan Press*, 37; Pasley, *"Tyranny of Print- ers,"* 190; Halperin, *Alien and Sedition Acts*, 93.

3. John Adams, letter to the Attorney-General and the District-Attorney of Pennsylvania, in *Works of John Adams*, 56; Pollard, *Presidents and the Press*, 43; A. C. Clark, *William Duane*, 17–18; Phillips, *William Duane*, 81–91; Stone, *Perilous Times*, 65–66; Senate Historical Office, "Senate Holds Editor in Con- tempt," U.S. Senate, March 27, 1800, https://www.senate.gov/artandhistory

/history/minute/Senate_Holds_Editor_in_Contempt.htm; Daniel, *Scandal & Civility*, 262; Halperin, *Alien and Sedition Acts*, 93.

4. *Aurora*, August 4, 1800, cited in Rosenfeld, *American Aurora*, 831; "Communication," *American Citizen and General Advertiser*, July 1, 1800, 2; Pasley, *"Tyranny of Printers,"* 188.

5. Brown, *John Adams and the America Press*, 2–3, 10; Tagg, *Benjamin Franklin Bache*, 88–89; Sheppard, *Partisan Press*, 46; Chernow, *Alexander Hamilton*, 569.

6. McCullough, *John Adams*, 17, 23, 92, 112–13, 285, 334; Chernow, *Alexander Hamilton*, 520.

7. Chernow, *Alexander Hamilton*, 518; McCullough, *John Adams*, 98, 116, 118–20, 122–23, 126–28, 131–32, 140–41, 177–87, 242–56, 278–85, 328, 384; Grant, *John Adams*, 5–6.

8. McCullough, *John Adams*, 393–94; Chernow, *Alexander Hamilton*, 509–10; Ellis, *Founding Brothers*, 167.

9. Butterfield, Friedlaender, and Kline, *Book of Abigail and John*, 6; McCullough, *John Adams*, 404–8.

10. Tagg, *Benjamin Franklin Bache*, 92; Brown, *John Adams and the America Press*, 5–6; Avery, "Battle without a Rule Book," 24–25; Clive Thompson, "Tweet All about It," *Smithsonian*, May 2016, 43–49.

11. *Gazette of the United States*, April 27, 1791; Rubin, *Press, Party, and Presidency*, 9; C. H. Smith, *Press, Politics and Patronage*, 13–14; Brown, "Federal Era III," 125; Sheppard, *Partisan Press*, 24; Halperin, *Alien and Sedition Acts*, 13; T. E. V. Smith, *City of New York*, 223.

12. "The Union: Who Are Its Real Friends?" *National Gazette*, April 2, 1792, 2; Bowden, *Philip Freneau*, 19–20, 81; C. H. Smith, *Press, Politics and Patronage*, 15; Brown, "Federal Era III," 125; Sheppard, *Partisan Press*, 25.

13. Pasley, *"Tyranny of Printers,"* 67; Risjord, *Thomas Jefferson*, 84–87; Sheppard, *Partisan Press*, 23; Halperin, *Alien and Sedition Acts*, 4, 397.

14. Jonathan Green, "John Adams's Montesquieuean Moment," 232; Halperin, *Alien and Sedition Acts*, 12, 41; McCullough, *John Adams*, 421–22, 434, 441; Ellis, *Founding Brothers*, 168–69; Pollard, *Presidents and the Press*, 37; Chernow, *Alexander Hamilton*, 518.

15. M. E. Clark, "Peter Porcupine in America," 46–47; Halperin, *Alien and Sedition Acts*, 25–26; McCullough, *John Adams*, 449, 456.

16. *Boston Independent Chronicle*, November 23, 1795, cited in Brown, *John Adams and the America Press*, 21; Brown, *John Adams and the America Press*, 20; Halperin, *Alien and Sedition Acts*, 26–27; McCullough, *John Adams*, 456–57.

17. Mark A. Smith, "Andrew Brown's 'Earnest Endeavor': The 'Federal Gazette's Role in Philadelphia's Yellow Fever Epidemic of 1793," *Pennsylvania Magazine*

of History and Biography 120, no. 4 (October 1996): 324–25, 342; Halperin, *Alien and Sedition Acts*, 12–14; Avery, "Battle without a Rule Book," 26; Sheppard, *Partisan Press*, 22, 31; George Washington, letter to Alexander Hamilton, June 26, 1796, Mount Vernon, available at "Founders Online," National Archives, https://founders.archives.gov/documents/Hamilton/01-20-02-0151.

18. "From a Correspondent," *Aurora*, May 18, 1797, 3; Brown, *John Adams and the America Press*, 24, 25; Halperin, *Alien and Sedition Acts*, 39; Scherr, "Inventing the Patriot President," 369; Chernow, *Alexander Hamilton*, 514; *Aurora*, October 29, 1796, cited in McCullough, *John Adams*, 462; "1796," American Presidency Project, University of California Santa Barbara, https://www.presidency.ucsb.edu/statistics/elections/1796.

19. Grant, *John Adams*, 379; McCullough, *John Adams*, 467–68, 519–20; Ellis, *First Family*, 178; Chernow, *Alexander Hamilton*, 523.

20. See *Porcupine's Gazette*, June 12, 1798, 1; Brown, *John Adams and the America Press*, 30; McCullough, *John Adams*, 395–96, 398; James Gigantino, "Slavery and the Slave Trade," *The Encyclopedia of Greater Philadelphia*, https://philadelphiaencyclopedia.org/archive/slavery-and-the-slave-trade/.

21. Grant, *John Adams*, 379–80, 382–83; Chernow, *Alexander Hamilton*, 523; Skowronek, *Politics Presidents Make*, 22; McCullough, *John Adams*, 471–73.

22. "From a Correspondent," *Aurora*, May 18, 1797, 3; Scherr, "Inventing the Patriot President," 386–90; Halperin, *Alien and Sedition Acts*, 43; Sheppard, *Partisan Press*, 33; "Presidential Conundrum," *Aurora*, May 19, 1797, 3; "To the Editor of the Aurora," *Aurora*, July 28, 1797, 2.

23. "Communications," *Aurora*, May 22, 1797, 3; "Philadelphia," *Aurora*, June 19, 1797, 2; Tagg, *Benjamin Franklin Bache*, 104–6; Sheppard, *Partisan Press*, 30; Scherr, "Inventing the Patriot President," 397.

24. Risjord, *Thomas Jefferson*, 103; Chernow, *Alexander Hamilton*, 529–43; Stone, *Perilous Times*, 61; Halperin, *Alien and Sedition Acts of 1798*, 87; Sheppard, *Partisan Press*, 44–46; Brown, "Federal Era III," 126; McCullough, *John Adams*, 492–93.

25. *Porcupine's Gazette*, June 18, 1798, 2; M. C. Clark, "Peter Porcupine in America," 5, 94–95; "Report on an Action"; Daniel, *Scandal & Civility*, 281; Sheppard, *Partisan Press*, 35–36.

26. *Gazette of the United States*, January 30, 1797, 3; McCullough, *John Adams*, 471; M. A. Smith, "Andrew Brown's 'Earnest Endeavor,'" 324–25; Pollard, *Presidents and the Press*, 40; John Adams diary, January 2, 1794, in Adams, *Works of John Adams*, 461; Grant, *John Adams*, 381–82; Chernow, *Alexander Hamilton*, 611–12.

27. *Aurora*, May 23, 1798, 2–3; Brown, *John Adams and the American Press*, 24; Halperin, *Alien and Sedition Acts*, 27–28, 41; Chernow, *Alexander Hamilton*, 546; Grant, *John Adams*, 388–91; McCullough, *John Adams*, 477–79.

28. Ellis, *Founding Brothers*, 189–90; Brown, *John Adams and the America Press*, 27–29; Halperin, *Alien and Sedition Acts*, 41–46; Chernow, *Alexander Hamilton*, 549–50.

29. "Philadelphia, June 20," *Courier of New Hampshire*, July 10, 1798, 3; "Horrors of French Invasion," *Porcupine's Gazette*, June 12, 1798, 2; "Important," *Porcupine's Gazette*, June 18, 1798, 3; Brown, *John Adams and the America Press*, 27–29; Chernow, *Alexander Hamilton*, 552.

30. Grant, *John Adams*, 396–97; Halperin, *Alien and Sedition Acts*, 1–3; McCullough, *John Adams*, 498–501; Pasley, *"Tyranny of the Printers,"* 117–18.

31. Chernow, *Alexander Hamilton*, 552.

32. J. M. Smith, "Political Suppression of Seditious Criticism," 41–42; Ellis, *Founding Brothers*, 191; R. G. Kennedy, *Burr, Hamilton, and Jefferson*, 106–7; Bird, *Press and Speech under Assault*, 253–54; Daniel, *Scandal & Civility*, 224; Halperin, *Alien and Sedition Acts*, 6, 47–48; McCullough, *John Adams*, 504–5; Stone, *Perilous Times*, 33.

33. Halperin, *Alien and Sedition Acts*, 6, 74–77; Chernow, *Alexander Hamilton*, 570; Daniel, *Scandal & Civility*, 278.

34. Senate Historical Office, "Senate Holds Editor in Contempt," U.S. Senate, March 27, 1800, https://www.senate.gov/artandhistory/history/minute/Senate_Holds_Editor_in_Contempt.htm; Pollard, *Presidents and the Press*, 41; Ellis, *Founding Brothers*, 190–91; Bird, *Press and Speech under Assault*, 248, 333–35; Pasley, *"Tyranny of Printers,"* 120, 136.

35. Stone, *Perilous Times*, 44, 67–69; Avery, "Battle without a Rule Book," 42–43; Daniel, *Scandal & Civility*, 278; Grant, *John Adams*, 406; Bird, *Press and Speech under Assault*, 248–49; Halperin, *Alien and Sedition Acts*, 70–71; Brown, *John Adams*, 32.

36. United States Congress, *Annals of Congress*, 766; Bird, *Press and Speech under Assault*, 251, 474; Chernow, *Alexander Hamilton*, 572.

37. John Adams, letter to Timothy Pickering, August 13, 1799, in Adams, *Works of John Adams*, 13–14; Halperin, *Alien and Sedition* Acts, 74.

38. Stone, *Perilous Times*, 15–18; Pasley, *"Tyranny of the Printers,"* 109–11; Brown, *John Adams and the America Press*, 12; Austin, *Matthew Lyon*, 7–44, 96–101; Brown, *John Adams and the America Press*, 26.

39. Austin, *Matthew Lyon*, 105–6.

40. Austin, *Matthew Lyon*, 110–11.

41. Austin, *Matthew Lyon*, 110–13, 117.

42. Austin, *Matthew Lyon*, 109–13, 117, 119–27; Brown, *John Adams and the America Press*, 26, 33.

43. Pasley, "Thomas Greenleaf," 371; Chernow, *Alexander Hamilton*, 575–76; Pasley, *"Tyranny of Printers,"* 125; Brown, *John Adams and the America Press*, 33;

Halperin, *Alien and Sedition Acts*, 84–86, 95–96; Bird, *Press and Speech under Assault*, 280–82; T. Cooper, *Account of the Trial*; Pollard, *Presidents and the Press*, 43; Stone, *Perilous Times*, 54–58.

44. Pasley, *"Tyranny of Printers,"* 136, 140; Bird, *Press and Speech under Assault*, 308–9; J. M. Smith, "Political Suppression of Seditious Criticism," 41–56; Pollard, *Presidents and the Press*, 49.

45. Previous estimates put the number of prosecutions at seventeen, but scholar Wendell Bird discovered additional cases that other historians hadn't counted. See Bird, *Press and Speech under Assault*, xxi–xxii, 258, 388.

46. Bird, *Press and Speech under Assault*, 388–89; Grant, *John Adams*, 408–9; Chernow, *Alexander Hamilton*, 621–25.

47. Brown, *John Adams and the America Press*, 36; Halperin, *Alien and Sedition Acts*, 94; Alvin K. Benson, "Luther Baldwin," *The First Amendment Encyclopedia*, https://www.mtsu.edu/first-amendment/article/1428/luther-baldwin.

48. Bird, *Press and Speech under Assault*, 251, 256, 266; Ellis, *Founding Brothers*, 201; Daniel, *Scandal & Civility*, 256.

49. Bird, *Press and Speech under Assault*, 326; Pasley, *"Tyranny of Printers,"* 128–29, 131, 326; Chernow, *Alexander Hamilton*, 572–73.

50. Burleigh, "To the People of the United States," *Connecticut Courant*, September 15, 1800, 1; Avery, "Battle without a Rule Book," 24; McCullough, *John Adams*, 543–44; "Full Text: Donald Trump Announces a Presidential Bid," *Washington Post*, June 16, 2015.

51. Halperin, *Alien and Sedition Acts*, 112–13; Stone, *Perilous Times*, 62–63; McCullough, *John Adams*, 536–37, 544.

52. The election was held in the days before there were separate ballots for president and vice president, and the candidate with the most votes became president, and the one with the second most votes became vice president. Jefferson and Burr received the same number of electoral votes, and the winner of the presidency was decided by the House of Representatives. "Historical Election Results," National Archives and Records Administration, https://www.archives.gov /federal-register/electoral-college/scores.html; McCullough, *John Adams*, 556.

53. John Adams, letter to Christopher Gadsden, April 16, 1801, cited in Bird, *Press and Speech under Assault*, 263; John Adams, letter to John Trumbull, April 23, 1800, in Adams, *Works of John Adams*, 83–84; Bird, *Press and Speech under Assault*, xxxiii; Ellis, *Founding Brothers*, 203–4.

54. Ellis, *Founding Brothers*, 202; Skowronek, *Politics Presidents Make*, 67–68; McCullough, *John Adams*, 523, 552, 566–67; Pollard, *Presidents and the Press*, 43; Halperin, *Alien and Sedition Acts*, 84–86; Stone, *Perilous Times*, 54–58; *Aurora*, March 11, 1801, cited in McCullough, *John Adams*, 564–65.

55. Halperin, *Alien and Sedition Acts*, 90–91; Chernow, *Alexander Hamilton*, 663; McCullough, *John Adams*, 577–80.

56. Daniel, *Scandal & Civility*, 282–83.

57. Thomas Jefferson, letter to Edward Carrington, January 16, 1787, "Founders Online," National Archives, https://founders.archives.gov/documents /Jefferson/01-11-02-0047; Stone, *Perilous Times*, 72–73; Ellis, *Founding Brothers*, 205; Halperin, *Alien and Sedition Acts*, 6, 120–21; Chernow, *Alexander Hamilton*, 667; McCullough, *John Adams*, 577.

58. Bird, *Press and Speech under Assault*, 467–69; Halperin, *Alien and Sedition Acts*, 125–27; Chernow, *Alexander Hamilton*, 667–71; Thomas Jefferson, letter to John Norvell, June 14, 1807, in Jefferson, *Works of Thomas Jefferson*, 10:417–18.

2. ABRAHAM LINCOLN

1. "Emancipation Jubilee," *Liberator*, January 2, 1863, 1; J. L. Thomas, *Liberator*, 207; Blight, *Frederick Douglass*, 382; Lois Leveen, "The Civil War's Oratorical Wunderkind," *New York Times*, May 21, 2013; Harrold, *Lincoln and the Abolitionists*, 91; Risley, *Abolition and the Press*, 168.

2. Gates, "Abraham Lincoln on Race," xxx–xxxii.

3. "Emancipation Jubilee," *Liberator*, January 2, 1863, 1; Harrold, *Lincoln and the Abolitionists*, 1, 91; Oakes, *Radical and the Republican*, 173.

4. "Emancipation Jubilee," *Liberator*, January 2, 1863, 1; Risley, *Abolition and the Press*, 168; McFeely, *Frederick Douglass*, 215–16; "African American Churches of Beacon Hill," National Park Service, https://www.nps.gov/boaf/learn /historyculture/churches.htm; "History—Anti-Slavery Meeting House," Twelfth Baptist Church, https://www.tbcboston.org/history-anti-slavery -meetinghouse/; Blight, *Frederick Douglass*, 383–84; Harrold, *Lincoln and the Abolitionists*, 91, 382–83.

5. Bacon, *Freedom's Journal*, 211; Delbanco, *Abolitionist Imagination*, 4–6; Tripp, "Journalism for God and Man," 50, 52–55, 63; Risley, *Abolition and the Press*, 9, 188.

6. Kaplan, *Lincoln and the Abolitionists*, 25, 56; Guelzo, *Lincoln's Emancipation Proclamation*, 17–18; Risley, *Abolition and the Press*, 40; Chernow, *Alexander Hamilton*, 628–29; Gates, "Abraham Lincoln on Race," xxi, xxx.

7. "Abolition of Slavery," *Freedom's Journal*, September 19, 1828; "Runaway Slave," *Freedom's Journal*, December 21, 1827; Bacon, *Freedom's Journal*, 212–13, 218.

8. Bacon, *Freedom's Journal*, 37, 241, 251–52, 262–63, 270–72; Washburn, *African American Newspaper*, 19, 23,24, 27.

9. W. L. Katz, introduction to Walker, *Walker's Appeal*, 1; Walker, *Walker's Appeal*, 58, 80; Kaplan, *Lincoln and the Abolitionists*, 311.

10. Gabrial, *Press and Slavery in America*, 38–39; Bacon, *Freedom's Journal*, 260; Risley, *Abolition and the Press*, 26.

11. Description based on photograph, *William Lloyd Garrison*, Library of Congress Prints and Photographs Division, https://www.loc.gov/item /2004672098/; Thomas, *The Liberator*, 7, 130; Risley, *Abolition and the Press*, 18–19, 22–24, 34; Kaplan, *Lincoln and the Abolitionists*, 58; Gabrial, *Press and Slavery in America*, 38; Blight, *Frederick Douglass*, 104.

12. "To the Public," *Liberator*, January 1, 1831, 1.

13. Risley, *Abolition and the Press*, 39–41; Harrold, *Lincoln and the Abolitionists*, 12–13.

14. Blight, *Frederick Douglass*, 9, 91–99, 102, 160, 190–92; Washburn, *African American Newspaper*, 28–33; Holzer, *Lincoln and the Power*, 110.

15. "Slave Catching Revived," *Frederick Douglass' Paper*, June 2, 1854.

16. Blight, *Frederick Douglass*, 107, 186, 195–97; Chesebrough, *Frederick Douglass*, 36–38; Tripp, "Journalism for God and Man," 50.

17. Gabrial, *Press and Slavery*, 52; Risley, *Abolition and the Press*, 26, 28–29, 43–44; J. L. Thomas, *The Liberator*, 126–27.

18. Simon, *Freedom's Champion*, 3–4, 29, 41, 59; Kaplan, *Lincoln and the Abolitionists*, 27; Borchard and Bulla, *Lincoln Mediated*, 100.

19. Simon, *Freedom's Champion*, 38.

20. Logan Jaffe, "Slavery Existed in Illinois, but Schools Don't Always Teach That History," *ProPublica Illinois*, June 19, 2020; Harrold, *Lincoln and the Abolitionists*, 8; Simon, *Freedom's Champion*, 55–57; Kaplan, *Lincoln and the Abolitionists*, 27–28, 39–45; Borchard and Bulla, *Lincoln Mediated*, 100; Holzer, *Lincoln and the Power*, 35–36.

21. Simon, *Freedom's Champion*, 153–54, 168; Tripp, "Journalism for God and Man," 58–59; Borchard and Bulla, *Lincoln Mediated*.

22. Kaplan, *Lincoln and the Abolitionists*, 64–65; Borchard and Bulla, *Lincoln Mediated*, 100; Donald, *Lincoln*, 82; Simon, *Freedom's Champion*, 150; Gabrial, *Press and Slavery in America*, 49; Risley, *Abolition and the Press*, 42, 45–47; Delbanco, *Abolitionist Imagination*, 3–4; Holzer, *Lincoln and the Power*, xvii, 149; Harrold, *Lincoln and the Abolitionists*, 19.

23. Klingaman, *Abraham Lincoln*, 27; Harrold, *Lincoln and the Abolitionists*, 8–9, 15.

24. Herndon, *Herndon on Lincoln*, xi, 5, 91, 159; Holzer, *Lincoln and the Power*, 36–37; Donald, *Lincoln*, 82, 521–22; Harrold, *Lincoln and the Abolitionists*, 15; Simon, *Freedom's Champion*, 164.

25. Abraham Lincoln, "Honors to Henry Clay," July 6, 1852, in Lincoln, *Collected Works of Abraham Lincoln*, 2:130; Gates, "Abraham Lincoln on Race," xviii,

xxii–xxiii; "AL to Josephus Hewett," in Gates and Yacovone, *Lincoln on Race and Slavery*, 20–21; Kaplan, *Lincoln and the Abolitionists*, 26; Guelzo, *Lincoln's Emancipation Proclamation*, 25–26; Donald, *Lincoln*, 63–64.

26. Harrold, *Lincoln and the Abolitionists*, 2, 23–24; Kaplan, *Lincoln and the Abolitionists*, 14–15, 26; Gates, "Abraham Lincoln on Race," xviii, xxv, xxxvi.

27. Dicken-Garcia, *Journalistic Standards*, 51; Gabrial, *Press and Slavery in America*, xv, 58, 60; Risley, *Abolition and the Press*, 41–42.

28. Holzer, *Lincoln and the Power*, xv; Borchard and Bulla, *Lincoln Mediated*, 6.

29. "Why Douglas Refuses to Face the Music," *Chicago Press and Tribune*, August 30, 1858, 2; Holzer, *Presidents vs. the Press*, 160–61; Charles J. Johnson, "The Times Abraham Lincoln Got Mad at the Tribune," *Chicago Tribune*, June 9, 2019, 23; Donald, *Lincoln*, 203; Borchard and Bulla, *Lincoln Mediated*, 6–7, 18–19.

30. "Abraham Lincoln's Speech," *New York Tribune*, reprinted in *Chicago Press and Tribune*, March 2, 1860, 1; Borchard and Bulla, *Lincoln Mediated*, 20.

31. Donald, *Lincoln*, 240, 248; Borchard and Bulla, *Lincoln Mediated*, 20, 22.

32. Herndon, *Herndon on Lincoln*, 177–78; Harrold, *Lincoln and the Abolitionists*, 57; "The Western Anti-Slavery Society," *National Anti-Slavery Standard*, October 13, 1860, 1; Wendell Phillips, "Abraham Lincoln, the Slave-Hound of Illinois," *Liberator*, June 22, 1860, 99; Klingaman, *Abraham Lincoln*, 9; J. L. Thomas, *The Liberator*, 399–400.

33. "The Territorial Issue," *Liberator*, September 28, 1860, 1.

34. "The Chicago Nominations," *Douglass' Monthly*, June 1860.

35. "Historical Election Results," National Archives and Records Administration, https://www.archives.gov/federal-register/electoral-college/scores.html#1860; Harold Holzer, "Election Day 1860," *Smithsonian*, November 2008; Harrold, *Lincoln and the Abolitionists*, 75–76; "The Late Election," *Douglass' Monthly*, December 1860.

36. "The Inaugural Address," *Douglass' Monthly*, April 1861; "The New President," *Douglass' Monthly*, March 1861; Donald, *Lincoln*, 257, 267–68, 276, 292.

37. Klingaman, *Abraham Lincoln*, 24–33; Donald, *Lincoln*, 269, 270, 282–84; "Abraham Lincoln Inaugural Address," March 4, 1861, Abraham Lincoln Historical Society, http://www.abraham-lincoln-history.org/first-inaugural-address/; Gates, "Abraham Lincoln on Race," xlii; Harrold, *Lincoln and the Abolitionists*, 76.

38. "The Inaugural Address," *Douglass' Monthly*, April 1861; Harrold, *Lincoln and the Abolitionists*, 77–78; Risley, *Abolition and the Press*, 157–58; Blight, *Frederick Douglass*, 336–37.

39. *New York Herald*, February 5, 1861, cited in Borchard and Bulla, *Lincoln Mediated*, 25.

40. *Principia*, May 4, 1861, cited in J. M. McPherson, *Struggle for Equality*, 65; Risley, *Abolition and the Press*, 159; Blight, *Frederick Douglass*, 351; Risley, *Abolition and the Press*, 156.

41. Harrold, *Lincoln and the Abolitionists*, 78; Risley, *Abolition and the Press*, 162–63; Blight, *Frederick Douglass and Abraham Lincoln*, 10.

42. J. L. Thomas, *The Liberator*, 413–14.

43. *Principia*, December 21, 1861, cited in J. M. McPherson, *Struggle for Equality*, 81; Oakes, *Radical and the Republican*, 179; Risley, *Abolition and the Press*, 160–61.

44. Harrold, *Lincoln and the Abolitionists*, 83–85.

45. "The Abolition in the District," *National Anti-Slavery Standard*, April 26, 1862, 2; Blight, *Frederick Douglass*, 363–64; Harrold, *Lincoln and the Abolitionists*, 85–86; Oakes, *Radical and the Republican*, 182–83.

46. "The President and His Speeches," *Douglass' Monthly*, September 1862; J. L. Thomas, *The Liberator*, 414–15; Oakes, *Radical and the Republican*, 191–93; Gates, "Abraham Lincoln on Race," xxvi; Harrold, *Lincoln and the Abolitionists*, 88; Blight, *Frederick Douglass*, 371–73; Klingaman, *Abraham Lincoln and the Road*, 167.

47. Blight, *Frederick Douglass*, 365; Gates, "Abraham Lincoln on Race," xxvi–xxvii; Risley, *Abolition and the Press*, 166; Oakes, *Radical and the Republican*, 189; Harrold, *Lincoln and the Abolitionists*, 87–88.

48. Oakes, *Radical and the Republican*, 178, 202–5; Blight, *Frederick Douglass*, 378; Harrold, *Lincoln and the Abolitionists*, 87; Delbanco, *Abolitionist Imagination*, 14–15; Gates, "Abraham Lincoln on Race," xxix, xxvii–viii; Risley, *Abolition and the Press*, 171.

49. "Emancipation Proclaimed," *Douglass' Monthly*, October 1962; Borchard and Bulla, *Lincoln Mediated*, 104; Harrold, *Lincoln and the Abolitionists*, 89; Oakes, *The Radical and the Republican*, 196–97, 200–201; Risley, *Abolition and the Press*, 166–67; Kaplan, *Lincoln and the Abolitionists*, 294; Blight, *Frederick Douglass*, 254.

50. *Liberator*, January 2, 1863, cited in Samito, *Lincoln and the Thirteenth Amendment*, 39; Harrold, *Lincoln and the Abolitionists*, 91; Oakes, *Radical and the Republican*, 197–99; Blight, *Frederick Douglass*, 380; Gates, "Abraham Lincoln on Race," xxxiii.

51. "Frederick Douglass at the Cooper Institute," *Douglass' Monthly*, March 1863; Harrold, *Lincoln and the Abolitionists*, 97.

52. Fagan, *Black Newspaper*, 139–40; Blight, *Frederick Douglass*, 385–86, 402–3, 406; Risley, *Abolition and the Press*, 173.

53. *Proceedings of the American Anti-Slavery Society*, 116–17; Blight, *Frederick Douglass*, 408–9; Blight, *Frederick Douglass and Abraham Lincoln*, 10–11; Oakes, *Radical and the Republican*, 212–13.

54. *Proceedings of the American Anti-Slavery Society*, 117; Oakes, *Radical and the Republican*, 213–14; Blight, *Frederick Douglass and Abraham Lincoln*, 10–11; Blight, *Frederick Douglass*, 409–10.

55. Frederick Douglass, "Our Work Is Not Done," speech delivered at the annual meeting of the American Anti-Slavery Society, Philadelphia, December 3–4, 1863, reprinted in *Proceedings of the American Anti-Slavery Society*, 110–18, https://rbscp.lib.rochester.edu/4403; Borchard and Bulla, *Lincoln Mediated*, 109; Samito, *Lincoln and the Thirteenth Amendment*, 63; Risley, *Abolition and the Press*, 168–69; Blight, *Frederick Douglass*, 425–26.

56. "A Word to Republicans," *Liberator*, March 18, 1864, 46; Harrold, *Lincoln and the Abolitionists*, 98–102; J. L. Thomas, *The Liberator*, 424–25; Risley, *Abolition and the Press*, 175–77; Samito, *Lincoln and the Thirteenth Amendment*, 58.

57. "National Union Convention," *New York Times*, June 8, 1864, 1; Donald, *Lincoln*, 505; Oakes, *Radical and the Republican*, 227; Harrold, *Lincoln and the Abolitionists*, 101; Risley, *Abolition and the Press*, 177.

58. Donald, *Lincoln*, 500; J. L. Thomas, *The Liberator*, 425–26; Harrold, *Lincoln and the Abolitionists*, 98, 101.

59. W. L. Miller, *President Lincoln*, 383; Oakes, *Radical and the Republican*, xxi, 229–30; Blight, *Frederick Douglass and Abraham Lincoln*, 12; Harrold, *Lincoln and the Abolitionists*, 103; Blight, *Frederick Douglass*, 431–35.

60. W. L. Miller, *President Lincoln*, 104; Blight, *Frederick Douglass and Abraham Lincoln*, 12–13; Oakes, *Radical and the Republican*, 230–31, 237–38; Blight, *Frederick Douglass*, 437–38; Harrold, *Lincoln and the Abolitionists*, 103–4.

61. Frederick Douglass to Abraham Lincoln, August 29, 1864, image 4, Abraham Lincoln Papers, Series 1, General Correspondence, 1833–1916, Library of Congress, https://www.loc.gov/resource/mal.3565200/?sp=4&r=0.036,0.241,1.326 ,0.627,0; Blight, *Frederick Douglass and Abraham Lincoln*, 13; Harrold, *Lincoln and the Abolitionists*, 104.

62. "Presidential Election of 1864: A Resource Guide," Web Guides, Library of Congress, https://www.loc.gov/rr/program/bib/elections/election1864.html; Risley, *Abolition and the Press*, 179.

63. "The Late Presidential Struggle," *Liberator*, November 18, 1864, issue 47, 186; Risley, *Abolition and the Press*, 180.

64. Gates, "Abraham Lincoln on Race," xliv; Samito, *Lincoln and the Thirteenth Amendment*, 59, 63, 73; Harrold, *Lincoln and the Abolitionists*, 105–6.

65. *Scene in the House on the passage of the proposition to amend the Constitution, January 31, 1865*, illustration in *Harper's Weekly*, February 18, 1865, Library of Congress, https://www.loc.gov/resource/cph.3c27599/; "Laus Deo! Hallelujah," *Liberator*, February 3, 1865, 18; Congressional Research Service, *Constitution of the United States of America*, 30; Samito, *Lincoln and the Thirteenth Amendment*, 92–93; Blight, *Frederick Douglass*, 454; Donald, *Lincoln*, 553–54; Risley, *Abolition and the Press*, 180; Harrold, *Lincoln and the Abolitionists*, 106–7.

66. Abraham Lincoln, "Second Inaugural Address; Endorsed by Lincoln," March 4, 1865, image 2, Abraham Lincoln Papers, Series 3, Miscellaneous, 1837–1897, Library of Congress, https://www.loc.gov/resource/mal.4361300/?sp=2; Gates, "Abraham Lincoln on Race," xxxiii–xxxv.

67. Rice, *Reminiscences of Abraham Lincoln*, 191–93; Blight, *Frederick Douglass and Abraham Lincoln*, 9; Blight, *Frederick Douglass*, 459–60; Oakes, *Radical and the Republican*, 241–43.

68. Abraham Lincoln to William Lloyd Garrison, February 7, 1865, image 2, Abraham Lincoln Papers, Series 1, General Correspondence, 1833–1916, Library of Congress, https://www.loc.gov/resource/mal.4020200/?sp=2&r=-0.59,-0.516,2.18,1.031,0; Lincoln, *Collected Works of Abraham Lincoln*, 8:266; Harrold, *Lincoln and the Abolitionists*, 109.

69. Gates, "Abraham Lincoln on Race," xxxvi, xlii; Blight, *Frederick Douglass*, 454–55; Donald, *Lincoln*, 585.

70. Gates, "Abraham Lincoln on Race," xxxvi; Donald, *Lincoln*, 585; DeWitt, "Abraham Lincoln," 116.

71. "The Death of President Lincoln," *Liberator*, April 21, 1865, 2; Risley, *Abolition and the Press*, 185.

72. Risley, *Abolition and the Press*, 185–86, 174, 186.

73. Frederick Douglass, "Oration in Memory of Abraham Lincoln," speech delivered in Washington DC, April 14, 1876, in Douglass, *Selected Speeches and Writings*, 693.

74. Gates, "Abraham Lincoln on Race," xxi; Blight, *Frederick Douglass and Abraham Lincoln*, 7; Harrold, *Lincoln and the Abolitionists*, 112–14.

75. Abraham Lincoln to Erastus Corning and Others, June 1863, Draft of Reply to Resolutions concerning Military Arrests and Suspension of Habeas Corpus, Abraham Lincoln Papers, Series 1, General Correspondence, 1833–1916, Library of Congress, https://www.loc.gov/item/mal2399500/; Banning, "'Determined to Suppress Everything,'" 113; Bulla, "Palpable Injury," 41–42; Holzer, *Presidents vs. the Press*, 70, 73–74; Donald, *Lincoln*, 304; DeWitt, "Abraham Lincoln," 111; Stone, *Perilous Times*, 80–81.

3. WOODROW WILSON

1. James Kates, "Berger's Paper Is Barred under Espionage Act," *Chicago Daily Tribune*, October 4, 1917, 3; Kates, "Editor, Publisher, Citizen, Socialist," 79–88; Wagner, "Socialist Newspaper"; "Representative Victor Berger of Wisconsin, the First Socialist Member of Congress," United States House of Representatives, History, Art & Archives, https://history.house.gov/Historical -Highlights/1851-1900/Representative-Victor-Berger-of-Wisconsin,-the-first -Socialist-Member-of-Congress/.

2. Leidholdt, "Mysterious Mr. Maxwell," 285; Kates, "Editor, Publisher, Citizen, Socialist," 79–88; "Victor Berger Dies; Socialist Leader," *New York Times*, August 8, 1929, 18; Nash, "Victor L. Berger," 301–8; Kates, "Berger's Paper Is Barred," 3; "Representative Victor Berger of Wisconsin," United States House of Representatives.

3. Rosenberg, "War and the Health," 57; Sweeney, *Military and the Press*, 51; Beschloss, *Presidents of War*, 325; Starr, *Creation of the Media*, 278; Berg, *Wilson*, 14; Juergens, "Woodrow Wilson," 8; Startt, *Woodrow Wilson*, 151, 325.

4. Berg, *Wilson*, 12.

5. Cornwell, "Wilson, Creel, and the Presidency," 189. For a detailed examination of Wilson's use of propaganda, see Hamilton, *Manipulating the Masses*.

6. Berg, *Wilson*, 298, 300; Beschloss, *Presidents of War*, 301; J. M. Cooper, *Woodrow Wilson*, 11; Greenberg, *Republic of Spin*, 79–81.

7. Julian E. Zelizer, "A Century of Feuding between Presidents and the Press," *Atlantic*, April 28, 2018, https://www.theatlantic.com/politics/archive/2018/04 /president-press/559037/; Startt, *Woodrow Wilson*, 40–41; Tebbel and Watts, *Press and the Presidency*, 363; Greenberg, *Republic of Spin*, 89.

8. Tebbel and Watts, *Press and the Presidency*, 2.

9. Brands, *Woodrow Wilson*, 28; Juergens, "Woodrow Wilson," 5; Tebbel and Watts, *Press and the Presidency*, 367.

10. Tebbel and Watts, *Press and the Presidency*, 367–68.

11. Tebbel and Watts, *Press and the Presidency*, 366–68.

12. Juergens, "Woodrow Wilson," 6; Tebbel and Watts, *Press and the Presidency*, 368–69, 373.

13. Stuckey, "'Domain of Public Conscience,'" 1–3; Juergens, "Woodrow Wilson," 7–8; Tebbel and Watts, *Press and the Presidency*, 370, 372.

14. Startt, *Woodrow Wilson*, 10; Greenberg, *Republic of Spin*, 35, 52.

15. "April 8, 1913: Message Regarding Tariff Duties," Presidential Speeches, Miller Center, University of Virginia, https://millercenter.org/the-presidency /presidential-speeches/april-8-1913-message-regarding-tariff-duties; Howard,

"Woodrow Wilson," 173; Brands, *Woodrow Wilson*, 1; Berg, *Wilson*, 8; Greenberg, *Republic of Spin*, 79–81; Juergens, "Woodrow Wilson," 12; Tebbel and Watts, *Press and the Presidency*, 379.

16. Tebbel and Watts, *Press and the Presidency*, 369; Greenberg, *Republic of Spin*, 87.

17. Brands, *Woodrow Wilson*, 27; Startt, *Woodrow Wilson*, 7, 9; Edward M. House, *The Intimate Papers of Colonel House*, 1:114, cited in Brands, *Woodrow Wilson*, 27.

18. Cooper, *Woodrow Wilson*, 206–7; Startt, "Colonel Edward M. House," 28, 31–38.

19. J. M. Cooper, *Woodrow Wilson*, 200; Juergens, "Woodrow Wilson," 12; Tebbel and Watts, *Press and the Presidency*, 370, 376–77; Startt, *Woodrow Wilson*, 7.

20. Greenberg, *Republic of Spin*, 6; J. M. Cooper, *Woodrow Wilson*, 201; Juergens, "Woodrow Wilson," 16; Tebbel and Watts, *Press and the Presidency*, 371, 374.

21. J. M. Cooper, *Woodrow Wilson*, 201.

22. Juergens, "Woodrow Wilson," 101; Tebbel and Watts, *Press and the Presidency*, 371–72.

23. Grantham, review of *The Papers of Woodrow Wilson*, vol. 49, 1079–81; Juergens, review of *The Papers of Woodrow Wilson*, vol. 50, 1010; Brands, *Woodrow Wilson*, 63–65; Tebbel and Watts, *Press and the Presidency*, 372, 374; Juergens, "Woodrow Wilson," 16; Pollard, *Presidents and the Press*, 673–74.

24. Juergens, "Woodrow Wilson," 11; J. M. Cooper, *Woodrow Wilson*, 213–36, 344–46; Berg, *Wilson*, 9–10; Brands, *Woodrow Wilson*, 34–38.

25. Rothstein, *Color of Law*, 43; Startt, *Woodrow Wilson*, 12, 155; J. M. Cooper, *Woodrow Wilson*, 205–6; Washburn, *African American Newspaper*, 174.

26. Stone, *War and Liberty*, 41; Startt, *Woodrow Wilson*, 31, 38.

27. Grieves, "'It Would Be the Best,'" 52; Greenberg, "Ominous Clang," 50–52.

28. Beschloss, *Presidents of War*, 303–5; Brands, *Woodrow Wilson*, 58–59, 69; Startt, *Woodrow Wilson*, 45, 76.

29. Anderson, *Woodrow Wilson*, 132; Tebbel and Watts, *Press and the Presidency*, 377; *Chicago Tribune*, October 23, 1916, cited in Beschloss, *Presidents of War*, 307; Startt, *Woodrow Wilson*, 91–92, 94.

30. Berg, *Wilson*, 10; Beschloss, *Presidents of War*, 307; Startt, *Woodrow Wilson*, 95.

31. "Unarmed American Steamers Sunk by German Submarines," *Herald Democrat*, March 19, 1917, https://www.coloradohistoricnewspapers.org/?a=d&d=THD19170319-01.2.4&e=-------en-20--1--img-txIN%7ctxCO%7ctxTA-------0------; "Sinking of Three American Ships Virtually Causes State of War," *Cornell Daily Sun*, March 19, 1917, https://cdsun.library.cornell.edu/cgi-bin/cornell?a=d&d=CDS19170319.2.2; Startt, *Woodrow Wilson*, 116; Beschloss, *Presidents of War*, 293–395, 306, 310–11, 313.

32. Anderson, *Woodrow Wilson*, 134; Beschloss, *Presidents of War*, 314–16; Startt, *Woodrow Wilson*, 117–18.

33. Woodrow Wilson, "The President's Statement on Food Control," May 19, 1917, cited in *Information Quarterly* 3, no. 1 (January–March 1917): 461; Hyman, *Quiet Past and Stormy Present?*, 33; Berg, *Wilson*, 10; Beschloss, *Presidents of War*, 300–301, 355–56; Rosenberg, "War and the Health," 56.

34. Dubbs, *American Journalists*, 2, 203; Rosenberg, "War and the Health," 49.

35. D. Johnson, "Wilson, Burleson, and Censorship," 45–46; Sweeney, *Military and the Press*, 35; Berg, *Wilson*, 450; J. M. Cooper, *Woodrow Wilson*, 397; Hyman, *Quiet Past and Stormy Present?*, 33; Rosenberg, "War and the Health," 54–55; Brands, *Woodrow Wilson*, 84; Stone, *War and Liberty*, 49–50.

36. United States House of Representatives, "Hearing before the Subcommittee of the House Committee on Appropriations," 14; Berg, *Wilson*, 449–50; Tebbel and Watts, *Press and the Presidency*, 375, 384; Pollard, *Presidents and the Press*, 659.

37. Fishman, "George Creel," 34–35; United States House of Representatives, "Hearing before the Subcommittee of the House Committee on Appropriations," 4, 8, 12, 82; Cornwell, "Wilson, Creel, and the Presidency," 189–90; Brands, *Woodrow Wilson*, 82; Berg, *Wilson*, 451–52; Starr, *Creation of the Media*, 276, 315–16; Startt, *Woodrow Wilson*, 122.

38. United States House of Representatives, "Hearing before the Subcommittee of the House Committee on Appropriations," 5, 8–9; Berg, *Wilson*, 451–52; Starr, *Creation of the Media*, 316; Juergens, "Woodrow Wilson," 12–13; Rosenberg, "War and the Health," 51–53.

39. Rosenberg, "War and the Health," 49; Greenberg, "Ominous Clang," 55; United States House of Representatives, "Hearing before the Subcommittee of the House Committee on Appropriations," 14; Berg, *Wilson*, 449–50; Tebbel and Watts, *Press and the Presidency*, 375, 383–84; Pollard, *Presidents and the Press*, 669–70.

40. Startt, *Woodrow Wilson*, 31; Griffith, *Home Town News*, 203.

41. J. M. Cooper, *Woodrow Wilson*, 406–8, 411–15; Startt, *Woodrow Wilson*, 153–57; Anderson, *Woodrow Wilson*, 135.

42. *New York Times*, May 26, 1917, 1; Berg, *Wilson*, 455; Pollard, *Presidents and the Press*, 660–64.

43. Cited in "Conferees Offer Censorship Bill with Jury Trial," *New York Times*, May 26, 1917, 1, 4.

44. Mock, *Censorship 1917*, 48–51; Pollard, *Presidents and the Press*, 660–64; Berg, *Wilson*, 455; Starr, *Creation of the Media*, 276–77, 324; Beschloss, *Presidents of War*, 324; Startt, *Woodrow Wilson*, 152.

45. United States Congress, *United States Code*, 7466.

46. Leidholdt, "Mysterious Mr. Maxwell," 289; Mock, *Censorship 1917*, 51–52; Starr, *Creation of the Media*, 278; Rosenberg, "War and the Health," 50, 55; Fondren, "'This Is an American Newspaper,'" 1.

47. J. M. Cooper, *Woodrow Wilson*, 415; Rosenberg, "War and the Health," 156–57; Startt, *Woodrow Wilson*, 149–51.

48. U.S. House of Representatives, "The Sedition Act of 1798," https://history .house.gov/Historical-Highlights/1700s/The-Sedition-Act-of-1798/; Mock, *Censorship 1917*, 53–54; Berg, *Wilson*, 455; Stone, *War and Liberty*, 57.

49. Sweeney, *Military and the Press*, 51; Berg, *Wilson*, 455, 497; Rosenberg, "War and the Health," 57.

50. "Disloyalists and Aliens," *New York Times*, November 22, 1917, 12, https:// www.nytimes.com/1917/11/22/archives/disloyalists-and-aliens.html; Stone, *War and Liberty*, 49; Goff, "Masses Magazine," 137.

51. Starr, *Creation of the Media*, 316; Stone, *War and Liberty*, 55–56.

52. "Amnesty and Pardon," 177; Stone, *War and Liberty*, 44–45, 54–55; J. M. Cooper, *Woodrow Wilson*, 398.

53. Starr, *Creation of the Media*, 276–77.

54. D. Johnson, "Wilson, Burleson, and Censorship," 48; J. M. Cooper, *Woodrow Wilson*, 398; Stone, *War and Liberty*, 53–54; Mock, *Censorship 1917*, 148–49.

55. Johnson, "Wilson, Burleson, and Censorship," 55; Brands, *Woodrow Wilson*, 100; Pollard, *Presidents and the Press*, 667–68.

56. Hyman, *Quiet Past and Stormy Present?*, 34–35; Rosenberg, "War and the Health," 58; Stone, *War and Liberty*, 50; Mock, *Censorship 1917*, 35–37; Starr, *Creation of the Media*, 279–80.

57. Max Eastman, letter to Woodrow Wilson, September 8, 1917, Woodrow Wilson Papers, Library of Congress, https://www.loc.gov/exhibitions/world -war-i-american-experiences/about-this-exhibition/over-here/surveillance-and -censorship/suppression-of-the-masses/.

58. Debs v. United States, 249 U.S. 211 (1919), cited in Starr, *Creation of the Media*, 281–82; Erick Trickey, "When America's Most Prominent Socialist Was Jailed for Speaking Out against World War I," *Smithsonian*, June 15, 2018, https://www.smithsonianmag.com/history/fiery-socialist-challenged-nations -role-wwi-180969386/; Stone, *War and Liberty*, 44, 51; Berg, *Wilson*, 496–97; Rosenberg, "War and the Health," 57.

59. "Abrams v. United States," Oyez, https://www.oyez.org/cases/1900-1940 /250us616; Stone, *War and Liberty*, 60–62.

60. Estimates of the number of deaths and casualties vary. "Armistice Terms Granted to Central Powers"; Beschloss, *Presidents of War*, 334–35; J. M. Cooper, *Woodrow Wilson*, 451–52; Berg, *Wilson*, 20.

61. *New York Times*, November 12, 1918, 14.

62. Startt, "Wilson's Trip to Paris," 737–42; Dubbs, *American Journalists in the Great War*, 258–60; Brands, *Woodrow Wilson*, 103–4; Berg, *Wilson*, 520.

63. Dubbs, *American Journalists*, 261–62; Berg, *Wilson*, 12, 540–41; Juergens, "Woodrow Wilson," 17; Tebbel and Watts, *Press and the Presidency*, 386.

64. Juergens, "Woodrow Wilson," 10; Startt, *Woodrow Wilson*, 13–14; Berg, *Wilson*, 540–41; Tebbel and Watts, *Press and the Presidency*, 387–88.

65. "The League of Nations, 1920," Office of the Historian, U.S. Department of State, https://history.state.gov/milestones/1914-1920/league; J. M. Cooper, *Woodrow Wilson*, 508; Hyman, *Quiet Past and Stormy Present?*, 36; Brands, *Woodrow Wilson*, 99–107; Tebbel and Watts, *Press and the Presidency*, 387–88.

66. Brands, *Woodrow Wilson*, 122.

67. Anderson, *Woodrow Wilson*, 140; Brands, *Woodrow Wilson*, 122–28; J. M. Cooper, *Woodrow Wilson*, 520–32; Juergens, "Woodrow Wilson," 10; Startt, *Woodrow Wilson*, 14; Beschloss, *Presidents of War*, 349–50; Tebbel and Watts, *Press and the Presidency*, 390; Berg, *Wilson*, 634–42.

68. Brands, *Woodrow Wilson*, 132; Starr, *Creation of the Media*, 286.

69. Margaret Sullivan, "Shocked by Trump Aggression against Reporters and Sources? The Blueprint Was Drawn by Obama," *Washington Post*, June 8, 2018; Rosenberg, "War and the Health," 52, 56.

70. Sivowitch, "Technological Survey," 1–20; Sloan, *Media in America*, 352; Tebbel and Watts, *Press and the Presidency*, 391, Starr, *Creation of the Media*, 331.

4. FRANKLIN DELANO ROOSEVELT

1. Frederick A. Storm, "Biggest Crowd in Chicago's History Greets F.D.R.," *Atlanta Constitution*, October 15, 1936, 1; "Roosevelt Says New Deal Saved Business," *Boston Herald*, October 15, 1936, 1; Associated Press, "Windy City Gives F.D.R. Wild Cheers," *Baton Rouge Advocate*, October 15, 1936, 10; J. E. Edwards, *Foreign Policy*, 118; Looker, *This Man Roosevelt*, 2–4; Buhite and Levy, *FDR's Fireside Chats*, xii; Hurd, *When the New Deal*, 248, 281; "Campaign Address at Chicago, Ill.," October 14, 1936, in Roosevelt, *Public Papers and Addresses*, 5:480; Associated Press, "Windy City Gives F.D.R. Wild Cheers," 10.

2. R. N. Smith, *The Colonel*, xvii; J. E. Edwards, *Foreign Policy*, 118; "The Roosevelt Parade," *Chicago Tribune*, October 16, 1936, 1.

3. G. J. White, *FDR and the Press*, 97; J. E. Edwards, *Foreign Policy*, 118.

4. G. J. White, *FDR and the Press*, 70.

5. Becker, "Presidential Power," 10, 15–16.

6. Wapshott, *The Sphinx*, x–xv; Bureau of Labor Statistics, CPI Inflation Calculator, https://data.bls.gov/cgi-bin/cpicalc.pl.

7. Wapshott, *The Sphinx*, xi; Winfield, *FDR and the News Media*, 14, 16; Dallek, *Franklin D. Roosevelt*, 138.

8. Winfield, *FDR and the News Media*, 17–18; Buhite and Levy, *FDR's Fireside Chats*, xii; Hurd, *When the New Deal*, 248, 281; Looker, *This Man Roosevelt*, 2–4; Dallek, *Franklin D. Roosevelt*, 127.

9. Lebovic, "When the 'Mainstream Media,'" 66; Starr, *Creation of the Media*, 382; Tebbel, *Life and Good Times*, 14.

10. Wapshott, *The Sphinx*, 7; Winfield, *FDR and the News Media*, 21.

11. Tebbel, *Life and Good Times*, 250; Winfield, *FDR and the News Media*, 21; Wapshott, *The Sphinx*, 23–25.

12. Wapshott, *The Sphinx*, 26–27.

13. "U.S. Electoral College: Electoral Votes for President and Vice President, 1929–1941," National Archives and Records Administration, https://www .archives.gov/federal-register/electoral-college/votes/1929_1941.html#1932; Dallek, *Franklin D. Roosevelt*, 129–30.

14. Hamby, *Man of Destiny*, 200; R. N. Smith, *The Colonel*, 323; Dallek, *Franklin D. Roosevelt*, 144–59; 165; Hurd, *When the New Deal*, 11.

15. Schlesinger, *Imperial Presidency*, 223–24; Porter, *Assault on the Media*, 5; G. J. White, *FDR and the Press*; Winfield, *FDR and the News Media*, 5; Paul Y. Anderson, "Hoover and the Press," *Nation* 133 (1931): 382, cited in G. J. White, *FDR and the Press*, 6.

16. Winfield, *FDR and the News Media*, 1, 12, 15; G. J. White, *FDR and the Press*, 10.

17. Lipstadt, *Beyond Belief*, 7–8; G. J. White, *FDR and the Press*, 24; Steele, *Propaganda in an Open Society*, 11, 15–16.

18. Franklin D. Roosevelt Press Conference, March 8, 1933, American Presidency Project, University of California Santa Barbara, https://www.presidency.ucsb .edu/documents/press-conference-25; Hurd, *When the New Deal*, 229–44; Rosten, *Washington Correspondents*, 49–50; Dallek, *Franklin D. Roosevelt*, 139–40; Winfield, *FDR and the News Media*, 28–29.

19. "Presidential News Conferences," American Presidency Project, University of California Santa Barbara, https://www.presidency.ucsb.edu/statistics/data /presidential-news-conferences; Winfield, *FDR and the News Media*, 32–33.

20. Winfield, *FDR and the News Media*, 32–34; G. J. White, *FDR and the Press*, 21.

21. G. J. White, *FDR and the Press*, 20–21; Winfield, *FDR and the News Media*, 29; Franklin Roosevelt, *Complete Press Conferences*, PC 160, November 23, 1934, 4:232, cited in Winfield, *FDR and the News Media*, 40.

22. G. J. White, *FDR and the Press*, 10–11.

23. Beasley, *Women of the Washington Press*, 57–90; "Towards Adjournment," *Time*, June 19, 1933, 11; Allida M. Black, "Eleanor Roosevelt," Social Welfare History Project, Virginia Commonwealth University, https://socialwelfare

.library.vcu.edu/eras/great-depression/eleanor-roosevelt/; Winfield, *FDR and the News Media*, 59; Robert S. Mann, "Capital Corps No Propaganda Victims, Writers Tell Journalism Teachers," *Editor and Publisher*, January 4, 1936, 3, cited in G. J. White, *FDR and the Press*, 12.

24. Winfield, *FDR and the News Media*, 88; Rothstein, *Color of Law*, 19–20, 64–67; Dallek, *Franklin D. Roosevelt*, 146–47; Kevin Boyle, review of *The Black Cabinet: The Untold Story of African Americans and Politics during the Age of Roosevelt*, by Jill Watts, *New York Times Book Review*, June 7, 2020, 10; J. E. Smith, *FDR*, 401; Washburn, *African American Newspaper*, 173–76.

25. G. J. White, *FDR and the Press*, 1, 49, 69, 73–75, 90.

26. D. M. Kennedy, *Freedom from Fear*, 401; Swanberg, *Luce and His Empire*, 2, 56–57, 81–82; Winfield, *FDR and the News Media*, 19; Brinkley, *The Publisher*, 166–68; G. J. White, *FDR and the Press*, 52.

27. "The Paramount Issue," *Chicago Tribune*, March 11, 1933, 10; G. J. White, *FDR and the Press*, 52; J. E. Edwards, *Foreign Policy*, 13–15, 87, 89.

28. "Fear Congress Is Abdicating to a Dictator," *Chicago Tribune*, May 1, 1933, 1; J. E. Edwards, *Foreign Policy*, 87, 89; Ritchie, *Reporting from Washington*, 9.

29. Rosten, *Washington Correspondents*, 196; Tebbel, *Life and Good Times*, 252–53.

30. G. J. White, *FDR and the Press*, 51; Tebbel, *Life and Good Times*, 252–53.

31. G. J. White, *FDR and the Press*, 94.

32. Steele, *Propaganda in an Open Society*, 25–27; Winfield, *FDR and the News Media*, 116–18.

33. Culbert, *News for Everyman*, 3; Starr, *Creation of the Media*, 354, 379.

34. Becker, "Presidential Power," 10–12; Starr, *Creation of the Media*, 373–74; Winfield, *FDR and the News Media*, 5; Buhite and Levy, *FDR's Fireside Chats*, xiii; Rosenman, *Working with Roosevelt*, 39; Winfield, *FDR and the News Media*, 18; J. E. Smith, *FDR*, 238.

35. "Proclamation 2039—Declaring Bank Holiday," March 6, 1933, American Presidency Project, University of California Santa Barbara, https://www.presidency.ucsb.edu/documents/proclamation-2039-bank-holiday-march-6-9-1933-inclusive; Dallek, *Franklin D. Roosevelt*, 139; Rosenman, *Working with Roosevelt*, 92–93; Levin, *Making of FDR*, 109; Arthur M. Schlesinger Jr., *The Coming of the New Deal* (Boston: Houghton Mifflin, 1958), 12–13, cited in J. E. Smith, *FDR*, 718n34.

36. "March 12, 1933: Fireside Chat 1: On the Banking Crisis," Presidential Speeches, Franklin D. Roosevelt Presidency, Miller Center, University of Virginia, https://millercenter.org/the-presidency/presidential-speeches/march-12-1933-fireside-chat-1-banking-crisis; Buhite and Levy, *FDR's Fireside Chats*, 12.

37. Winfield, *FDR and the News Media*, 105; Buhite and Levy, *FDR's Fireside*, 12; J. E. Smith, *FDR*, 315–16; Dallek, *Franklin D. Roosevelt*, 140–41.

38. Dighe, "Saving Private Capitalism," 42; J. E. Smith, *FDR*, 315–16.

39. "A Week of Great Events," *Wall Street Journal*, March 13, 1933, 6; J. E. Smith, *FDR*, 315.

40. Historians differ on whether some of Roosevelt's talks broadcast on radio should count as a fireside chat. See Buhite and Levy, *FDR's Fireside Chats*, xv; Steele, *Propaganda in an Open Society*, 22; Winfield, *FDR and the News Media*, 105; Starr, *Creation of the Media*, 374–75.

41. Winfield, *FDR and the News Media*, 106–7; G. J. White, *FDR and the Press*, 22; Sherwood, *Roosevelt and Hopkins*, 213–18; Buhite and Levy, *FDR's Fireside Chats*, xvi–xviii; Rosenman, *Working with Roosevelt*, 93, 172–73.

42. Steele, *Propaganda in an Open Society*, 17, 20, 22; Winfield, *FDR and the News Media*, 109.

43. Associated Press, "Coughlin Asks Voters to Oust 'This Dictator,'" *Chicago Daily Tribune*, November 2, 1936, 4; Associated Press, "Stock Mart Bill Lauded by Father Coughlin," *Baltimore Sun*, April 9, 1934, 2; Wapshott, *The Sphinx*, 28–29; Dallek, *Franklin D. Roosevelt*, 186–87; J. E. Smith, *FDR*, 348, 371; D. M. Kennedy, *Freedom from Fear*, 216.

44. Dallek, *Franklin D. Roosevelt*, 185–88; Steele, *Propaganda in an Open Society*, 24–25; Starr, *Creation of the Media*, 376.

45. "Vote for Republican Congressmen," *Chicago Tribune*, November 6, 1934, 12; J. E. Smith, *FDR*, 350; John Boettiger, "Tugwell Named by Dr. Wirt as Revolt Leader," *Chicago Tribune*, April 11, 1934, 1.

46. *New York Times*, June 29, 1934, 2; Buhite and Levy, *FDR's Fireside Chats*, 48–49; Rosenman, *Working with Roosevelt*, 96–97.

47. William Allen White, "In the Wake of the Returns," *Los Angeles Times*, November 9, 1934, A4; J. E. Smith, *FDR*, 349; Dallek, *Franklin D. Roosevelt*, 193.

48. Rosenman, *Working with Roosevelt*, 97; J. E. Smith, *FDR*, 352–58.

49. Franklin D. Roosevelt, Acceptance Speech on Renomination for the Presidency, June 27, 1936, Franklin D. Roosevelt Library and Museum Collection, Grace Tully Archive Series, Grace Tully Papers, Box 5, Folder FDR Inscribed Speeches, http://www.fdrlibrary.marist.edu/_resources/images/tully/5_14.pdf; Hurd, *When the New Deal*, 270–73; Winfield, *FDR and the News Media*, 61–62; J. E. Smith, *FDR*, 366–68.

50. "The Democratic Keynoter Makes Some Comparisons," *Chicago Tribune*, June 26, 1936, 1; Leuchtenburg, *FDR Years*, 107; Tebbel, *Life and Good Times*, 259–60.

51. Donald Day, "Moscow Orders U.S. Reds to Back Roosevelt," *Chicago Tribune*, August 9, 1936, 3; Meyers, "Chicago Newspaper Hoax," 356–64; J. E. Edwards, *Foreign Policy*, 114–15.

52. Wayne Thomis, "Roosevelt Area in Wisconsin Is Hotbed of Vice," *Chicago Tribune*, October 16, 1936, 15.

53. American Presidency Project, University of California Santa Barbara, https://www.presidency.ucsb.edu/statistics/elections/1936; Arthur Sears Henning, "President Sets a Record with Electoral Vote," *Chicago Daily Tribune*, November 4, 1936, 1; Hurd, *When the New Deal*, 281; J. E. Edwards, *Foreign Policy*, 119–20; J. E. Smith, *FDR*, 374.

54. "Press Speaks on Roosevelt's Larger Supreme Court Plan," *Christian Science Monitor*, February 8, 1937, 6; Ritchie, *Reporting from Washington*, 19; D. M. Kennedy, *Freedom from Fear*, 323–27.

55. Walter Lippmann, "Change by Usurpation," *Detroit Free Press*, February 11, 1937, 1; Hemmer, *Messengers of the Right*, 16.

56. J. E. Smith, *FDR*, 388.

57. "Fear," *Detroit Free Press*, April 7, 1938, 8; "President 'Dared' by Mrs. Patterson," *New York Times*, April 6, 1938, 13; J. E. Smith, *FDR*, 396–97; Tebbel, *Life and Good Times*, 171–72.

58. Buhite and Levy, *FDR's Fireside Chats*, 320.

59. Rosenman, *Working with Roosevelt*, 175; J. E. Smith, *FDR*, 398; Dallek, *Franklin D. Roosevelt*, 336.

60. "Congress Profiles," 75th Congress and 76th Congress, United States House of Representatives, History, Art & Archives, https://history.house.gov/Congressional-Overview/Profiles/75th/ and https://history.house.gov/Congressional-Overview/Profiles/76th/; "Vital Statistics on Congress," Brookings, April 7, 2014, https://www.brookings.edu/wp-content/uploads/2016/06/Vital-Statistics-Chapter-2-Congressional-Elections.pdf.

61. J. E. Smith, *FDR*, 419.

62. "Stop Foreign Meddling; America Wants Peace," *Wall Street Journal*, October 8, 1937, 1.

63. *Jackson Citizen Patriot*, April 3, 1938, cited in Lipstadt, *Beyond Belief*, 9; Dallek, *Franklin D. Roosevelt*, 445; Lipstadt, *Beyond Belief*, 86, 104–9; J. E. Smith, *FDR*, 607–8.

64. "The Refugees," *New York Times*, November 16, 1938, 22.

65. "Under the Axis," *Jewish Frontier*, November 1942, cited in Serrin and Serrin, "Holocaust Exposed," 283–86.

66. Sweeney, *Military and the Press*, 94–95.

67. "1940. Edward R. Murrow from a Rooftop during the London Blitz: The Sights and Sounds in London," Bill Downs, War Correspondent, September 14, 2015, https://www.billdownscbs.com/2015/09/1940-edward-r-murrow-from-london.html; Bob Edwards, "Edward R. Murrow Broadcast from

London," Library of Congress, 2004, http://www.loc.gov/static/programs
/national-recording-preservation-board/documents/murrow.pdf; Kendrick,
Prime Time, 173–75, 200–205, 208; Culbert, *News for Everyman*, 3–7, 11;
Casey, *War Beat, Europe*, 204–5; Sweeney, *Military and the Press*, 95–96; Teel,
Public Press, 170, 200.

68. Casey, *War Beat, Europe*, 204; Kendrick, *Prime Time*, 173–75, 200–206; D. M.
Kennedy, *Freedom from Fear*, 472; Sweeney, *Military and the Press*, 96; Teel,
Public Press, 200.

69. G. J. White, *FDR and the Press*, 12; J. E. Smith, *FDR*, 469–70; Hurd, *When
the New Deal*, 266–67.

70. D. M. Kennedy, *Freedom from Fear*, 488–91.

71. Roosevelt, *Public Papers and Addresses*, 10:134.

72. "Pearl Harbor National Memorial," U.S. Park Service, https://www.nps
.gov/perl/learn/historyculture/people.htm#:~:text=A%20total%20of%202
%2C390%20American,Arizona%2C%20a%20total%20of%201%2C177;
Kendrick, *Prime Time*, 238–41; B. Edwards, *Edward R. Murrow*, 62; J. E.
Smith, *FDR*, 538.

73. Roosevelt, *Public Papers and Addresses*, 10:523–25.

74. Roosevelt, *Public Papers and Addresses*, 11:32–42, 78–79, 112, 116–17; "The
Pacific War," War Times Journal, http://www.wtj.com/articles/pacific
_summary/timeline.htm; Dallek, *Franklin D. Roosevelt*, 445.

75. Sweeney, *Military and the Press*, 65–73.

76. Washburn and Sweeney, "Grand Jury Transcripts," 2–11; Sweeney, *Military
and the Press*, 112–14.

77. J. E. Smith, *FDR*, 603–5, 622–23.

78. "The Old Magic," *Time*, October 2, 1944, 23.

79. "U.S. Electoral College Historical Election Results," National Archives and
Records Administration, https://www.archives.gov/federal-register/electoral
-college/scores.html#1944; D. M. Kennedy, *Freedom from Fear*, 798, 808; J. E.
Smith, *FDR*, 628, 635–36.

80. J. E. Smith, *FDR*, 601–2.

81. Greenberg, *Republic of Spin*, 257–58; Ritchie, *Reporting from Washington*, 185,
188; Becker, "Presidential Power," 16–17.

82. M. A. Watson, "Television and the Presidency," 205–7.

83. Parry, *Eisenhower*, 67–69.

84. M. A. Watson, "Television and the Presidency," 209; Allen, *Eisenhower and the
Mass Media*, 161.

85. M. A. Watson, "Television and the Presidency," 222–27; O'Brien, *John F.
Kennedy*, 817.

5. RICHARD NIXON

1. Tom Condon, "From Hartford 25 Years Later, a Watergate Player Reflects," *Hartford Courant*, June 15, 1997, https://www.courant.com/news/connecticut/hc-xpm-1997-06-15-9706150059-story.html; Nelson, *Scoop*, 61–68, 122–28; Elaine Woo, "Jack Nelson, Pulitzer Prize–Winning Reporter, Dies at 80; Journalist Helped Raise L.A. Times to National Prominence," *Los Angeles Times*, October 22, 2009, https://www.latimes.com/archives/la-xpm-2009-oct-22-me-jack-nelson22-story.html; Jack Nelson, "Orangeburg Students Unarmed, Study Shows," *Los Angeles Times*, February 18, 1968, A3; E. Roberts and Klibanoff, *Race Beat*, 402–3; Marrone, "Oral History Interview."

2. Jack Nelson and Ronald J. Ostrow, "Wiretap Witness Says He Gave Logs to Officials," *Los Angeles Times*, October 5, 1972, A1; "Excerpts from Interview with Man Who Says He Helped Bugging of Democrats," *New York Times*, October 7, 1972, 22; Woo, "Jack Nelson, Pulitzer Prize-Winning Reporter"; Transcript of Baldwin Interview by Reporters Ostrow and Nelson, 1827–72, U.S. v. Liddy, National Archives, https://www.archives.gov/files/research/investigations/watergate/59162111.pdf; R. T. Cooper, "Epilogue," 176; Kutler, *Wars of Watergate*, 260; Alicia C. Shepard, "The Myth of Watergate, Woodward and Bernstein," Poynter Online, June 15, 2007.

3. Porter, *Assault on the Media*, 3; Lashner, *Chilling Effect in TV News*, 57; Spear, *Presidents and the Press*, 39.

4. Schlesinger, *Imperial Presidency*, 227.

5. Perlstein, *Nixonland*, 748; Farrell, *Richard Nixon*, 23, 36.

6. Farrell, *Richard Nixon*, 145; Porter, *Assault on the Media*, 9.

7. Perlstein, *Nixonland*, 58; Spear, *Presidents and the Press*, 47.

8. "Address of Senator Nixon to the American People: The 'Checkers Speech,'" September 23, 1952, American Presidency Project, University of California Santa Barbara, https://www.presidency.ucsb.edu/documents/address-senator-nixon-the-american-people-the-checkers-speech; Ambrose, *Nixon*, 276–93; Rick Perlstein, "When Nixon Was Channeled on TV," *Wall Street Journal*, December 6–7, 2008, W3; Spear, *Presidents and the Press*, 50; Greenberg, *Nixon's Shadow*, 135; Interview with Ted Rogers, cited in Farrell, *Richard Nixon*, 208.

9. Perlstein, *Nixonland*, 53; Kutler, *Wars of Watergate*, 49, 53.

10. Gladwin Hill, "Nixon Denounces Press as Biased," *New York Times*, November 8, 1962, 1, 18; Perlstein, *Nixonland*, 59, 61.

11. James Reston, "Cats and Dogs: Mr. Nixon and the Press," *New York Times*, October 30, 1968, 46; Greenberg, *Nixon's Shadow*, 137, 141; Greenberg, *Republic of Spin*, 388–90.

12. Kutler, *Wars of Watergate*, 78–79.

13. Greenberg, *Nixon's Shadow*, 128, 132; Kutler, *Wars of Watergate*, 77–78, 166; Farrell, *Richard Nixon*, 373.

14. Herblock cartoon, March 1, 1970, reprinted in Block, *Herblock's State of the Union*, 72; Orman, "Covering the American Presidency," 387; Schlesinger, *Imperial Presidency*, 226; Schell, *Time of Illusion*, 31.

15. "Oral History Interview with H. R. Haldeman Conducted by Raymond H. Geselbracht in Mr. Haldeman's Home in Santa Barbara, California, on April 12, 1988," 28–30, Richard Nixon Presidential Library and Museum, https://www.nixonlibrary.gov/sites/default/files/forresearchers/find/histories/haldeman-1988-04-12.pdf; Spear, *Presidents and the Press*, 41–42; Liebovich, *Richard Nixon*, 3; Kutler, *Wars of Watergate*, 85; Associated Press, "Nixon's Note Tell of an Early Distrust of the Press," *New York Times*, May 31, 1987.

16. Eleanor Randolph, "Nixon White House Sought FBI Data on Gay Journalists," *Washington Post*, December 23, 1987, A3.

17. "Oral History Interview with H. R. Haldeman," 9–12; Bruce Ladd, "Nixon Press Operation," memorandum to Ron Ziegler, November 25, 1968, copy provided to the author; H. Thomas, *Front Row at the White House*, 86, 142; Lashner, *Chilling Effect in TV News*, 58; Greenberg, *Republic of Spin*, 299, 398–99.

18. William Beecher, "Raids in Cambodia by U.S. Unprotested," *New York Times*, May 9, 1969, 1; Richard Nixon and H. R. Haldeman, July 1, 1971, conversation in Oval Office, Tape #534-012(2), Richard Nixon Presidential Library and Museum, https://www.nixonlibrary.gov/media/14865; Bud McFarlane, "Leaks Early in the Administration," memorandum to Jon Howe, September 7, 1973, H. R. Haldeman Diaries Collection, July 24, 1969, National Archives and Records Administration, Online Public Access Identifier 7787364; Lukas, *Nightmare*, 60; Kutler, *Wars of Watergate*, 119–20; Safire, *Before the Fall*, 357, 656; Liebovich, *Richard Nixon*, 4.

19. "Oral History Interview with H. R. Haldeman," 63–68; McClendon, *Mr. President, Mr. President!*, 129; Mascaro, *Into the Fray*, 321.

20. Safire, *Before the Fall*, 360.

21. "Oral History Interview with H. R. Haldeman," 63–68; Safire, *Before the Fall*, 341, 351; Schudson, *Watergate in American Memory*, 117.

22. Greenberg, *Nixon's Shadow*, 145.

23. Spiro Theodore Agnew, "On the National Media," speech, Des Moines, Iowa, November 13, 1969, American Rhetoric, https://www.americanrhetoric.com/speeches/spiroagnewtvnewscoverage.htm; Spear, *Presidents and the Press*, 39; Kutler, *Wars of Watergate*, 177.

24. Safire, *Before the Fall,* 352.

25. Liebovich, *Richard Nixon,* 8–9.

26. "Transcript of Address by Agnew Extending Criticism of News Coverage to Press," *New York Times,* November 21, 1969, 22; Safire, *Before the Fall,* 353.

27. Vietnam Task Force, "United States—Vietnam Relations, 1945–1967," Office of the Secretary of Defense, https://nara-media-001.s3.amazonaws.com /arcmedia/research/pentagon-papers/Pentagon-Papers-Index.pdf; Kincaid, "Secrecy and Democracy," 152; Olson, *Watergate,* 17–18; Liebovich, *Richard Nixon,* 35–38; Kutler, *Wars of Watergate,* 109.

28. Kincaid, "Secrecy and Democracy," 153; Lashner, *Chilling Effect in TV News,* 204–5; Greenberg, *Nixon's Shadow,* 155–56.

29. Seymour M. Hersh, "Colson Asserts Kissinger Wanted Ellsberg Stopped," *New York Times,* April 30, 1974, 33.

30. Kincaid, "Secrecy and Democracy," 154–62; Lukas, *Nightmare,* 94–101; T. H. White, *Breach of Faith,* 150–51.

31. "September 8, 1972, President Nixon and Haldeman Discuss the IRS and an Enemies List," White House tapes, Richard Nixon Presidential Library and Museum, https://www.nixonlibrary.gov/media/31486.

32. "Lists of White House 'Enemies' and Memorandums Relating to Those Named," *New York Times,* June 28, 1973, 38.

33. "August 3, 1972, President Nixon, Ehrlichman, and Haldeman Discuss Using the IRS against Political Enemies," White House tapes, Richard Nixon Presidential Library and Museum, https://www.nixonlibrary.gov/media/31485; Morris, *Mary McGrory,* 146–47.

34. Associated Press, "Caulfield Testified That He Ordered Audit of Newsman," *New York Times,* May 28, 1974, 25; Memo from J. Edgar Hoover to John W. Dean III, December 20, 1971, Richard Nixon Presidential Library and Museum, https://www.nixonlibrary.gov/sites/default/files/virtuallibrary /documents/dec08/122071_Hoover.pdf; Morris, *Mary McGrory,* 147–48, 156; Kutler, *Wars of Watergate,* 180; Greenberg, *Nixon's Shadow,* 155.

35. Bob Woodward, "Hunt Told Associates of Orders to Kill Jack Anderson," *Washington Post,* September 21, 1975, 1; Perlstein, *Nixonland,* 635–36; Olson, *Watergate,* 20; Feldstein, *Poisoning the Press,* 280.

36. Bob Woodward and Carl Bernstein, "Bugging Suspect Investigated Writer," *Washington Post,* September 27, 1972, A1; Feldstein, *Poisoning the Press,* 278–82.

37. Feldstein, *Poisoning the Press,* 282, 285–90.

38. Dean, *Blind Ambition,* 79–84.

39. Dean, *Blind Ambition,* 85; Perlstein, *Nixonland,* 636–37, 85–86; Olson, *Watergate,* 36–40; James Rosen, *Strong Man,* 262–75.

40. Sussman, *Great Coverup*, 5–11; Perlstein, *Nixonland*, 666–67; Olson, *Watergate*, 38–40; Lukas, *Nightmare*, 196–209.

41. Associated Press, "GOP Consultant Charged in Democratic Break-In," *Baltimore Sun*, June 19, 1972, A1; Edward Jay Epstein, "How Press Handled Watergate Scandal," *Los Angeles Times*, September 14, 1973, 3A, 18A; Bob Woodward and E. J. Bachinski, "White House Consultant Tied to Bugging Figure," *Washington Post*, June 20, 1972, A1.

42. Woodward and Bachinski, "White House Consultant."

43. G. W. Johnson, *Nixon Presidential Press Conferences*, 248; Bob Woodward and Jim Mann, "Bond Cut for Bugging Suspects," *Washington Post*, June 23, 1972, C1.

44. Nixon, *Nixon Presidential Press Conferences*, 258–80.

45. Katharine Graham, "The Watergate Watershed: A Turning Point for a Nation and a Newspaper," *Washington Post*, January 28, 1997, D01; Ritchie, *Reporting from Washington*, 206.

46. "The Watergate Issue," *Time*, August 28, 1972, 22.

47. "The Watergate Probe," *Time*, July 24, 1972, 36.

48. Walter Rugaber, "Cash in Capital Raid Traced to Mexico," *New York Times*, July 31, 1972, 1; Sussman, *Great Cover-Up*, 74–75.

49. Carl Bernstein and Bob Woodward, "Bug Suspect Got Campaign Funds," *Washington Post*, August 1, 1972, A1.

50. Shepard, *Woodward and Bernstein*, 2–10, 14–16, 35–36; Bernstein and Woodward, *All the President's Men*, 51; Bernstein, "Reporter's Assessment," 223.

51. Shepard, *Woodward and Bernstein*, 17–29; Alicia C. Shepard, "Woodward and Bernstein Uncovered," *Washingtonian*, September 1, 2003, https://www.washingtonian.com/2003/09/01/woodward-and-bernstein-uncovered/; Shepard, "Myth of Watergate"; "The Watergate Three," *Time*, May 7, 1973.

52. Carl Bernstein and Bob Woodward, "Spy Funds Linked to GOP Aides," *Washington Post, Times Herald*, September 17. 1972, A1.

53. Carl Bernstein and Bob Woodward, "2 Linked to Secret GOP Fund," *Washington Post*, September 18, 1972, A1.

54. Carl Bernstein and Bob Woodward, "Watergate Data Destruction Charged," *Washington Post*, September 20, 1972, A1.

55. Carl Bernstein and Bob Woodward, "Mitchell Controlled Secret GOP Fund," *Washington Post*, September 29, 1972, A1; Graham, "Watergate Watershed," D01.

56. Carl Bernstein and Bob Woodward, "FBI Finds Nixon Aides Sabotaged Democrats," *Washington Post*, October 10, 1972, A1; Carl Bernstein and Bob Woodward, "Key Nixon Aide Named as 'Sabotage' Contact," *Washington Post*, October 15, 1972, A1.

57. Carl Bernstein and Bob Woodward, "Testimony Ties Top Nixon Aide to Secret Fund," *Washington Post*, October 25, 1972, A1; Bernstein and Woodward, *All the President's Men*, 174–96.

58. "Watergate, Contd.," *Time*, August 14, 1972, 23; "The Watergate Issue," *Time*, August 28, 1972, 22; "More Fumes from the Watergate Affair," *Time*, October 23, 1972, 25.

59. Ritchie, *Reporting from Washington*, 219; Schudson, *Watergate in American Memory*, 105; Lashner, *Chilling Effect in TV News*, 62.

60. Seymour M. Hersh, "Watergate Days," *New Yorker*, June 13, 2005.

61. Lang and Lang, *Battle for Public Opinion*, 27–30; Liebovich, *Richard Nixon*, Appendix C.

62. Lukas, *Nightmare*, 274; Shepard, "Myth of Watergate."

63. Lang and Lang, *Battle for Public Opinion*, 29–30; Ritchie, *Reporting from Washington*, 207: Perlstein, *Nixonland*, 738–39; Walter Pincus and George Lardner Jr., "Nixon Hoped Antitrust Threat Would Sway Network Coverage," *Washington Post*, December 1, 1997, A1; Shepard, "Myth of Watergate."

64. Dickinson, *Watergate*, 9.

65. "Transcript Prepared by the Impeachment Inquiry Staff for the House Judiciary Committee of a Recording of a Meeting among the President, H. R. Haldeman and John Dean of September 15, 1972, from 5:24 to 6:17 P.M.," August 6, 1974, 35, Richard Nixon Presidential Library and Museum, https://www.nixonlibrary.gov/sites/default/files/forresearchers/find/tapes/finding_aids/tapesubjectlogs/oval779-2.pdf.

66. Graham, "Watergate Watershed," DOI.

67. Safire, *Before the Fall*, 361.

68. Lang and Lang, *Battle for Public Opinion*, 28; Kutler, *Wars of Watergate*, 164–65; T. H. White, *Breach of Faith*, 169–70.

69. Hersh, *Reporter*, 175–79; Seymour M. Hersh, "4 Watergate Defendants Reported Still Being Paid," *New York Times*, January 14, 1973, 1, 180.

70. Congressional Quarterly, *Watergate*, 1:22, 3; Sussman, *Great Coverup*, 151–66; Olson, *Watergate*, 72–77; T. H. White, *Breach of Faith*, 203–5; Epstein, "How Press Handled Watergate Scandal," 3A, 18A.

71. Associated Press, "'I Apologize,' Ziegler Tells Washington Post," *Los Angeles Times*, May 1, 1973, 3; Carl Bernstein and Bob Woodward, "Watergate Data Destruction Charged," *Washington Post*, September 20, 1972, A1; "It's Inoperative. They Misspoke Themselves," *Time*, April 30, 1973, 16; R. J. Harris, *Pulitzer's Gold*, 222–35.

72. Ritchie, *Reporting from Washington*, 208; David Greenberg, "Nabobs Revisited: What Watergate Reveals about Today's Washington Press Corps," *Washington Monthly* 35, no. 10 (October 2003): 45–48.

73. Greenberg, "Nabobs Revisited," 45–48; Epstein, "How Press Handled Watergate Scandal," 3A, 18A.

74. Nixon, *Nixon Presidential Press Conferences*, 341–45.

75. Associated Press, "Jack White, 63; News Story on Nixon's Taxes Prompted, 'I Am Not a Crook' Line," *Los Angeles Times*, October 13, 2005; J. Anthony Lukas, "Nixon's Retreats—Public Funds Finance His Privacy," *Boston Globe*, January 15, 1974, 2.

76. Lukas, *Nightmare*, 426–41; Liebovich, *Richard Nixon*, 97–98; Kutler, *Wars of Watergate*, 413.

77. "An Editorial: The President Should Resign," *Time*, November 12, 1973, 42.

78. "The President Should Be Impeached," *Los Angeles Times*, May 10, 1974, B6; Olson, *Watergate*, 144–46.

79. Liebovich, *Richard Nixon*, 104–6; Sussman, *Great Coverup*, 286–99; W. J. Campbell, *Getting It Wrong*, 115.

80. Schudson, *Watergate in American Memory*, 104; W. J. Campbell, *Getting It Wrong*, 115–17, 122; Woodward, *Secret Man*, 5–6; Shepard, "Myth of Watergate"; Epstein, "How Press Handled Watergate Scandal," 3A, 18A.

81. Transcript of a recording of a meeting between the president, John Ehrlichman, and Ronald Ziegler, April 16, 1973, from 3:27 to 4:02 p.m., Executive Office Building, EOB #427-5 and #426-6, Richard Nixon Presidential Library and Museum.

82. Memorandum from David Gergen to the President, April 28, 1973, Watergate Memos folder, box 106, White House Central Files: Staff Member & Office Files, Richard Nixon Presidential Library and Museum, https://www .nixonlibrary.gov/sites/default/files/virtuallibrary/documents/jul11/gergen35 .pdf; Memorandum from David Gergen to Leonard Garment, May 5, 1973, Watergate Memos folder, box 106, WHCF: SMOF, Richard Nixon Presidential Library and Museum, https://www.nixonlibrary.gov/sites/default/files /virtuallibrary/documents/jul11/gergen36.pdf.

83. Porter, *Assault on the Media*, 2; R. Campbell, *60 Minutes and the News*, 160; Blum, *Tick . . . Tick . . . Tick*, 1.

6. RONALD REAGAN

1. "President Reagan Remarks at the 30th Anniversary of the National Review Magazine at the Plaza Hotel in New York City, New York on December 5, 1985," Reagan Library, https://www.youtube.com/watch?v=Rm_FPbqFEZk;

White House Diaries, November 25–December 2, 1985, Ronald Reagan Presidential Foundation & Institute, https://www.reaganfoundation.org /ronald-reagan/white-house-diaries/diary-entry-11251985/ and https:// www.reaganfoundation.org/ronald-reagan/white-house-diaries/diary-entry -11261985/; Kim Mills, "Reagan Praises Conservative Magazine for Intellectual, Political Influence," Associated Press, December 6, 1985, https://apnews .com/898c0d095117ad9264d135f410fc011c; Robert Suro, "National Review, Now 30, Takes a Bow at Plaza," *New York Times*, December 6, 1985, B3; Paula Span, "Reagan for the Review," *Washington Post*, December 6, 1985, C1; Associated Press, "Buckley, Pals Celebrate Review's 30th," *Boston Globe*, December 6, 1986, 14.

2. "President Reagan," *National Review*, December 31, 1985, 127–29; Suro, "National Review"; Hemmer, *Messengers of the Right*, 252; "President Reagan Remarks at the 30th Anniversary of the National Review."

3. Richard Brookhiser, "National Review 30th Anniversary," *National Review*, December 31, 1985, 4–5.

4. David A. Walsh, "In Their Right Mind," *Washington Monthly* 50, no. 7/8 (July/August 2018): 46; Hemmer, *Messengers of the Right*, xii–xiii, 22–31.

5. "The Who, What, How and Why of Your Washington Service," *Human Events*, April 21, 1961, 1–2; Harry Hurt III, "A Sweeping Tale of Four Giants of Texas Oil," *New York Times*, January 17, 2009; Hemmer, *Messengers of the Right*, 31, 253.

6. Hemmer, *Messengers of the Right*, 43.

7. D. A. Walsh, "In Their Right Mind," 46–47.

8. J. B. McPherson, *Conservative Resurgence and the Press*, 142–45; "Firing Line," American Archive of Public Broadcasting, https://americanarchive.org/special _collections/firing-line.

9. Bill Peterson, "The Word According to Human Events," *Washington Post*, March 14, 1982; Perlstein, *Invisible Bridge*, 25–28; Cannon, *President Reagan*, 33, 40; Reagan, *American Life*, 63–65, 169; Deaver, *Different Drummer*, 56, 176; Ritter and Henry, *Ronald Reagan*, 5; Schaller, *Ronald Reagan*, 1–4.

10. Reagan, *American Life*, 80–81; Cannon, *President Reagan*, 33, 45; Schaller, *Ronald Reagan*, 4–5; Deaver, *Different Drummer*, 52; Ritter and Henry, *Ronald Reagan*, 5–6, 14.

11. Ritter and Henry, *Ronald Reagan*, 23; Perlstein, *Invisible Bridge*, 380.

12. Ronald Reagan, "A Time for Choosing," speech, October 27, 1964, Ronald Reagan Presidential Library and Museum, https://www.reaganlibrary.gov/archives /speech/time-choosing-speech; Ronald Reagan, "Reagan Campaign Address for Goldwater," C-SPAN, October 27, 1964, https://www.c-span.org/video/?153897

-1/ronald-reagans-a-time-choosing-speech; K. B. McPherson, *Conservative Resurgence and the Press*, 83–84; Ritter and Henry, *Ronald Reagan*, 16.

13. Deaver, *Different Drummer*, 51; Ritter and Henry, *Ronald Reagan*, 24,

14. Cannon, *President Reagan*, 11–13; Ritter and Henry, *Ronald Reagan*, 6; Deaver, *Different Drummer*, 21; Gladwin Hill, "Reagan Emerging in 1968 Spotlight," *New York Times*, November 10, 1968, 1.

15. "Ronald Reagan Citizen Governor 1968," presidential campaign film, Reagan Library, https://www.youtube.com/watch?v=9lbJn7SwHSw; Ron Moskowitz, "Reagan Shuts the Colleges," *San Francisco Chronicle*, May 7, 1970, 1, 28; Dallek, *Ronald Reagan*, 49; Cannon, *President Reagan*, 48; J. B. McPherson, *Conservative Resurgence and the Press*, 85–86.

16. Ritter and Henry, *Ronald Reagan*, 95; Dallek, *Ronald Reagan*, 49.

17. Perlstein, *Invisible Bridge*, 25–28; Schaller, *Ronald Reagan*, 770–804; Spear, *Presidents and the Press*, 266.

18. "1980 Presidential Candidate Debate," Reagan Foundation, October 28, 1980, https://www.youtube.com/watch?v=_8YxFc_1b_0; "Debate Transcript," *New York Times*, October 30, 1980, B18; "October 28, 1980 Debate Transcript," Commission on Presidential Debates, https://www.debates.org/voter-education/debate-transcripts/october-28-1980-debate-transcript/; Ritter and Henry, *Ronald Reagan*, 102; Schaller, *Ronald Reagan*, 26–27; 1980 Electoral College Results, National Archives, https://www.archives.gov/electoral-college/1980.

19. J. B. McPherson, *Conservative Resurgence and the Press*, 89–90; Hertsgaard, *On Bended Knee*, 44, 47.

20. Garment, *Scandal*, 43–56.

21. Hertsgaard, *On Bended Knee*, 3–4.

22. Deaver, *Behind the Scenes*, 144.

23. Dallek, *Ronald Reagan*, 76; "Ronald Reagan Inaugural Address," CBS News, January 20, 1981, https://www.youtube.com/watch?v=G8jV_1G9Yj4; Reagan, *American Life*, 208; Kumar, *Managing the President's Message*, 149; Smoller, *Six O'Clock Presidency*, 1; Sherman, *Loudest Voice in the Room*, xix; J. B. McPherson, *Conservative Resurgence and the Press*, 88–89; Ritter and Henry, *Ronald Reagan*, 104–5.

24. Ritter and Henry, *Ronald Reagan*, 103; Ronald Reagan, "1982 State of the Union," C-SPAN, January 26, 1982, https://www.c-span.org/video/?88293-1/1982-state-union-address; "Who Gets Invited to the State of the Union," *New York Times*, January 30, 2018, https://www.youtube.com/watch?v=1tA9sjxrbZg; Brian Resnick and National Journal, "What's a Skutnik and Why Is One Sitting Next to Michelle Obama at the State of the Union?"

Atlantic, February 11, 2013, https://www.theatlantic.com/politics/archive/2013
/02/whats-a-skutnik-and-why-is-one-sitting-next-to-michelle-obama-at-the
-state-of-the-union/454281/; Ritter and Henry, *Ronald Reagan*, 105–6.

25. Deaver, *Behind the Scenes*, 140–41; Hertsgaard, *On Bended Knee*, 24–25.

26. David S. Broder, "Reagan Issues an Appeal for New Consensus," *Washington Post*, July 17, 1980, A1; Drew, *Portrait of an Election*, 218; Ritter and Henry, *Ronald Reagan*, 95, 97, 218; Perlstein, *Reaganland*, 102.

27. Reagan, "1982 State of the Union"; "Transcript of the President's State of the Union Message to the Nation," *New York Times*, January 27, 1982, A16.

28. Bill Gray, "Blacks Will Suffer from Reaganomics," *Philadelphia Tribune*, March 6, 1981, 1; Howell Raines, "Benefits and Bruises," *New York Times*, March 22, 1981, E1; Nacos, *Press, Presidents, and Crises*, 135–36; Dallek, *Ronald Reagan*, 64, 70.

29. United Press International, "Reagan Wonders Why He Wasn't Shot Before," *Marietta Journal*, April 23, 1981, 1; Nacos, *Press, Presidents, and Crises*, 133–34; Schaller, *Ronald Reagan*, 37; Deaver, *Different Drummer*, 131–42; Hertsgaard, *On Bended Knee*, 20.

30. Deaver, *Different Drummer*, 140.

31. H. Thomas, "Ronald Reagan," 35; Helen Thomas, United Press International, "The Pain Hangs On," *Fresno Bee*, April 23, 1981, 1; Dallek, *Ronald Reagan*, 68.

32. Nacos, *Press, Presidents, and Crises*, 156; Dallek, *Ronald Reagan*, 68; Schaller, *Ronald Reagan*, 44–46; J. B. McPherson, *Conservative Resurgence and the Press*, 102–3; Walter Isaacson, Douglas Brew, and Neil MacNeil, "Yeas 238–Nays 195," *Time*, August 10, 1981, 20.

33. "Ship of State to Starboard," *National Review*, August 21, 1981.

34. "President Reagan and Nancy Reagan Depart via Marine One for Camp David," Reagan Library, March 12, 1982, https://www.youtube.com/watch?v=IRSVFUcUEsU; Donaldson, *Hold On, Mr. President!*, 201–2; Cannon, *President Reagan*, 536.

35. Steven V. Roberts, "Washington Talk: The Presidency; Shouting Questions at Reagan," *New York Times*, October 21, 1987, B4.

36. Lance Morrow, "In the Kingdom of Television," *Time*, February 8, 1988, 27.

37. Smoller, *Six O'Clock Presidency*, 15–17; Hertsgaard, *On Bended Knee*, 51; Schaller, *Ronald Reagan*, 38.

38. J. B. McPherson, *Conservative Resurgence and the Press*, 88; Hertsgaard, *On Bended Knee*, 27–28; Cannon, *President Reagan*, 536–37; Maltese, *Spin Control*, 199.

39. Lou Cannon, "President's Deeds Reveal His Real Opinion of Press Freedom," *Washington Post*, November 28, 1983, A3.

40. Hertsgaard, *On Bended Knee*, 139; Ritter and Henry, *Ronald Reagan*, 98–99; Cannon, *President Reagan*, 58–59; Donaldson, *Hold On, Mr. President!*, 171–72.

41. Hertsgaard, *On Bended Knee*, 148–49.

42. Hertsgaard, *On Bended Knee*, 8.

43. United Press International, "Is 'Some Fella's' Layoff Really News?" *Richmond Times-Dispatch*, March 18, 1982, 59; Hertsgaard, *On Bended Knee*, 152; Cannon, *President Reagan*, 496; Thomas, "Ronald Reagan and the Management of the News," 39; J. B. McPherson, *Conservative Resurgence and the Press*, 102; Schaller, *Ronald Reagan*, 44–46.

44. Sally Bedell Smith, "Rather Cites White House Criticism," *New York Times*, November 14, 1983, C18.

45. "Reagan/Corporate Tax," NBC *Nightly News*, January 26, 1983, Vanderbilt Television News Archive; Alan Richman, "Hey, Look Who Dropped In!" *Boston Globe*, January 27, 1983, 41; Hertsgaard, *On Bended Knee*, 17–20, 25–26.

46. "Lebanon/Bombing," NBC *Evening News*, October 24, 1983; Eric Weiner, "Remembering the 1983 Suicide Bombings in Beirut," U.S. Department of State, April 18, 2018, https://2017-2021.state.gov/remembering-the-1983 -suicide-bombings-in-beirut-the-tragic-events-that-created-the-diplomatic -security-service/index.html; Richard Ernsberger Jr., "1983 Beirut Barracks Bombing: 'The BLT Building Is Gone!'" *Marine Corps Times*, October 23, 2019, https://www.marinecorpstimes.com/news/your-marine-corps/2019/10 /23/1983-beirut-barracks-bombing-the-blt-building-is-gone/; "President Reagan's Remarks on the Grenada Rescue Mission on October 25, 1983," Reagan Library, https://www.youtube.com/watch?v=upU-RNPEJmY; "Grenada/ United States Invasion," NBC *Nightly News*, October 25, 1983; Maltese, *Spin Control*, 197; J. B. McPherson, *Conservative Resurgence and the Press*, 93–94.

47. Cannon, "President's Deeds Reveal His Real Opinion," A3.

48. Maltese, *Spin Control*, 197.

49. Cannon, *President Reagan*, 494, 501.

50. Rich Jaroslovsky and James M. Perry, "New Question in Race: Is Oldest U.S. President Now Showing His Age," *Wall Street Journal*, October 9, 1984, 1; Cannon, *President Reagan*, 495.

51. Sherman, *Loudest Voice in the Room*, 118–19; Cannon, *President Reagan*, 550–51.

52. Cannon, *President Reagan*, 493.

53. Ivo Daalder, "Nuclear War Was Barely Averted in 1983," *Chicago Tribune*, February 26, 2021, 15.

54. Associated Press, "Reagan Wins Bipartisan Praise for Talks," *Evening Post*, December 11, 1987, 1; Rudy Abramson, "'A Clear Success,'" *Daily Advocate*,

December 11, 1987, 1; Stan Jones, "Summit 'First Step' toward Peace," *Fort Worth Star-Telegram*, December 11, 1987, 1; Schaller, *Ronald Reagan*, 60–63, 84; Cannon, *President Reagan*, 775.

55. Byrne, *Iran-Contra*, 253–54; Schaller, *Ronald Reagan*, 78.

56. White House Diaries, August 14, 1985, Ronald Reagan Presidential Foundation & Institute, https://www.reaganfoundation.org/ronald-reagan/white-house-diaries/diary-entry-08141985/; Byrne, *Iran-Contra*, xx, 1–2; Schaller, *Ronald Reagan*, 77.

57. White House Diaries, August 14, 1985, and November 12, 1986, Ronald Reagan Presidential Foundation & Institute, https://www.reaganfoundation.org/ronald-reagan/white-house-diaries/diary-entry-08141985/ and https://www.reaganfoundation.org/ronald-reagan/white-house-diaries/diary-entry-11121986/; Byrne, *Iran-Contra*, 256–58; Schaller, *Ronald Reagan*, 78.

58. "President Reagan's Address to the Nation on the Iran-Contra Controversy from the Oval Office," Reagan Library, November 13, 1986, https://www.youtube.com/watch?v=rYdvBZxPhLY.

59. L. E. Walsh, *Firewall*, 10; Byrne, *Iran-Contra*, 262.

60. "Ronald Reagan Holds a News Conference and Takes Question on the Iran Arms and Contra Aid," AP Archive, November 19, 1986, https://www.youtube.com/watch?v=HnpmdVVK2-4; Byrne, *Iran-Contra*, 265; L. E. Walsh, *Firewall*, 11; Cannon, *President Reagan*, 690.

61. Eleanor Randolph, "For Journalists, Shock—and Hot Pursuit," *Washington Post*, November 26, 1986, D1, D13; Byrne, *Iran-Contra*, 2; Schaller, *Ronald Reagan*, 78.

62. "Presidential Approval Ratings—Gallup Historical Statistics and Trends," Gallup, https://news.gallup.com/poll/116677/presidential-approval-ratings-gallup-historical-statistics-trends.aspx; Cohen, *Presidency in the Era*, 6–7, 9–10; Fitzwater, *Call the Briefing!*, 117–18.

63. L. E. Walsh, *Firewall*, 3–4, 12–15; Byrne, *Iran-Contra*, 276–77.

64. Byrne, *Iran-Contra*, 3–4, 264–69, 275; Cannon, *President Reagan*, 590.

65. Kumar, *Managing the President's Message*, 170; Byrne, *Iran-Contra*, 4; Cohen, 6–7.

66. Fitzwater, *Call the Briefing!*, 108; Thomas Ferraro, United Press International, "Are American Media Guilty of Overkill on Iran Arms Dealing," *San Diego Union*, March 29, 1987, 48.

67. Schaller, *Ronald Reagan*, 79; Ferraro, "Are American Media Guilty," 48; Fitzwater, *Call the Briefing!*, 108–9.

68. Simpson, *Right in the Old Gazoo*, 1–3; Terrence Hunt, Associated Press, "Reagan Vows Not to Repeat Iran Policy," *State* (Columbia SC), March 20,

1987, 1A, 10A; "Simpson Apologizes in Public to 'Gazoo-Sticking' Reporters," *Houston Chronicle*, March 25, 1987, 6; Ferraro, "Are American Media Guilty," 48; Fitzwater, *Call the Briefing!*, 110.

69. "President Reagan's 40th Press Conference in the East Room on March 19, 1987," Reagan Library, https://www.youtube.com/watch?v=P42fS72JIJU; Fitzwater, *Call the Briefing!*, 111–15, 120–22; Ferraro, "Are American Media Guilty," 48.

70. Bill Carter, "Reagan Steers around Issues of Iran Crisis," *Baltimore Sun*, March 20, 1987, 1E, 8E.

71. *Report of the Congressional Committees*, 11; L. E. Walsh, *Final Report*, 445.

72. Frank Newport, Jeffrey M. Jones, and Lydia Saad, "Ronald Reagan from the People's Perspective: A Gallup Poll Review," June 7, 2004, https://news.gallup .com/poll/11887/ronald-reagan-from-peoples-perspective-gallup-poll-review .aspx; Cohen, *Presidency in the Era*, 6–7; Cannon, *President Reagan*, 20, 829–31; Shawn Langlois, "How Much Each U.S. President Has Contributed to the National Debt," *MarketWatch*, October 29, 2018, https://www.marketwatch .com/story/how-much-each-us-president-has-contributed-to-the-national -debt-2018-10-29; Kimberly Amadeo, "U.S. Debt by President by Dollar and Percentage," *Balance*, January 10, 2020, https://www.thebalance.com/us-debt -by-president-by-dollar-and-percent-3306296.

73. "Fairness in Broadcasting Act of 1987," U.S. Senate hearing, March 18, 1987, C-SPAN, https://www.c-span.org/video/?171860-1/fairness-broadcasting-act -1987; Associated Press, "Merits of Fairness Doctrine Debated by Broadcasters," *New York Times*, March 20, 1987; Hemmer, *Messengers of the Right*, 258; Starr, *Creation of the Media*, 380; J. E. Zelizer, "How Washington Helped Create," 178–79, 183–84; Hendershot, *What's Fair on the Air?*, 9–10, 16–19.

74. Myer Feldman, "Memorandum for the President: Right-Wing Groups," August 15, 1963, Presidential Papers, President's Office Files, box 106, folder Right Wing Movements, Part 1, 1, John F. Kennedy Presidential Library and Museum, https://www.jfklibrary.org/asset-viewer/archives/JFKPOF/106 /JFKPOF-106-013; Peter Applebome, "The Hunts: A Dynasty Built on Poker and Oil," *New York Times*, August 30, 1986, 1; Martin Waldron, "The Right-Wing 'Life Line' Program, Lacking H. L. Hunt's Aid, Has Lost Radio Outlets and Revenue," *New York Times*, April 13, 1975, 19; J. E. Zelizer, "How Washington Helped Create," 179; Hendershot, *What's Fair on the Air?*, 17, 21–22.

75. Caroline E. Mayer, "FCC Chief's Fears," *Washington Post*, February 6, 1983, K1.

76. Ronald Reagan, "Message Returning to the Senate without Approval the Fairness in Broadcasting Bill," June 19, 1987, Ronald Reagan Presidential Library and Museum, https://www.reaganlibrary.gov/research/speeches/061987h;

Jamieson and Cappella, *Echo Chamber*, 45; Jon Pepper, "FCC Repeals Fairness Doctrine," *Detroit News*, August 5, 1987, 3; Hemmer, *Messengers of the Right*, 259; J. E. Zelizer, "How Washington Helped Create," 177, 186–87.

77. Tom Shales, "Repeal of Fairness Doctrine Leaves Audience in the Lurch," *Cleveland Plain Dealer*, August 7, 1987, 65.

78. Hemmer, *Messengers of the Right*, 260; David Remnick, "Day of the Dittohead," *Washington Post*, February 20, 1994, C4; Clarence Page, "Rush Limbaugh Can Dish It Out, but He Sure Can't Take It," *Chicago Tribune*, May 5, 1993; Nick Robins-Early and Christopher Mathias, "Rush Limbaugh, Bigoted King of Talk Radio, Dies at 70," *HuffPost*, February 17, 2021, https://www.huffpost.com/entry/rush-limbaugh-talk-radio-dies_n_5fe4e082c5b66809cb30ad57?uod&fbclid=IwAR2K6mxMBrNtNYVESf3nWMaxz4lEqZ84Ea76VaQBfBd28vjX5mmHmf90K3U.

79. Remnick, "Day of the Dittohead," C4; "Al Gore's Greatest Hoax," *Limbaugh eLetter*, December 1997, http://www.thelimbaughletter.com/thelimbaughletter/february_2019/MobilePagedArticle.action?articleId=1459907#articleId1459907.

80. Jamieson and Cappella, *Echo Chamber*, 44–45; Walsh, "In Their Right Mind," 49; Hemmer, *Messengers of the Right*, 262.

7. BILL CLINTON

1. Matt Drudge, "Speech to the National Press Club on the Media and the Internet," June 2, 1998, American Rhetoric, Online Speech Bank, https://www.americanrhetoric.com/speeches/mattdrugdenationalpressclub.htm; Eddie Dean, "Hard Times and Jalapeño Bologna," *Washington City Paper*, March 13, 1988; Alterman, *What Liberal Media?*, 77; Ritchie, *Reporting from Washington*, 276.

2. Drudge, "Speech to the National Press Club"; King, *Free for All*, 238; Dean, "Hard Times and Jalapeño Bologna"; Alterman, *What Liberal Media?*, 78; Ritchie, *Reporting from Washington*, 278.

3. Drudge, "Speech to the National Press Club."

4. "Presidential Heights," POTUS: Presidents of the United States, https://www.potus.com/presidential-facts/presidential-heights/; Maraniss, *First in His Class*, 407, 418; "Gov. William Jefferson Clinton," National Governors Association, https://www.nga.org/governor/william-jefferson-clinton/.

5. Maraniss, *First in His Class*, 444–47; Takiff, *Complicated Man*, 90–91.

6. "Clinton Appearance on Arsenio Hall Show," C-SPAN, June 3, 1992, https://www.c-span.org/video/?26472-1/clinton-appearance-arsenio-hall-show; J. F. Harris, *The Survivor*, xvi, xxii; Hayden, *Covering Clinton*, 18.

7. Riley, *Inside the Clinton White House*, 36; Woodward, *Shadow*, 306; J. F. Harris, *The Survivor*, xxii; Julian E. Zelizer, "Bill Clinton's Nearly Forgotten 1992 Sex Scandal," CNN Opinion, April 6, 2016, https://www.cnn.com/2016/04/06/opinions/zelizer-presidential-election-campaign-scandals-bill-clinton/index.html; Kevin Merida, "It's Come to This: A Nickname That's Proven Hard to Slip," *Washington Post*, December 20, 1998, FI.

8. Larry Edelman, "The Economy Cost George H. W. Bush a Second Term. Will the Same Happen to Trump?" *Boston Globe*, December 3, 2018, https://www.bostonglobe.com/news/politics/2018/12/03/the-economy-cost-bush-second-term-will-same-happen-trump/FXE0ILm4lF3qKw1pXhwshK/story.html; "1992 Electoral College Results," National Archives, https://www.archives.gov/electoral-college/1992; J. F. Harris, *The Survivor*, xxv, 3–4.

9. J. F. Harris, *The Survivor*, 7–8.

10. CNBC, May 2, 1994, transcript in box 6, Office of the Press Secretary, Dee Dee Myers, "Media File—Paula Jones," Clinton Digital Library, https://clinton.presidentiallibraries.us/items/show/99922.

11. J. F. Harris, *The Survivor*, 35.

12. Rose, *American Presidency under Siege*, 3; Kumar, *Managing the President's Message*, 50; Memorandum for the President from Mark Gearan, December 10, 1993, David Gergen Collection, White House Office of Records Management System and FG001-07, "047625 SS," Clinton Digital Library, https://clinton.presidentiallibraries.us/items/show/96264.

13. Memo from George Condon of the White House Correspondents' Association to Dee Dee Myers, box 11, Press Corps [1], Office of the Press Secretary, Dee Dee Myers, "Press Corps [1]," Clinton Digital Library, https://clinton.presidentiallibraries.us/items/show/99955; Kumar, *Managing the President's Message*, 35.

14. Jeff Gerth, "Clintons Joined S&L Operator in an Ozark Real-Estate Venture," *New York Times*, March 8, 1992, A1; Ritchie, *Reporting from Washington*, 238; Hayden, *Covering Clinton*, 53; "Whitewater Time Line," *Washington Post*, 1998, https://www.washingtonpost.com/wp-srv/politics/special/whitewater/timeline.htm.

15. Dee Dee Myers, letter to Max Frankel, executive editor of the *New York Times*, March 26, 1994, box 6, Office of the Press Secretary, Dee Dee Myers, 2011-0587-F, Clinton Presidential Records: White House Staff and Office Files, William J. Clinton Presidential Library and Museum, https://clinton.presidentiallibraries.us/items/show/99872; Ritchie, *Reporting from Washington*, 238; J. F. Harris, *The Survivor*, 101.

16. "Arkansas Anxieties," *Wall Street Journal*, December 15, 1993, A16.

17. "Use of Government Vehicles," Memorandum for the Heads of Executive Departments and Agencies, White House Office of the Press Secretary, February 10, 1993, Coptergate [1], box 3, Dee Meyers, 2011-0587-F, Clinton Presidential Records: White House Staff and Office Files, William J. Clinton Presidential Library and Museum, https://clinton.presidentiallibraries.us/items/show/99813; Kumar, *Managing the President's Message*, 53; Roger Simon, "Information, Please: How to Mismanage a Scandal," *Baltimore Sun*, April 3, 1994; Woodward, *Shadow*, 251; J. F. Harris, *The Survivor*, 36–39.

18. "The Body Count," *Newsweek*, August 6, 1995; Woodward, *Shadow*, 287.

19. Remnick, "Day of the Dittohead"; Gallup Presidential Election Trial-Heat Trends, 1936–2008, https://news.gallup.com/poll/110548/gallup-presidential-election-trial-heat-trends.aspx; Hemmer, *Messengers of the Right*, 262; Sherman, *Loudest Voice in the Room*, 134; Jamieson and Cappella, *Echo Chamber*, 42.

20. Page, "Rush Limbaugh Can Dish It Out."

21. Molly Ivins, "It Ain't Funny, Rush," *Washington Post*, October 14, 1993, https://www.washingtonpost.com/archive/opinions/1993/10/14/it-aint-funny-rush/5dfc5618-c9f3-41a2-b88b-7f07ab4c5bf2/; Hemmer, *Messengers of the Right*, 270; Remnick, "Day of the Dittohead."

22. Warren Rojas, "The G-Man Signs Off," *Roll Call*, September 25, 2021, https://www.rollcall.com/2012/09/25/the-g-man-signs-off/; Laurie Asseo, "Liddy Goes 'on Trial' for Inciting Radio Listener to Violence," Associated Press, August 8, 1995, https://apnews.com/article/f3378e93961d689840c33210df1094ca.

23. Alterman, *What Liberal Media?*, 3–5; "Ann Coulter Net Worth," *Celebrity Net Worth*, https://www.celebritynetworth.com/richest-politicians/republicans/ann-coulter-net-worth/.

24. Hemmer, *Messengers of the Right*, 267.

25. Alterman, *What Liberal Media?*, 246–51.

26. Robert B. Fiske Jr., Independent Counsel, "Statement of Washington, D.C. Investigations," June 30, 1994, Office of the Press Secretary, Dee Dee Myers, "Media File—Vincent Foster," Clinton Digital Library, https://clinton.presidentiallibraries.us/items/show/99923; Alterman, *What Liberal Media?*, 252–53; J. F. Harris, *The Survivor*, 74.

27. Russell Watson, "Vince Foster's Suicide: The Rumor Mill Churns," *Newsweek*, March 20, 1994, https://www.newsweek.com/vince-fosters-suicide-rumor-mill-churns-185900; Matthew Yglesias, "Vince Foster's Death and Subsequent Conspiracy Theories, Explained," *Vox*, May 25, 2016, https://www.vox.com/2016/5/25/11761128/vince-foster.

28. David Brock, "His Cheatin' Heart," *American Spectator*, January 1994; Brock, *Blinded by the Light*, xviii, 150; Alterman, *What Liberal Media?*, 253–55.

29. Brock, *Blinded by the Light*, 165–75.

30. Joel Williams, Associated Press, "Former Arkansas Employee Files Suit against Clinton," May 6, 1994, Office of the Press Secretary, Dee Dee Myers, box 9, 2011-0587, Clinton Presidential Records: White House Staff and Office Files, William J. Clinton Presidential Library and Museum, https://clinton.presidentiallibraries.us/items/show/99922; William C. Rempel and Douglas Frantz, "Troopers Say Clinton Sought Silence on Personal Affairs," *Los Angeles Times*, December 21, 1993, A1.

31. Brock, *Blinded by the Light*, 174.

32. J. F. Harris, *The Survivor*, 287–88; "Press Conference of Robert Bennett," May 6, 1994, box 6, Office of the Press Secretary, Dee Dee Myers, "Media File—Paula Jones," Clinton Digital Library, https://clinton.presidentiallibraries.us/items/show/99922; Woodward, *Shadow*, 243, 254.

33. Amy Goldstein, "How the Demise of Her Health-Care Plan Led to the Politician Clinton Is Today," *Washington Post*, August 25, 2016, https://www.washingtonpost.com/politics/after-health-care-missteps-a-chastened-hillary-clinton-emerged/2016/08/25/2d200cb4-64b4-11e6-be4e-23fc4d4d12b4_story.html.

34. Takiff, *Complicated Man*, 239; "Majority Changes in the House of Representatives, 1856 to Present," U.S. House of Representatives, https://history.house.gov/Institution/Majority-Changes/Majority-Changes/; Adam Clymer, "The 1994 Elections," *New York Times*, November 10, 1994; Hemmer, *Messengers of the Right*, 271.

35. Woodward, *Shadow*, 332–33.

36. CNBC, May 2, 1994, transcript in box 6, Office of the Press Secretary, Dee Dee Myers, 2011-0587-F, Clinton Presidential Records: White House Staff and Office Files, William J. Clinton Presidential Library and Museum, https://clinton.presidentiallibraries.us/items/show/99872; J. F. Harris, *The Survivor*, 64–65; Kumar, *Managing the President's Message*, 37, 41, 47, 64.

37. Richard Lei, "The Commander in Briefs," *Washington Post*, April 20, 1994; Memorandum from George Stephanopolous to Al Hunt and Jeff Birnbaum, April 15, 1993, box 11, Office of the Press Secretary, Dee Dee Myers, "Press Corps [1]," Clinton Digital Library, https://clinton.presidentiallibraries.us/items/show/99955; Kumar, "President as Message and Messenger," 422; J. F. Harris, *The Survivor*, 34–35. 56.

38. J. F. Harris, *The Survivor*, 35.

39. J. F. Harris, *The Survivor*, 88–91; Hayden, *Covering Clinton*, 119; Agence France-Press, "The 1990s Balkan Wars in Key Dates," Voice of America,

November 22, 2017, https://www.voanews.com/europe/1990s-balkan-wars
-key-dates; Jessica Lussenhop, "Clinton Crime Bill: Why Is It So Controversial?" *BBS News Magazine*, April 18, 2016, https://www.bbc.com/news/world
-us-canada-36020717.

40. J. F. Harris, *The Survivor*, 218–19.

41. Sherman, *Loudest Voice in the Room*, 160–70; Dan McCrum, "How to Build an
Empire, the Full Murdoch Timeline," *Financial Times*, July 16, 2014, https://
www.ft.com/content/07a1385d-7923-39d4-b0c2-fbe6adc8e71d; Ritchie,
Reporting from Washington, 216–17; Howard Rosenberg, "Cutting across the
Bias of the Fox News Channel," *Los Angeles Times*, October 11, 1996, F1.

42. Paul Farhi, "The Life of O'Reilly," *Washington Post*, December 13, 2000.

43. "Bill O'Reilly: TV's Angriest Man," ABC News, January 6, 2006, https://
abcnews.go.com/Primetime/story?id=132175&page=1; Hemmer, *Messengers of
the Right*, 266; Farhi, "Life of O'Reilly"; Rosenberg, "Cutting across the Bias."

44. Kurtz, *Spin Cycle*, xxiii.

45. Auletta, *Three Blind Mice*, 4; David Zurawik, "At TV's Halfway Mark, Good
News and Bad," *Baltimore Sun*, January 17, 1993; Kumar, "President as Mes-
sage and Messenger," 417; J. F. Harris, *The Survivor*, 144; Kumar, *Managing the
President's Message*, 48.

46. Katz, Barris, and Jain, *Social Media President*, 22; King, *Free for All*, 216, 225.

47. Kalb, *One Scandalous Story*, 47; Woodward, *Shadow*, 283; Ritchie, *Reporting
from Washington*, 239.

48. Glenn Garvin, "Who Blabbed about Gary Hart–Donna Rice Affair?" *Miami
Herald*, September 20, 2014; Rose, *American Presidency under Siege*, 33.

49. Kalb, *One Scandalous Story*, 35; "A Chronology: Key Moments in the
Clinton-Lewinsky Scandal," CNN All Politics, 1998, https://www.cnn.com
/ALLPOLITICS/1998/resources/lewinsky/timeline/; Woodward, *Shadow*,
264–65, 289.

50. Ritchie, *Reporting from Washington*, 239; Kovach and Rosenstiel, *Warp Speed*, 53.

51. Howard Kurtz, "Newsweek's Melted Scoop," *Washington Post*, January 22,
1998, C1; Ritchie, *Reporting from Washington*, 239.

52. *Drudge Report*, Library of Congress Web Archive, https://www.loc.gov/item
/lcwaN0019734/; Allan, *Online News*, 40–41; Harris, *The Survivor*, 301; Kalb,
One Scandalous Story, 82.

53. Olivia B. Waxman and Merrill Farby, "From an Anonymous Tip to an
Impeachment," *Time*, May 4, 2018, https://time.com/5120561/bill-clinton
-monica-lewinsky-timeline/.

54. Kurtz, "Newsweek's Melted Scoop"; Katz, Barris, and Jain, *Social Media President*, 24.

55. Kurtz, "Newsweek's Melted Scoop"; Riley, *Inside the Clinton White House*, 321–22; "Scandal Puts Internet in the Spotlight," CNN Interactive, January 30, 1988, http://edition.cnn.com/TECH/9801/30/scandal.online/; King, *Free for All*, 214.

56. Woodward, *Shadow*, 398, 415–16; Kovach and Rosenstiel, *Warp Speed*, 100, 119.

57. "President Bill Clinton—Jan. 21, 1998," transcript of the PBS *NewsHour with Jim Lehrer*, CNN All Politics, http://edition.cnn.com/ALLPOLITICS/1998/01/21/transcripts/lehrer/; Woodward, *Shadow*, 389–90; J. F. Harris, *The Survivor*, 304.

58. "USA: Clinton Denies Having an Affair with Monica Lewinsky Update," AP Archive, posted July 21, 2015, https://www.youtube.com/watch?v=kMu-2tXfPQI; J. F. Harris, *The Survivor*, 306–7.

59. Takiff, *Complicated Man*, 323; Howard Kurtz, "For the Press, a Lot of Ink over the Dam," *Washington Post*, February 13, 1999, C1.

60. Woodward, *Shadow*, 431; "A Chronology: Key Moments in the Clinton-Lewinsky Scandal"; Peter Baker, "Clinton Settles Paula Jones Lawsuit for $850,000," *Washington Post*, November 14, 1998, A1.

61. J. F. Harris, *The Survivor*, 312; Kurtz, "Newsweek's Melted Scoop"; Ann Coulter, "High Crimes and Misdemeanors," *Human Events* 54, no. 31 (August 14, 1998): 14–18.

62. Office of Management and Budget, "Summary of Receipts, Outlays, and Surpluses or Deficits"; Kumar, *Managing the President's Message*, 70; Woodward, *Shadow*, 399.

63. Ritchie, *Reporting from Washington*, 281; J. F. Harris, *The Survivor*, 346; "A Chronology: Key Moments in the Clinton-Lewinsky Scandal"; Peter Baker and Susan Schmidt, "Starr Submits Report to House," *Washington Post*, September 10, 1998.

64. Riley, *Inside the Clinton White House*, 323; Woodward, *Shadow*, 473; J. F. Harris, *The Survivor*, 347; David Maraniss, "Catching a Break on the Brink: Video Release May Help More Than Hurt Clinton," *Washington Post*, September 22, 1998, A19.

65. Nate House, "City Residents Eager for End of Clinton-Lewinsky Affairs," *Philadelphia Tribune*, September 22, 1998, 5A.

66. Woodward, *Shadow*, 476–77.

67. King, *Free for All*, 215; Alison Mitchell, "The Speaker Steps Down," *New York Times*, November 7, 1998; Associated Press, "Gingrich Admits Having an Affair in Clinton Era," NBC News, March 8, 2007, https://www.nbcnews.com/id/wbna17527506; William Neikirk and Mike Dorning, "Speaker-Elect Admits Illicit Sexual Affairs," *Chicago Tribune*, December 18, 1998; J. F. Harris, *The Survivor*, 355.

68. Articles of Impeachment Against William Jefferson Clinton, Congress of the United States of America, in the House of Representatives, December 19, 1998, 105th Congress, 2nd sess., https://www.congress.gov/105/bills/hres611 /BILLS-105hres611enr.pdf.

69. Frank Newport, "Clinton Receives Record High Job Approval Rating after Impeachment Vote and Iraq Air Strikes," Gallup News Service, December 24, 1998, https://news.gallup.com/poll/4111/clinton-receives-record-high -job-approval-rating-after-impeachment-vot.aspx; Olivia B. Waxman and Merrill Fabry, "Timeline of Key Moments in the Clinton-Lewinsky Scandal," *Time*, May 4, 2018, https://time.com/5120561/bill-clinton-monica-lewinsky -timeline/; Kurtz, "For the Press."

8. GEORGE W. BUSH

1. Poling, "Unattributed Prepackaged News Stories," 3; Roth, "Karen Ryan, Revisited"; Laura Miller, "Thanks for the (False) Memories: The 2004 Falsie Awards," Center for Media and Democracy's PR Watch, December 28, 2004; Robert Pear, "U.S. Videos, for T.V. News, Come under Scrutiny," *New York Times*, March 15, 2004, A1; Greenberg, *Republic of Spin*, 431–32; "Karen Ryan PR Story," *Omaha News*, https://www.youtube.com/watch?v=xBze5atYyCo; Potter, "Virtual News Reports."

2. Miller, "Thanks for the (False) Memories."

3. Poling, "Unattributed Prepackaged News Stories," 5–6; Pear, "U.S. Videos"; Miller, "Thanks for the (False) Memories."

4. "'Truthiness': Can Something 'Seem,' without Being, True?" *Merriam-Webster*, April 2020, https://www.merriam-webster.com/words-at-play /truthiness-meaning-word-origin.

5. "Presidential News Conferences"; *Newsweek*, October 19, 1987, cover; J. E. Mueller, *Towel Snapping the Press*, 30; Mann, *George W. Bush*, 23.

6. Bush, *American Press*, 7, 14; Kumar, "President as Message and Messenger," 412.

7. Mann, *George W. Bush*, 2, 5, 7, 9, 15.

8. J. E. Mueller, *Towel Snapping the Press*, 4; Mann, *George W. Bush*, 3, 15–19, 20–23.

9. Mann, *George W. Bush*, 29–36, 48; Jamieson and Wildman, *Press Effect*, 28.

10. Ryan, *Presidency in Black and White*, 89–90; Jamieson and Wildman, *Press Effect*, 97–98; Greenberg, *Republic of Spin*, 428–29; J. E. Mueller, *Towel Snapping the Press*, 42; Mann, *George W. Bush*, 39–40; "Supreme Court, Split 5–4, Halts Florida Count in Blow to Gore," *New York Times*, December 10, 2000; "Members of the Supreme Court of the United States," Supreme Court of the United States, https://www.supremecourt.gov/about/members.aspx; Andrew

Glass, "Gore Concedes Presidential Election to Bush, December 13, 2000," *Politico*, December 13, 2017, https://www.politico.com/story/2017/12/13/gore -concedes-presidential-election-to-bush-dec-13-2000-287285.

11. Lawrence J. Korb, Laura Conley, and Alex Rothman, "A Historical Perspective on Defense Budgets," Center for American Progress, July 6, 2011, https://www .americanprogress.org/issues/economy/news/2011/07/06/10041/a-historical -perspective-on-defense-budgets/; Mann, *George W. Bush*, 45, 50–52; Chuck Jones, "Don't Blame Obama for Doubling the Federal Debt," *Forbes*, January 15, 2018, https://www.forbes.com/sites/chuckjones/2018/01/15/obamas-federal -debt-grew-at-a-slower-rate-than-reagan-h-w-bush-or-w-bush/#651fa1891917.

12. Isikoff and Corn, *Hubris*, 3–4; Marder, "Press and the Presidency," 8.

13. Marder, "Press and the Presidency," 8; Montgomery, "Presidential Materials," 102–3, 126; Layton, "Information Squeeze," 20–30.

14. Isikoff and Corn, *Hubris*, 2; Gup, "Working in a Wartime Capital," 24.

15. Ken Auletta, "Fortress Bush," *New Yorker*, January 19, 2004, 53–65; Page, "Washington," 23.

16. Kumar, *Managing the President's Message*, 75, 92; Mann, *George W. Bush*, 27; J. E. Mueller, *Towel Snapping the Press*, 1, 44–45, 55.

17. Kumar, *Managing the President's Message*, 78.

18. "Bush Family Pets," George W. Bush Presidential Center, https://www .bushcenter.org/about-the-center/bush-family/bush-family-pets.html; Video by April Ryan, "Barney Bites Reporter," *Austin American-Statesman*, August 18, 2008, https://www.youtube.com/watch?v=IT8Ds2_Iwd4; Kumar, *Managing the President's Message*, 79; Katz, Barris, and Jain, *Social Media President*, 27–28.

19. "Presidential News Conferences"; Auletta, "Fortress Bush," 53.

20. Auletta, "Fortress Bush"; Ron Suskind, "Faith, Certainty and the Presidency of George W. Bush," *New York Times Magazine*, October 17, 2014; Glenn Kessler, Salvador Rizzo, and Meg Kelly, "President Trump Has Made More Than 5,000 False or Misleading Claims," *Washington Post*, September 13, 2018.

21. "U.S.-Mexico: A State Dinner," White House Photos, White House— President George W. Bush, https://georgewbush-whitehouse.archives.gov /president/statedinner-mexico-200109/; R. Roberts, "Guess Who's Not Coming," 25; Christopher Marquis, "A Spicy Welcome to the White House," *New York Times*, September 6, 2001, A10.

22. Beschloss, *Presidents of War*, 581.

23. "Bin Laden Determined to Strike in US," memorandum for the president only, August 6, 2001, National Security Archive, declassified and approved for release April 10, 2004, https://nsarchive2.gwu.edu/NSAEBB/NSAEBB116

/pdb8-6-2001.pdf; Thomas S. Blanton, "The President's Daily Brief," National Security Archive, April 12, 2004, https://nsarchive2.gwu.edu/NSAEBB /NSAEBB116/; Mann, *George W. Bush*, 57.

24. "Setting the Record Straight: President Bush's Actions against Terrorism before 9/11," White House Press Office, Dana Perino—Subject Files, folder 3, box 5, George W. Bush Presidential Library and Museum; Mann, *George W. Bush*, 59.

25. "A Nation Challenged; A Snapshot Gives Bush 90% Approval," *New York Times*, September 24, 2001.

26. Beschloss, *Presidents of War*, 582.

27. Ellen Knickmeyer, "Costs of the Afghanistan War, in Lives and Dollars," Associated Press, August 16, 2021, https://apnews.com/article/middle-east -business-afghanistan-43d8f53b35e80ec18c130cd683e1a38f.

28. Isikoff and Corn, *Hubris*, 3–20.

29. Howard Kurtz, "The Post on WMDs: An Inside Story," *Washington Post*, August 12, 2004, A1; Lewis, "Selling the Iraq War"; Greenberg, *Republic of Spin*, 434.

30. "Text: Cheney on Bin Laden Tape," *Washington Post Online*, December 9, 2001, https://www.washingtonpost.com/wp-srv/nation/specials/attacked /transcripts/cheneytext_120901.html; Isikoff and Corn, *Hubris*, 102, 119.

31. Jamieson and Wildman, *Press Effect*, 137–38.

32. Shapiro, "Washington," 22; Gup, "Working in a Wartime Capital," 21.

33. Isikoff and Corn, *Hubris*, 56; Umansky, "Failures of Imagination," 17–18.

34. "The Times and Iraq," *New York Times*, May 26, 2004, A10; Isikoff and Corn, *Hubris*, 49–51, 57–58.

35. Judith Miller, "Iraqi Tells of Renovations at Sites for Chemical and Nuclear Arms," *New York Times*, December 20, 2001, A1; "Times and Iraq"; Isikoff and Corn, *Hubris*, 55–59.

36. Isikoff and Corn, *Hubris*, 29, 53–55.

37. Michael R. Gordon and Judith Miller, "U.S. Says Hussein Intensifies Quest for a-Bomb Parts," *New York Times*, September 8, 2002, 1.

38. Isikoff and Corn, *Hubris*, 34–37, 41–41; Bennett, Lawrence, and Livingston, *When the Press Fails*, 19.

39. Judith Miller and Michael R. Gordon, "White House Lists Iraq Steps to Build Banned Weapons," *New York Times*, September 13, 2002, A1; Isikoff and Corn, *Hubris*, 60–61.

40. Bob Kemper, "Bush Repeats Vow on Terror," *Daily Advocate* (Stamford CT), September 12, 2002, A1, A11; Bennett Roth, "Bush Will Urge U.N. to Take Strong Action against Iraq," *Houston Chronicle*, September 12, 1A, 14A;

Elisabeth Bumiller, "Bush's Pilgrimage Ends with Vow to Prevail over 'Terror-ist or Tyrant,'" *New York Times*, September 12, 2002, B8; Elisabeth Bumiller, "Bush Aides Set Strategy to Sell Policy on Iraq," *New York Times*, September 7, 2002, A1; Greenberg, *Republic of Spin*, 434.

41. Howard Kurtz, "The Post on WMDs: An Inside Story," *Washington Post*, August 12, 2004, A1; "Setting the Course on Iraq," *Washington Post*, October 10, 2002, A32.

42. Kurtz, "Post on WMDs," A1.

43. Max Follmer, "The Reporting Team That Got Iraq Right," *HuffPost*, March 25, 2011, https://www.huffpost.com/entry/the-reporting-team-that-g_n _91981; Matt Taibbi, "16 Years Later, How the Press That Sold the Iraq War Got Away with It," *Rolling Stone*, March 22, 2019, https://www.rollingstone .com/politics/politics-features/iraq-war-media-fail-matt-taibbi-812230/.

44. Press Briefing by Ari Fleischer, Office of the Press Secretary, May 1, 2002, https://georgewbush-whitehouse.archives.gov/news/releases/2002/05 /20020501-9.html.

45. "In Iraq Crisis, Networks Are Megaphones for Official Views," Fairness & Accuracy in Reporting, March 18, 2003, https://fair.org/take-action/action -alerts/in-iraq-crisis-networks-are-megaphones-for-official-views/.

46. Beschloss, *Presidents of War*, 582; Mann, *George W. Bush*, 78; Jeffrey Goldberg, "The Great Terror," *New Yorker*, March 25, 2002, https://www.newyorker.com /magazine/2002/03/25/the-great-terror.

47. Auletta, "Fortress Bush"; Beschloss, *Presidents of War*, 583; Greenberg, *Republic of Spin*, 436; Bennett, Lawrence, and Livingston, *When the Press Fails*, 16–17.

48. "5/1/2003: 'Mission Accomplished' in Iraq," *Nightline*, ABC News, May 1, 2003, https://abcnews.go.com/Archives/video/2003-mission-accomplished -iraq-9099537; Kumar, *Managing the President's Message*, 103–4; Beschloss, *Presidents of War*, 583; "Casualty Status," U.S. Department of Defense, Febru-ary 17, 2020, https://www.defense.gov/casualty.pdf; "Costs of War," Watson Institute, Brown University, November 2018; Taibbi, "16 Years Later"; Philip Bump, "15 Years After Iraq War Began, the Death Toll Is Still Murky," *Wash-ington Post*, March 20, 2018; Mann, *George W. Bush*, 86; Dana Milbank, "Bush Disavows Hussein–Sept. 11 Link," *Washington Post*, September 18, 2003, A18; Auletta, "Fortress Bush"; *Time*, October 6, 2003, cover.

49. Auletta, "Fortress Bush"; "The Times and Iraq," *New York Times*, May 26, 2004, A10.

50. Brian Stelter, "Was Press a War 'Enabler'? 2 Offer a Nod from Inside," *New York Times*, May 30, 2008, A18.

NOTES TO PAGES 175–178

51. Seymour M. Hersh, "Torture at Abu Ghraib," *New Yorker*, May 10, 2004; Olmsted and Rauchway, "George W. Bush," 460; Major, *Unilateral Presidency*, 40–41.

52. Anthony Lewis, "A President beyond the Law," *New York Times*, May 7, 2004, A31.

53. Derek Buckaloo, "Swift Boat Veterans for Truth," Center for Presidential History, Southern Methodist University, http://cphcmp.smu.edu/2004election /swift-boat-veterans-for-truth/; Lempert and Silverstein, *Creatures of Politics*, 46, 69–71; "Swift Boat Veterans Political Ad," C-SPAN, August 15, 2004, https://www.c-span.org/video/?183127-1/swift-boat-veterans-political-ad; "Swiftboat Veterans Ad on John Kerry—Any Questions (2004)," BattleCryofFreedom, https://www.youtube.com/watch?v=V4Zk9YmED48; "Swiftboat Ad on John Kerry—Sellout," BattleCryofFreedom, https://www.youtube.com /watch?v=phqOuEhg9yE.

54. Kate Zernike, "Veterans Rebut 'Swift Boat' Charges against Kerry in Answer to Challenge," *New York Times*, June 22, 2008; David Mikkelson, "John Kerry Swift Boats," Snopes.com, July 29, 2004, https://www.snopes.com/fact-check /swift-justice/; Lempert and Silverstein, *Creatures of Politics*, 46, 69–71; "Swift Boat Veterans Political Ad," C-SPAN; "Swiftboat Veterans Ad on John Kerry— Any Questions (2004)"; "Swiftboat Ad on John Kerry—Sellout (2004)"; Buckaloo, "Swift Boat Veterans for Truth."

55. Felix Gillette, "The Revolution Will Be Televised (It'll Just Have Low Production Values)," *Bloomberg Businessweek*, July 24, 2017, 44–49; "Sinclair: Stations Won't Run Entire Anti-Kerry Film," CNN Politics, October 20, 2004, https://www.cnn.com/2004/ALLPOLITICS/10/20/sinclair.kerry/; Lempert and Silverstein, *Creatures of Politics*, 3, 69; "News," Sinclair Broadcast Group, https://web.archive.org/web/20040606111325/http://sbgi.net /business/news.shtml.

56. Andrew Glass, "George W. Bush Suspended from Texas Air National Guard, Aug. 1, 1972," *Politico*, August 1, 2013, https://www.politico.com/story/2013 /08/this-day-in-politics-aug-1-1972-095023; Mann, *George W. Bush*, 12–13; Betsy Ashton, "The CBS Debacle," *Quill*, 2005, 34–35.

57. Rainie, "The State of Blogging"; King, *Free for All*, 229–31, 233–34.

58. "For the Record: CBS Memos Controversy on Free Republic," September 18, 2004, http://www.freerepublic.com/focus/f-news/1220090/posts; Ashton, "CBS Debacle," 34–35; Paul Fahri, "'Lamestream Media Hit by Little Green Footballs,'" *Los Angeles Times*, August 11, 2006.

59. Gallup and Newport, *Public Opinion 2004*, 399; Beschloss, *Presidents of War*, 584.

60. Eshbaugh-Soha and Peake, *Breaking through the Noise*, 196; Kumar, *Managing the President's Message*, 71–72, 82; Mann, *George W. Bush*, 103.

61. Bruce Alpert, "George W. Bush Never Recovered Politically from Katrina," NOLA.com and *Times-Picayune*, August 28, 2015, https://www.nola.com/news /article_9b0ff883-2078-5662-8e6b-b8296249a161.html.

62. Sheryl Gay Stolberg, "With Eye on Political Reality, a Shorter Vacation for Bush," *New York Times*, August 6, 2006; White House Photos, August 31, 2005, White House of President George W. Bush, https://georgewbush -whitehouse.archives.gov/news/releases/2005/08/images/20050831 _p083105pm-0117jas-515h.html; Dyson, *Come Hell or High Water*, 65–68; Ryan, *Presidency in Black and White*, 107; Mark Knoller, "A Look Back to 2005: President Bush and Katrina," CBS News, August 29, 2010, https://www .cbsnews.com/news/a-look-back-to-2005-president-bush-and-katrina/.

63. Dyson, *Come Hell or High Water*, 90–94.

64. Press Gaggle with Scott McClellan, September 2, 2005, 7, White House Press Office, Dana Perino Subject Files, folder 3, box 4, George W. Bush Presidential Library and Museum.

65. Julie Mason, "Shake-up at FEMA Sends Chief Back to D.C.," *Houston Chronicle*, September 10, 2005, 1.

66. Katrina Talking Points 9-7-05, White House Press Office, Dana Perino Subject Files, folder 2, box 4, George W. Bush Presidential Library and Museum; Memo from Dana M. Perino, September 4, 2005, White House Press Office, Dana Perino Subject Files, folder 2, box 4, George W. Bush Presidential Library and Museum; Mann, *George W. Bush*, 100.

67. "Briefing Book: Tony Snow, Press Secretary," May 1, 2006, White House Staff Member Office Files—Press Office, Robert (Tony) Snow, folder 23, box 3, George W. Bush Presidential Library and Museum.

68. Dana Priest, "CIA Holds Terror Suspects in Secret Prisons," *Washington Post*, November 2, 2005, A1.

69. James Risen and Eric Lichtblau, "Bush Lets U.S. Spy on Callers without Courts," *New York Times*, December 16, 2005; Olmsted and Rauchway, "George W. Bush," 454; Scott Shane, "Behind Bush's Fury, a Vow Made in 2001," *New York Times*, June 29, 2006, A12.

70. "Views of Press Values and Performance: 1985–2007," Pew Research Center for the People and the Press, Washington DC, August 9, 2007.

71. "Bush Administration Thwarts Access," Center for Public Integrity, January 6, 2004, updated May 19, 2014, https://publicintegrity.org/politics/bush -administration-thwarts-access/; Marder, "Press and the Presidency," 8.

72. Heidi Shierholz, "Job Losses Ballooned in Final Quarter of 2008," Economic Policy Institute, January 9, 2009, https://www.epi.org/publication /job_losses_ballooned_in_final_quarter_of_2008/; Mann, *George W. Bush*,

90–92, 124–25; David Pilling, "Why George W Bush Is Africa's Favourite US President," *Financial Times*, July 17, 2019, https://www.ft.com/content /72424694-a86e-11e9-984c-fac8325aaa04; Eugene Robinson, "George W. Bush's Greatest Legacy—His Battle against AIDS," *Washington Post*, July 26, 2012; Chuck Jones, "Don't Blame Obama for Doubling the Federal Debt," *Forbes*, January 15, 2018, https://www.forbes.com/sites/chuckjones/2018/01/15 /obamas-federal-debt-grew-at-a-slower-rate-than-reagan-h-w-bush-or-w-bush/ #651fa1891917; "Foreclosures in the U.S. in 2008," Pew Research Center, May 12, 2009, https://www.pewresearch.org/hispanic/2009/05/12/v-foreclosures-in -the-u-s-in-2008/.

73. "Bush Warns of 'Long and Painful Recession,'" Associated Press, September 24, 2008, https://www.youtube.com/watch?v=dw_USyFqFMY; "President Bush's Speech to the Nation on the Economic Crisis," *New York Times*, September 24, 2008; "Absence of Leadership," *New York Times*, September 25, 2008, A28.

74. Schedule of the President, January 13, 2009, Lunch with Rush Limbaugh, Lunch with Rich Wolf and Susan Page memo, and Interview with Larry King of CNN's *Larry King Live* briefing papers, Records Pertaining to a Lunch President George W. Bush Had with Rush Limbaugh on January 13, 2009, 13124, George W. Bush Presidential Library and Museum.

75. Daily Diary of George W. Bush, August 2, 2007, and briefing paper on Meeting with Rush Limbaugh of *The Rush Limbaugh Show*, White House Office of Records Management 2017, Subject Files FG001-07 (Briefing Papers), White House Office of Appointments and Scheduling, box 1, 11908/12046 12141, George W. Bush Presidential Library and Museum; "Rush Meets with President Bush," *The Rush Limbaugh Show*, August 3, 2007, https://www.rushlimbaugh.com/daily/2007/08/03/rush_meets_with _president_bush2/.

76. Hemmer, *Messengers of the Right*, 276; Rosenwald, *Talk Radio's America*, 130–31; Brian Lowry, "How Conservatives Dominate TV/Radio Talk Game," *Variety*, January 3, 2014.

77. The top seven in the spring 2006 were Rush Limbaugh, Sean Hannity, Michael Savage, Laura Schlessinger, Laura Ingraham, Neal Boortz, and Michael Gallagher. Bill O'Reilly, Glenn Beck, and Bill Bennett weren't far behind. See "The Top Talk Radio Audiences," *Talkers Magazine*, November 14, 2006, https://web.archive.org/web/20061114200439/http://www.talkers .com/main/index.php?option=com_content&task=view&id=17&Itemid=34.

78. Press Party #1 Guest List, December 18, 2003, White House Staff Member Office Files—Press Office, Robert (Tony) Snow, OA/NARA #7531/7632 6198,

folder 1, box 3, George W. Bush Presidential Library and Museum; Kumar, *Managing the President's Message*, 99.

79. Meeting with Talk Radio Hosts briefing paper, September 15, 2006, and the Daily Diary of President George W. Bush, September 15, 2006, White House Office of Records Management 2016 0130-F, Subject Files FG-00107, box 1, George W. Bush Presidential Library and Museum; Daily Diary of President George W. Bush, Appendix B, White House Office of Records Management 2016 0130-F, Subject Files FG-00107, box 1, George W. Bush Presidential Library and Museum.

9. BARACK OBAMA

1. "President Obama Hangs Out with America," White House of President Barack Obama, January 30, 2012, https://obamawhitehouse.archives.gov /blog/2012/01/30/president-obama-hangs-out-america; Erik Kain, "A Look at President Obama's First Google+ Hangout," *Forbes*, February 2, 2012; Alex Fitzpatrick, "President Obama's First Google+ Hangout," *Mashable*, January 31, 2012, https://mashable.com/2012/01/31/obama-hangout/.

2. Katz, Barris, and Jain, *Social Media President*, 51.

3. "White House 2.0," White House—Barack Obama, May 1, 2009, https:// obamawhitehouse.archives.gov/blog/2009/05/01/whitehouse-20; Jennifer Epstein, "Obama Google+ Chat Gets Personal," *Politico*, January 30, 2012, https://www.politico.com/story/2012/01/obama-send-me-the-resume-072185; "I Am Barack Obama, President of the United States—AMA," Reddit, August 29, 2012, https://www.reddit.com/r/IAmA/comments/z1c9z/i_am_barack _obama_president_of_the_united_states/.

4. Tammerlin Drummond, "Barack Obama's Law," *Los Angeles Times*, March 12, 1990, E1; Fox Butterfield, "First Black Elected to Head Harvard's Law Review," *New York Times*, February 6, 1990, A20; Michael J. Ybarra, "Activist in Chicago Now Heads Harvard Law Review," *Chicago Tribune*, February 7, 2020, A3; McClelland, *Young Mr. Obama*, 2, 62; Maraniss, *Barack Obama*, 466, 516–64; D'Antonio, *Consequential President*, 5.

5. Jackson, "Making of a Senator," 22; McClelland, *Young Mr. Obama*, 142–43, 176–77, 202–6, 215–17, 225–29; Todd, *The Stranger*, 24, 138.

6. Adam Nagourney, "Baffled in Loss, Democrats Seek Road Forward," *New York Times*, November 7, 2004, 33.

7. D'Antonio, *Consequential President*, 10, 14; Godfrey Sperling, "Why Not an Obama-Romney Match-up in 2008," *Christian Science Monitor*, July 5, 2008, 9.

8. Greenberg, *Republic of Spin*, 441–42; D'Antonio, *Consequential President*, 14; Todd, *The Stranger*, 5.

9. Garrow, *Rising Star*, 1036; Howard Kurtz, "MSNBC, Leaning Left and Getting Flak from Both Sides," *Washington Post*, May 28, 2008.

10. King, *Free for All*, 235–36; Katz, Barris, and Jain, *Social Media President*, 30–32.

11. Martin, *The First*, 326, 364; Parlett, *Demonizing a President*, 8; "Fist at Fox: The Obamas' Dap Gets Prime Attention," *Pittsburgh Post-Gazette*, June 11, 2008, https://www.post-gazette.com/opinion/2008/06/12/Fist-at-Fox-The -Obamas-dap-gets-prime-attention/stories/200806120444; Ari Berman, "Fox's 'Terrorist Fist Jab,'" *Nation*, June 10, 2008.

12. D'Antonio, *Consequential President*, 14.

13. "Federal Elections 2008," Federal Election Commission, July 2009, 5, https:// transition.fec.gov/pubrec/fe2008/federalelections2008.pdf; "2008 Electoral College Results," National Archives, https://www.archives.gov/electoral -college/2008; Dowdle, van Raemdonck, and Maranto, "Barack Obama," 4.

14. Maureen Dowd, "Bring on the Puppy and the Rookie," *New York Times*, November 6, 2008, A33.

15. Martin, *The First*, 388.

16. "All Employees, Total Nonfarm (PAYEMS)," Federal Reserve Bank of St. Louis, September 12, 2021, https://fred.stlouisfed.org/series/PAYEMS; Chuck Jones, "Trump's Job Losses Will Exceed the Great Recession's," *Forbes*, April 4, 2020, https://www.forbes.com/sites/chuckjones/2020/04/04/trumps-job-losses -will-exceed-the-great-recessions/?sh=4bbda47d3723; Steve Thomma, "With Historic Oath Comes Promise to Lift Nation Up," *Houston Chronicle*, January 21, 2009, 1; Todd, *The Stranger*, 74, 172.

17. "Limbaugh: I Hope Obama Fails," *The Rush Limbaugh Show*, January 16, 2009, https://www.rushlimbaugh.com/daily/2009/01/16/limbaugh_i_hope _obama_fails/; J. E. Zelizer, "Tea Partied," 13–15, 17.

18. "Unemployment in 2009," *Ted: The Economics Daily*, Bureau of Labor Statistics, December 8, 2009, https://www.bls.gov/opub/ted/2009/ted_20091208 .htm?view_full; Ryan, *Presidency in Black and White*, 126; Todd, *The Stranger*, 12, 68–71, 102, 172.

19. "Santelli's Tea Party Rant, February 19, 2009," CNBC, https://www.cnbc .com/video/2015/02/06/santellis-tea-party-rant-february-19-2009.html; Chris Good, "Rick Santelli: Campaign Meme?" *Atlantic*, February 20, 2009, https://www.theatlantic.com/politics/archive/2009/02/rick-santelli-campaign -meme/848/.

20. "Tea Party Origins: Santelli," CNBC, February 24, 2014, https://www.cnbc .com/video/2014/02/24/tea-party-origins-santelli.html.

21. Skocpol and Williams, *Tea Party*, 129; Good, "Rick Santelli"; Mutz, *In-Your-Face Politics*, 44; J. E. Zelizer, "Tea Partied," 15, 18–19.

22. "News Audiences Increasingly Politicized"; DellaVigna and Kaplan, "Fox News Effect."

23. "News Audiences Increasingly Politicized."

24. Kurtz, "MSNBC, Leaning Left."

25. Sam Roberts, "Alan Colmes, Sean Hannity's Liberal Partner on Fox News, Dies at 66," *New York Times*, February 23, 2017; Hemmer, *Messengers of the Right*, 272; David Folkenflik, "Glenn Beck's Show on Fox News to End," National Public Radio, April 6, 2011, https://www.npr.org/2011/04/06 /135181398/glenn-beck-to-leave-daily-fox-news-show; Matea Gold, "Fox News' Glenn Beck Strikes Ratings Gold by Challenging Barack Obama," *Los Angeles Times*, March 6, 2009.

26. Gold, "Fox News' Glenn Beck."

27. Lowry, "How Conservatives Dominate"; Han, *Hatred of America's Presidents*, 362; David Folkenflik, "Fox News Thrives in the Age of Obama," *All Things Considered*, NPR, March 23, 2009, https://www.npr.org/templates/story/story .php?storyId=102254703&ft=1&f=1014.

28. Gold, "Fox News' Glenn Beck."

29. Skocpol and Williams, *Tea Party*, 121, 131.

30. Chris Good, "More Tea Party Symbiotics," *Atlantic*, April 10, 2009; James Rainey, "Crashing the Tea Party," *Los Angeles Times*, April 15, 2009, A2; Hemmer, *Messengers of the Right*, 272–73; Skocpol and Williams, *Tea Party*, 121, 133–34.

31. "Radio Giant Clear Channel to Lay Off 1,850 workers," *Denver Business Journal*, January 21, 2009, https://www.bizjournals.com/denver/stories/2009 /01/19/daily21.html; Sarah McBride, "Clear Channel, Limbaugh Ink $400 Million New Contract," *Wall Street Journal*, July 3, 2008; Paul Farhi, "Limbaugh's Audience Size? It's Largely Up in the Air," *Washington Post*, March 7, 2009; "From the Climate Hoax to Health Care to 'Hope,' Liberalism Is Lies," *The Rush Limbaugh Show*, May 19, 2011, https://www.rushlimbaugh.com/daily /2011/05/19/from_the_climate_hoax_to_health_care_to_hope_liberalism_is _lies/; Daynes and Sussman, "Environmental Policy," 179.

32. Hemmer, *Messengers of the Right*, 272.

33. Hacker and Pierson, *Let Them Eat Tweets*, 99; "Radio Transmission," *A Science Odyssey*, PBS, https://www.pbs.org/wgbh/aso/tryit/radio/radiorelayer.html; Rosenwald, *Talk Radio's America*, 180–81; Hemmer, *Messengers of the Right*, 264–65.

34. "Greenville Tea Party with Mike Gallagher," Upstate Update, April 18, 2009, https://www.youtube.com/watch?v=7rhDuEjsUGk; Skocpol and Williams, *Tea Party*, 130.

35. Skocpol and Williams, *Tea Party*, 139, 150.
36. "Loud, Disruptive Healthcare Town Halls," ABC News, August 7, 2009, https://www.youtube.com/watch?v=w4G9RGxahTM; Skocpol and Williams, *Tea Party*, 139.
37. Angie Drobnic Holan, "PolitiFact's Lie of the Year: 'Death Panels,'" PolitiFact, Poynter Institute, December 18, 2009, https://www.politifact.com/article/2009/dec/18/politifact-lie-year-death-panels/; Rosenwald, *Talk Radio's America*, 183.
38. Skidmore, "Legislative Leadership," 101; J. E. Zelizer, "Tea Partied," 17.
39. Axelrod, *Believer*, 427; J. E. Zelizer, "Tea Partied," 18.
40. "Presidential Approval Ratings—Barack Obama," Gallup, https://news.gallup.com/poll/116479/barack-obama-presidential-job-approval.aspx; Todd, *The Stranger*, 92, 325; Axelrod, *Believer*, 483; Skidmore, "Legislative Leadership," 99–111; Miriam Berger, "Invaders, Allies, Occupiers, Guests: A Brief History of U.S. Military Involvement in Iraq," *Washington Post*, January 11, 2020; Brattebo and Watson, "Making History," 412.
41. "2012 Electoral College Results," National Archives, https://www.archives.gov/electoral-college/2012; "Presidential Election Results," Decision 2012, NBC News, http://elections.nbcnews.com/ns/politics/2012/all/president/#.Xlh3ixNKjm0; Wilkerson, *Caste*, 321.
42. "Remarks by the President at the Gridiron Dinner," Office of the Press Secretary, White House, March 9, 2013, https://obamawhitehouse.archives.gov/the-press-office/2013/03/10/remarks-president-gridiron-dinner.
43. Barack Obama, "Transparency and Open Government," Memorandum for the Heads of Executive Departments and Agencies, January 21, 2009, Obama White House Archives, https://obamawhitehouse.archives.gov/the-press-office/transparency-and-open-government.
44. Obama White House website, https://open.obamawhitehouse.archives.gov/; Cuillier, "Referee Madness," 31; Brainard, "Transparency Watch"; Society of Professional Journalists, "Letter Urges President Obama to Be More Transparent," *SPJ News*, July 8, 2014, https://www.spj.org/news.asp?ref=1253.
45. "100 Days, 100 Mistakes," *New York Post*, April 25, 2009, https://nypost.com/2009/04/25/100-days-100-mistakes/; Todd, *The Stranger*, 382–84.
46. Kumar, "Continuity and Change," 96, 101; Downie, "Obama Administration and the Press"; Matthew Cooper, "Is Obama Too Mean to the Media, or Are Reporters Just Whiny," *Atlantic*, February 19, 2013, https://www.theatlantic.com/politics/archive/2013/02/is-obama-too-mean-to-the-media-or-are-reporters-just-whiny/273302/.
47. Downie, "Obama Administration and the Press."

48. Dahmen and Coyle, "Obama White House Photos," 440–45; Letter to Jay Carney, Press Secretary, November 21, 2013, https://corpcommap.files .wordpress.com/2013/11/white-house-photo-letter-final-00591175.pdf.

49. "White House Denies Independent Press Photographers Request to Photograph Obama and Dalai Lama," White House News Photographers Association, February 21, 2014, https://www.whnpa.org/main/white-house-denies-independent -press-photographers-request-to-photograph-obama-and-dalai-lama/.

50. Benjamin Mullin, "Obama Administration Sets Record for Unfulfilled FOIA Requests," Poynter, March 18, 2016, https://www.poynter.org/business-work /2016/obama-administration-sets-record-for-unfulfilled-foia-requests/; Jason Leopold, "It Took a FOIA Lawsuit to Uncover How the Obama Administration Killed FOIA Reform," *Vice News*, March 9, 2016, https://www.vice.com /en_us/article/7xamnz/it-took-a-foia-lawsuit-to-uncover-how-the-obama -administration-killed-foia-reform; Munno and Long, "Tracking Litigation," 15; Society of Professional Journalists, "Letter Urges President Obama."

51. Jim VandeHei and Mike Allen, "Obama, the Puppet Master," *Politico*, February 18, 2013; Kumar, "Continuity and Change," 101–4; Axelrod, *Believer*, 444; Paul Farhi, "Obama Keeps Newspaper Reporters at Arm's Length," *Washington Post*, February 10, 2013.

52. Interview with Matt Lauer of "NBC's Today," February 1, 2009, Public Papers of the Presidents of the United States: Barack Obama (2009, Book 1), 29–38, https://www.govinfo.gov/content/pkg/PPP-2009-book1/xml/PPP-2009 -book1-doc-pg29-2.xml.

53. Andy Katz, "President Obama Chooses Kansas to Win It All in Tournament," ESPN, May 16, 2016, https://www.espn.com/mens-college-basketball /story/_/id/14984934/president-barack-obama-chooses-kansas-jayhawks-win -tournament; Rosenwald, *Talk Radio's America*, 178; Farhi, "Obama Keeps Newspaper Reporters"; VandeHei and Allen, "Obama, the Puppet Master"; *The Oprah Winfrey Show*, August 16, 2015, https://www.youtube.com/watch?v =nUdBpR5Ha3w.

54. "President Barack Obama: Between Two Ferns with Zach Galifianakis," Funny or Die, March 13, 2014, https://www.youtube.com/watch?v= UnW3xkHxIEQ; Juliet Elperin, "Remember When Zach Galifiankis Asked Obama about Being 'the Last Black President'? How That Happened," *Washington Post*, August 16, 2016, https://www.washingtonpost.com/graphics /national/obama-legacy/funny-or-die-video-history.html; Rosenwald, *Talk Radio's America*, 178.

55. Ryan, *Presidency in Black and White*, 127; "Factbox: Highlights of 'The Oprah Winfrey Show,'" Reuters, May 25, 2011; Lesley Clark, "Obama Official Who

Bettered Hispanic Media Access Steps Down," McClatchy Newspapers, March 8, 2013, https://www.mcclatchydc.com/news/politics-government /white-house/article24746341.html.

56. "Press Briefing by Press Secretary Jay Carney, 2/22/12," Office of the Press Secretary, White House, February 22, 2012, https://obamawhitehouse.archives.gov /the-press-office/2012/02/22/press-briefing-press-secretary-jay-carney-22212; "White House Daily Briefing," C-SPAN, February 22, 2012, https://www.c -span.org/video/?304535-1/white-house-daily-briefing; David Carr, "Blurred Line between Espionage and Truth," *New York Times*, February 26, 2012.

57. Downie, "Trump Administration and the Media"; Olmsted, "Terror Tuesdays," 223–25; Downie, "Obama Administration and the Press"; Carr, "Blurred Line."

58. Siobhan Gorman, "NSA Rejected System That Sifted Phone Data Legally," *Baltimore Sun*, May 18, 2006, 1A; Downie, "Obama Administration and the Press"; Andrew Beaujon, "The Day in Government Scooping," Poynter, May 20, 2013.

59. Downie, "Obama Administration and the Press"; Matt Apuzzo, "C.I.A. Officer Is Found Guilty in Leak Tied to Times Reporter," *New York Times*, January 26, 2015, A1.

60. David Leigh, "How 250,000 US Embassy Cables Were Leaked," *Guardian*, November 28, 2010, https://www.theguardian.com/world/2010/nov/28/how -us-embassy-cables-leaked.

61. Noam Cohen, "A Renegade Site, Now Working with the News Media," *New York Times*, August 2, 2010, B3; Adam Liptak, "Court Rulings Blur the Line between a Spy and a Leaker," *New York Times*, August 2, 2013; Downie, "Obama Administration and the Press"; Charlie Savage, "Manning to Be Released Early as Obama Commutes Sentence," *New York Times*, January 17, 2017, A1.

62. Kim Zetter, "Obama Administration Secretly Obtains Phone Records of AP Journalists," *Wired*, May 13, 2013, https://www.wired.com/2013/05/doj -got-reporter-phone-records/; Gary B. Pruitt, Associated Press, letter to Attorney General Eric Holder, May 13, 2013, https://www.wired.com/images _blogs/threatlevel/2013/05/Letter-to-Eric-Holder_reporter-call-records.pdf; Downie, "Obama Administration and the Press."

63. Ann E. Marrimow, "A Rare Peak into a Justice Department Leak Probe," *Washington Post*, May 19, 2013; Liptak, "Court Rulings Blur the Line"; Downie, "Obama Administration and the Press."

64. United States Department of Justice, "Report on Review of News Media Policies"; Charlie Savage, "Holder Tightens Rules on Getting Reporters' Data,"

New York Times, July 12, 2013; Downie, "Obama Administration and the Press."

65. Barton Gellman and Laura Poitras, "U.S., British Intelligence Mining Data from Nine U.S. Internet Companies in Broad Secret Program," *Washington Post*, June 7, 2013; Ellen Nakashima, "NSA Gathered Thousands of Americans' E-mails before Court Ordered It to Revise Its Tactics," *Washington Post*, August 21, 2013; Olmsted, "Terror Tuesdays," 222–23; Downie, "Obama Administration and the Press."

66. Downie, "Obama Administration and the Press."

67. "What's Happening," White House—President Barack Obama, January 19, 2017, https://obamawhitehouse.archives.gov/blog; Katz, Barris, and Jain, *Social Media President*, 42; "Obama White House Archived," Flickr, https://www.flickr.com/people/obamawhitehouse/; "The Obama White House," Facebook (archive), https://www.facebook.com/ObamaWhiteHouse/; Obamawhitehouse, Instagram (archive), https://www.instagram.com/obamawhitehouse/?hl=en; Rosenwald, *Talk Radio's America*, 177; Greenberg, *Republic of Spin*, 443; Downie, "Obama Administration and the Press."

68. Dahmen and Coyle, "Obama White House Photos," 445.

69. @POTUS 44, Obama Administration archive, https://twitter.com/potus44; Farhi, "Obama Keeps Newspaper Reporters."

70. Brattebo and Watson, "Making History," 412–14; Han, *Hatred of America's Presidents*, 358–59; Rosenwald, *Talk Radio's America*, 198; J. E. Zelizer, "Tea Partied," 26; Todd, *The Stranger*, 255.

71. D'Antonio, *Consequential President*, 263–64; "The Top Talk Radio Audiences: September 2014," *Talkers*, October 6, 2014, https://web.archive.org/web/20141006082413/http://www.talkers.com/top-talk-radio-audiences/; Mark de la Viña, "The Man behind the 'Savage Nation': Neo-Conservative Host Once Embraced the Counterculture," *Mercury News*, July 20, 2003, https://web.archive.org/web/20030801234541/http://www.bayarea.com/mld/mercurynews/entertainment/television/6336570.htm; Brian Tashman, "Michael Savage: Obama Should Be Called 'Obola,' Will Destroy America with Abe Lincoln Praise," *Right Wing Watch*, October 10, 2014, https://www.rightwingwatch.org/post/michael-savage-obama-should-be-called-obola-will-destroy-america-with-abe-lincoln-praise/.

72. Brian Resnick, "Can Conservative Talk Radio Derail Immigration Reform—Again?" *Atlantic*, April 22, 2013, https://www.theatlantic.com/politics/archive/2013/04/can-conservative-talk-radio-derail-immigration-reform-again/275183/.

73. "Full Transcript of President Obama's Remarks on Immigration Reform," *New York Times*, January 29, 2013; Molly Ball, "The Immigration Fight Is

the Battle for the Soul of the GOP," *Atlantic*, July 17, 2013, https://www
.theatlantic.com/politics/archive/2013/07/the-immigration-fight-is-the-battle
-for-the-soul-of-the-gop/277867/; Joshua Green, *Devil's Bargain*, 107–
10; Rosenwald, *Talk Radio's America*, 212; Stephen Dinan, "Sean Hannity
Turns on Immigration Deal," *Washington Times*, June 19, 2013, https://www
.washingtontimes.com/blog/inside-politics/2013/jun/19/sean-hannity-turns
-immigration-deal/.

74. "Levin: Immigration Reform Bill Is a 'Disgusting Disgrace,'" Media Matters for America, June 12, 2013, https://www.mediamatters.org/mark-levin
/levin-immigration-reform-bill-disgusting-disgrace; Rosenwald, *Talk Radio's
America*, 215; Mackenzie Weinger, "Limbaugh, Hannity Lead Talkers Top
100," *Politico*, March 13, 2013, https://www.politico.com/blogs/media/2013/03
/limbaugh-hannity-lead-talkers-top-100-159206.

75. Zachary Pleat, Thomas Bishop, Olivia Marshall, and Libby Watson, "Laura
Ingraham Campaigned against Eric Cantor to Push Her Perfect Anti-
Immigrant Candidate to Victory," Media Matters for America, June 10, 2014,
https://www.mediamatters.org/laura-ingraham/laura-ingraham-campaigned
-against-eric-cantor-push-her-perfect-anti-immigrant.

76. Ann Coulter, "GOP Crafts Plan to Wreck the Country, Lose Voters," January
29, 2014, http://www.anncoulter.com/columns/2014-01-29.html#read_more;
"Why Immigration Reform Died in Congress," NBC News, June 30, 2014,
https://www.nbcnews.com/politics/first-read/why-immigration-reform-died
-congress-n145276.

77. Brandon Darby, "Mexican Nationals Sentenced in Large Idaho Narco Bust,"
Breitbart, June 1, 2013, http://www.breitbart.com/Big-Government/2013/05
/31/4-Mexican-Nationals-Sentenced-in-Large-Narco-Op-In-Idaho; Matthew Boyle, "National Immigration Forum Funded by Soros and the Left,"
Breitbart, June 2, 2013, http://www.breitbart.com/Big-Government/2013
/06/02/National-Immigration-Forum-lead-evangelical-Jim-Wallis-funded
-by-George-Soros-other-bastions-of-institutional-left; Caroline May, "Illegal Immigrants Accounted for Nearly 37 Percent of Federal Sentences in FY
2014," Breitbart, July 7, 2015, https://www.breitbart.com/politics/2015/07/07
/illegal-immigrants-accounted-for-nearly-37-percent-of-federal-sentences-in
-fy-2014/.

78. David Carr, "The Provacateur," *New York Times*, April 13, 2012; Steve Oney,
"Citizen Breitbart," *Time*, April 5, 2010, 34–37; "Who Breitbart Is . . . Really,"
Breitbart, https://media.breitbart.com/media/2019/11/about-breitbart-news
.pdf; Ryan, *Presidency in Black and White*, 134–35; Rosenwald, *Talk Radio's
America*, 172–74.

79. Oney, "Citizen Breitbart," 34–37.

80. Ryan, *Presidency in Black and White*, 134–35; Rosenwald, *Talk Radio's America*, 172; Carr, "The Provacateur."

81. Carr, "The Provacateur."

82. Tina Nguyen, "Steve Bannon Has a Nazi Problem," *Vanity Fair*, September 12, 2017, https://www.vanityfair.com/news/2017/09/steve-bannon-has-a-nazi -problem; "Steve Bannon: The Downfall of Trump's Chief Strategist," BBC News, January 9, 2018; Joshua Green, *Devil's Bargain*, 148; Jeremy W. Peters, "Steve Bannon Steps Down from Breitbart Post," *New York Times*, January 9, 2018, A1. For examples of Breitbart's content, see https://web.archive.org/web /20130101000000*/Breitbart.com.

83. Joshua Green, *Devil's Bargain*, 46, 109–10.

84. Ryan, *Presidency in Black and White*, 121; J. E. Zelizer, "Tea Partied," 23–24, 26; Gerstle, "Civic Ideals, Race, and Nation," 271; Todd, *The Stranger*, 252.

85. Emma Margolin, "Donald Trump's History of Questioning Others' Religion," NBC News, June 22, 2016, https://www.nbcnews.com/politics/2016-election /donald-trump-s-history-questioning-others-religion-n596666; Joshua Green, *Devil's Bargain*, 39; J. E. Zelizer, "Tea Partied," 25.

86. J. E. Zelizer, "Tea Partied," 25–26; Todd, *The Stranger*, 254–58.

87. "President Obama at the 2011 White House Correspondents' Dinner," C-SPAN, April 30, 2011, https://www.youtube.com/watch?v=n9mzJhvC-8E; Joshua Green, *Devil's Bargain*, 32–36.

10. DONALD TRUMP AND THE ART OF THE LIE

1. "InfoWars: Alex Jones Interviews Donald Trump—December 2, 2015," YouTube, posted November 3, 2017, https://www.youtube.com/watch?v= 4LeChPL0sLE; Manuel Roig-Franzia, "How Alex Jones, Conspiracy Theorist Extraordinaire, Got Donald Trump's Ear," *Washington Post*, November 17, 2016; "United States of Conspiracy," *Frontline*, July 28, 2020, https://www .pbs.org/wgbh/frontline/film/united-states-of-conspiracy/; Zach Beauchamp, "Alex Jones, Pizzagate Booster and America's Most Famous Conspiracy Theorist, Explained," *Vox*, December 7, 2016, https://www.vox.com/policy -and-politics/2016/10/28/13424848/alex-jones-infowars-prisonplanet; "Alex Jones," Southern Poverty Law Center, https://www.splcenter.org/fighting-hate /extremist-files/individual/alex-jones; William Finnegan, "Donald Trump and the 'Amazing' Alex Jones," *New Yorker*, June 23, 2016, https://www.newyorker .com/news/daily-comment/donald-trump-and-the-amazing-alex-jones.

2. Finnegan, "Donald Trump"; @realDonaldTrump, Twitter, March 28, 2014, https://twitter.com/realDonaldTrump/status/449525268529815552.

3. "InfoWars: Alex Jones Interviews Donald Trump—December 2, 2015," YouTube, posted November 3, 2017, https://www.youtube.com/watch?v=4LeChPL0sLE.

4. "United States of Conspiracy."

5. Eric Bradner, "Trump Praises 9/11 Truther's 'Amazing' Reputation," CNN Politics, December 2, 2015, https://www.cnn.com/2015/12/02/politics/donald-trump-praises-9-11-truther-alex-jones/index.html; Roig-Franzia, "How Alex Jones."

6. Benkler, Faris, and Roberts, *Network Propaganda*, 32.

7. B. Zelizer, "Why Journalism," 14.

8. Karl, *Front Row*, 314; Jan Ransom, "Trump Will Not Apologize for Calling for Death Penalty over Central Park Five," *New York Times*, June 18, 2019.

9. Poniewozik, *Audience of One*, xii, 66–68, 132, 160–61; Manuel Roig-Franzia and Sarah Ellison, "A History of the Trump War on Media," *Washington Post*, March 29, 2020; Mike McIntire, Russ Buettner, and Susanne Craig, "How Reality-TV Fame Handed Trump a $427 Million Lifeline," *New York Times*, September 28, 2020; Joshua Green, *Devil's Bargain*, 95.

10. Jane Mayer, "The Making of the Fox News White House," *New Yorker*, March 11, 2019; Poniewozik, *Audience of One*, 141, 159, 169.

11. Parks, "Ultimate News Value," 512; "10 Donald Trump Business Failures," *Time*, April 29, 2011, updated October 11, 2016; Tim Carman, "Trump Steaks Are So Rare, We Can't Even Find One," *Washington Post*, March 23, 2016.

12. Poniewozik, *Audience of One*, 188; Holzer, *Presidents vs. the Press*, 409–10; Waisbord, Tucker, and Lichtenheld, "Trump and the Great Disruption," 29.

13. Joshua Green, *Devil's Bargain*, 6–7, 9, 46, 143, 167, 208; Michael Patrick Leahy, "Six Diseases Return to Us as Migration Advocates Celebrate 'World Refugee Day,'" Breitbart, June 19, 2016, https://www.breitbart.com/politics/2016/06/19/diseases-thought-eradicated-world-refugee-day/; Benkler, Faris, and Roberts, *Network Propaganda*, 4.

14. Joshua Green, *Devil's Bargain*, 145–48, 212; "Pepe the Frog," Anti-Defamation League, https://www.adl.org/education/references/hate-symbols/pepe-the-frog; Ben Collins, "On Reddit, Russian Propagandists Try New Tricks," NBC News, September 25, 2018, https://www.nbcnews.com/tech/tech-news/reddit-russian-propagandists-try-new-tricks-n913131.

15. Uscinski, "Down the Rabbit Hole," 7; Benkler, Faris, and Roberts, *Network Propaganda*, 3, 14.

16. Waisbord, Tucker, and Lichtenheld, "Trump and the Great Disruption," 28.

17. Andrew Marantz, "Antisocial Media," *New Yorker*, March 19, 2018; Faiz Siddiqui and Susan Svrluga, "N.C. Man Told Police He Went to D.C. Pizzeria

with Gun to Investigate Conspiracy Theory," *Washington Post*, December 5, 2016; James Doubek, "Conspiracy Theorist Alex Jones Apologizes for Promoting 'Pizzagate,'" National Public Radio, March 26, 2017, https://www.npr.org /sections/thetwo-way/2017/03/26/521545788/conspiracy-theorist-alex-jones -apologizes-for-promoting-pizzagate; Kathy Francovic, "Belief in Conspiracies Largely Depends on Political Identity," YouGov, December 27, 2016, https://today.yougov.com/topics/politics/articles-reports/2016/12/27/belief -conspiracies-largely-depends-political-iden; Collins, "On Reddit"; McCormick, "One America News Was Desperate."

18. Craig Silverman and Lawrence Alexander, "How Teens in the Balkans Are Duping Trump Supporters with Fake News," *BuzzFeed*, November 3, 2016.

19. Tucker et al., *Social Media, Political Polarization*, 22; Hindman and Barash, *Disinformation, "Fake News," and Influence Campaigns*; Craig Silverman, "This Analysis Shows How Viral Fake Election News Stories Outperformed Real News on Facebook," *BuzzFeed News*, November 16, 2016, https:// www.buzzfeednews.com/article/craigsilverman/viral-fake-election-news -outperformed-real-news-on-facebook.

20. Shorenstein Center of Media, Politics and Public Policy, "Combating Fake News"; Benkler et al., "Study"; Benkler, Faris, and Roberts, *Network Propaganda*, 14.

21. Joshua Green, *Devil's Bargain*, 168–74, 194–96; Levitsky and Ziblatt, *How Democracies Die*, 58; McCormick, "One America News Was Desperate"; Waisbord, Tucker, and Lichtenheld, "Trump and the Great Disruption," 29; Poniewozik, *Audience of One*, 205–7; Ben Smith, "Jeff Zucker Helped Create Donald Trump: That Show May Be Ending," *New York Times*, October 20, 2020; Jeremy Barr, "What's Up with Tucker Carlson's Leaked Tapes of Michael Cohen's Secret CNN Conversations," *Washington Post*, September 10, 2020.

22. Pickard, "When Commercialism Trumps Democracy," 195; Waisbord, Tucker, and Lichtenheld, "Trump and the Great Disruption," 30; Poniewozik, *Audience of One*, 207.

23. Mohammed and Trumpbour, "The Carnivalesque"; Parks, "Covering Trump's 'Carnival,'" 1–3, 5–6; Delli Carpini, "Alternative Facts," 20; Pickard, "When Commercialism Trumps Democracy," 196.

24. "Lesley Stahl: Trump Admitted Mission to 'Discredit' Press," CBS News, May 23, 2018, https://www.cbsnews.com/news/lesley-stahl-donald-trump-said -attacking-press-to-discredit-negative-stories/.

25. Finnegan, "Donald Trump"; Levitsky and Ziblatt, *How Democracies Die*, 64.

26. "2016 Electoral College Results," National Archives, https://www.archives .gov/electoral-college/2016; Sides, Tesler, and Vavreck, "How Trump Lost

and Won," 34; "Why Voting Matters: Supreme Court Edition," *Axios*, June 28, 2018, https://www.axios.com/hillary-clinton-2016-election-votes-supreme -court-liberal-justice-1b4bc4fc-9fad-44b4-ab54-9ef86aa9c1f1.html; Joshua Green, *Devil's Bargain*, 13–14; Roig-Franzia, "How Alex Jones"; "United States of Conspiracy."

27. "Trump CIA Speech Transcript," CBS News, January 23, 2017, https://www .cbsnews.com/news/trump-cia-speech-transcript/; Karl, *Front Row at the Trump Show*, 117–19.

28. "Spicer Rips Media's Trump Coverage (Full Remarks)," CNN, January 21, 2017, https://www.youtube.com/watch?v=Z3c8Fh8FdGI; Jay Rosen, "Send the Interns," *Press Think*, January 22, 2017, https://pressthink.org/2017/01 /send-the-interns/; Poniewozik, *Audience of One*, 246; Karl, *Front Row*, 119–20.

29. Karl, *Front Row*, 120; Ezra Klein, "Trump's Real War Isn't with the Media, It's with Facts," *Vox*, January 21, 2017, https://www.vox.com/policy-and-politics /2017/1/21/14347952/trump-spicer-press-conference-crowd-size-inauguration.

30. Margaret Sullivan, "Kellyanne Conway Undermined the Truth like No Other Trump Official: And Journalists Enabled Her," *Washington Post*, August 20, 2020.

31. Karpf, "We All Stand Together," 223–34; George Packer, "A Political Obituary for Donald Trump," *Atlantic*, December 9, 2020, https://www.theatlantic .com/magazine/archive/2021/01/the-legacy-of-donald-trump/617255/; Fact Checker, "In Four Years, President Trump Made 30,573 False or Misleading Claims," *Washington Post*, January 20, 2021, https://www.washingtonpost.com /graphics/politics/trump-claims-database/.

32. Maggie Haberman and Alexander Burns, "A Week of Whoppers from Trump," *New York Times*, September 25, 2016, 26; Poniewozik, *Audience of One*, 253.

33. See, for instance, Karen Travers and Jordyn Phelps, "'If They Had Spies in My Campaign, That Would Be a Disgrace to This Country': Trump," ABC News, May 22, 2018, https://abcnews.go.com/Politics/spies-campaign-disgrace -country-trump/story?id=55357830; "President Trump Coronavirus News Conference," C-SPAN, July 30, 2020, https://www.c-span.org/video/?474399 -1/president-trump-remarks-passing-herman-cain-addresses-tweet-mail -voting; "President Trump with Coronavirus Task Force in Press Briefing," C-SPAN, April 10, 2020, https://www.c-span.org/video/?471115-1/white-house -coronavirus-curve-starting-level; Muirhead and Rosenbaum, *Lot of People*, 1–3.

34. Brian Stelter, "President Trump Is Suddenly Using the Word 'Treason' a Lot," CNN Business, June 17, 2019, https://www.cnn.com/2019/06/17/media

/reliable-sources-06-16-19/index.html; A. G. Sulzberger, "Accusing the *New York Times* of 'Treason,' Trump Crosses a Line," *Wall Street Journal*, June 19, 2019; Michael M. Grynbaum and Eileen Sullivan, "Trump Attacks The Times, in a Week of Unease for the American Press," *New York Times*, February 20, 2019.

35. Muirhead and Rosenbaum, *Lot of People*, 1, 26.

36. Figure for followers based on @realDonaldTrump as of December 11, 2020; Holzer, *Presidents vs. the Press*, 423.

37. @RealDonaldTrump, Twitter, February 17, 2017, https://twitter.com /realDonaldTrump/status/832708293516632065; Karl, *Front Row*, 144; "'Enemies of the People': Trump Remark Echoes History's Worst Tyrants," BBC News, February 18, 2017; Levitsky and Ziblatt, *How Democracies Die*, 181; Steve LeVine, "When You Became the Enemy," *Axios*, August 1, 2018; Karl, *Front Row*, 145; David Remnick, "Donald Trump and the Enemies of the American People," *New Yorker*, February 19, 2017.

38. Michael M. Grynbaum, "After Another Year of Trump Attacks, 'Ominous Signs' for the American Press," *New York Times*, December 30, 2019; "Poll: One-Third of Americans Say News Media is the 'Enemy of the People,'" *Hill*, July 2, 2019.

39. Levitsky and Ziblatt, *How Democracies Die*, 200.

40. "Trump to CNN Reporter: What a Stupid Question," CNN, November 9, 2018, https://www.youtube.com/watch?v=9dSpBbTWigE.

41. "President Trump Says CNN's Jim Acosta Is 'Unprofessional,' Slams April Ryan as 'Loser,'" NBC News, November 9, 2018, https://www.youtube.com /watch?v=iOmscp6qpFo; Tom Jones, "Trump's Treatment of Women Reporters," Poynter, August 10, 2020; "JAWS and NABJ Stand against Unacceptable Treatment of Yamiche Alcindor," JAWS.org, March 31, 2020, https://jaws.org /2020/03/31/jaws-and-nabj-stand-against-unacceptable-treatment-of-yamiche -alcindor/.

42. "Trump Continues Attacks against Media, Democrats," AP Archive, July 6, 2018, https://www.youtube.com/watch?v=CV0uFfmQ8VI; Brian Stelter, "Trump Calls Journalists 'Bad People' at Rally Week after Newsroom Shooting," CNN Media, June 6, 2018.

43. Brian Stelter, "Why Trump's Constant Attacks on an Independent Press Are So Dangerous," CNN Business, September 2, 2019, https://www.cnn.com /2019/09/02/media/trump-press-attacks-media/index.html.

44. A. G. Sulzberger, "The Growing Threat to Journalism around the World," *New York Times*, September 23, 2019; Downie, "Trump Administration and the Media," 43; Grynbaum, "After Another Year."

45. Julian E. Barnes and David E. Sanger, "Saudi Crown Prince Is Held Responsible for Khashoggi Killing in U.S. Report," *New York Times*, February 26, 2021; Karen DeYoung, "Saudi Crown Prince Approved Operation That Led to Death of Journalist Jamal Khashoggi, U.S. Intelligence Report Concludes," *Washington Post*, February 26, 2021.

46. Levitsky and Ziblatt, *How Democracies Die*, 182.

47. Christal Hayes, "Trump Praises GOP Congressman Who Assaulted a Reporter," *USA Today*, October 18, 2018.

48. Mark Follman, "Trump's 'Enemy of the People' Rhetoric Is Endangering Journalists' Lives," *Mother Jones*, September 13, 2018; Downie, "Trump Administration and the Media"; Alex Kotlowitz, "Journalists Are Pushing Back against Trump's Attacks on Press Freedom: Where Is Everybody Else?" *Los Angeles Times*, August 17, 2018.

49. "CPJ's Backgrounder on US Press Freedom," Committee to Protect Journalists, August 15, 2018.

50. Packer, "Political Obituary for Donald Trump"; "On the Bench: Federal Judiciary," American Constitution Society, December 4, 2020, https://www.acslaw.org/judicial-nominations/on-the-bench/; Damian J. Troise and Alex Veiga, "Stocks End Year at Record Highs," *Chicago Sun-Times*, January 1, 2021.

51. "What Is the National Debt Today?" Peter G. Peterson Foundation, https://www.pgpf.org/national-debt-clock; "Protests Erupt at Airports following Trump Travel Ban," Associated Press, January 29, 2017, https://apnews.com/article/98d4bed7e9414a86bfefc28c5f7595b1; Lauren Gambino, Sabrina Siddiqui, Paul Owen, and Edward Helmore, "Thousands Protest against Trump Travel Ban in Cities and Airports Nationwide," *Guardian*, January 29, 2017, https://www.theguardian.com/us-news/2017/jan/29/protest-trump-travel-ban-muslims-airports; Miriam Jordan, "U.S. Shutters Warehouse Where Migrants Were Kept in 'Cages,'" *New York Times*, November 25, 2020.

52. Kathryn Dunn Tenpas, "Tracking Turnover in the Trump Administration," Brookings, December 2020, https://www.brookings.edu/research/tracking-turnover-in-the-trump-administration/.

53. Karl, *Front Row*, 190.

54. Tom Jones, "Arrogant, Inexperienced and Ineffective: White House Press Secretary Kayleigh McEnany Is Overmatched in Her New Job," Poynter, May 26, 2020; Downie, "Trump Administration and the Media"; Grynbaum, "After Another Year"; Elizabeth Williamson, "Stephanie Grisham's Turbulent Ascent to a Top White House Role," *New York Times*, August 22, 2019.

55. Daniel Dale, Marshall Cohen, and Tara Subramaniam, "Fact Check: New White House Press Secretary Makes False Claims in First Briefing," CNN, May 1, 2020.

56. T. Jones, "Arrogant, Inexperienced and Ineffective"; Erik Wemple, "Kayleigh McEnany's Shameful Tryout for Fox News," *Washington Post*, January 27, 2021.

57. Dana Milbank, "The White House Revoked My Press Pass," *Washington Post*, May 8, 2019; Russell, "Making Journalism Great Again," 205; Levitsky and Ziblatt, *How Democracies Die*, 200; Grynbaum, "After Another Year."

58. Jason Abbruzzese and Dennis Romero, "CNN Journalist Jim Acosta Banned from White House after Trump Calls Him 'Rude, Terrible Person,'" NBC News, November 7, 2018, https://www.nbcnews.com/news/all /trump-unloads-cnn-journalist-jim-acosta-you-are-rude-terrible-n933571; Downie, "Trump Administration and the Media," 23–24; Karl, *Front Row*, 258–59.

59. FOIA Project, "September 2020 FOIA Litigation"; Downie, "Trump Administration and the Media," 19.

60. Emily Flitter, "Treasury Official Charged with Leaking Bank Reports to Journalists," *New York Times*, October 17, 2018; Downie, "Trump Administration and the Media," 29–35.

61. Karl, *Front Row*, 129, 225; Downie, "Trump Administration and the Media," 29–30.

62. Joshua Green, *Devil's Bargain*, xvi; Margaret Sullivan, "Kellyanne Conway Undermined the Truth Like No Other White House Official," *Washington Post*, August 20, 2020; Downie, "Trump Administration and the Media," 31.

63. Mayer, "Making of the Fox News White House"; "This Invasion Can't Be Organic—and It Must Be Stopped," *The Rush Limbaugh Show*, October 22, 2018, https://www.rushlimbaugh.com/daily/2018/10/22/the-caravan-cant-be -organic-and-it-must-be-stopped/.

64. Mayer, "Making of the Fox News White House"; "United States House of Representatives Elections, 2018," Ballotpedia, https://ballotpedia.org/United _States_House_of_Representatives_elections,_2018.

65. Hacker and Pierson, *Let Them Eat Tweets*, 100; Stelter, *Hoax*, 202, 222; Mayer, "Making of the Fox News White House."

66. Piore, "Tuned Out," 98.

67. "Donald Trump Press Conference Transcript September 10: Coronavirus, Bob Woodward Recording," Rev, September 10, 2020, https://www.rev.com /blog/transcripts/donald-trump-press-conference-transcript-september-10 -coronavirus-bob-woodward-recording; Stelter, *Hoax*, 208.

68. Mayer, "Making of the Fox News White House"; Matt Gertz, "STUDY: Trump Sent 657 Live Tweets of Fox Programming in 2019," Media Matters for America, January 19, 2020, https://www.mediamatters.org/fox-news/study -trump-sent-657-live-tweets-fox-programming-2019.

69. Bob Bryan, "The Government Shutdown Is Now the Longest on Record and the Fight between Trump and Democrats Is Only Getting Uglier," *Business Insider*, January 21, 2019, https://www.businessinsider.com/government -shutdown-timeline-deadline-trump-democrats-2019-1; Mayer, "Making of the Fox News White House."

70. Mayer, "Making of the Fox News White House"; Jacob Pramuk, "Trump Signs Bill to Temporarily Reopen Government after Longest Shutdown in History," CNBC, January 25, 2019, https://www.cnbc.com/2019/01/25/senate -votes-to-reopen-government-and-end-shutdown-without-border-wall.html; Jeffrey M. Jones, "Trump Job Approval Sets New Record for Polarization," Gallup News, January 16, 2019, https://news.gallup.com/poll/245996/trump -job-approval-sets-new-record-polarization.aspx; Stelter, *Hoax*, 226–28.

71. Mayer, "Making of the Fox News White House"; Brian Stelter, "'Hannity Has Said to Me More Than Once, "He's Crazy"': Fox News Staffers Feel Trapped in the Trump Cult," *Vanity Fair*, August 20, 2020.

72. Shawna Chen, "Sarah Huckabee Sanders to Join Fox News as a Contributor," *Politico*, August 22, 2019, https://www.politico.com/story/2019/08/22/sarah -sanders-fox-news-contributor-1472104; Stelter, *Hoax*, 239; Niraj Chokshi, "Sarah Huckabee Sanders to Join Fox News as a Contributor," *New York Times*, August 22, 2019; Ryan Lizza, "Anthony Scaramucci Called Me to Unload about White House Leakers, Reince Priebus, and Steve Bannon," *New Yorker*, July 27, 2017, https://www.newyorker.com/news/ryan-lizza /anthony-scaramucci-called-me-to-unload-about-white-house-leakers-reince -priebus-and-steve-bannon; Karl, *Front Row*, 183–84.

73. Michael D. Shear, Glenn Thrush, and Maggie Haberman, "John Kelly, Assert-ing Authority, Fires Anthony Scaramucci," *New York Times*, July 31, 2017; Stelter, *Hoax*, 204; Chokshi, "Sarah Huckabee Sanders"; Mayer, "Making of the Fox News White House."

74. Mayer, "Making of the Fox News White House."

75. Felix Gillette, "The Revolution Will Be Televised (It'll Just Have Low Produc-tion Values)," *Bloomberg Businessweek*, July 24, 2017, 44–49; Claire Atkinson, "Sinclair Drops Boris Epshteyn and Other Political Analysts," NBC News, December 11, 2019; Jacey Fortin and Jonah Engel Bromwich, "Sinclair Made Dozens of Local News Anchors Recite the Same Script," *New York Times*, April 2, 2018.

76. Colin Woodard, "WGME, Other Sinclair Stations Run Stories Touting New Trump Campaign Hats," *Portland (ME) Press Herald*, August 19, 2019, https://www.pressherald.com/2019/08/19/wgme-other-sinclair-stations-run-stories-promoting-trump-campaign-merchandise/; Lachlan Markay, "Sinclair Stations Run 'Stories' That Help Trump Sell Campaign Swag," *Daily Beast*, August 19, 2019.

77. Joe Palazzolo, Nicole Hong, Michael Rothfeld, Rebecca Davis O'Brien, and Rebecca Ballhaus, "Donald Trump Played Central Role in Hush Payoffs to Stormy Daniels and Karen McDougal," *Wall Street Journal*, November 9, 2018; Toobin, *True Crimes and Misdemeanors*, 207, 216–17; Mayer, "Making of the Fox News White House."

78. Michael Rothfeld and Joe Palazzolo, "Trump Lawyer Arranged $130,000 Payment for Adult Film-Star's Silence," *Wall Street Journal*, January 12, 2018; Glenn Kesler, "Not Just Misleading. Not Merely False. A Lie," *Washington Post*, August 22, 2018; Toobin, *True Crimes and Misdemeanors*, 207, 254; Mayer, "Making of the Fox News White House."

79. David A. Fahrenthold, "Trump Used $258,000 from His Charity to Settle Legal Problems," *Washington Post*, September 20, 2016.

80. David A. Fahrenthold, "Trump Recorded Having Extremely Lewd Conversation about Women in 2005," *Washington Post*, October 8, 2016.

81. Sam Wolfson, "The Ethics Scandals That Eventually Forced Scott Pruitt to Resign," *Guardian*, July 5, 2018, https://www.theguardian.com/us-news/2018/jul/05/scott-pruitt-what-it-took-to-get-him-to-resign-from-his-epa-job; Tara Law, "Here Are All the Controversies That Led to Interior Secretary Ryan Zinke's Resignation," *Time*, December 15, 2018, https://time.com/5480865/controversies-interior-secretary-ryan-zinke-resignation/; Dan Diamond, Rachana Pradhan, and Adriel Bettelheim, "Price Resigns from HHS after Facing Fire for Travel," *Politico*, September 29, 2017, updated September 30, 2017, https://www.politico.com/story/2017/09/29/price-has-resigned-as-health-and-human-services-secretary-243315.

82. David Barstow, Susanne Craig, and Russ Buettner, "Trump Engaged in Suspect Tax Schemes as He Reaped Riches from His Father," *New York Times*, October 2, 2018.

83. David Ignatius, "Why Did Obama Dawdle on Russia's Hacking?" *Washington Post*, January 12, 2017; Bonnie Berkowitz, Denise Lu, and Julie Vitkovskaya, "Here's What We Learned about Team Trump's Ties to Russian Interests," *Washington Post*, March 31, 2017, updated February 23, 2018, https://www.washingtonpost.com/graphics/national/trump-russia/; Jeffrey Toobin, "Why the Mueller Investigation Failed," *New Yorker*, June 29, 2020.

84. Greg Miller and Greg Jaffe, "Trump Revealed Highly Classified Information to Russian Foreign Minister and Ambassador," *Washington Post*, May 15, 2017.

85. Ned Parker, Jonathan Landay, and Warren Strobel, "Exclusive: Trump Had at Least 18 Undisclosed Contacts with Russians: Sources," Reuters, May 18, 2017, https://www.reuters.com/article/us-usa-trump-russia-contacts/exclusive -trump-campaign-had-at-least-18-undisclosed-contacts-with-russians-sources -idUSKCN18E106.

86. Jo Becker, Matt Apuzzo, and Adam Goldman, "Trump Team Met with Lawyer Linked to Kremlin during Campaign," *New York Times*, July 8, 2017.

87. Toobin, *True Crimes and Misdemeanors*, 37; Toobin, "Why the Mueller Investigation Failed"; @RealDonaldTrump, Twitter, March 17, 2018.

88. Mayer, "Making of the Fox News White House"; "Hannity: Proof the Deep State Is Real," Fox News, March 20, 2018, https://video.foxnews.com/v /5754542698001#sp=show-clips; Muirhead and Rosenbaum, *Lot of People*, 36–37.

89. "Here's a Breakdown of Indictments and Cases in Mueller's Probe," ABC News, November 15, 2019, https://abcnews.go.com/Politics/breakdown -indictments-cases-muellers-probe/story?id=61219489; Michael S. Schmidt, "Justice Dept. Never Fully Examined Trump's Ties to Russia, Ex-Officials Say," *New York Times*, August 30, 2020; Spencer S. Hsu, Ann E. Marimow, and Rachel Weiner, "Rick Gates Sentenced to 45 days in Jail, 3 Years Probation for Conspiracy and Lying to FBI in Mueller Probe," *Washington Post*, December 17, 2019; Toobin, "Why the Mueller Investigation Failed"; "All the President's Crooks," *New York Times*, August 21, 2018.

90. Isaac Stanley-Becker, "In Trump's Right-Wing Media Universe, It Was a Day like Any Other," *Washington Post*, August 22, 2018; Margaret Sullivan, "This Is the Moment All of Trump's Anti-Media Rhetoric Has Been Working Toward," *Washington Post*, August 22, 2018; Screenshot of Breitbart.com, August 22, 2018.

91. "Text of Letter Summarizing Special Counsel's Report," Associated Press, March 24, 2019, https://apnews.com/article /07eb3adcff3645db8dd1ff2999ca37ee.

92. R. S. Mueller, *Report on the Investigation*, 1:1, 9, https://www.justice.gov /storage/report.pdf; Margaret Sullivan, "Journalists Can't Repeat Their Watergate-Hero Act," *Washington Post*, June 9, 2019; Sullivan and Jordan, *Trump on Trial*, 18; Schmidt, *Donald Trump v. The United States*, 361; Toobin, *True Crimes and Misdemeanors*, 311; "Highlights from the Mueller Report, Annotated," National Public Radio, April 18, 2019, https://www .npr.org/2019/04/18/708965026/highlights-from-the-mueller-report;

Mark Sherman, "The 10 Instances of Possible Obstruction in Mueller Report," Associated Press, April 18, 2019, https://apnews.com/article/e0d125d737be4a21a81bec3d9f1dffd8.

93. Sullivan, "Journalists Can't Repeat"; R. S. Mueller, *Report on the Investigation*; Al Tompkins, "Mueller Proves 'Fake News' to Be True," Poynter, April 18, 2019; Matt Taibbi, "It's Official: Russiagate Is This Generation's WMD," *RealClear Politics*, March 24, 2019.

94. Schmidt, *Donald Trump v. The United States*, 363.

95. Caitlin Emma and Connor O'Brien, "Trump Holds Up Ukraine Military Aid Meant to Confront Russia," *Politico*, August 28, 2019, https://www.politico.com/story/2019/08/28/trump-ukraine-military-aid-russia-1689531; Joe Gould and Howard Altman, "Here's What You Need to Know about the U.S. Aid Package to Ukraine That Trump Delayed," *Defense News*, September 25, 2019, https://www.defensenews.com/congress/2019/09/25/what-you-need-to-know-about-the-us-aid-package-to-ukraine-that-trump-delayed/.

96. "Trump Tries to Force Ukraine to Meddle in the 2020 Election," *Washington Post*, September 5, 2019.

97. "Document: Read the Whistle-Blower Complaint," *New York Times*, September 26, 2019; Jo Becker, Walt Bogdanich, Maggie Haberman, and Ben Protess, "Why Giuliani Singled Out 2 Ukrainian Oligarchs to Help Look for Dirt," *New York Times*, November 25, 2019.

98. United States House of Representatives, "Trial Memorandum of the United States House of Representatives in the Impeachment Trial of President Donald J. Trump"; Amber Phillips, "The Articles of Impeachment against President Trump, Explained," *Washington Post*, December 10, 2019; Dareh Gregorian, "Trump Impeached by the House for Abuse of Power, Obstruction of Congress," NBC News, December 18, 2019, https://www.nbcnews.com/politics/trump-impeachment-inquiry/trump-impeached-house-abuse-power-n1104196.

99. Ryan Broderick, "Republicans' Conspiracy Theory–Ridden Counterprogramming to Impeachment Is Working," *BuzzFeed News*, November 20, 2019.

100. Tobin Smith, "Why Fox News Slimed a Purple Heart Recipient," *New York Times*, November 22, 2019; Michael M. Grynbaum and Dave Alba, "After Vindman's Testimony Went Public, Right-Wing Conspiracies Fired Up," *New York Times*, October 29, 2019.

101. Sullivan, "Journalists Can't Repeat"; Grynbaum, "After Another Year"; Broderick, "Republicans' Conspiracy Theory–Ridden Counterprogramming."

102. Sullivan and Jordan, *Trump on Trial*, 426, 447.

103. "How Senators Voted on Trump's Impeachment," *Politico*, February 5, 2020, https://www.politico.com/interactives/2019/trump-impeachment-vote-count-senate-results/.

104. "A Full Transcript of Trump's Remarks from the White House on Impeachment Acquittal," *Boston Globe*, February 6, 2020, https://www.bostonglobe.com/2020/02/06/nation/full-transcript-trumps-remarks-white-house-impeachment-acquittal/; "President Trump Speaks following Acquittal in Impeachment Trial," CNBC, February 6, 2020, https://www.youtube.com/watch?v=GFPqfmXr0U8.

105. Jeffrey M. Jones, "Trump Job Approval at Personal Best 49%," Gallup, February 4, 2020, https://news.gallup.com/poll/284156/trump-job-approval-personal-best.aspx.

11. DONALD TRUMP AND THE YEAR OF CRISES

1. "Watch: Full 2020 Trump Super Bowl Interview with Sean Hannity," *Real-Clear Politics*, February 2, 2020, https://www.realclearpolitics.com/video/2020/02/02/watch_full_2020_trump_super_bowl_interview_with_sean_hannity.html. For data on the economy, see Kimberly Amadeo, "Unemployment Rate by Year since 1929 Compared to Inflation and GDP," *Balance*, updated March 16, 2021, https://www.thebalance.com/unemployment-rate-by-year-3305506.

2. Woodward, *Rage*, xiii; Ayesha Roscoe and Colin Dwyer, "Trump Received Intelligence Briefings on Coronavirus Twice in January," National Public Radio, May 2, 2020, https://www.npr.org/sections/coronavirus-live-updates/2020/05/02/849619486/trump-received-intelligence-briefings-on-coronavirus-twice-in-january.

3. Margaret Sullivan, "The Data Is In: Fox News May Have Kept Millions from Taking the Coronavirus Threat Seriously," *Washington Post*, June 28, 2020.

4. Anne Gearan, Seung Min Kim, and Erica Werner, "Trump Administration Tries to Play Down the Health and Economic Risks of the Coronavirus," *Washington Post*, February 28, 2020.

5. "Presidential Address on the Coronavirus Outbreak," C-SPAN, March 11, 2020, https://www.c-span.org/video/?470284-1/president-trump-travel-europe-us-suspended-30-days-uk.

6. Domenico Cucinotta and Maurizio Vanelli, "WHO Declares COVID-19 a Pandemic," National Library of Medicine, March 19, 2020, https://pubmed.ncbi.nlm.nih.gov/32191675/#:~:text=The%20World%20Health%20Organization%20(,outbreak%20a%20global%20pandemic.

7. Fred Imbert and Thomas Franck, "Dow Plunges 10% amid Coronavirus Fears for Its Worst Day since the 1987 Market Crash," CNBC, March 11, 2020, https://www.cnbc.com/2020/03/11/futures-are-steady-wednesday-night-after-dow-closes-in-bear-market-traders-await-trump.html; Woodward, *Rage*, 279; Doug Bock Clark, "Unmasked," *New York Times Magazine*, November 22, 2020, 24–25.

8. J. M. Barrie, *Peter Pan*, chapter 13, "Do You Believe in Fairies?" Lit2Go, https://etc.usf.edu/lit2go/86/peter-pan/1607/chapter-13-do-you-believe-in-fairies/.

9. Bilinski and Emanuel, "COVID-19 and Excess All-Cause Mortality," table 1; "Coronavirus (COVID-19) Deaths," Our World in Data, accessed September 25, 2021, https://ourworldindata.org/covid-deaths, updated daily.

10. @RealDonalTrump, Twitter, March 8, 2020.

11. Charlie Warzel, "What We Pretend to Know about the Coronavirus Could Kill Us," *New York Times*, April 3, 2020; "Coronavirus in the U.S.: Latest Map and Case Count," *New York Times*, updated December 12, 2020, https://www.nytimes.com/interactive/2020/us/coronavirus-us-cases.html.

12. Katie Rogers and Maggie Haberman, "Kayleigh McEnany Heckles the Press. Is That All?" *New York Times*, August 2, 2020; Michael M. Grynbaum, "Trump's Briefings Are a Ratings Hit: Should Networks Cover Them Live?" *New York Times*, March 25, 2020; Michael M. Grynbaum, "'Don't Try This at Home': Even 'Fox & Friends' Balked at Trump's Advice," *New York Times*, April 24, 2020.

13. Michael M. Grynbaum, "At Fox News, Mixed Message on Malaria Drug," *New York Times*, May 19, 2020.

14. @RealDonaldTrump, Twitter, May 18, 2020, https://twitter.com/realDonaldTrump/status/1262563582086184970; Matthew Choi, "Trump Goes after Fox News Host, and the Network, in Twitter Flurry," *Politico*, May 18, 2020.

15. "Top Talk Audiences," *Talkers*, November 2020, http://www.talkers.com/top-talk-audiences/; Brian Stelter, "Rush Limbaugh Renews Radio Show Contract in a 'Long-Term' Deal," CNN Business, January 5, 2020, https://www.cnn.com/2020/01/05/media/rush-limbaugh-show-contract/index.html; Jackson Katz, "Trump Giving Rush Limbaugh the Medal of Freedom Was Controversial—and Fitting," NBC News, February 7, 2020, https://www.nbcnews.com/think/opinion/trump-giving-rush-limbaugh-medal-freedom-was-controversial-fitting-ncna1132121.

16. "Algore's Idiotic Poem and All the Latest from the ClimateGate Stack," *The Rush Limbaugh Show*, December 7, 2009, https://www.rushlimbaugh.com

/daily/2009/12/07/algore_s_idiotic_poem_and_all_the_latest_from_the
_climategate_stack/; "Democrats Push to Kill Capitalism; Obama Uses Alin-
sky Plan on Banks," *The Rush Limbaugh Show*, January 14, 2010, https://www
.rushlimbaugh.com/daily/2010/01/14/democrats_push_to_kill_capitalism
_obama_uses_alinsky_plan_on_banks/.

17. "ClimateGate Hoax: The Universe of Lies versus the Universe of Reality,"
The Rush Limbaugh Show, November 24, 2009, https://www.rushlimbaugh
.com/daily/2009/11/24/climategate_hoax_the_universe_of_lies_versus_the
_universe_of_reality/.

18. Funk et al., "Science and Scientists Held in High Esteem."

19. "I'm the Only Guy Getting the Coronavirus Right!" *The Rush Limbaugh
Show*, February 26, 2020, https://www.rushlimbaugh.com/daily/2020/02/26
/im-the-only-guy-getting-the-coronavirus-right/; Jeremy W. Peters, "Alarm,
Denial, Blame: The Pro-Trump Media's Coronavirus Distortion," *New York
Times*, April 1, 2020.

20. World Health Organization, "Coronavirus Disease."

21. "In the Face of COVID-19, We're Not Acting at All like Americans," *The Rush
Limbaugh Show*, July 14, 2020, https://www.rushlimbaugh.com/daily/2020/07
/14/were-not-acting-at-all-like-americans-in-this-pandemic/.

22. Oliver Darcy, "Flashback: Right-Wing Media Downplayed Coronavirus
Death Toll Potential in Spring," CNN Business, September 22, 2020, https://
www.cnn.com/2020/09/22/media/coronavirus-right-wing-media-reliable
-sources/index.html; Tiffany Hsu, "Right-Wing Media Stars Mislead on
Covid-19 Death Toll," *New York Times*, September 24, 2020; "United States of
Conspiracy"; Emily Bazelon, "Freedom of Speech Will Preserve Our Democracy," *New York Times Magazine*, October 18, 2020.

23. Matt Gertz, "Misinformation of the Year: Fox News," Media Matters for
America, December 30, 2020, https://www.mediamatters.org/fox-news
/misinformer-year-fox-news.

24. Stelter, "'Hannity Has Said to Me'"; Jeremy W. Peters, "Alarm, Denial, Blame:
The Pro-Trump Media's Coronavirus Distortion," *New York Times*, April 1, 2020.

25. Sheera Frankel, Ben Decker, and Davey Alba, "How the 'Plandemic Movie'
and Its Falsehoods Spread Widely Online," *New York Times*, May 21, 2020;
Oliver Darcy, "Local TV Stations across the Country Set to Air Discredited
'Plandemic' Researcher's Conspiracy Theory about Fauci," CNN Business, July
25, 2020, https://www.cnn.com/2020/07/24/media/sinclair-fauci-conspiracy
-bolling/index.html.

26. Emily Baumgaertner and James Rainey, "Trump Administration Ended
Pandemic Early-Warning Program to Detect Coronavirus," *Los Angeles*

Times, April 6, 2020; Bill Whitaker, "Sick Doctors, Nurses and Not Enough Equipment: NYC Health Care Workers on the Fight against Coronavirus," *60 Minutes*, April 12, 2020, https://www.cbsnews.com/news/personal-protective -equipment-ppe-doctors-nurses-short-supply-60-minutes-2020-04-12/; Margaret Sullivan, "What It Really Means When Trump Calls a Story 'Fake News,'" *Washington Post*, April 13, 2020.

27. Shawn Boburg, Robert O'Harrow Jr., Neena Satija, and Amy Goldstein, "Inside the Corona Testing Failure," *Washington Post*, April 3, 2020; Richard A. Oppel Jr., Robert Gebeloff, K. K. Rebecca Lai, Will Wright, and Mitch Smith, "The Fullest Look Yet at the Racial Inequity of Coronavirus," *New York Times*, July 5, 2020.

28. Grace Goins, "Too Many Patients Are Still Suffering and Dying Alone," *Star Tribune*, September 16, 2020; Tatiana Sanchez, "COVID Patients Are Dying Alone in Bay Area Hospitals," *San Francisco Chronicle*, December 18, 2020.

29. John Gramlich, "5 Facts about Fox News," *Fact Tank*, Pew Research Center, April 8, 2020; Jamieson and Albarracin, "Relation between Media Consumption and Misinformation," 1–7; Zacc Ritter, "Amid Pandemic, News Attention Spikes; Media Favorability Flat," Gallup, April 9, 2020; Sullivan, "Data Is In."

30. @KevinVesey, Twitter, May 14, 2020, https://twitter.com/KevinVesey/status /1261001977598808065; Tom Brune, "Trump Cheers 'Reopen LI' Protesters Who Heckled News 12 Reporter Kevin Vesey," *Newsday*, May 16, 2020, https://www.newsday.com/news/health/coronavirus/trump-kevin-vesey-news -12-1.44696404.

31. Richard A. Oppel Jr., Derrick Bryson Taylor, and Nicholas Bogel-Burroughs, "What to Know about Breonna Taylor's Death," *New York Times*, October 30, 2020.

32. Initial accounts said the officer had his knee on Floyd's neck for eight minutes, forty-six seconds, but prosecutors later said the length of time was nine minutes, twenty-nine seconds. See Nicholas Bogel-Burroughs, "Prosecutors Say Derek Chauvin Knelt on George Floyd for Nine Minutes 29 Seconds, Longer than Initially Reported," *New York Times*, March 30, 2021.

33. Larry Buchanan, Quoctrung Bui, and Jugal K. Patel, "Black Lives Matter May Be the Largest Movement in U.S. History," *New York Times*, July 3, 2020; Leonard Pitts Jr., "Respect Your Local Police—or Else?" *Seattle Times*, December 8, 2019; "George Floyd: Timeline of Black Deaths and Protests," BBC News, September 23, 2020, https://www.bbc.com/news/world-us-canada -52905408.

34. Sanders, "Presidents and Social Movements," 226.

35. Charlie Warzel, "The Protests Show That Twitter Is Real Life," *New York Times*, June 14, 2020; Sarah L. Jackson, "Twitter Made Us Better," *New York Times*, December 27, 2019; Yamiche Alcindor, "#BlackOnCampus Describes Personal Experiences with Racism," *USA Today*, November 12, 2015.

36. Michael T. Heaney, "The George Floyd Protests Generated More Media Coverage than Any Protest in 50 Years," *Washington Post*, July 6, 2020; Matthew Yglesias, "Brick by Brick," *New York Times Book Review*, February 7, 2021, 15.

37. Sanders, "Presidents and Social Movements," 223, 239; Davey Alba, "Misinformation about George Floyd Protests Surges on Social Media," *New York Times*, June 1, 2020; "Tucker: Black Lives Matter Is Now a Political Party," Fox News, June 8, 2020, https://www.youtube.com/watch?v=l7aQ02YX7qo&feature=youtu.be; Elyse Samuels, "Trump Retweets Video Tying BLM, Antifa to an Assault," *Washington Post*, September 1, 2020; Davey Alba, Kate Conger, and Raymond Zhong, "Twitter Adds Warnings to Trump and White House Tweets, Fueling Tensions," *New York Times*, May 29, 2020.

38. Marc Tracy and Rachel Abrams, "Police Target Journalists as Trump Blames 'Lamestream Media' for Protests," *New York Times*, June 1, 2020.

39. Katharine Jacobsen, "In 2020, U.S. Journalists Faced Unprecedented Attacks," Committee to Protect Journalists, December 14, 2020, https://cpj.org/2020/12/in-2020-u-s-journalists-faced-unprecedented-attacks/; "RSF and 19 Other Groups Call on US Governors and Mayors to Ensure Safety of Journalists," Reporters without Borders, June 5, 2020; Paul Farhi and Elahe Izadi, "The Norms Have Broken Down," *Washington Post*, May 31, 2020; "U.S. Press Freedom Tacker," Freedom of the Press, https://pressfreedomtracker.us/all-incidents/; "US: Fueled by Years of Trump's Demonization of the Media, Unprecedented Violence Breaks Out against Journalists Covering Protests," Reporters without Borders, May 31, 2020; Sullivan, "Trump Has Sown Hatred."

40. "Australian Journalist Amelia Brace Testified before US Congress about Being Struck by Police during Black Lives Matter Protest," Australian Broadcasting Corporation, June 29, 2020, https://www.abc.net.au/news/2020-06-30/australian-journalist-testifies-us-congress-black-lives-matter/12404958; Peter Hermann, Sarah Pulliam Bailey, and Michelle Boorstein, "Fire Set at Historic St. John's Church during Protests of George Floyd's Death," *Washington Post*, May 31, 2020; Dalton Bennett, Sarah Cahlan, Aaron C. Davis, and Joyce Lee, "The Crackdown before Trump's Photo Op," *Washington Post*, June 8, 2020; Dan Zak, Monica Hesse, Ben Terris, Maura Judkis, and Travis M. Andrews, "'This Can't Be Happening': An Oral History of 48 Surreal, Violent, Biblical Minutes in Washington,"

Washington Post, June 2, 2020; "Australia Investigates Treatment of Journalists at US Protest," Voice of America, June 3, 2020, https://www.voanews .com/usa/nation-turmoil-george-floyd-protests/australia-investigates -treatment-journalists-us-protest; Ashley Park, Josh Dawsey, and Rebecca Tan, "Inside the Push to Tear-Gas Protesters ahead of a Trump Photo Op," *Washington Post*, June 1, 2020; Egan Millard, "After 'Sickening and Haunting' Encounter with Police in D.C., Priest and Seminarian Turn Focus Back to Racial Justice," Episcopal News Service, June 4, 2020, https://www .episcopalnewsservice.org/2020/06/04/episcopal-priest-seminarian-who -shared-sickening-and-haunting-experience-being-ambushed-by-police -turn-the-focus-back-to-racial-justice/; Jack Jenkins, "Ahead of Trump Bible Photo Op, Police Forcibly Expel Priest from St. John's Church near White House," Religion News Service, June 2, 2020.

41. @RealDonaldTrump, Twitter, June 9, 2020, https://twitter.com /realDonaldTrump/status/1270333484528214018; Glenn Kessler, "Trump Tweets Outrageous Conspiracy Theory about Injured Buffalo Man," *Washington Post*, June 9, 2020; Alex Feuer, "Trump Falsely Targets Buffalo Protester, 75, as 'Antifa Provocateur,'" *New York Times*, June 9, 2020.

42. "Trump, in Crisis Mode, Tweets His 2000th Attack on the Press," U.S. Press Freedom Tracker, April 12, 2020, https://pressfreedomtracker.us/blog/trump -crisis-mode-tweets-his-2000th-attack-press/; Downie, "Trump Administration and the Media," 11.

43. @RealDonaldTrump, Twitter, September 2, 2019; Stelter, "Why Trump's Constant Attacks."

44. @MarkKnoller, Twitter, August 5, 2020, https://twitter.com/markknoller /status/1290991859997839372.

45. "Donald Trump Interview Transcript with Jonathan Swan of Axios on HBO," Rev, August 3, 2020, https://www.rev.com/blog/transcripts/donald-trump -interview-transcript-with-axios-on-hbo; "Fact-checking 22 Claims from Donald Trump's Axios Interview," PolitiFact, August 4, 2020, https://www .politifact.com/article/2020/aug/04/fact-checking-donald-trumps-axios -interview/; Tom Jones, "Does President Trump's Astonishing Interview with Axios Even Matter? Yes, and Here's Why," Poynter, August 5, 2020.

46. Moser, "Interference 2020"; Katie Rogers and Kevin Roose, "Trump Says QAnon Followers Are People Who Love 'Our Country,'" *New York Times*, August 19, 2020; Michelle Goldberg, "QAnon Believers Are Obsessed with Hillary Clinton," *New York Times*, February 5, 2021.

47. Tony Romm, "Amazon, Apple, Facebook and Google Grilled on Capitol Hill over Their Market Power," *Washington Post*, July 29, 2020.

48. Kate Conger, "Another Tweet from Trump Gets a Label from Twitter," *New York Times*, June 23, 2020; Heather Kelly, "Facebook, Twitter Penalize Trump for Posts Containing Coronavirus Misinformation," *Washington Post*, August 5 2020.

49. Barbara Ortutay, Associated Press, "Twitter to Combat Misleading Election Claims," *Chicago Tribune*, September 11, 2020; Drew Harwell and Craig Timberg, "Pro-Trump Message Board 'Quarantined' by Reddit following Violent Threats," *Washington Post*, June 26, 2019; Mike Isaac, "Reddit, Acting against Hate Speech, Bans 'The_Donald' Subreddit," *New York Times*, June 29, 2020; Kevin Roose, "Goodbye to the Wild Wild Web," *New York Times*, July 2, 2020.

50. Morgan Greene, "Summer Derecho Left $11B in Damage," *Chicago Tribune*, January 20, 2021, 1; John Bacon and Trevor Hughes, "Smoke, Flames alter Western Skies as 'Unprecedented' Wildfires the Size of Connecticut Burn," *USA Today*, September 9, 2020; Jocelyn Gecker, "Fires Torch 'Unfathomable' 4 Million Acres in California," *Chicago Tribune*, October 5, 2020; David Leonhardt, "Remember Climate Change?" *New York Times*, November 15, 2020.

51. Abraham Lustgarten, "How Climate Change Will Remap Where Americans Live," *New York Times Magazine*, September 20, 2020, 36–38; Kevin McGill, Stacey Plaisance, and Rebecca Santana, "At Least 1 Dead as Hurricane Zeta Hammers Gulf Coast," Associated Press, October 28, 2020, https://apnews.com/article/donald-trump-virus-outbreak-alabama-kay-ivey-mississippi-62ac94b1114344c592f11fef63d5b87a; Peter Baker, Lisa Friedman, and Thomas Kaplan, "As Trump Again Rejects Science, Biden Calls Him a 'Climate Arsonist,'" *New York Times*, September 15, 2020; Leonhardt, "Remember Climate Change?"; Henry Fountain, Blacki Migliozzi, and Nadja Popovich, "Where 2020's Record Heat Was Felt the Most," *New York Times*, January 14, 2021.

52. Michael M. Grynbaum and Tiffany Hsu, "'Nothing to Do with Climate Change': Conservative Media and Trump Align on Fires," *New York Times*, September 15, 2020.

53. Rachel Siegel and Andrew Van Dam, "2020 Was the Worst Year for Economic Growth since the Second World War," *Washington Post*, January 28, 2021; Kimberly Amadeo, "US GDP by Year Compared to Recessions and Events: The Strange Ups and Downs of the U.S. Economy since 1929," *Balance*, July 30, 2020, https://www.thebalance.com/us-gdp-by-year-3305543; "Federal Deficit Trends over Time," Data Lab, 2020, https://datalab.usaspending.gov/americas-finance-guide/deficit/trends/; Jeff Stein and Andrew Van Dam,

"U.S. Budget Deficit Breached $3.1 trillion in 2020 as Pandemic Slammed Economy," *Washington Post*, October 16, 2020.

54. Hamza Shaban and Heather Long, "The Stock Market Is Ending 2020 at Record Highs, Even as the Virus Surges and Millions Go Hungry," *Washington Post*, December 31, 2020; Stan Choe, Damian J. Troise, and Alex Veiga, Associated Press, "Markets Hit New Records as Biden Takes Helm," *Chicago Tribune*, January 21, 2021.

55. "All Employees, Total Nonfarm (PAYEMS)," Federal Reserve Bank of St. Louis, Economic Research, updated January 8, 2021, https://fred.stlouisfed.org/series /PAYEMS; John Harwood, "Trump Will Leave Office with a Historically Bad Economic Record," CNN Politics, December 13, 2020; Bureau of Labor Statistics, "Labor Force Statistics."

56. Woodward, *Fear*, 354–57.

57. Peter Baker, "For a President Who Needs to 'Touch the Flame,' Bob Woodward Was Irresistible," *New York Times*, September 10, 2020.

58. Woodward, *Rage*, xviii, 386, 392; Robert Costa and Philip Rucker, "Woodward Book: Trump Says He Knew Coronavirus Was 'Deadly,'" *Washington Post*, September 9, 2020.

59. Jeffrey Goldberg, "Trump: Americans Who Died in War Are 'Losers' and 'Suckers,'" *Atlantic*, September 3, 2020.

60. Russ Buettner, Susanne Craig, and Mike McIntire, "Long-Concealed Records Show Trump's Chronic Losses and Years of Tax Avoidance," *New York Times*, September 27, 2020; David Leonhardt, "18 Revelations from a Trove of Trump Tax Records," *New York Times*, September 27, 2020; Tom Jones, "The New York Times' Bombshell Report on the President's Taxes," *Poynter Report*, September 28, 2020.

61. David A. Fahrenthold, Josh Dawsey, Jonathan O'Connell, and Anu Narayanswamy, "Ballrooms, Candles and Luxury Cottages," *Washington Post*, October 27, 2020.

62. Margaret Sullivan, "The Media Never Fully Learned How to Cover Trump," *Washington Post*, November 8, 2020.

63. @realDonaldTrump, Twitter, October 1, 2020, https://twitter.com /realdonaldtrump/status/1311892190680014849?lang=en; James Poniewozik, "Sick with Covid, Trump Tries to Paint the Picture of Health on TV," *New York Times*, October 4, 2020, updated October 6, 2020; Peter Baker and Maggie Haberman, "As Trump Seeks to Project Strength, Doctors Disclose Alarming Episodes," *New York Times*, October 4, 2020; Josh Wingrove, Jennifer Jacobs, and Justin Sink, "Trump Return Trailed by Doubts on Recovery,

White House Outbreak," *Bloomberg*, October 5, 2020, updated October 6, 2020.

64. Janie Boschma, Christopher Hickey, Kevin Liptak, and Heather Fulbright, "Who Has Tested Positive for Coronavirus in Trump's Orbit," CNN Politics, December 17, 2020, https://www.cnn.com/2020/12/09/politics/white-house -trump-covid-cases/index.html; Elahe Izadi, "Which Trump Official Has Coronavirus Now? This Reporter Always Seems to Know First," *Washington Post*, November 24, 2020; Joe Pompeo, "'People Are Livid': White House Reporters Fume over Team Trump's 'Reckless' COVID Response," *Vanity Fair*, October 5, 2020, https://www.vanityfair.com/news/2020/10/white-house -reporters-fume-over-reckless-covid-response; Michael M. Grynbaum, "As Virus Invades West Wing, White House Reporters Face Heightened Risks," *New York Times*, October 5, 2020.

65. @BenSTracy, Twitter, October 5, 2020, https://twitter.com/benstracy/status /1313146869573464064; Michael M. Grynbaum, "As Trump Flouts Safety Protocols, News Outlets Balk at Close Coverage," *New York Times*, October 12, 2020.

66. Linda Qiu and Michael D. Shear, "Rallies Are the Core of Trump's Campaign, and a Font of Lies and Misinformation," *New York Times*, October 26, 2020; Todd Richmond and Frank Jordans, "Europe and US Facing New Round of Shutdowns amid Virus Surge," Associated Press, October 28, 2020, https://apnews.com/article/europe-us-shutdowns-virus-surge-covid-19 -a8b0d7b63fde5b9d289cabf06ae367bf; Alexander Burns, "Trump's Closing Argument on Virus Clashes with Science and Voters' Lives," *New York Times*, October 28, 2020.

67. Alexander Burns, "Trump Attacks an Election He Is at Risk of Losing," *New York Times*, July 30, 2020.

68. Tiffany Hsu, "Conservative News Sites Fuel Voter Misinformation," *New York Times*, October 25, 2020; Davey Alba, Kellen Browning, and Jacob Silver, "How Three Election-Related Falsehoods Spread," *New York Times*, October 30, 2020; Michael Anton, "The Coming Coup?" *American Mind*, September 4, 2020, https://americanmind.org/salvo/the-coming-coup/; Emily Bazelon, "Freedom of Speech Will Preserve Our Democracy," *New York Times Magazine*, October 18, 2020, 28.

69. Bazelon, "Freedom of Speech," 28.

70. Bazelon, "Freedom of Speech," 28; "Explore Key 2020 Survey Data," Pew Research Center, https://www.pewresearch.org/pathways-2020 /knowmailfraud/main_source_of_election_news/us_adults/.

71. Nick Corasaniti and Jim Rutenberg, "Record Turnout Hints at Future of Vote in U.S.," *New York Times*, December 6, 2020; Tom Jones, "Election Day Continues—and We Shouldn't Be Surprised," *Poynter Report*, November 4, 2020.

72. Nancy LeToruneau, "How Fox News Spoiled Trump's Plan to Steal the Election," *Washington Monthly*, November 10, 2020, https://washingtonmonthly.com/2020/11/10/how-fox-news-foiled-trumps-plan-to-steal-the-election/.

73. LeToruneau, "How Fox News Spoiled Trump's Plan"; Sarah Ellison and Josh Dawsey, "The Long Love Affair between Fox News and Trump May Be Over," *Washington Post*, November 9, 2020; "Biden Campaign Optimistic as 2020 Vote Count Stretches On (Updated)," *Vanity Fair*, November 5, 2020, https://www.vanityfair.com/news/2020/11/2020-election-live-polls-and-results; Michael M. Grynbaum and John Koblin, "Fox News Helped Fuel Trump's Rise: Now It's Reporting on a Possible Fall," *New York Times*, November 4, 2020, updated November 10, 2020.

74. "President Trump Remarks on Election Status," C-SPAN, November 3, 2020, https://www.c-span.org/video/?477710-1/president-trump-remarks-election-status; Alexander Burns and Jonathan Martin, "As America Awaits a Winner, Trump Falsely Claims He Prevailed," *New York Times*, November 4, 2020; Fox News, election coverage, November 4, 2020.

75. Tom Jones, "Outrage," *Poynter Report*, November 4, 2020; Michael M. Grynbaum and John Koblin, "TV Anchors and Pundits Criticize Trump's Baseless Claims of Fraud," *New York Times*, November 4, 2020.

76. Grynbaum and Koblin, "Fox News Helped Fuel."

77. @GabrielSherman, Twitter, November 4, 2020, https://twitter.com/gabrielsherman/status/1324147150901661697; Grynbaum and Koblin, "Fox News Helped Fuel."

78. @JudgeJeanine, Twitter, November 5, 2020, https://twitter.com/JudgeJeanine/status/1324393751679242240.

79. Matthew Rosenberg, Jim Rutenberg, and Nick Corasanti, "The Disinformation Is Coming from Inside the White House," *New York Times*, November 5, 2020.

80. Tiffany Hsu and John Koblin, "Fox News Meets Trump's Fraud Claims with Skepticism," *New York Times*, November 5, 2020.

81. Ellison and Dawsey, "Long Love Affair."

82. David Folkenflik, "Newsmax Rises on Wave of Resentment toward Media—Especially Fox News," National Public Radio, November 30, 2020, https://www.npr.org/2020/11/30/939030504/newsmax-rises-on-wave-of-resentment

-toward-media-especially-fox-news; Brian Stelter, "Newsmax TV Scores a Rat-ings Win over Fox News for the First Time Ever," CNN Business, December 8, 2020, https://www.cnn.com/2020/12/08/media/newsmax-fox-news-ratings /index.html; Greg Weiner, "How Do We Get to Herd Immunity for Fake News?" *New York Times*, December 14, 2020; Hsu and Koblin, "Fox News Meets."

83. Rosenberg, Rutenberg, and Corasanti, "Disinformation Is Coming from Inside."

84. Patricia Mazzei and Nicole Perlroth, "False News Targeting Latinos Trails the Election," *New York Times*, November 4, 2020, updated November 7, 2020.

85. Sheera Frenkel, "How Misinformation 'Superspreaders' Seed False Election Theories," *New York Times*, November 23, 2020.

86. Alex Newhouse, "Who Is behind This Growing Conservative Social Media Platform?" *Chicago Tribune*, December 20, 2020; Tina Nguyen, "On Parler, MAGA's Post-Election World View Blossoms with No Pushback," *Politico*, November 22, 2020, https://www.politico.com/news/2020/11/22/parler -maga-election-echo-chamber-439056; Donie O'Sullivan, "In Georgia, Some Trump Supporters Turn to Parler, a Platform for a Parallel Universe," CNN Business, December 3, 2020, https://www.cnn.com/2020/12/03/tech/parler -trump-supporters/index.html; Kellen Browning, "Parler C.E.O. Says He Was Fired," *New York Times*, February 3, 2021.

87. Brooke Singman and Paul Steinhauser, "Biden Wins Presidency, Trump Denied Second Term in White House, Fox News Projects," Fox News, November 7, 2020, https://www.foxnews.com/politics/biden-wins-presidency -trump-fox-news-projects; John Koblin, Michael M. Grynbaum, and Tiffany Hsu, "Tension, Then Some Tears, as TV News Narrates a Moment for His-tory," *New York Times*, November 7, 2020.

88. "It's Joe Time," *New York Post*, November 8, 2020, https://nypost.com/cover /november-8-2020/.

89. James M. Lindsay, "The 2020 Election by the Numbers," Council on Foreign Relations, December 15, 2020, https://www.cfr.org/blog/2020-election -numbers.

90. Christopher Ingraham, "How Experts Define the Deadly Mob Attack at the U.S. Capitol," *Washington Post*, January 13, 2021; Zeynep Tufekci, "This Must Be Your First," *Atlantic*, December 7, 2020, https://www.theatlantic .com/ideas/archive/2020/12/trumps-farcical-inept-and-deadly-serious-coup -attempt/617309/; Charles T. Call, "No, It's Not a Coup—It's a Failed 'Self-Coup' That Will Undermine US Leadership and Democracy Worldwide," Brookings, January 8, 2021.

91. Rosalind S. Halderman, "Wisconsin Recount Confirms Biden's Win over Trump," *Washington Post*, November 29, 2020; Philip Rucker, Ashley Parker, Josh Dawsey, and Amy Gardner, "20 Days of Fantasy and Failure: Inside Trump's Quest to Overturn the Election," *Washington Post*, November 28, 2020; David Atkins, "Trump Is Staging a Comically Incompetent Coup," *Washington Monthly*, November 21, 2020, https://washingtonmonthly.com /2020/11/21/trump-is-staging-a-comically-incompetent-coup/; Alanna Durkin Richer and Nomaan Merchant, "EXPLAINER: Trump's Election Challenges Falling Flat in Court," Associated Press, November 21, 2020, https://apnews.com/article/election-2020-joe-biden-donald-trump-elections -18c9a1eef016f2e7f2cda7e443620dcl.

92. William Cummings, Joey Garrison, and Jim Sergent, "By the Numbers: President Donald Trump's Failed Efforts to Overturn the Election," *USA Today*, January 6, 2021; Louis Jacobson and Amy Sherman, "Donald Trump Has Lost Dozens of Election Lawsuits: Here's Why," PolitiFact, December 10, 2020, https://www.politifact.com/article/2020/dec/10/donald-trump-has-lost -dozens-election-lawsuits-her/.

93. "Joint Statement from Elections Infrastructure Government Coordinating Council & the Election Infrastructure Sector Coordinating Committees," Cybersecurity and Infrastructure Security Agency, November 12, 2020, https://www.cisa.gov/news/2020/11/12/joint-statement-elections-infrastructure -government-coordinating-council-election; David E. Sanger, Matt Stevens, and Nicole Perlroth, "Election Officials Directly Contradict Trump on Voting System Fraud," *New York Times*, November 12, 2020, updated November 16, 2020; Michael Balsamo, "Disputing Trump, Barr Says No Widespread Election Fraud," Associated Press, December 1, 2020, https://apnews.com/article /barr-no-widespread-election-fraud-b1f1488796c9a98c4b1a9061a6c7f49d.

94. Nick Corasaniti, Reid J. Epstein, and Jim Rutenberg, "The Times Called Officials in Every State: No Evidence of Voter Fraud," *New York Times*, November 10, 2020, updated November 19, 2020.

95. @RealDonaldTrump, Twitter, November 24, 2020, https://twitter.com /realDonaldTrump/status/1331214247955738624; @RealDonaldTrump, November 4, 2020, https://twitter.com/realDonaldTrump/status /1324108200141082624.

96. "I'm Not Advocating for Secession!" *The Rush Limbaugh Show*, December 10, 2020, https://www.rushlimbaugh.com/daily/2020/12/10/im-not-advocating-for -seccesion/; Tom Jones, "Rush Limbaugh Backtracked a Reckless Claim That Part of the Country Was 'Trending toward Secession," Poynter, December 13, 2020, https://www.poynter.org/newsletters/2020/rush-limbaugh-backtracked

-a-reckless-claim-that-part-of-the-country-was-trending-toward-secession/; Nancy LeTourneau, "Why Rush Limbaugh Is Laughing All the Way to the Bank," *Washington Monthly*, December 15, 2020, https://washingtonmonthly .com/2020/12/15/why-rush-limbaugh-is-laughing-all-the-way-to-the-bank/; "The State of Texas Isn't Asking SCOTUS to Pick a Winner," *The Rush Limbaugh Show*, December 10, 2020, https://www.rushlimbaugh.com/daily/2020 /12/10/what-the-state-of-texas-is-asking-scotus-to-do/.

97. "Right-Wing Host Eric Metaxas: 'We Need to Fight to the Death, to the Last Drop of Blood,'" Media Matters for America, December 10, 2020, https:// www.mediamatters.org/charlie-kirk/right-wing-radio-host-eric-metaxas-we -need-fight-death-last-drop-blood; "About Eric," *The Eric Metaxas Show*, https://metaxastalk.com/about-eric/.

98. Eric Wemple, "Sean Hannity, America's No. 2 Threat to Democracy," *Washington Post*, December 14, 2020; Lis Power, "In the 2 Weeks After It Called the Election, Fox News Cast Doubt on the Results Nearly 800 Times," Media Matters for America, January 14, 2021, https://www.mediamatters.org/fox -news/2-weeks-after-it-called-election-fox-news-cast-doubt-results-nearly-800 -times.

99. Chris Kahn, "Half of Republicans Say Biden Won Because of a 'Rigged' Election: Reuters/Ipsos Poll," Reuters, November 18, 2020.

100. @realDonaldTrump, Twitter, December 2, 2020, https://twitter.com /realDonaldTrump/status/1334303260279234562; Tom Jones, "President Trump's Latest Speech Is a Greatest Hits of Election Lies," *Poynter Report*, December 3, 2020; Aamer Madhani and Kevin Freking, "In Video, Trump Recycles Unsubstantiated Voter Fraud Claims," Associated Press, December 2, 2020, https://apnews.com/article/joe-biden-donald-trump-media-social -media-elections-71d5469ac0bbccbfe601528a2517b239.

101. Nomaan Merchant, Alanna Durkin Richer, and Mark Sherman, Associated Press, "Supreme Court Rejects Republican Attack on Biden Victory," *Chicago Tribune*, December 12, 2020.

102. @realDonaldTrump, Twitter, December 11, 2020, https://twitter.com /realDonaldTrump/status/1337629306919538694; @realDonaldTrump, Twitter, December 12, 2020, https://twitter.com/realDonaldTrump/status /1337749020706549762; @realDonaldTrump, Twitter, December 12, 2020, https://twitter.com/realDonaldTrump/status/1337754366569295874; @realDonaldTrump, Twitter, December 12, 2020, https://twitter.com /realDonaldTrump/status/1337755964339081216; @realDonaldTrump, Twitter, December 12, 2020, https://twitter.com/realDonaldTrump/status /1337774011376340992.

103. Matt Mathers, "Conspiracy Theorist Alex Jones Accused of Inciting Violence after Saying Biden Will Be Removed 'One Way or the Other,'" *Independent*, December 14, 2020.

104. "Proud Boys," Southern Poverty Law Center, 2021, https://www.splcenter.org /fighting-hate/extremist-files/group/proud-boys; Anisa Holmes, "Protesters Ripped, Set Fire to BLM Signs at Two DC Churches, Organizers Respond," NBC-4 Washington, December 13, 2020, https://www.nbcwashington.com/news /protesters-rip-set-fire-to-blm-signs-at-two-dc-churches-organizers-respond /2507057/; Ashraf Khalil, "DC Police Seeking Church Vandals after Weekend Clashes," Associated Press, December 14, 2020, https://apnews.com/article/donald -trump-politics-race-and-ethnicity-arrests-e1f2a2c9c471e101c945482766744d1f; Hailey Fuchs, Pranshu Verma, and Nicholas Bogel-Burroughs, "4 Stabbed and One Shot as Trump Supporters and Opponents Clash," *New York Times*, December 12, 2020; Ellie Hall, "Four People Were Stabbed and One Shot during Pro-Trump Rallies," *BuzzFeed News*, December 13, 2020, https://www .buzzfeednews.com/article/ellievhall/pro-trump-dc-rally-stabbing.

105. "Confirmed US Virus Cases Top 20M," *Chicago Tribune*, January 2, 2021; Heather Hollingsworth and Marion Renault, "One-Day US Deaths Top 3,000, More than D-Day or 9/11," Associated Press, December 10, 2020, https://apnews.com/article/public-health-new-york-new-york-city -coronavirus-pandemic-a203294d021661100b57ddaeaa08bda9; "Fact Check: US COVID-19 Deaths from Dec. 1–5 Rival the Toll from the Pearl Harbor Attack," *USA Today*, December 10, 2020, https://www.usatoday.com/story /news/factcheck/2020/12/10/fact-check-covid-19-deaths-rival-pearl-harbor-toll /6506431002/; "Coronavirus in the U.S.: Latest Map and Case Count," *New York Times*, December 17, 2020, https://www.nytimes.com/interactive/2020 /us/coronavirus-us-cases.html.

106. @realDonaldTrump, Twitter, December 14, 2020, https://twitter.com /LLinWood/status/1338715369566048256; @realDonaldTrump, Twitter, December 18, 2020, https://twitter.com/realDonaldTrump/status /1339953001847525379; @realDonaldTrump, Twitter, December 25, 2020, https://twitter.com/realDonaldTrump/status/1342624069687062528; @realDonaldTrump, Twitter, December 31, 2020, https://twitter.com /realDonaldTrump/status/1344867566456627201.

107. Amy Gardner, "'I Just Want to Find 11,780 Votes,'" *Washington Post*, January 3, 2021; Ben Collins, Brandy Zadrozny, and Jane C. Timm, "Trump Pushed QAnon and 4chan-Created Conspiracy Theories in Georgia Call," NBC News, January 4, 2021, https://www.nbcnews.com/tech/internet/trump-pushed -qanon-4chan-created-conspiracy-theories-georgia-call-n1252769.

108. @realDonaldTrump, Twitter, January 5, 2021 https://twitter.com
/realDonaldTrump/status/1346488314157797389; @realDonaldTrump,
Twitter, January 5, 2020, https://twitter.com/realDonaldTrump/status
/1346693906990305280; Lynn Sweet, "Republican Rep Fears Potential for
Violence over Electoral College," *Chicago Sun-Times*, December 28, 2020.

109. Michael M. Grynbaum, Tiffany Hsu, Katie Robertson, and Keith Collins,
"How Right-Wing Radio Stoked Anger before the Capitol Siege," *New York
Times*, February 10, 2021; Paul Farhi, "Talk-Radio Owner Orders Conservative Hosts to Temper Election Fraud Rhetoric," *Washington Post*, January 11,
2021.

110. Dan Barry, Mike McIntire, and Matthew Rosenberg, "Mob's Battle Cry: 'Our
President Wants Us Here,'" *New York Times*, January 10, 2021, A1.

111. Sheera Frenkel, Associated Press, "How the Storming of Capitol Hill Was
Organized on Social Media," *New York Times*, January 6, 2021; Tali Arbel,
"Extremists Find Escape in Podcasts," *Chicago Tribune*, January 18, 2021, 11.

112. Charlie Savage, "Incitement to Riot? What Trump Told Supporters Before
Mob Stormed Capitol," *New York Times*, January 10, 2021; Rachel Chason
and Samantha Schmidt, "Lafayette Square, Capitol Rallies Met Starkly Different Police Response," *Washington Post*, January 14, 2021; Ashley Parker, Josh
Dawsey, and Philip Rucker, "Six Hours of Paralysis: Inside Trump's Failure
to Act After a Mob Stormed the Capitol," *Washington Post*, January 11, 2021;
Blake, "What Trump Said."

113. Lauren Leatherby, Arielle Ray, Anjali Singhvi, Christiaan Triebert, Derek
Watkins, and Haley Willis, "How a Presidential Rally Turned into a Capitol
Rampage," *New York Times*, January 12, 2021; James Poniewozik, "The Attack
on the Capitol Was Even Worse Than It Looked," *New York Times*, January
11, 2021; Chason and Schmidt, "Lafayette Square, Capitol Rallies"; Sabrina
Tavernise and Matthew Rosenberg, "These Are the Rioters Who Stormed
the Nation's Capitol," *New York Times*, January 7, 2021; Nicholas Fandos and
Emily Cochrane, "After Pro-Trump Mob Storms Capitol, Congress Confirms
Biden's Win," *New York Times*, January 6, 2021; Tom Jackman, "Police Union
Says 140 Officers Injured in Capitol Riot," *Washington Post*, January 27, 2021;
Jan Wolfe, "Four Officers Who Responded to U.S. Capitol Attack Have
Died by Suicide," Reuters, August 2, 2021, https://www.reuters.com/world/us
/officer-who-responded-us-capitol-attack-is-third-die-by-suicide-2021-08-02/.

114. David Bauder, "Journalists Recount Harrowing Attacks amid Capitol Riot," Associated Press, January 8, 2021, https://apnews.com
/article/donald-trump-new-york-journalists-media-social-media
-cba6bd7b93be0ade1da714a32c33d74c; Joseph Choi, "Videos Show

Protestors outside Capitol Destroying Journalists' Equipment," *Hill*, January 6, 2021, https://thehill.com/homenews/news/533022-videos-show-protesters-outside-capitol-destroying-journalists-equipment.

115. Michael M. Grynbaum, John Koblin, and Tiffany Hsu, "TV Networks Shift from Coverage of Electoral Tally to Storming of Capitol," *New York Times*, January 6, 2021; Tom Jones, "Looking Back at the Media Coverage from Wednesday's Astonishing Day in America," *Poynter Report*, January 6, 2021.

116. @realDonaldTrump, Twitter, January 6, 2021, Trump Twitter Archive, http://www.thetrumparchive.com/; Jamie Gangel, Kevin Liptak, Michael Warren, and Marshall Cohen, "New Details about Trump-McCarthy Shouting Match Show Trump Refused to Call Off the Rioters," CNN Politics, February 12, 2021, https://www.cnn.com/2021/02/12/politics/trump-mccarthy-shouting-match-details/index.html; Parker, Dawsey, and Rucker, "Six Hours of Paralysis."

117. Nicholas Fandos and Emily Cochrane, "After Pro-Trump Mob Storms Capitol, Congress Confirms Biden's Win," *New York Times*, January 6, 2021; Colby Itkowitz, Felicia Sonmez, John Wagner, Amy B. Yang, and Marisa Iati, "Pelosi, Schumer Call for Trump's Removal," *Washington Post*, January 7, 2021.

118. Grynbaum, Koblin, and Hsu, "TV Networks Shift from Coverage"; Astead W. Herndon, "How Republicans Are Warping Reality around the Capitol Attack," *New York Times*, January 17, 2021; Tom Jones, "Shameful," *Poynter Report*, January 7, 2021.

119. "Rules for Rioters," *The Rush Limbaugh Show*, January 7, 2021, https://www.rushlimbaugh.com/daily/2021/01/07/rules-for-rioters-it-doesnt-matter-what-you-do-its-who-you-are-when-youre-doing-it/.

120. Tom Jones, "Chilling Words," *Poynter Report*, January 7, 2021; "Trump Caused the Assault on the Capitol: He Must Be Removed," *Washington Post*, January 6, 2021; "Invoke the 25th Amendment: Trump Needs to Go," *Chicago Tribune*, January 8, 2021, 13; "Donald Trump's Final Days," *Wall Street Journal*, January 7, 2021.

121. Clerk of United States House of Representatives, "Roll Call 17; Bill Number H. Res. 24," January 13, 2021, 117th Congress, 1st sess., https://clerk.house.gov/Votes/202117; Nicholas Fandos, "Trump Impeached for Inciting Insurrection," *New York Times*, January 13, 2021; Ashlyn Still, JM Rieger, and Adrian Blanco, "How Democratic and Republican Senators Voted on Trump's Second Impeachment," *Washington Post*, February 13, 2021; Aaron Blake, "199 Legal Experts Say Senate Must Not Acquit Trump over Constitutionality Issue," *Washington Post*, February 12, 2021.

122. Lisa Kashinsky, "Full Text of Trump's Statement on Impeachment," *Boston Herald*, February 13, 2021.

123. John Koblin and Michael M. Grynbaum, "From Trump to Biden, TV Captures a Dramatic Shift," *New York Times*, January 20, 2021; Meridith McGraw and Marc Caputo, "Trump Builds 'Turnkey' Campaign Operation for 2024," *Politico*, September 7, 2021, https://www.politico.com/news/2021/09/07/trump-campaign-operation-2024-510013.

124. Will Stone, "On Trump's Last Full Day, Nation Records 400,000 COVID Deaths," *Kaiser Health News*, January 19, 2021, https://khn.org/news/nation-records-400000-covid-deaths-on-last-day-of-donald-trump-presidency/; "America's Wars," Department of Veterans Affairs, November 2020, https://www.va.gov/opa/publications/factsheets/fs_americas_wars.pdf; Shoshana Zuboff, "The Knowledge Coup," *New York Times*, January 31, 2021; "Mortality Analyses," Coronavirus Resource Center, Johns Hopkins University School of Medicine, updated January 28, 2021, https://coronavirus.jhu.edu/data/mortality.

125. Joel Rose, "Even If It's 'Bonkers,' Poll Finds Many Believe QAnon and Other Conspiracy Theories," National Public Radio, December 30, 2020, https://www.npr.org/2020/12/30/951095644/even-if-its-bonkers-poll-finds-many-believe-qanon-and-other-conspiracy-theories; Daniel A. Cox, "After the Ballots Are Counted: Conspiracies, Political Violence, and American Exceptionalism," Survey Center on American Life, February 13, 2021, https://www.americansurveycenter.org/research/after-the-ballots-are-counted-conspiracies-political-violence-and-american-exceptionalism/.

126. Sarah E. Needleman, "Facebook Says It Is Removing All Content Mentioning 'Stop the Steal,'" *Wall Street Journal*, January 11, 2011; Tony Romm and Elizabeth Dwoskin, "Trump Banned from Facebook Indefinitely, CEO Mark Zuckerberg Says," *Washington Post*, January 7, 2021; Kevin Roose, "Who's Boss? 2 Tech Giants," *New York Times*, January 10, 2021, A1; Kate Conger and Mike Isaac, "Twitter Permanently Bans Trump, Capping Online Revolt," *New York Times*, January 8, 2021; Brendan Cole, "Donald Trump Sent Record 12,200 Tweets in 2020, Ends Year with Stock Market Boast," *Newsweek*, January 1, 2021, https://www.newsweek.com/donald-trump-record-12200-tweets-2020-stock-market-boast-1558415.

127. Tony Romm and Rachel Lerman, "Amazon Suspends Parler, Taking Pro-Trump Site Offline Indefinitely," *Washington Post*, January 11, 2021; Elizabeth Dwoskin and Craig Timberg, "Misinformation Dropped Dramatically the Week After Twitter Banned Trump and Some Allies," *Washington Post*, January 16, 2021.

12. PRESIDENTS AND THE CRISIS OF THE PRESS

1. Tiffany Hsu and Katie Robertson, "War-Zone Experience Carries Journalists into Inauguration Coverage," *New York Times*, January 19, 2021.

2. "Inaugural Address by President Joseph R. Biden, Jr.," White House, January 20, 2021, https://www.whitehouse.gov/briefing-room/speeches-remarks/2021/01/20/inaugural-address-by-president-joseph-r-biden-jr/.

3. "Two Pieces That Come Close to Explaining What I Felt Watching the Inauguration," *The Rush Limbaugh Show*, January 21, 2021, https://www.rushlimbaugh.com/daily/2021/01/21/two-pieces-that-come-close-to-explaining-what-i-felt-watching-the-inauguration/; "Why Are You a Republican?" *The Rush Limbaugh Show*, January 21, 2021, https://www.rushlimbaugh.com/daily/2021/01/21/why-are-you-a-republican/; "Tucker: What Biden's War on White Supremacy Is Really About," Fox News, January 20, 2021; Helen Coster, "From 'See You Soon' to Call for 'Unity': How America's Transfer of Power Played Out on TV," Reuters, January 20, 2021, https://www.reuters.com/article/us-usa-biden-inauguration-tv/from-see-you-soon-to-call-for-unity-how-americas-transfer-of-power-played-out-on-tv-idUSKBN29P23E.

4. Margaret Sullivan, "The Media Can Be Glad for the Biden White House's Return to Normalcy: But Let's Not Be Lulled," *Washington Post*, January 21, 2021.

5. Zachary Evans, "Biden Admonishes Reporter for Questioning Whether Vaccine Goal Is Ambitious Enough: 'Give Me a Break,'" *National Review*, January 21, 2021, https://news.yahoo.com/biden-admonishes-reporter-questioning-whether-211143831.html; "'Give Me a Break!' President Joe Biden Snaps Back at Reporter for Question on Vaccine Roll Out," Fox News Now, January 21, 2021, https://www.youtube.com/watch?v=VbQL9lvmBdo.

6. "Biden Promise Tracker," PolitiFact, https://www.politifact.com/truth-o-meter/promises/biden-promise-tracker/; Linda Qiu, "The First Week in the Oval Office," *New York Times*, January 31, 2021, A19.

7. Deakin, "Problem of Presidential-Press Relations," 17.

8. Timothy Snyder, "The American Abyss: Trump, the Mob and What Comes Next," *New York Times Magazine*, January 17, 2021, 32–33.

9. "Tribune Tower," Chicago Architecture Center, https://www.architecture.org/learn/resources/buildings-of-chicago/building/tribune-tower/; Ryan Ori, "Chicago Tribune to Exit Prudential Plaza, Move Newsroom to Printing Facility," *Chicago Tribune*, January 11, 2021; David Roeder, "Tribune Publishing Selling Itself to N.Y. Hedge Fund," *Chicago Sun-Times*, February 17, 2021,

16; Rick Edmonds, "Alden Buyouts Have Eliminated More Than 10 Percent of Tribune Publishing Newsroom Staffing in Just Six Weeks," Poynter, July 1, 2021, https://www.poynter.org/locally/2021/alden-buyouts-have-eliminated-more-than-10-of-tribune-publishing-newsroom-staffing-in-just-six-weeks/.

10. Ritchie, *Reporting from Washington*, ix; Gillmor, *We the Media*, xxvi.

11. Pickard, "When Commercialism Trumps Democracy," 198; Rick Edmonds, "Chatham Asset Management, a Hedge Fund, Has Won the Auction to Buy the McClatchy Newspaper Chain," Poynter, July 12, 2020; A. S. Jones, *Losing the News*, xv–xvi.

12. A. S. Jones, *Losing the News*, 20; "Google Benefit from News Content," News Media Alliance Economic Study, June 2019, 3, http://www.newsmediaalliance.org/wp-content/uploads/2019/06/Google-Benefit-from-News-Content.pdf; Kurt Wagner, "Digital Advertising in the US Is Finally Bigger than Print and Television," *Recode by Vox*, February 20, 2019, https://www.vox.com/2019/2/20/18232433/digital-advertising-facebook-google-growth-tv-print-emarketer-2019; Steven Hill, "Biden Should Revoke Section 230 Before We Lose Our Democracy," *Chicago Tribune*, January 29, 2021, 15.

13. Galen Stocking, Patrick Van Kessel, Michael Barthel, Katerina Eva Matisa, and Maya Khuzam, "Many Americans Get News on YouTube, Where News Organizations and Independent Producers Thrive Side by Side," Pew Research Center, September 28, 2020, https://www.journalism.org/2020/09/28/many-americans-get-news-on-youtube-where-news-organizations-and-independent-producers-thrive-side-by-side/; Wagner, "Digital Advertising."

14. Steven Waldman, "The Coming Era of 'Civic News,'" *Washington Monthly*, November–December 2020, https://washingtonmonthly.com/magazine/november-december-2020/the-coming-era-of-civic-news/; *Expanding News Desert*, University of North Carolina Hussman School of Journalism and Media, 2021, https://www.usnewsdeserts.com/reports/news-deserts-and-ghost-newspapers-will-local-news-survive/the-news-landscape-in-2020-transformed-and-diminished/; Robert Channick, "COVID-19 Pandemic Hits Chicago Media Hard," *Chicago Tribune*, July 10, 2020; Marc Tracy, "News Media Outlets Have Been Ravaged by the Pandemic," *New York Times*, April 10, 2020.

15. Hamilton, *Democracy's Detectives*, 16, 46–47.

16. Sara Fischer, "Trump Bump: NYT and WaPo Digital Subscriptions Tripled since 2016," *Axios*, November 24, 2020, https://www.axios.com/washington-post-new-york-times-subscriptions-8e888fd7-5484-44c7-ad43-39564e06c84f.html; Ben Smith, "It's the End of an Era for the Media, No Matter Who Wins the Election," *New York Times*, November 1, 2020.

17. Piore, "Tuned Out," 91; "2Q Is Most-Watched Quarter in CNN's 40 Year History," CNN Press Room, June 30, 2020.

18. Felix Richter, "The Steady Rise of Podcasts," Statista, May 26, 2020, https://www.statista.com/chart/10713/podcast-listeners-in-the-united-states/.

19. Starr, *The Creation of the Media*, 88–89; Pickard, *America's Battle for Media Democracy*, 215.

20. Eli Meixler, "Google Has Announced a $300 Million Initiative to Support News Organizations," *Fortune*, March 21, 2018; Paul Farhi, Sarah Ellison, and Elahe Izadi, "The Coronavirus Crisis Is Devastating the News Industry," *New York Times*, April 8, 2020; Craig Timberg, "Facebook to Offer 'News' Tab for Users—and Pay (Some) Publishers for Their Work," *New York Times*, October 23, 2019.

21. David McCabe, "Maryland Approves Country's First Tax on Big Tech's Ad Revenue," *New York Times*, February 12, 2021; United States House of Representatives, Subcommittee on Antitrust, Commercial, and Administrative Law of the Committee on the Judiciary, *Investigation of Competition in Digital Markets*, 6–7; Tony Romm, Cat Zakrzewski, and Rachel Lerman, "House Investigation Faults Amazon, Apple, Facebook and Google for Engaging in Anti-Competitive Monopoly Tactics," *Washington Post*, October 6, 2020; Mike Isaac and Damien Cave, *New York Times*, February 22, 2021.

22. H.R. 3940—Local Journalism Sustainability Act, 117th Congress (2021–22), https://www.congress.gov/bill/117th-congress/house-bill/3940; Waldman, "Coming Era of 'Civic News.'"

23. Corporation for Public Broadcasting, "CPB Operating Budget 2020" and "Federal Appropriation," https://www.cpb.org/aboutcpb/financials/budget/.

24. Mona Charen, "Even Post-Trump, Republicans Must Confess Complicity in the Big Lie," *Chicago Sun-Times*, January 23, 2021.

25. Jeremy Barr and Elahe Izadi, "Smartmatic Files $2.7 Billion Defamation Suit against Fox News over Election Fraud Claims," *Washington Post*, February 4, 2021; "Facts about Dominion, Smartmatic You Should Know," Newsmax, December 19, 2020, https://www.newsmax.com/us/smartmatic-dominion-voting-systems-software-election/2020/12/19/id/1002355/.

26. Shoshana Zuboff, "The Knowledge Coup," *New York Times*, January 31, 2021.

27. Jonathan Chait, "How Trumpism Has Become a Cult of Losing," *New York*, February 26, 2021, https://nymag.com/intelligencer/article/donald-trump-cpac-golden-calf-election-loser.html.

28. Kevin Roose, Mike Isaac, and Sheera Frenkel, "Facebook Struggles to Balance Civility and Growth," *New York Times*, November 24, 2020.

29. Shorenstein Center of Media, Politics and Public Policy, "Combating Fake News"; Kevin Roose, "How the Biden Administration Can Help Solve Our Reality Crisis," *New York Times*, February 2, 2021.

30. Will, *Conservative Sensibility*, 107; Greenberg, *Republic of Spin*, 47–48; David Greenberg, "How Teddy Roosevelt Invented Spin," *Atlantic*, January 24, 2016.

31. Parks, "Covering Trump's 'Carnival,'" 1–3, 5–6.

32. Pope, "Time of Opportunity," 7.

33. Rosen, "Send the Interns."

34. Karpf, "We All Stand Together," 226.

35. Jason Leopold and Anthony Cormier, "President Trump Directed His Attorney Michael Cohen to Lie to Congress about the Moscow Tower Project," *BuzzFeed News*, January 17, 2019, https://www.buzzfeednews.com/article/jasonleopold/trump-russia-cohen-moscow-tower-mueller-investigation.

36. Brian Flood, "CNN, MSNBC Mentioned Trump Impeachment Nearly 200 Times Friday Before BuzzFeed Report Was Discredited," Fox News, January 21, 2019, https://www.foxnews.com/entertainment/cnn-msnbc-mentioned -trump-impeachment-nearly-200-times-friday-before-buzzfeed-report-was -discredited.

37. Mark Mazzetti and Sharon LaFraniere, "Mueller Statement Refutes Report That Trump Directed Cohen to Lie," *New York Times*, January 18, 2019; @ RealDonaldTrump, Twitter, January 19, 2020.

38. Michael M. Grynbaum and Sydney Ember, "CNN Corrects a Trump Story, Fueling Claims of 'Fake News,'" *New York Times*, December 8, 2017; Steven Arons, "Deutsche Bank Records Said to Be Subpoenaed by Mueller," *Bloomberg*, December 5, 2017, corrected December 6, 2017, https:// www.bloomberg.com/news/articles/2017-12-05/deutsche-bank-said-to-be -subpoenaed-by-mueller; Manu Raja and Jeremy Herb, "Email Pointed Trump Campaign to WikiLeaks Documents," CNN Politics, December 8, 2017, https://www.cnn.com/2017/12/08/politics/email-effort-give-trump -campaign-wikileaks-documents/index.html.

39. Helen Stubbs, "Bias in Others' News a Greater Concern Than Bias in Own News," Gallup News, September 10, 2020, https://news.gallup.com/poll /319724/bias-others-news-greater-concern-bias-own-news.aspx; Benkler, Faris, and Roberts, *Network Propaganda*, 16.

40. Padgett, Dunaway, and Darr, "As Seen on TV?"

41. Eli J. Finkel et al., "Political Sectarianism in America," *Science*, October 30, 2020, 533–36; Rani Molla, "Social Media Is Making a Bad Political Situation Worse," *Recode by Vox*, November 10, 2020; Mason, *Uncivil Agreement*, 6; Abramowitz, *Polarized Public?*, xii, xv, 8.

42. Levitsky and Ziblatt, *How Democracies Die*, 9.

43. Dwight D. Eisenhower, news conference, July 7, 1954, in *Public Papers of the Presidents*, 623–24; Associated Press, "Reply by Ike," *Sacramento Bee*, July 8, 1954, 18; "Resident Annoyed by Query on Travel Race Ban Support," *Washington Evening Star*, July 7, 1954, 1.

44. Women's Media Center, "Status of Women in U.S. Media 2019," 11; Durham, review of *No Longer Newsworthy*, 549–50; "2018 Survey," News Leaders Association, November 15, 2018, https://members.newsleaders.org/diversity-survey-2018; Radio Television Digital News Association, "2020 Research."

45. Gillmor, *We the Media*, xviii.

46. Amy Yee, "To Recognize Misinformation in Media, Teach a Generation While It's Young," *New York Times*, October 23, 2020; Kristy Roschke, "Why Teach Students about Media Literacy—and How," *Intelligencer*, January 23, 2021, https://ajha.wildapricot.org/Intelligencer/9980218.

47. Center for News Literacy, Stony Brook University School of Journalism, https://www.centerfornewsliteracy.org/; News Literary Project, https://newslit.org/about/; Yee, "To Recognize Misinformation"; Media Literacy Now, https://medialiteracynow.org/.

48. "Universities with Courses in News or Media Literacy," Center for News Excellence & Engagement, https://www.news-excellence.org/universities-with-courses-in-news-or-media-literacy/; "Media Literacy Minor," Academic Catalog, Ithaca College, https://catalog.ithaca.edu/undergrad/schools/school-humanities-sciences/interdisciplinary-studies/media-literacy/; "Media Literacy Minor," Metropolitan State University, https://www.metrostate.edu/academics/programs/media-literacy-minor; University Catalog 2020–21, "Media Literacy—Minor," Kent State University, http://catalog.kent.edu/colleges/ci/mdj/media-literacy-minor/; "Minor in Media Literacy," Academic Bulletin (2020–21), San Francisco State University, http://bulletin.sfsu.edu/colleges/liberal-creative-arts/broadcast-electronic-communication-arts/minor-media-literacy/.

49. S. 2240—Digital Citizenship and Media Literacy Act, 116th Congress (2019–20), https://www.congress.gov/bill/116th-congress/senate-bill/2240/actions; Yee, "To Recognize Misinformation."

50. "Presidential Historians Survey 2017," C-SPAN, https://www.c-span.org/presidentsurvey2017/?page=overall; "American Presidents: Greatest and Worst," Siena College Research Institute, February 13, 2019, https://scri.siena.edu/wp-content/uploads/2019/02/2019_Release_2018_Final.pdf; American Political Science Association survey, in Brandon Rottinghaus and Justin S. Vaughn, "Measuring Obama against the Great Presidents," Brookings, February 13, 2015.

BIBLIOGRAPHY

One of the joys of researching this book was finding articles, editorials, cartoons, and other material in more than six dozen newspapers and magazines stretching back to the 1790s. I was able to access these primary sources using the digital archives of America's Historical Newspapers, Gale's Nineteenth Century U.S. Newspapers, NewsBank, ProQuest, and Readex's African American Newspapers series. In addition, I gathered information and ideas from the following archives, collections, books, journal articles, and other published works.

ARCHIVES AND MANUSCRIPT MATERIALS

Abraham Lincoln Papers. Library of Congress, Washington DC. https://www.loc
.gov/collections/abraham-lincoln-papers/.

American Presidency Project. University of California Santa Barbara. https://www
.presidency.ucsb.edu/.

American Rhetoric. Online Speech Bank. https://www.americanrhetoric.com/.

Associated Press Collections Online. Gale Cengage Learning. https://www.gale
.com/primary-sources/associated-press-collections-online.

Barack Obama Presidential Library. https://www.obamalibrary.gov/research.

Collected Works of Abraham Lincoln. Abraham Lincoln Association, University of
Michigan, Ann Arbor. https://quod.lib.umich.edu/l/lincoln/.

Commission on Presidential Debates. https://www.debates.org/.

Corporation for Public Broadcasting. Annual Budgets. https://www.cpb.org
/aboutcpb/financials/budget/.

C-SPAN Executive Branch Archive. https://www.c-span.org/executiveBranch/.

Electoral College Results. National Archives. https://www.archives.gov/electoral-college.

Franklin D. Roosevelt Presidential Library and Museum, Digitized Collections. https://fdrlibrary.org/archives.

Gallup Historical Statistics and Trends. Presidential Approval Ratings. https://news.gallup.com/poll/116677/presidential-approval-ratings-gallup-historical-statistics-trends.aspx.

George W. Bush Presidential Library and Museum, Dallas. https://www.georgewbushlibrary.gov/.

Historic American Newspapers, 1789–1963. Chronicling America. Library of Congress, Washington DC. https://chroniclingamerica.loc.gov/.

Internet Archive. www.archive.org.

John F. Kennedy Presidential Library and Museum, Archival Collections. https://www.jfklibrary.org/archives/about-archival-collections.

Memorandum, Bruce Ladd to Ron Ziegler. "Nixon Press Operation." November 25, 1968. Copy provided by Bruce Ladd to the author.

National Security Archive. George Washington University, Washington DC. https://nsarchive.gwu.edu/.

Presidential Speeches. Miller Center, University of Virginia, Charlottesville. https://millercenter.org/the-presidency/presidential-speeches.

Presidents of the United States. Library of Congress, Washington DC. http://www.loc.gov/rr/program/bib/presidents/.

Public Papers of the Presidents of the United States. Office of the Federal Register, National Archives and Records Administration, Washington DC. https://www.govinfo.gov/app/collection/PPP.

Richard Nixon Presidential Library and Museum, Yorba Linda CA. https://www.nixonlibrary.gov/research/guide-holdings.

Ronald Reagan Presidential Library and Museum, Simi Valley CA. https://www.reaganlibrary.gov/archives.

Roper Center for Public Opinion, Cornell University, Ithaca NY. https://ropercenter.cornell.edu.

Trump Twitter Archive. http://www.thetrumparchive.com/.

United States Census Bureau. History, Through the Decades. https://www.census.gov/history/www/through_the_decades/fast_facts/.

United States Elections Web Archive. Library of Congress, Washington DC. https://www.loc.gov/collections/united-states-elections-web-archive/about-this-collection/.

United States House of Representatives. History, Art & Archives. https://history.house.gov/.

Vanderbilt Television News Archive, Nashville TN. https://tvnews.vanderbilt.edu/.

White House Diaries. Ronald Reagan Presidential Foundation & Institute, Simi Valley CA. https://www.reaganfoundation.org/ronald-reagan/white-house-diaries/diary-entry-01201981/.

White House Transcripts. www.whitehouse.gov.

William J. Clinton Presidential Library and Museum, Little Rock AR. https://clinton.presidentiallibraries.us/.

Woodrow Wilson Papers. Library of Congress, Washington DC. https://www.loc.gov/collections/woodrow-wilson-papers/.

PUBLISHED WORKS

Abramowitz, Alan. *The Polarized Public? Why American Government Is So Dysfunctional.* Boston: Pearson, 2013.

Adams, John. *The Works of John Adams, Second President of the United States: With a Life of the Author.* Vol. 9. Edited by Charles Francis Adams. Boston: Little, Brown, 1856.

Allan, Stuart. *Online News: Journalism and the Internet.* New York: McGraw Hill Education, 2006.

Allen, Craig. *Eisenhower and the Mass Media: Peace, Prosperity & Prime-Time TV.* Chapel Hill: University of North Carolina Press, 1993.

Alterman, Eric. *What Liberal Media? The Truth about Bias and the News.* New York: Perseus Books, 2003.

Ambrose, Stephen E. *Nixon.* Vol. 1, *The Education of a Politician, 1913–1962.* New York: Simon & Schuster, 1987.

"Amnesty and Pardon for Political Prisoners." Hearings before a Subcommittee of the Committee on the Judiciary, U.S. Senate, 66th Congress, 1921.

Anderson, David D. *Woodrow Wilson.* Boston: Twayne, 1978.

"Armistice Terms Granted to Central Powers." Library of Congress, Articles and Essays. Accessed September 25, 2021. https://www.loc.gov/collections/world-war-i-rotogravures/articles-and-essays/events-and-statistics/armistice-terms/.

Auletta, Ken. *Three Blind Mice: How the TV Networks Lost Their Way.* New York: Random House, 1991.

Austin, Aleine. *Matthew Lyon: "New Man" of the Democratic Revolution, 1749–1822.* University Park: Pennsylvania State University Press, 1981.

Avery, Donald. "Battle without a Rule Book." In *The Press in Times of Crisis*, edited by Lloyd Chiasson Jr. Westport CT: Greenwood Press, 1995.

Axelrod, David. *Believer: My Forty Years in Politics.* New York: Penguin Press, 2015.

Bacon, Jacqueline. *Freedom's Journal: The First African-American Newspaper.* Lanham MD: Lexington Books, 2007.

Banner, James M., Jr., ed. *Presidential Misconduct from George Washington to Today.* New York: New Press, 2019.

Banning, Stephen. "'Determined to Suppress Everything like Free Speech': Lincoln's Private Letters Reveal Aggressive Use of Newspaper Censorship." *Journalism History* 46, no. 2 (June 2020): 106–23.

Beasley, Maurine H. *Women of the Washington Press: Politics, Prejudice, and Persistence.* Medill School of Journalism Visions of the American Press. Evanston IL: Northwestern University Press, 2012.

Becker, Samuel L. "Presidential Power: The influence of Broadcasting." *Quarterly Journal of Speech* 47, no. 1 (February 1961): 10–18.

Benkler, Yochai, Robert Faris, and Hal Roberts. *Network Propaganda: Manipulation, Disinformation, and Radicalization in American Politics.* New York: Oxford University Press, 2018.

Benkler, Yochai, Robert Faris, Hal Roberts, and Ethan Zuckerman. "Study: Breitbart-Led Right-Wing Media System Altered Broader Media Agenda." *Columbia Journalism Review*, March 3, 2017. https://www.cjr.org/analysis /breitbart-media-trump-harvard-study.php.

Bennett, W. Lance, Regina G. Lawrence, and Steven Livingston. *When the Press Fails: Political Power and the News Media from Iraq to Katrina.* Chicago: University of Chicago Press, 2007.

Berg, A. Scott. *Wilson.* New York: G. P. Putnam's Sons, 2013.

Bernstein, Carl. "A Reporter's Assessment." In *Secret Man: The Story of Watergate's Deep Throat*, by Bob Woodward. New York: Simon & Schuster, 2005.

Bernstein, Carl, and Bob Woodward, *All the President's Men.* New York: Simon & Schuster, 1974; Pocket Books, 2005.

Beschloss, Michael. *Presidents of War.* New York: Crown, 2018.

Bilinski, Alyssa, and Ezekiel J. Emanuel. "COVID-19 and Excess All-Cause Mortality in the US and 18 Comparison Countries." *JAMA*, October 12, 2020, table 1. https://jamanetwork.com/journals/jama/fullarticle/2771841?guestAccessKey =0b2df654-b775-4691-bf01-b6e762f46c6c&utm_source=For_The_Media& utm_medium=referral&utm_campaign=ftm_links&utm_content=tfl&utm _term=101220.

Bird, Wendell. *Press and Speech under Assault: The Early Supreme Court Justices, the Sedition Act of 1798, and the Campaign against Dissent.* Oxford: Oxford University Press, 2016.

Blight, David W. *Frederick Douglass and Abraham Lincoln: A Relationship in Language, Politics, and Memory.* Frank L. Klement Lectures; Alternative Views of the Sectional Conflict. Milwaukee: Marquette University Press, 2001.

―――. *Frederick Douglass: Prophet of Freedom*. New York: Simon & Schuster, 2018.

Block, Herbert. *Herblock's State of the Union*. New York: Simon and Schuster, 1972.

Blum, David. *Tick . . . Tick . . . Tick . . . : The Long Life and Turbulent Times of 60 Minutes*. New York: HarperCollins, 2004.

Boczkowski, Pablo J., and Zizi Papacharissi, eds. *Trump and the Media*. Cambridge MA: MIT Press, 2018.

Borchard, Gregory A., and David W. Bulla. *Lincoln Mediated: The President and the Press through Nineteenth-Century Media*. New Brunswick NJ: Transaction, 2015.

Bowden, Mary Weatherspoon. *Philip Freneau*. Boston: Twayne, 1976.

Bradlee, Ben. *A Good Life: Newspapering and Other Adventures*. New York: Simon & Schuster, 1995.

Brainard, Curtis. "Transparency Watch: A Closed Door." *Columbia Journalism Review*, September–October 2011.

Brands, H. W. *Woodrow Wilson*. The American Presidents Series. New York: Henry Holt, 2003.

Brattebo, Douglas M., and Robert P. Watson. "Making History." In *The Obama Presidency: A Preliminary Assessment*, edited by Robert P. Watson, Jack Covarrubias, Tom Lansford, and Douglas M. Brattebo. Albany: State University of New York Press, 2012.

Brinkley, Alan. *The Publisher: Henry Luce and His American Century*. New York: Alfred A. Knopf, 2010.

Brock, David. *Blinded by the Right: The Conscience of an Ex-Conservative*. New York: Three Rivers Press, 2002.

Brown, Walt. "The Federal Era III: Scissors, Paste, and Ink." In *The American Journalism History Reader*, edited by Bonnie Brennen and Hanno Hardt. New York: Routledge, 2011.

―――. *John Adams and the American Press: Politics and Journalism at the Birth of the Republic*. Jefferson NC: McFarland, 1995.

Buhite, Russell D., and David W. Levy, eds. *FDR's Fireside Chats*. Norman: University of Oklahoma Press, 1992.

Bulla, David W. "Palpable Injury: Abraham Lincoln and Press Suppression in the Civil War North." In *An Indispensable Liberty: The Fight for Free Speech in Nineteenth-Century America*, edited by Mary M. Cronin. Carbondale: Southern Illinois University Press, 2016.

Bureau of Labor Statistics. "Labor Force Statistics from the Current Population Survey." https://data.bls.gov/timeseries/LNS12000000.

Bush, George H. W. *The American Press and the American Presidency.* Gauer Distinguished Lecture in Law and Public Policy, vol. 7. Washington DC: National Legal Center for the Public Interest, 1998.

Butterfield, L. H., Marc Friedlaender, and Mary-Jo Kline, eds. *The Book of Abigail and John: Selected Letters of the Adams Family, 1762–1784.* Boston: Northeastern University Press, 2002.

Byrne, Malcolm. *Iran-Contra: Reagan's Scandal and the Unchecked Abuse of Presidential Power.* Lawrence: University Press of Kansas, 2014.

Campbell, Richard. *60 Minutes and the News: A Mythology for Middle America.* Urbana: University of Illinois Press, 1991.

Campbell, W. Joseph. *Getting It Wrong: Ten of the Greatest Misreported Stories in American Journalism.* Berkeley: University of California Press, 2010.

Cannon, Lou. *President Reagan: The Role of a Lifetime.* New York: Simon & Schuster, 1991.

Casey, Steven. *The War Beat, Europe: The American Media at War against Nazi Germany.* New York: Oxford University Press, 2017.

Chernow, Ron. *Alexander Hamilton.* New York: Penguin Press, 2004.

Chesebrough, David B. *Frederick Douglass: Oratory from Slavery.* Westport CT: Greenwood Press, 1998.

Chiasson, Lloyd, Jr. *The Press in Times of Crisis.* Westport CT: Greenwood Press, 1995.

Clark, Allan C. *William Duane.* Washington DC: W. F. Roberts, 1905.

Clark, Mary Elizabeth. "Peter Porcupine in America: The Career of William Cobbett, 1792–1800." PhD diss., University of Pennsylvania, 1939.

Cohen, Jeffrey E. *The Presidency in the Era of 24-Hour News.* Princeton NJ: Princeton University Press, 2008.

Congressional Quarterly. *Watergate: Chronology of a Crisis.* 2 vols. Washington DC: Congressional Quarterly, 1974.

Congressional Research Service. *The Constitution of the United States of America: Analysis and Interpretation.* Washington DC: U.S. Government Printing Office, 2013.

Cooper, John Milton, Jr. *Woodrow Wilson: A Biography.* New York: Alfred A. Knopf, 2009.

Cooper, Richard T. "Epilogue: The Washington Years." In *Scoop: The Evolution of a Southern Reporter,* by Jack Nelson. Jackson: University Press of Mississippi, 2012.

Cooper, Thomas. *An Account of the Trial of Thomas Cooper of Northumberland on a Charge of Libel against the President of the United States.* Philadelphia: John Bioren, 1800.

Cornwell, Elmer E., Jr. "Wilson, Creel, and the Presidency." *Public Opinion Quarterly* 23, no. 2 (Summer 1959): 189–202.

Creel, George. *How We Advertised America*. New York: Arno Press, 1920.

Cronin, Mary M. *An Indispensable Liberty: The Fight for Free Speech in Nineteenth-Century America*. Carbondale: Southern Illinois University Press, 2016.

Cuillier, David. "Referee Madness: PIOs Increasingly Thwart Access to Government Information." *IRE Journal*, Summer 2013.

Culbert, David Holbrook. *News for Everyman: Radio and Foreign Affairs in Thirties America*. Westport CT: Greenwood Press, 1976.

Dahmen, Nicole Smith, and Erin K. Coyle. "Obama White House Photos Limited by Access Policies." *Newspaper Research Journal* 38, no. 4 (Fall 2017): 439–48.

Dallek, Robert. *Franklin D. Roosevelt: A Political Life*. New York: Penguin Books, 2017.

———. *Ronald Reagan: The Politics of Symbolism*. Cambridge MA: Harvard University Press, 1984.

Daniel, Marcus. *Scandal & Civility: Journalism and the Birth of American Democracy*. New York: Oxford University Press, 2009.

D'Antonio, Michael. *A Consequential President: The Legacy of Barack Obama*. New York: St. Martin's Press, 2016.

Daynes, Byron W., and Glen Sussman. "Environmental Policy and Global Climate Change." In *The Obama Presidency: A Preliminary Assessment*, edited by Robert P. Watson, Jack Covarrubias, Tom Lansford, and Douglas M. Brattebo. Albany: State University of New York Press, 2012.

Deakin, James. "The Problem of Presidential-Press Relations." In *The White House Press on the Presidency: News Management and Co-Option*, edited by Kenneth W. Thompson. Vol. 4. Lanham MD: University Press of America, 1983.

Dean, John W., III. *Blind Ambition: The White House Years*. New York: Simon & Schuster, 1976.

Deaver, Michael K. *Behind the Scenes: In Which the Author Talks about Ronald and Nancy Reagan . . . and Himself*. With Mickey Herskowitz. New York: William Morrow, 1987.

———. *A Different Drummer: My Thirty Years with Ronald Reagan*. New York: HarperCollins, 2001.

Delbanco, Andrew. *The Abolitionist Imagination*. Cambridge MA: Harvard University Press, 2012.

DellaVigna, Stefano, and Ethan Kaplan. "The Fox News Effect: Media Bias and Voting." *Quarterly Journal of Economics* 122, no. 3 (August 2007): 1187–234.

Delli Carpini, Michael X. "Alternative Facts: Donald Trump and the Emergence of a New U.S. Media Regime." In Boczkowski and Papacharissi, *Trump and the Media*, 17–23.

DeWitt, Darin. "Abraham Lincoln." In *Hatred of America's Presidents: Personal Attacks on the White House from Washington to Trump*, edited by Lori Cox Han. Santa Barbara CA: ABC-CLIO, 2018.

Dicken-Garcia, Hazel. *Journalistic Standards in Nineteenth-Century America*. Madison: University of Wisconsin Press, 1989.

Dickinson, William B., ed. *Watergate: Chronology of a Crisis*. Vol. 1. Washington DC: Congressional Quarterly, 1973.

Dighe, Ranjit S. "Saving Private Capitalism: The U.S. Bank Holiday of 1933." *Essays in Economic & Business History* 39 (2011): 41–58.

Donald, David Herbert. *Lincoln*. New York: Simon & Schuster, 1995.

Donaldson, Sam. *Hold On, Mr. President!* Thorndike ME: Thorndike Press, 1987.

Douglass, Frederick. *Selected Speeches and Writings*. Edited by Philip Sheldon Foner. Chicago: Lawrence Hill Books, 1999.

Dowdle, Andrew J., Dirk C. van Raemdonck, and Robert Maranto. "Barack Obama: A Reagan of the Left?" In Dowdle, van Raemdonck, and Maranto, *Obama Presidency*, 3–16.

———, eds. *The Obama Presidency: Change and Continuity*. New York: Routledge, 2011.

Downie, Leonard, Jr. "The Obama Administration and the Press: Leak Investigations and Surveillance in Post-9/11 America." With reporting by Sara Rafsky. Committee to Protect Journalists, October 10, 2013. https://cpj.org/reports /2013/10/obama-and-the-press-us-leaks-surveillance-post-911.php.

———. "The Trump Administration and the Media: Attacks on Press Credibility Endanger US Democracy and Global Press Freedom." Committee to Protect Journalists, April 16, 2020. https://cpj.org/reports/2020/04/trump-media -attacks-credibility-leaks/.

Drew, Elizabeth. *Portrait of an Election: The 1980 Presidential Campaign*. New York: Simon & Schuster, 1981.

Dubbs, Chris. *American Journalists in the Great War*. Lincoln: University of Nebraska Press, 2017.

Durham, Frank. Review of *No Longer Newsworthy: How the Mainstream Media Abandoned the Working Class*, by Christopher R. Martin. *Journalism & Mass Communication Quarterly* 97, no. 2 (Summer 2020): 549–50.

Dyson, Michael Eric. *Come Hell or High Water: Hurricane Katrina and the Color of Disaster*. New York: Basic Civitas Books, 2006.

Edwards, Bob. *Edward R. Murrow and the Birth of Broadcast Journalism*. Hoboken NJ: John Wiley & Sons, 2004.

Edwards, Jerome E. *The Foreign Policy of Col. McCormick's Tribune, 1929–1941*. Reno: University of Nevada Press, 1971.

Ellis, Joseph J. *First Family: Abigail and John.* New York: Alfred A. Knopf, 2010.

———. *Founding Brothers: The Revolutionary Generation.* New York: Alfred A. Knopf, 2000.

Eshbaugh-Soha, Matthew, and Jeffrey S. Peake. *Breaking through the Noise: Presidential Leadership, Public Opinion, and the News Media.* Studies in the Modern Presidency. Stanford CA: Stanford University Press, 2011.

Fagan, Benjamin. *The Black Newspaper and the Chosen Nation.* Athens: University of Georgia Press, 2016.

Farrell, John A. *Richard Nixon: The Life.* New York: Doubleday, 2017.

Feldstein, Mark. *Poisoning the Press: Richard Nixon, Jack Anderson, and the Rise of Washington's Scandal Culture.* New York: Farrar, Straus and Giroux, 2010.

Fishman, Donald. "George Creel: Freedom of Speech, the Film Industry, and Censorship during World War I." *Free Speech Yearbook* 39, no. 1 (2001): 34–56.

Fitzwater, Marlin. *Call the Briefing! Bush and Reagan, Sam and Helen.* New York: Crown, 1995.

FOIA Project. "September 2020 FOIA Litigation with Five-Year Monthly Trends." November 3, 2020. http://foiaproject.org/2020/11/03/september-2020-foia -litigation-with-five-year-monthly-trends/.

Fondren, Elisabeth. "'This Is an American Newspaper': Editorial Opinions and the German Immigrant Press in 1917." *Media History*, 2019, 1–14.

Friedman, Leon, and William F. Levantrosser, eds. *Watergate and Afterward: The Legacy of Richard M. Nixon.* Westport CT: Greenwood Press, 1992.

Funk, Cary, Alec Tyson, Brian Kennedy, and Courtney Johnson. "Science and Scientists Held in High Esteem across Global Publics." Pew Research Center, September 29, 2020.

Gabrial, Brian. *The Press and Slavery in America, 1791–1859: The Melancholy Effect of Popular Excitement.* Columbia: University of South Carolina, 2016.

Gallup, Alec M., and Frank Newport, eds. *Public Opinion 2004.* Lanham MD: Rowman & Littlefield, 2006.

Garment, Suzanne. *Scandal: The Crisis of Mistrust in American Politics.* New York: Times Books, 1991.

Garrow, David J. *Rising Star: The Making of Barack Obama.* New York: Harper-Collins, 2017.

Gates, Henry Louis, Jr. "Abraham Lincoln on Race and Slavery." In *Lincoln on Race and Slavery*, edited by Henry Louis Gates Jr. and Donald Yacovone. Princeton NJ: Princeton University Press, 2009.

Gates, Henry Louis, Jr., and Donald Yacovone, eds. *Lincoln on Race and Slavery.* Princeton NJ: Princeton University Press, 2009.

Gerstle, Gary. "Civic Ideals, Race, and Nation in the Age of Obama." In J. E. Zelizer, *Presidency of Barack Obama*, 261–80.

Gillmor, Dan. *We the Media: Grassroots Journalism by the People, for the People.* Sebastopol CA: O'Reilly Media, 2006.

Goff, Victoria. "The Masses Magazine (1911–1917): Odyssey of an Era." *Journalism History* 23, no. 3 (Autumn 1997).

Graham, Katharine. *Personal History.* New York: Alfred A. Knopf, 1980.

Grant, James. *John Adams: Party of One.* New York: Farrar, Straus and Giroux, 2005.

Grantham, Dewey W. Review of *The Papers of Woodrow Wilson*, vol. 49, edited by Robert C. Hilderbrand. *Journal of American History* 74, no. 3 (December 1987): 1079–81.

Green, Jonathan. "John Adams's Montesquieuean Moment." *Journal of the History of Ideas* 77, no. 2 (April 2016): 227–51.

Green, Joshua. *Devil's Bargain: Steve Bannon, Donald Trump, and the Storming of the Presidency.* New York: Penguin Random House, 2017.

Greenberg, David. *Nixon's Shadow: The History of an Image.* New York: W. W. Norton, 2003.

———. "The Ominous Clang: Fears of Propaganda from World War I to World War II." In Schulman and Zelizer, *Media Nation*, 50–62.

———. *Republic of Spin: An Inside History of the American Presidency.* New York: W. W. Norton, 2016.

Grieves, Kevin. "'It Would Be the Best to Suspend Publication': The German-American Press and Anti-German Hysteria during World War I." *American Journalism* 37, no. 1 (Winter 2020): 47–65.

Griffith, Sally Foreman. *Home Town News: William Allen White and the Emporia Gazette.* New York: Oxford University Press, 1989.

Guelzo, Allen C. *Lincoln's Emancipation Proclamation: The End of Slavery in America.* New York: Simon & Schuster, 2004.

Gup, Ted. "Working in a Wartime Capital: An Uneasy Quiet and a Sense of Mission." *Columbia Journalism Review*, September–October 2002.

Hacker, Jacob S., and Paul Pierson. *Let Them Eat Tweets: How the Right Rules in an Age of Extreme Inequality.* New York: Liveright Publishing, 2020.

Halperin, Terri Diane. *The Alien and Sedition Acts of 1798: Testing the Constitution.* Baltimore: Johns Hopkins University Press, 2016.

Hamby, Alonzo. *Man of Destiny: FDR and the Making of the American Century.* New York: Basic Books, 2015.

Hamilton, James T. *Democracy's Detectives: The Economics of Investigative Journalism.* Cambridge MA: Harvard University Press, 2016.

Hamilton, John Maxwell. *Manipulating the Masses: Woodrow Wilson and the Birth of American Propaganda*. Baton Rouge: LSU Press, 2020.

Han, Lori Cox, ed. *Hatred of America's Presidents: Personal Attacks on the White House from Washington to Trump*. Santa Barbara CA: ABC-CLIO, 2018.

Harris, John F. *The Survivor: Bill Clinton in the White House*. New York: Random House, 2005.

Harris, Roy J., Jr. *Pulitzer's Gold: Behind the Prize for Public Service Journalism*. Columbia: University of Missouri Press, 2007.

Harrold, Stanley. *Lincoln and the Abolitionists*. Carbondale: Southern Illinois University Press, 2018.

Hayden, Joseph. *Covering Clinton: The President and the Press in the 1990s*. Praeger Series in Presidential Studies. Westport CT: Praeger, 2002.

Hemmer, Nicole. *Messengers of the Right: Conservative Media and the Transformation of American Politics*. Philadelphia: University of Pennsylvania Press, 2016.

Hendershot, Heather. *What's Fair on the Air? Cold War Right-Wing Broadcasting and the Public Interest*. Chicago: University of Chicago Press, 2011.

Herndon, William H. *Herndon on Lincoln: Letters*. Edited by Douglas L. Wilson and Rodney O. Davis. Urbana: University of Illinois Press for Knox College Lincoln Studies Center, 2016.

Hersh, Seymour M. *Reporter: A Memoir*. New York: Alfred A. Knopf, 2018.

Hertsgaard, Mark. *On Bended Knee: The Press and the Reagan Presidency*. New York: Farrar, Straus & Giroux, 1988.

Hindman, Matthew, and Vlad Barash. *Disinformation, "Fake News," and Influence Campaigns on Twitter*. Knight Foundation report, October 2018. https://knightfoundation.org/reports/disinformation-fake-news-and-influence-campaigns-on-twitter/.

Holzer, Harold. *Lincoln and the Power of the Press: The War for Public Opinion*. New York: Simon & Schuster, 2014.

———. *The Presidents vs. the Press: The Endless Battle between the White House and the Media from the Founding Fathers to Fake News*. New York: Dutton, 2020.

Howard, Vincent W. "Woodrow Wilson, the Press, and Presidential Leadership: Another Look at the Passage of the Underwood Tariff, 1913." *Centennial Review* 24, no. 2 (1980): 167.

Hurd, Charles. *When the New Deal Was Young and Gay*. New York: Hawthorn Books, 1965.

Hyman, Harold M. *Quiet Past and Stormy Present? War Powers in American History*. Washington DC: American Historical Association, 1986.

Isikioff, Michael, and David Corn. *Hubris: The Inside Story of Spin, Scandal, and the Selling of the Iraq War*. New York: Crown, 2006.

Jackson, John S. "The Making of a Senator: Barack Obama and the 2004 Illinois Senate Race." *Simon Review*, Paper no. 4. Paul Simon Public Policy Institute, Southern Illinois University Carbondale, August 2006. https://opensiuc.lib .siu.edu/cgi/viewcontent.cgi?article=1004&context=ppi_papers.

Jamieson, Kathleen Hall, and Dolores Albarracin. "The Relation between Media Consumption and Misinformation at the Outset of the SARS-CoV-2 Pandemic in the US." *Harvard Kennedy School Misinformation Review* 1 (April 2020).

Jamieson, Kathleen Hall, and Joseph N. Cappella. *Echo Chamber: Rush Limbaugh and the Conservative Media Establishment*. New York: Oxford University Press, 2008.

Jamieson, Kathleen Hall, and Paul Waldman. *The Press Effect: Politicians, Journalists, and the Stories That Shape the Political World*. Oxford: Oxford University Press, 2003.

Jefferson, Thomas. *The Works of Thomas Jefferson*. Edited by Paul Leicester Ford. Vol. 10. New York: G. P. Putnam's Sons, 1904–5.

Johnson, Donald. "Wilson, Burleson, and Censorship in the First World War." *Journal of Southern History* 28, no. 1 (1962): 46–58.

Jones, Alex S. *Losing the News: The Future of the News That Feeds Democracy*. Oxford: Oxford University Press, 2009.

Juergens, George. Review of *The Papers of Woodrow Wilson*, vol. 50, edited by Robert C. Hilderbrand. *American Historical Review* 91, no. 4 (October 1986): 1010.

———. "Woodrow Wilson." In *Ten Presidents and the Press*, edited by Kenneth W. Thompson. Washington DC: University Press of America, 1983.

Kalb, Marvin. *One Scandalous Story: Clinton, Lewinsky, and Thirteen Days That Tarnished American Journalism*. New York: Free Press, 2001.

Kaplan, Fred. *Lincoln and the Abolitionists: John Quincy Adams, Slavery, and the Civil War*. New York: Harper Perennial, 2017.

Karl, Jonathan. *Front Row at the Trump Show*. New York: Dutton, 2020.

Karpf, Dave. "We All Stand Together or We All Fall Apart: On the Need for an Adversarial Press in the Age of Trump." In Boczkowski and Papacharissi, *Trump and the Media*, 221–28.

Kates, James. "Editor, Publisher, Citizen, Socialist: Victor L. Berger and His *Milwaukee Leader*." *Journalism History* 44, no. 2 (Summer 2018): 79–88.

Katz, James E., Michael Barris, and Anshul Jain. *The Social Media President: Barack Obama and the Politics of Digital Engagement*. New York: Palgrave Macmillan, 2013.

Katz, William Loren. Introduction to *Walker's Appeal, in Four Articles: Together with a Preamble, to the Coloured Citizens of the World, but in Particular, and*

Very Expressly, to Those of the United States of America, by David Walker. New York: Arno Press and New York Times, 1969.

Kendrick, Alexander. *Prime Time: The Life of Edward R. Murrow.* Boston: Little, Brown, 1969.

Kennedy, David M. *Freedom from Fear: The American People in Depression and War, 1929–1945.* Oxford: Oxford University Press, 1999.

Kennedy, Roger G. *Burr, Hamilton and Jefferson: A Study in Character.* Oxford: Oxford University Press, 2000.

Kincaid, John. "Secrecy and Democracy: The Unresolved Legacy of the Pentagon Papers." In *Watergate and Afterward: The Legacy of Richard M. Nixon*, edited by Leon Friedman and William F. Levantrosser. Westport CT: Greenwood Press, 1992.

King, Elliot. *Free for All: The Internet's Transformation of Journalism.* Medill School of Journalism Visions of the American Press. Evanston IL: Northwestern University Press, 2010.

Klingaman, William K. *Abraham Lincoln and the Road to Emancipation, 1861–1865.* New York: Viking, 2001.

Kovach, Bill, and Tom Rosenstiel. *Warp Speed: America in the Age of Mixed Media.* New York: Century Press, 1999.

Kumar, Martha Joynt. "Continuity and Change in White House Communications: President Obama Meets the Press." In Dowdle, van Raemdonck, and Maranto, *Obama Presidency*, 91–106.

———. *Managing the President's Message: The White House Communications Operation.* Baltimore: Johns Hopkins University Press, 2010.

———. "The President as Message and Messenger." In *Presidential Power: Forging the Presidency for the Twenty-First Century*, edited by Robert Y. Shapiro, Martha Joynt Kumar, and Lawrence R. Jacobs. New York: Columbia University Press, 2000.

Kurtz, Howard. *Spin Cycle: Inside the Clinton Propaganda Machine.* New York: Free Press, 1998.

Kutler, Stanley I., ed. *Abuse of Power: The New Nixon Tapes.* New York: Free Press, 1997.

———. *The Wars of Watergate: The Last Crisis of Richard Nixon.* New York: Alfred A. Knopf, 1990.

Lang, Gladys Engel, and Kurt Lang. *The Battle for Public Opinion: The President, the Press, and the Polls during Watergate.* New York: Columbia University Press, 1983.

Lashner, Marilyn A. *The Chilling Effect in TV News: Intimidation by the Nixon White House.* New York: Praeger, 1984.

Layton, Charles. "The Information Squeeze." *American Journalism Review* 24, no. 7 (September 2002): 20–30.

Lebovic, Sam. "When the 'Mainstream Media' Was Conservative: Media Criticism in the Age of Reform." In Schulman and Zelizer, *Media Nation*, 63–76.

Leidholdt, Alexander S. "The Mysterious Mr. Maxwell and Room M-1: Clandestine Influences on American Postal Censorship during World War I." *American Journalism* 36, no. 3 (Summer 2019): 276–99.

Lempert, Michael, and Michael Silverstein. *Creatures of Politics: Media, Message, and the American Presidency.* Bloomington: Indiana University Press, 2012.

Leuchtenburg, William Edward. *The FDR Years: On Roosevelt and His Legacy.* New York: Columbia University Press, 1995.

Levin, Linda Lotridge. *The Making of FDR: The Story of Stephen T. Early, America's First Modern Press Secretary.* New York: Prometheus Books, 2008.

Levitsky, Steven, and Daniel Ziblatt, *How Democracies Die.* New York: Broadway Books, 2018.

Lewis, Charles. "Selling the Iraq War: Unearthing False Advertising." *Nieman Reports* 62, no. 1 (Spring 2008): 26.

Liebovich, Louis W. *Richard Nixon, Watergate and the Press.* Westport CT: Praeger, 2003.

Lincoln, Abraham. *Collected Works of Abraham Lincoln.* Edited by Roy P. Basler. New Brunswick NJ: Rutgers University Press, 2001.

Lipstadt, Deborah. *Beyond Belief: The American Press and the Coming of the Holocaust, 1933–1945.* New York: Free Press, 1986.

Looker, Earle. *This Man Roosevelt.* New York: Brewer, Warren & Putnam, 1932.

Lukas, J. Anthony. *Nightmare: The Underside of the Nixon Years.* New York: Viking, 1976.

Major, Mark. *The Unilateral Presidency and the News Media: The Politics of Framing Executive Power.* New York: Palgrave Macmillan, 2014.

Maltese, John Anthony. *Spin Control: The White House Office of Communications and the Management of the Presidential News.* Chapel Hill: University of North Carolina Press, 1992.

Mann, James. *George W. Bush.* The American Presidents. New York: Times Books, 2015.

Maraniss, David. *Barack Obama: The Story.* New York: Simon & Schuster, 2012.

———. *First in His Class: A Biography of Bill Clinton.* New York: Simon & Schuster, 1995.

Marder, Murrey. "The Press and the Presidency: Silencing the Watchdog." *Nieman Reports* 62, no. 1 (Spring 2008): 8–10.

Marrone, Matt. "Oral History Interview with Jack Nelson." Defining Civil Rights and the Press Symposium, April 24, 2004. S. I. Newhouse School of Public Communications, Syracuse University.

Martin, Roland S. *The First: President Barack Obama's Road to the White House as Originally Reported by Roland S. Martin.* Chicago: Third World Press, 2010.

Mascaro, Tom. *Into the Fray: How NBC's Washington Documentary Unit Reinvented the News.* Washington DC: Potomac Books, 2012.

Mason, Lilliana. *Uncivil Agreement: How Politics Became Our Identity.* Chicago: University of Chicago Press, 2018.

McClelland, Edward. *Young Mr. Obama: Chicago and the Making of a Black President.* New York: Bloomsbury Press, 2010.

McClendon, Sarah. *Mr. President, Mr. President! My Fifty Years of Covering the White House.* With Jules Minton. Los Angeles: General Publishing Group, 1996.

McCormick, Andrew. "One America News Was Desperate for Trump's Approval: Here's How It Got It." *Columbia Journalism Review*, May 27, 2020.

McCullough, David. *John Adams.* New York: Simon & Schuster, 2001.

McFeely, William S. *Frederick Douglass.* New York: Norton, 1981.

McPherson, James Brian. *The Conservative Resurgence and the Press: The Media's Role in the Rise of the Right.* Medill School of Journalism Visions of the American Press. Evanston IL: Northwestern University Press, 2008.

McPherson, James M. *The Struggle for Equality: Abolitionists and the Negro in the Civil War and Reconstruction.* Princeton NJ: Princeton University Press, 2014.

Meyers, W. Cameron. "The Chicago Newspaper Hoax in the '36 Election Campaign." *Journalism Quarterly* 37 (Summer 1960).

Miller, William Lee. *President Lincoln: The Duty of a Statesman.* New York: Vintage Books, 2009.

Mock, James R. *Censorship, 1917.* Princeton NJ: Princeton University Press, 1941.

Mohammed, Shaheed Nick, and Robert C. Trumpbour. "The Carnivalesque in the 2016 U.S. Presidential Campaign." *Presidential Studies Quarterly*, June 12, 2020.

Montgomery, Bruce P. "Presidential Materials: Politics and the Presidential Records Act." *American Archivist* 66, no. 1 (Spring–Summer 2003): 102–38.

Morris, John. *Mary McGrory: The Trailblazing Columnist Who Stood Washington on Its Head.* New York: Penguin Books, 2015.

Moser, Bob. "Interference 2020." *Columbia Journalism Review*, Fall 2019. https://www.cjr.org/special_report/interference-election-2020.php.

Mueller, James E. *Towel Snapping the Press: Bush's Journey from Locker-Room Antics to Message Control.* Lanham MD: Rowman & Littlefield, 2006.

Mueller, Robert S., III. *Report on the Investigation into Russian Interference in the 2016 Presidential Election.* 2 vols. Washington DC: U.S. Department of Justice, March 2019. https://www.justice.gov/storage/report.pdf and https://www.justice.gov/storage/report_volume2.pdf.

Muirhead, Russell, and Nancy L. Rosenblum. *A Lot of People Are Saying: The New Conspiracism and the Assault on Democracy.* Princeton NJ: Princeton University Press, 2019.

Munno, Greg, and Susan Long. "Tracking Litigation." *IRE Journal,* Fall 2014, 15.

Mutz, Diana C. *In-Your-Face Politics: The Consequences of Uncivil Media.* Princeton NJ: Princeton University Press, 2015.

Nacos, Brigitte Lebens. *The Press, Presidents and Crises.* New York: Columbia University Press, 1990.

Nash, Roderick. "Victor L. Berger: Making Marx Respectable." *Wisconsin Magazine of History* 47, no. 4 (Summer 1964): 301–8.

Nelson, Jack. *Scoop: The Evolution of a Southern Reporter.* Jackson: University Press of Mississippi, 2012.

"News Audiences Increasingly Politicized." Pew Research Center, June 8, 2004. https://www.people-press.org/2004/06/08/news-audiences-increasingly-politicized/.

Nixon, Richard M. *The Nixon Presidential Press Conferences.* New York: Earl M. Coleman Enterprises, 1978.

Oakes, James. *The Radical and the Republican: Frederick Douglass, Abraham Lincoln, and the Triumph of Antislavery Politics.* New York: W. W. Norton, 2007.

O'Brien, Michael. *John F. Kennedy: A Biography.* New York: Macmillan, 2006.

Office of Management and Budget. "Summary of Receipts, Outlays, and Surpluses or Deficits." Historical Tables. Accessed April 10, 2021. https://www.whitehouse.gov/omb/historical-tables/.

Olmsted, Kathryn. "Terror Tuesdays: How Obama Refined Bush's Counterterrorism Policies." In J. E. Zelizer, *Presidency of Barack Obama,* 212–16.

Olmsted, Kathryn S., and Eric Rauchway. "George W. Bush, 2001–2009." In *Presidential Misconduct: From George Washington to Today,* edited by James M. Banner Jr. New York: New Press, 2019.

Olson, Keith W. *Watergate: The Presidential Scandal That Shook America.* Lawrence: University Press of Kansas, 2003.

Orman, John. "Covering the American Presidency: Valenced Reporting in the Periodical Press, 1900–1982." *Presidential Studies Quarterly* 14, no. 3 (Summer 1984): 381–90.

Osgood, Kenneth, and Andrew K. Frank, eds. *Selling War in a Media Age: The Presidency and Public Opinion in the American Century.* Gainesville: University Press of Florida, 2010.

Padgett, Jeremy, Johanna L. Dunaway, and Joshua P. Darr. "As Seen on TV? How Gatekeeping Makes the U.S. House Seem More Extreme." *Journal of Communication* 69, no. 6 (December 2019): 696–719.

Page, Clarence. "Washington: New Climate, Old Culture." *Columbia Journalism Review*, September–October 2002.

Parks, Perry. "Covering Trump's 'Carnival': A Rhetorical Alternative to 'Objective' Reporting." *Journalism Practice* 13, no. 10 (February 2019): 1164–84.

———. "The Ultimate News Value: Journalism Textbooks, the U.S. Presidency, and the Normalization of Donald Trump." *Journalism Studies* 21, no. 4 (2020): 512–29.

Parlett, Martin A. *Demonizing a President: The "Foreignization" of Barack Obama.* Santa Barbara CA: Praeger, 2014.

Parry, Pam. *Eisenhower: The Public Relations President.* Lanham MD: Lexington Books, 2014.

Pasley, Jeffrey L. "Thomas Greenleaf: Printers and the Struggle for Democratic Politics and Freedom of the Press." In *Revolutionary Founders: Rebels, Radicals, and Reformers in the Making of the Nation*, edited by Alfred F. Young, Ray Raphael, and Gary B. Nash. New York: Vintage, 2012.

———. *"The Tyranny of the Printers": Newspaper Politics in the Early American Republic.* Charlottesville: University Press of Virginia, 2001.

Perlstein, Rick. *The Invisible Bridge: The Fall of Nixon and the Rise of Reagan.* New York: Simon & Schuster, 2014.

———. *Nixonland: The Rise of a President and the Fracturing of America.* New York: Scribner, 2008.

———. *Reaganland: America's Right Turn, 1976–1980.* New York: Simon & Schuster, 2020.

Phillips, Kim Tousley. *William Duane: Radical Journalist in the Age of Jefferson.* New York: Garland, 1989.

Pickard, Victor. *America's Battle for Media Democracy: The Triumph of Corporate Libertarianism and the Future of Media Reform.* New York: Cambridge University Press, 2015.

———. "When Commercialism Trumps Democracy: Media Pathologies and the Rise of the Misinformation Society." In Boczkowski and Papacharissi, *Trump and the Media*, 195–201.

Piore, Adam. "Tuned Out." *Columbia Journalism Review*, Summer 2020.

Poling, Susan A. Office of General Counsel, U.S. Government Accountability Office. "Unattributed Prepackaged News Stories Violate Publicity or Propaganda Prohibition." Testimony before the Committee on Commerce, Science, and Transportation, U.S. Senate, May 12, 2005.

Pollard, James E. *The Presidents and the Press*. London: Octagon Books, 1947.

Poniewozik, James. *Audience of One: Donald Trump, Television, and the Fracturing of America*. New York: Liveright, 2019.

Pope, Kyle. "A Time of Opportunity." *Columbia Journalism Review*, Summer 2020.

Porter, William E. *Assault on the Media: The Nixon Years*. Ann Arbor: University of Michigan Press, 1976.

Potter, Deborah. "Virtual News Reports." *American Journalism Review*, June/July 2004. https://ajrarchive.org/article.asp?id=3698&id=3698.

Proceedings of the American Anti-Slavery Society: At Its Third Decade, Held in the City of Philadelphia, Dec. 3d and 4th, 1864 [i.e., 1863]. New York: American Anti-Slavery Society, 1864.

Public Papers of the Presidents of the United States. Office of the Federal Register, National Archives and Records Service. Washington DC: General Services Administration, 1960.

Radio Television Digital News Association (RTDNA). "2020 Research: Newsroom Diversity." September 9, 2020. https://www.rtdna.org/article/2020_research _newsroom_diversity.

Rainie, Lee. "The State of Blogging." Pew Research Center, January 2, 2005. https://www.pewresearch.org/internet/2005/01/02/the-state-of-blogging/.

Reagan, Ronald. *An American Life*. New York: Simon & Schuster, 1990.

Report of the Congressional Committees Investigating the Iran-Contra Affair with Supplemental, Minority, and Additional Views. Submitted by Lee H. Hamilton and Daniel K. Inouye. 100th Congress, 1st session. H. Rept. No. 100-433; S. Rept. No 100-216. Washington DC: Government Printing Office, 1987.

"A Report on an Action for a Libel Brought by Dr. Benjamin Rush, against William Cobbett, in the Supreme Court of Pennsylvania, December Term, 1799." Evans Early American Imprint Collection. https://quod.lib.umich.edu/cgi/t /text/text-idx?c=evans;idno=N27847.0001.001.

Rice, Allen Thorndike, ed. *Reminiscences of Abraham Lincoln by Distinguished Men of His Time*. New York: North American Review, 1888.

Riley, Russell L. *Inside the Clinton White House: An Oral History*. New York: Oxford University Press, 2016.

Risjord, Norman K. *Thomas Jefferson*. Madison WI: Madison House, 1994.

Risley, Ford. *Abolition and the Press: The Moral Struggle against Slavery*. Medill School of Journalism Visions of the American Press. Evanston IL: Northwestern University Press, 2008.

Ritchie, Donald A. *Reporting from Washington: The History of the Washington Press Corps*. Oxford: Oxford University Press, 2005.

Ritter, Kurt W., and David Henry. *Ronald Reagan: The Great Communicator*. New York: Greenwood Press, 1992.

Roberts, Eugene, and Hank Klibanoff. *The Race Beat: The Press, the Civil Rights Struggle, and the Awakening of a Nation*. New York: Alfred A. Knopf, 2006.

Roberts, Roxanne. "Guess Who's Not Coming to Dinner." *Columbia Journalism Review*, September–October 2002.

Roosevelt, Franklin D. *The Public Papers and Addresses of Franklin D. Roosevelt*. 13 vols. New York: Random House, 1938–50.

Rose, Gary L. *The American Presidency under Siege*. Albany: State University of New York Press, 1997.

Rosen, James. *The Strong Man: John Mitchell and the Secrets of Watergate*. New York: Doubleday, 2008.

Rosenberg, Emily S. "War and the Health of the State: The U.S. Government and the Communications Revolution during World War I." In *Selling War in a Media Age: The Presidency and Public Opinion in the American Century*, edited by Kenneth Osgood and Andrew K. Frank. Gainesville: University Press of Florida, 2010.

Rosenfeld, Richard N. *American Aurora: A Democratic-Republican Returns*. New York: St. Martin's, 2014.

Rosenman, Samuel I. *Working with Roosevelt*. New York: Harper & Brothers, 1952.

Rosenwald, Brian. *Talk Radio's America: How an Industry Took Over a Political Party That Took Over the United States*. Cambridge MA: Harvard University Press, 2019.

Rosten, Leo C. *The Washington Correspondents*. New York: Harcourt, Brace, 1937.

Roth, Zachary. "Karen Ryan, Revisited." *Columbia Journalism Review*, April 20, 2004. https://archives.cjr.org/behind_the_news/karen_ryan_revisited.php.

Rothstein, Richard. *The Color of Law: A Forgotten History of How Our Government Segregated America*. New York: Liveright, 2017.

Rubin, Richard L. *Press, Party, and Presidency*. New York: W. W. Norton, 1981.

Russell, Adrienne. "Making Journalism Great Again: Trump and the New Rise of News Activism." In Boczkowski and Papacharissi, *Trump and the Media*, 203–12.

Ryan, April. *The Presidency in Black and White: My Up-Close View of Three Presidents and Race in America*. Lanham MD: Rowman and Littlefield, 2015.

Safire, William. *Before the Fall: An Inside View of the Pre-Watergate White House*. Garden City NY: Doubleday, 1975.

Samito, Christian G. *Lincoln and the Thirteenth Amendment*. Carbondale: Southern Illinois University Press, 2015.

Sanders, Elizabeth. "Presidents and Social Movements: A Logic and Preliminary Results." In *Formative Acts: American Politics in the Making*, edited by Stephen Skowronek and Matthew Glassman. Philadelphia: University of Pennsylvania Press, 2007.

Schaller, Michael. *Ronald Reagan*. Oxford: Oxford University Press, 2011.

Schell, Jonathan. *The Time of Illusion*. New York: Alfred A. Knopf, 1976.

Scherr, Arthur. "Inventing the Patriot President: Bache's 'Aurora' and John Adams." *Pennsylvania Magazine of History and Biography* 119, no. 4 (October 1995): 369–99.

Schlesinger, Arthur M., Jr. *The Imperial Presidency*. Boston: Houghton Mifflin, 1973.

Schmidt, Michael S. *Donald Trump v. The United States: Inside the Struggle to Stop a President*. New York: Random House, 2020.

Schudson, Michael. *Watergate in American Memory: How We Remember, Forget, and Reconstruct the Past*. New York: Basic Books, 1992.

Serrin, Judith, and William Serrin. "The Holocaust Exposed: How Could the World Not Know." In *Muckraking! The Journalism That Changed America*, edited by Serrin and Serrin. New York: New Press, 2002.

Shapiro, Robert Y., Martha Joynt Kumar, and Lawrence R. Jacobs, eds. *Presidential Power: Forging the Presidency for the Twenty-First Century*. New York: Columbia University Press, 2000.

Shapiro, Walter. "Washington: New Climate, Old Culture." *Columbia Journalism Review*, September–October 2002.

Shepard, Alicia. *Woodward and Bernstein: Life in the Shadow of Watergate*. Hoboken NJ: John Wiley & Sons, 2007.

Sheppard, Si. *The Partisan Press: A History of Media Bias in the United States*. Jefferson NC: McFarland, 2008.

Sherman, Gabriel. *The Loudest Voice in the Room: How the Brilliant, Bombastic Roger Ailes Built Fox News—and Divided a Country*. New York: Random House, 2014.

Sherwood, Robert E. *Roosevelt and Hopkins: An Intimate History*. New York: Harper, 1950.

Shorenstein Center of Media, Politics and Public Policy. "Combating Fake News: An Agenda for Research and Action." Conference held February 17–18, 2017, Harvard University Kennedy School. Executive Summary, May 2, 2017. https://shorensteincenter.org/combating-fake-news-agenda-for-research/.

Schulman, Bruce J., and Julian E. Zelizer, eds. *Media Nation: The Political History of News in Modern America*. Philadelphia: University of Pennsylvania Press, 2017.

Sides, John, Michael Tesler, and Lynn Vavreck. "How Trump Lost and Won." *Journal of Democracy* 28, no. 2 (April 2017): 34–44.

Simon, Paul. *Freedom's Champion, Elijah Lovejoy.* Carbondale: Southern Illinois University Press, 1984.

Simpson, Alan K. *Right in the Old Gazoo: A Lifetime of Scrapping with the Press.* New York: William Morrow, 1997.

Sivowitch, Elliot. "A Technological Survey of Broadcasting's 'Pre-History,' 1876–1920." *Journal of Broadcast* 15, no. 1 (May 2009): 1–20.

Skidmore, Max J. "Legislative Leadership." In *The Obama Presidency: A Preliminary Assessment,* edited by Robert P. Watson, Jack Covarrubias, Tom Lansford, and Douglas M. Brattebo. Albany: State University of New York Press, 2012.

Skocpol, Theda, and Vanessa Williams. *The Tea Party and the Remaking of Republican Conservatism.* Oxford: Oxford University Press, 2012.

Skowronek, Stephen. *The Politics Presidents Make: Leadership from John Adams to Bill Clinton.* Cambridge MA: Belknap Press of Harvard University Press, 1993.

Skowronek, Stephen, and Matthew Glassman, eds. *Formative Acts: American Politics in the Making.* Philadelphia: University of Pennsylvania Press, 2007.

Sloan, Wm. David. *The Media in America: A History.* Northport AL: Vision Press, 2008.

Smith, Culver H. *The Press, Politics, and Patronage: The American Government's Use of Newspapers, 1789–1875.* Athens: University of Georgia Press, 1977.

Smith, James Morton. "Political Suppression of Seditious Criticism: A Connecticut Case Study." *The Historian* 18, no. 1 (Autumn 1955): 41–56.

Smith, Jean Edward. *FDR.* New York: Random House, 2007.

Smith, Mark A. "Andrew Brown's 'Earnest Endeavor': The 'Federal Gazette's' role in Philadelphia's Yellow Fever Epidemic of 1793." *Pennsylvania Magazine of History and Biography* 120, no. 4 (October 1996): 321–42.

Smith, Richard Norton. *The Colonel: The Life and Legend of Robert R. McCormick, 1880–1955.* Evanston IL: Northwestern University Press, 1997.

Smith, Thomas Edward Vermilye. *The City of New York in the Year of Washington's Inauguration, 1789.* New York: A. D. F. Randolph, 1889.

Smoller, Frederic T. *The Six O'Clock Presidency: A Theory of Presidential Press Relations in the Age of Television.* Santa Barbara CA: Praeger, 1990.

Spear, Joseph C. *Presidents and the Press: The Nixon Legacy.* Cambridge MA: MIT Press, 1984.

Starr, Paul. *The Creation of the Media: Political Origins of Modern Communications.* New York: Basic Books, 2004.

Startt, James D. "Colonel Edward M. House and the Journalists." *American Journalism* 27, no. 3 (Summer 2010): 27–58.

———. "Wilson's Trip to Paris: Profile of Press Response." *Journalism Quarterly* 46, no. 4 (1969): 737–42.

———. *Woodrow Wilson, the Great War, and the Fourth Estate*. College Station: Texas A&M University Press, 2017.

Steele, Richard W. *Propaganda in an Open Society: The Roosevelt Administration and the Media, 1933–1941*. Westport CT: Greenwood, 1985.

Stelter, Brian. *Hoax: Donald Trump, Fox News, and the Dangerous Distortion of Truth*. New York: Simon & Schuster, 2020.

Stone, Geoffrey R. *Perilous Times: Free Speech in Wartime: From the Sedition Act of 1798 to the War on Terrorism*. New York: W. W. Norton, 2005.

———. *War and Liberty: An American Dilemma: 1790 to the Present*. New York: W. W. Norton, 2007.

Stuckey, Mary E. "'The Domain of Public Conscience': Woodrow Wilson and the Establishment of a Transcendent Political Order." *Rhetoric & Public Affairs* 6, no. 1 (2003): 1–3.

Sullivan, Kevin, and Mary Jordan. *Trump on Trial: The Investigation, Impeachment, Acquittal and Aftermath*. New York: Scribner, 2020.

Sussman, Barry. *The Great Cover-Up: Nixon and the Scandal of Watergate*. New York: Signet Classics, 1974.

Swanberg, W. A. *Luce and His Empire*. New York: Charles Scribner's Sons, 1972.

Sweeney, Michael S. *The Military and the Press: An Uneasy Truce*. Medill School of Journalism Visions of the American Press. Evanston IL: Northwestern University Press, 2006.

Tagg, James. *Benjamin Franklin Bache and the Philadelphia "Aurora."* Philadelphia: University of Pennsylvania Press, 1991.

Takiff, Michael. *A Complicated Man: The Life of Bill Clinton as Told by Those Who Know Him*. New Haven CT: Yale University Press, 2010.

Tebbel, John. *The Life and Good Times of William Randolph Hearst*. New York: E. P. Dutton, 1952.

Tebbel, John William, and Sarah Miles Watts. *The Press and the Presidency: From George Washington to Ronald Reagan*. New York: Oxford University Press, 1985.

Teel, Leonard Ray. *The Public Press, 1900–1945*. The History of American Journalism, no. 5. Westport CT: Praeger, 2006.

Thomas, Helen. *Front Row at the White House: My Life and Times*. New York: Scribner, 1999.

———. "Ronald Reagan and the Management of the News." In *The White House Press on the Presidency: News Management and Co-Option*, edited by Kenneth W. Thompson. Vol. 4. Lanham MD: University Press of America, 1983.

Thomas, John L. *The Liberator, William Lloyd Garrison: A Biography*. Boston: Little, Brown, 1963.

Todd, Chuck. *The Stranger: Barack Obama in the White House*. New York: Little, Brown, 2014.

Toobin, Jeffrey. *True Crimes and Misdemeanors: The Investigation of Donald Trump*. New York: Doubleday, 2020.

Tripp, Bernell. "Journalism for God and Man." In *The Press in Times of Crisis*, edited by Lloyd Chiasson Jr. Westport CT: Greenwood Press, 1995.

Tucker, Joshua A., Andrew Guess, Pablo Barberá, Cristian Vaccari, Alexandra Siegel, Sergey Sanovich, Denis Stukal, and Brendan Nyhan. *Social Media, Political Polarization, and Political Disinformation: A Review of the Scientific Literature*. Hewlett Foundation, March 2018. https://www.hewlett.org/wp-content/uploads/2018/03/Social-Media-Political-Polarization-and-Political-Disinformation-Literature-Review.pdf.

Umansky, Eric. "Failures of Imagination: American Journalists and the Coverage of American Torture." *Columbia Journalism Review*, September–October 2006.

United States Congress. *Annals of Congress: The Debates and Proceedings in the Congress of the United States*. Vol. 1. 1st Congress. Washington DC: Gales & Seaton, 1834.

———. *United States Code: Trading with the Enemy Act of 1917, 50a U.S.C. 1-40 1952*. https://www.loc.gov/item/uscode1952-005050a002/.

United States Department of Justice. "Report on Review of News Media Policies." July 12, 2013. https://www.justice.gov/iso/opa/resources/2202013712162851796893.pdf.

United States House of Representatives. "Hearing before the Subcommittee of the House Committee on Appropriations." Part 3. 65th Congress, June 11, 1918. Washington DC: Government Printing Office, 1918.

United States House of Representatives, Subcommittee on Antitrust, Commercial, and Administrative Law of the Committee on the Judiciary. *Investigation of Competition in Digital Markets: Majority Staff Report and Recommendations*. October 2020. https://assets.documentcloud.org/documents/7222833/House-Tech-Antitrust-Report.pdf.

Uscinski, Joseph E. "Down the Rabbit Hole We Go!" In *Conspiracy Theories and the People Who Believe Them*, edited by Joseph E. Uscinski. New York: Oxford University Press, 2019.

Wagner, A. Jay. "A Socialist Newspaper, the First Amendment, and the Espionage Act." *Journalism History*, July 16, 2019. https://journalism-history.org/2019/07/16/wagner-essay-the-milwaukee-leader/.

Waisbord, Silvio, Tina Tucker, and Zoey Lichtenheld. "Trump and the Great Disruption in Public Communication." In Boczkowski and Papacharissi, *Trump and the Media*, 25–32.

Walker, David. *Walker's Appeal, in Four Articles: Together with a Preamble, to the Coloured Citizens of the World, but in Particular, and Very Expressly, to Those of the United States of America.* Boston, 1829; rev., 1830; rev. New York: Arno Press and New York Times, 1969.

Walsh, Lawrence E. *Final Report of the Independent Counsel on Iran/Contra Matters.* Washington DC: United States Court of Appeals for the District of Columbia, 1993.

———. *Firewall: The Iran-Contra Conspiracy and Cover-Up.* New York: W. W. Norton, 1997.

Wapshott, Nicholas. *The Sphinx: Franklin Roosevelt, the Isolationists, and the Road to World War II.* New York: W. W. Norton, 2015.

Washburn, Patrick S. *The African American Newspaper: Voice of Freedom.* Medill School of Journalism Visions of the American Press. Evanston IL: Northwestern University Press, 2006.

Washburn, Patrick S., and Michael S. Sweeney. "Grand Jury Transcripts in the *Chicago Tribune's* 1942 Espionage Act Case: What Is Missing Is Significant." Paper presented to the American Journalism Historians Association annual conference, Little Rock, Arkansas, October 12, 2017.

Watson, Mary Ann. "Television and the Presidency—Eisenhower and Kennedy." In *The Columbia History of American Television*, edited by Gary R. Edgerton. New York: Columbia University Press, 2007.

Watson, Robert P., Jack Covarrubias, Tom Lansford, and Douglas M. Brattebo. *The Obama Presidency: A Preliminary Assessment.* Albany: State University of New York Press, 2012.

White, Graham J. *FDR and the Press.* Chicago: University of Chicago Press, 1979.

White, Theodore H. *Breach of Faith: The Fall of Richard Nixon.* New York: Atheneum, 1975.

Wilkerson, Isabel. *Caste: The Origins of Our Discontents.* New York: Random House, 2020.

Will, George F. *The Conservative Sensibility.* New York: Hachette Books, 2019.

Winfield, Betty Houchin. *F.D.R. and the News Media.* Urbana: University of Illinois Press, 1990.

Women's Media Center. "The Status of Women in U.S. Media 2019." WMC Reports, February 21, 2019. https://www.womensmediacenter.com/reports/the-status-of-women-in-u-s-media-2019.

Woodward, Bob. *Fear: Trump in the White House*. New York: Simon & Schuster, 2018.

———. *Rage*. New York: Simon & Schuster, 2020.

———, ed. *The Secret Man: The Story of Watergate's Deep Throat*. New York: Simon & Schuster, 2005.

———. *Shadow: Five Presidents and the Legacy of Watergate, 1974–1999*. New York: Simon & Schuster, 1999.

World Health Organization. "Coronavirus Disease (COVID-19)—Situation Report 174." July 12, 2020. https://www.who.int/docs/default-source/coronaviruse /situation-reports/20200712-covid-19-sitrep-174.pdf?sfvrsn=5d1c1b2c_2.

Zelizer, Barbie. "Why Journalism in the Age of Trump Shouldn't Surprise Us." In Boczkowski and Papacharissi, *Trump and the Media*, 9–16.

Zelizer, Julian E. "How Washington Helped Create the Contemporary Media: Ending the Fairness Doctrine in 1987." In Schulman and Zelizer, *Media Nation*, 176–89.

———, ed. *The Presidency of Barack Obama: A First Historical Assessment*. Princeton NJ: Princeton University Press, 2018.

———. "Tea Partied: President Obama's Encounters with the Conservative-Industrial Complex." In J. E. Zelizer, *Presidency of Barack Obama*, 11–29.

INDEX